W9-BGO-806

RETURN TARGETS AND SHORTFALL RISKS

RETURN TARGETS AND SHORTFALL RISKS

Studies in Strategic Asset Allocation

MARTIN L. LEIBOWITZ
LAWRENCE N. BADER
STANLEY KOGELMAN

IRWIN
Professional Publishing®
Chicago • London • Singapore

Irwin Professional Book Team

Publisher: *Wyne McGuirt*

Executive editor: *Kevin Commins*

Marketing manager: *Kelly Sheridan*

Project editor: *Rebecca Dodson*

Production supervisor: *Laurie Kersch*

Assistant manager, desktop services: *Jon Christopher*

Jacket designer: *Chip Butzko*

Compositor: *Precision Graphic Services, Inc.*

Typeface: *10/12 Palatino*

Printer: *Quebecor/Book Press*

Times Mirror
Higher Education Group

Library of Congress Cataloging-in-Publication Data

Leibowitz, Martin L.,
    Return targets and shortfall risks : studies in strategic asset allocation / Martin L. Leibowitz, Lawrence N. Bader, Stanley Kogelman.
        p.   cm.
    Includes index.
    ISBN 1-55738-916-0
    1. Portfolio management.   2. Asset allocation.   I. Bader, Lawrence N.   II. Kogelman, Stanley.   III. Title.
HG4529.5.L45   1996
332.6—dc20   95–33464

Printed in the United States of America

1 2 3 4 5 6 7 8 9 0 QBP 2 1 0 9 8 7 6 5

To
Kim, Becky, and Karen
and to
Peggy, Christine, Carrie, Sam, and Lexy
and to
Laura

Contents

Chapter 4   Asset Allocation under Liability Uncertainty   61

Chapter 5   "Optimal" Portfolios Relative to Benchmark
            Allocations   89

Chapter 6   Total Portfolio Duration and Relative
            Returns   113

Part III—Global Fixed-Income Investments 391

About the Authors

MARTIN L. LEIBOWITZ

In June 1995, Martin Leibowitz became Chief Investment Officer of the College Retirement Equity Fund (CREF), the largest retirement system in the world. For the previous 26 years, he was associated with Salomon Brothers Inc, where the research studies in this volume were prepared. Most recently, he served as the Director of Research and as a member of the firm's Executive Committee. He joined Salomon Brothers in 1969 to form the first research unit directed toward portfolio analysis in the fixed-income area. He and his associates developed structured portfolio techniques, performance benchmarks, and new approaches for constructing "optimal" bond portfolios.

In 1972, Dr. Leibowitz coauthored a book with Sidney Homer entitled *Inside the Yield Book*, which described a conceptual foundation for analyzing bond portfolios. He has written or coauthored over 130 articles on a wide variety of topics, ranging from immunization techniques to "total portfolio duration" to surplus management for pension funds. Many of these papers were published in *Financial Analysts Journal*, *The Journal of Portfolio Management*, *The Journal of Investing*, and *The Journal of Fixed Income*. Over the years, Dr. Leibowitz has received eight Graham & Dodd Awards for excellence in financial writing. In 1992, a volume of his collected writings was published under the title *Investing*, with a foreword by William F. Sharpe, the 1990 Nobel Laureate in Economics. In 1994, he coauthored (with Stanley Kogelman) a collection of studies on equity valuation entitled *Franchise Value and the Price/Earnings Ratio*.

Dr. Leibowitz received his bachelor's and master's degrees from the University of Chicago and his doctorate in mathematics from New York University. He is currently President-Elect of the Board of Trustees for The New York Academy of Sciences. He also serves on the Board of Overseers for NYU's Stern School of Business and on the Board of Directors of the Institute for Quantitative Research in Finance.

In 1995, the Association for Investment Management and Research (AIMR) named Dr. Leibowitz to be the recipient of the Nicholas Molodovsky Award. This Award is one of the highest honors in the field and is presented to "those individuals who have made outstanding contributions of such significance as to change the direction of the profession."

LAWRENCE N. BADER

Lawrence N. Bader is a Vice President in the Research Department of Salomon Brothers Inc. His work has addressed investment strategies and other financial issues for both private and public entities, including corporations, public retirement systems, and the Pension Benefit Guaranty Corporation. He was previously a Managing Director at William M. Mercer, Incorporated, an employee benefits and compensation consulting firm, where he was an actuarial consultant to corporate and multiemployer benefit plan sponsors. Mr. Bader received his B.A. in Mathematics from Yale University, where he was elected to Phi Beta Kappa, and did graduate work in economics at Gonville and Caius College, Cambridge University. He is a Fellow of the Society of Actuaries and has served on the Board of Directors of the Academy, the Pension Section Council of the Society, and numerous other organizations.

Mr. Bader is a frequent speaker and writer on employee benefit and investment topics, including pension investment strategy, pension funding and accounting, employee stock ownership plans, and retiree medical benefits.

STANLEY KOGELMAN

Stanley Kogelman is a Director in the Research Department at Salomon Brothers Inc. Prior to joining Salomon Brothers in 1985, he was Chairman of the Mathematics Department at the State University of New York College at Purchase. Dr. Kogelman received his B.S., M.S., and Ph.D. degrees in Mathematics from Rensselaer Polytechnic Institute.

Dr. Kogelman has written or coauthored over 40 articles on a wide range of financial topics. His recent research includes studies on asset allocation strategies for private investors, the shortfall approach to asset allocation and surplus management, "franchise factor" models for equity valuation, and the use of hedging in global investing. Many of these studies have been published in *Financial Analysts Journal*, *The Journal of Portfolio Management*, *The Journal of Investing*, and *The Journal of Fixed Income*. Two papers (written jointly with Martin Leibowitz) received Graham & Dodd Scrolls from the Association for Investment Management and Research (1992 and 1994). He is also coauthor (with Martin L. Leibowitz) of the book *Franchise Value and the Price/ Earnings Ratio*, published by AIMR.

Preface

We developed the research and ideas in this volume during a period of several years and with the support of Salomon Brothers Inc, for which we are most grateful. The chapters that form the body of this work (Chapters 2–25) were originally published as papers by Salomon Brothers Inc (SB). Later, the articles that provided the bases of Chapters 2–5, 8, 10, 12, 17–21, and 24–25 were published in slightly revised form in *The Journal of Portfolio Management*, *The Journal of Fixed Income*, *The Journal of Investing*, or *Financial Analysts Journal*. The published titles and dates are as follows:

PART I—ASSET ALLOCATION

Chapter 2:   "Asset Allocation Under Shortfall Constraints," *The Journal of Portfolio Management*, Winter 1991

Chapter 3:   "Asset Performance and Surplus Control: A Dual-Shortfall Approach," *Journal of Portfolio Management*, Winter 1992

Chapter 4:   "Asset Allocation Under Liability Uncertainty," *The Journal of Fixed Income*, September 1992

Chapter 5:   "'Optimal' Portfolios Relative to Benchmark Allocations," *The Journal of Portfolio Management*, Summer 1993

Chapter 6:   "Total Portfolio Duration and Relative Returns," SB, August 1992

Chapter 7:   "Return Targets, Shortfall Risks and Market Realities," SB, July 1993

Chapter 8:   "Interest Rate Sensitive Asset Allocation: A New Approach to Strategic Asset Allocation," *The Journal of Portfolio Management*, Spring 1994

Chapter 9:   "Strategic Allocation Under Changing Market Conditions," SB, January 1994

Chapter 10:   "Funding Ratio Return: A More 'Universal' Measure for Asset/Liability Management," *The Journal of Portfolio Management*, Fall 1994

Chapter 11:   "Pension Fund Risk Capacity: Surplus and Time Horizon Effects on Asset Allocation," SB, September 1994

PART II—YIELD CURVE POSITIONING

PART III—GLOBAL FIXED-INCOME INVESTMENTS

We wish to thank Ajay Dravid and Thomas Klaffky, our coauthors on several of these chapters, and to express our appreciation for helpful comments and suggestions from Niso Abuaf, Dennis Adler, Keith Ambachtsheer, Peter Bernstein, Rick Bookstaber, Allan Emkin, Don Ezra, Vilas Gadkari, Nicholas Glinsman, Jeremy Gold, Michael Granito, Steven Guterman, Gil Hammer, W. Van Harlow, Antti Ilmanen, Milton Irvin, Ray Iwanowski, Cal Johnson, Tony Kao, Richard Klotz, Edward Leventhal, John Lipsky, Y. Y. Ma, Joe Mezrich, Richard Noble, Peter Noris, Nancy Noyes, Ardavan Nozari, Judy Otterman, Richard Pagan, Greg Parseghian, Murali Ramaswami, Robert Salomon, Leo Schlinkert, William Sharpe, David Shulman, Eric Sorensen, Leon Tatevossian, and Michael Waldman.

We also owe a special debt of gratitude to Rachel Gold, Eileen Contrucci, and Ann Scavetta, without whose dedication and meticulous work this volume would not have been possible.

Martin L. Leibowitz
Lawrence N. Bader
Stanley Kogelman
New York
1995

Chapter 1

Introduction

For most professional investors, the ultimate risk is the failure to meet one or more of their goals. These goals may include ensuring a certain minimum asset return, staying reasonably close to a performance benchmark (such as Standard & Poor's 500 Stock Index), surpassing the median performance of a peer group of funds, or maintaining a prescribed surplus of assets over liabilities. To measure the danger of such failures, we have made use of the concept of "shortfall risk"—the risk of failing to earn the minimum return that a manager regards as critical. The more traditional risk measure, volatility (or standard deviation of returns), fails to distinguish between upward and downward return fluctuations. In contrast, we believe that the shortfall risk's focus on downside variation more closely reflects the investor's true sense of risk. The shortfall risk measure also has the advantage of explicitly treating higher expected returns as a cushion against the full impact of volatility.

As an example, consider a pension plan sponsor who must deal with multiple goals over various time horizons. The sponsor may need a 90% probability of achieving a one-year return greater than zero, as well as a five-year return that does not trail a peer group average by more than a cumulative 3%. From a liability perspective, another constraint may be to keep the funding ratio above 115%, again with 90% probability. The relative importance of various goals is reflected in the latitude afforded by the corresponding shortfall thresholds. Some thresholds may be liberal, while others may be quite confining. By identifying asset allocations that meet each of these shortfall constraints, the sponsor can determine the range of possible investment choices.

1

Another feature of the shortfall approach is that it can be used to help the fund maintain its minimum target levels as interest rates change. The level of interest rates plays a more fundamental role in asset allocation than is generally recognized. Most allocation studies use a "building block" approach to estimate asset class return. Risk premiums, usually derived at least in part from historical experience, are layered onto a foundation that corresponds to the current structure of interest rates. At the same time, a fund's objectives may include a target level and/or a minimum threshold defined in terms of nominal return values. By specifying these target level objectives as shortfall constraints, one can readily determine the required allocation adjustment following any major change in rate levels.

The equity allocation can also be viewed in terms of the "risk capacity" of the fund—the amount of shortfall risk the fund can accept relative to a given benchmark or liability. This view enables us to explore how the maximum equity allocation changes with the fund's time horizon. The results are quite surprising. The allowable equity exposure actually *decreases* as the sponsor's view shifts from short to intermediate horizons and then increases only slowly as the horizon grows quite long.

A fund with minimal risk tolerance (perhaps due to statutory requirements or the absence of a back-up funding source) would probably be constrained to follow a "low-risk path" with little or no equity. In general, such a fund would exercise rigorous duration control, and monitor the management closely for even minor risks.

In contrast, equities are the asset of choice for funds that follow the "high-risk path." As a consequence of the dominant role of equities, these funds have a broad latitude for strategies that entail *relatively* minor incremental risks, especially in terms of their impact at the total fund level. For example, substantial shifts in the duration of bonds will significantly alter the volatility of the bond component, but may have little impact on the total fund volatility. Similarly, a modest shift from Treasuries to corporate bonds will have only a minimal effect on total fund risk. Even within the equity component, departures from the benchmark (toward more small-capitalization stocks, for example) may add little overall risk.

In general, productive, low-correlation departures from asset class benchmarks, whether motivated by strategic or tactical views, can enjoy enhanced reward/risk ratios at the total fund level, because the *return* pass-through is greater than the *volatility* pass-through. This "total fund effect" creates incentives for more aggressive departures from the ultimate benchmark. Active positions with bona fide expectations of incremental return—whether over short- or long-term horizons—will almost always be more compelling when viewed from the vantage point of the overall fund. The standard approach to fund management fails to capitalize on the potential benefits that can be derived from this total fund effect.

The common practice is for a fund to set its allocation as a mixture of standard asset class benchmarks. This mixture forms the ultimate benchmark for the fund as a whole. The components of this single benchmark are then parceled out to the various managers, who in turn pursue performance *solely* with an eye on their assigned benchmarks. To facilitate the use of productive active departures, we suggest an alternative approach that replaces the standard single benchmark with a "hierarchy of benchmarks." At the top of the hierarchy is a *policy benchmark* corresponding to the ultimate benchmark in the standard format. At the next level down, a *strategic benchmark* incorporates all portfolio tilts that fund management believes should be pursued over longer time horizons.

The strategic benchmark might, for example, reflect the ongoing substitution of corporate bonds for some percentage of the Treasury position in a market-weighted index. The strategic benchmark, which incorporates any "easy improvements" to the policy benchmark, should then be disaggregated for distribution to individual portfolio managers. Moreover, these management assignments should be clearly segregated into active and passive roles. With this delineation, the active managers can be more readily encouraged (and monitored) in their reach for the level of aggressiveness that best serves the overall fund.

The asset allocation problem is typically described in terms of an asset-only framework. However, as noted at the outset, the top level of the benchmark hierarchy—the policy benchmark—should be designed as the best balance point among *all* the fund's objectives, including the need to fulfill the fund's liabilities over time. For some funds, the liability objective may be both imminent and paramount. In such instances, the asset allocation is often cast as a problem of "liability management."

In liability management, the first issue is to determine the appropriate yardsticks for measuring success or failure. For example, for a given liability, the fund can focus on surplus dollars or funding ratio. When the funding ratio is critical, we show how a new measure—the funding ratio return (FRR)—can serve as a convenient and more universal method for choosing the best allocation.

Another key issue in liability management is the clarity of the liabilities. Although the cash flows for many traditional life insurance products or for a group of retired pension plan participants can be forecast with reasonable precision, other obligations, such as payouts of property/casualty claims or the deferred pensions earned by young workers, can be quite fuzzy. If the liabilities are well defined, a sponsor with low tolerance for asset/liability mismatch will benefit from a tightly constrained asset allocation that matches the liability cash flows (or at least their duration) with high-quality bonds. In contrast, if the liabilities are uncertain, the liability volatility may dominate the asset-side volatility. Equity additions may then bring incremental expected surplus return that outweighs the incremental volatility of the surplus measure. In a sense, the liability uncertainty affords latitude for productive asset risk taking with little added surplus risk.

The interest-rate sensitivity of the assets is a critical variable in matching the movements of the liabilities. For obvious reasons, most funds look to their fixed-income component to control this factor. However, we show how the rate sensitivity of equities can also play an important role in the asset/ liability context. This "equity duration" factor is often underappreciated, especially in light of equity's dominant position in typical allocations.[1]

With regard to the fixed-income component itself, the key problem is to determine optimal positions along the yield curve and risk-controlled ways to capture incremental spreads. The overall duration will probably be largely guided by broader fund-level considerations. However, for a given overall fund duration, there still remains a wide range of choices for the individual durations of the Treasury and non-Treasury components. In a series of studies, we show how significant return enhancements can be attained through risk-controlled techniques such as "spread immunization" and optimal yield-curve positioning.

The current yield curve usually serves as a starting point in estimating expected bond returns. However, the assumed evolution of the yield curve over time has a critical impact on the expected pattern of return. For example, a yield curve that migrates in accordance with "forward rates" produces flat returns along the entire curve, eliminating the rationale for any yield-seeking behavior. In contrast, a yield curve that tends to "persist" and maintain its current shape offers a wealth of opportunities for active managers. These managers can use their knowledge of the yield curve to position their investments at maturities that offer the best combination of yield and anticipated capital gains.

Managers can augment their expected returns by shifting to non-Treasury investments such as mortgage-backed securities, investment-grade corporate bonds, and currency-hedged foreign bonds. For non-Treasury U.S. securities, we illustrate how strategic positioning along the "spread" curve can enhance returns while still maintaining the prescribed interest-rate and

---

[1]For details, see *Franchise Value and the Price/Earnings Ratio*, Martin L. Leibowitz and Stanley Kogelman, The Research Foundation of The Institute of Chartered Financial Analysts, 1994.

spread sensitivity. We find that currency-hedged foreign bonds are not a pure investment in foreign markets, but rather a combination of exposures to domestic bonds and to particular segments of the foreign yield curve. Insight into the sources of return and volatility of these investments is necessary to balance hoped-for rewards with the volatility risks and loss of duration control.

The studies in this book develop these themes in a variety of contexts. They were written to be read singly; readers ambitious enough to read several in succession will be able to skip portions that merely recapitulate earlier studies. The chapters are collected into three main groupings: Asset Allocation, Yield-Curve Positioning, and Global Fixed-Income Investments. A brief description of the chapters in each grouping follows.

PART I—ASSET ALLOCATION

Chapter 2. Asset Allocation under Shortfall Constraints develops the notion of shortfall risk using a simple investment set consisting of cash and equity. The shortfall threshold includes three elements: a minimum level of return that the fund needs to attain, a required probability of achieving that level, and a measurement horizon—for example, attaining a return of at least 5% annually over a 3-year period with 90% assurance. When portfolios are plotted in terms of the mean and standard deviation of their returns, all portfolios with a specified shortfall threshold lie on a straight line (the "shortfall line"). The point at which this line intersects the cash/equity efficient frontier indicates the maximum amount of equity that can be held in any portfolio that achieves the shortfall threshold. Variations in the horizon, return target, and required probability have distinct effects on the shortfall line and the maximum equity percentage.

Chapter 3. Asset Performance and Surplus Control: A Dual-Shortfall Approach extends the concept of shortfall risk to two dimensions: asset-only risk and surplus risk. A "dual-shortfall" approach enables a sponsor to maximize expected return while minimizing the risks of either an inadequate asset return or a dangerous erosion of surplus. Using the full yield curve to provide a range of durations, we demonstrate the effects of varying the asset/liability ratios of the funds and the "tension" between the two risk constraints.

Chapter 4. Asset Allocation under Liability Uncertainty studies the effect of real-world uncertainties on the standard surplus management model, which assumes perfect knowledge of the timing and amounts of the liability payments. A known payment stream can be matched risklessly with a bond portfolio; departures from the matching portfolio introduce significant risk. When substantial uncertainty exists about the liability payments, however, perfect surplus control is a delusion, and modest asset return uncertainty adds little to the surplus risk that already exists. Under these conditions, the opportunity costs of attempting precise liability matching are substantial, and return-seeking departures from the minimum-risk portfolio can be generously rewarded in relation to their incremental surplus risk.

Chapter 5. "Optimal" Portfolios Relative to Benchmark Allocations broadens the traditional asset/liability problem to "liabilities" that can be any benchmark that a sponsor wishes to outperform, such as a market index or peer-group performance level. With a market benchmark that consists of a prescribed mix of equity and bonds, there is a limit to the departures in equity percentage and/or bond duration that can provide acceptable performance relative to the benchmark. Adding equity is the strategy most likely to improve the relative return, but the sponsor may do better to add slightly less than the maximum possible equity to preserve the freedom for bond duration shifts as well. The shortfall approach accommodates the introduction of performance benchmarks as a third concern, in addition to the asset-only and surplus control objectives addressed in previous chapters.

Chapter 6. Total Portfolio Duration and Relative Returns partitions the tracking error relative to a benchmark into two components, interest-rate risk and residual equity risk. Interest-rate risk is measured by the *total portfolio duration,* which combines the interest-rate sensitivity (duration) of bonds and equity. Residual equity risk refers to the large portion of equity volatility that is not explained by interest-rate movements. Equity duration is treated as a statistical concept, and we review its fluctuations and their causes over the past decade. Efficient asset allocation reflects an appropriate balance of interest-rate risk and residual equity risk.

Chapter 7. Return Targets, Shortfall Risks, and Market Realities considers how falling interest rates influence asset allocation decisions. Written during the 1993 bond rally, this study begins with the premise that a decline in rates magnifies shortfall risk—for example, the danger of a negative total return on a 30-year Treasury bond is greater when its initial yield is 6% than when it is 8%. If risk premiums and volatilities are unchanged, it follows that all asset classes must experience a similar reduction in expected returns as well as a corresponding increase in shortfall risks. Thus, lower rates, together with fixed return targets, present investors a menu of unpalatable choices: They can hold their allocations constant and accept both a lower expected return and a heightened level of risk; they can rectify the risk increase by a more conservative investment posture, undermining their already weakened return expectations; or they can "reach for return," for example by easing credit constraints or increasing equity commitments, thus inflating their risk even further.

Chapter 8. Interest-Rate Sensitive Asset Allocation: A New Approach to Strategic Asset Allocation shows how changing interest rates affect investors who seek a fixed level of shortfall risk. For these investors, the strategic allocation is not a static mix, but a prescription for recalibrating the mix in response to interest-rate movements. These investors can extend duration and increase equity holdings when a rate rise diminishes their shortfall risk, but must temper their funds' volatility by contracting their equity and duration exposure when rates decline. These adaptations to rate changes are independent of any tactical views about risk premiums or future rate movements.

Chapter 9. Strategic Allocation under Changing Market Conditions broadens the scope of the two preceding chapters to encompass the other changes in market conditions that can accompany interest-rate changes. Falling interest rates tend to be accompanied by declining rate volatility, which lowers risk and may moderate or even reverse the bond portfolio changes that the rate decline alone would suggest. Changing equity volatilities, risk premiums, and bond/equity correlations can also undermine a fund's balance between risks and rewards.

Chapter 10. Funding Ratio Return: A More "Universal" Measure for Asset/Liability Management introduces the funding ratio return (FRR), a new yardstick for regulating surplus. The FRR is the percentage change in the ratio of assets to liabilities. Unlike standard surplus measures that depend on the initial funding status, the FRR is *independent* of the starting position and reflects *only* the asset and liability returns. The FRR thus offers a universal standard of surplus performance for funds with disparate funding positions, and a specific FRR shortfall constraint has the same significance for all funds. Sponsors with similar risk tolerances and liability structures would thus gravitate toward the same asset allocations. Thus, sponsors who can accept the risk of a −10% FRR would be free to invest heavily in equities and over a wide range of bond durations, regardless of differences in their levels of funding. On the other hand, those who require 90% assurance that their FRR will not be worse than −1% are forced into "virtual immunization."

Chapter 11. Pension Fund Risk Capacity: Surplus and Time-Horizon Effects on Asset Allocation spotlights the influence of asset/liability risk tolerance and time horizons in determining how much equity a fund can hold. FRR is used as a measure of asset/liability risk, permitting risk tolerance to be expressed as an FRR shortfall constraint. Under simple but plausible conditions, the maximum allowable equity is directly proportional to the FRR shortfall constraint. The time-horizon effects are quite sensitive to the capital market assumptions and the desired probability of avoiding a shortfall. Surprisingly, the admissible equity holding tends to fall as the investment horizon shifts from short to intermediate. Only over quite extended periods do the effects of time begin to favor greater equity commitments.

Chapter 12. The Opportunity for Greater Flexibility in the Bond Component: The Total Fund Effect explores the impact of the bond duration choice on total portfolio risk. During the decade ending in 1994, a period of broadly declining rates, duration extension was generously rewarded, but at a cost of added volatility. If the duration extension occurred in the bond component of a 60% equity/40% bond portfolio, the total portfolio return increased by 40% of the incremental bond return, as would be expected. However, only about 20% of the incremental bond volatility passed through to the total portfolio. This risk dilution, which we label "the total fund effect," arises from the diversification benefits produced by the imperfect correlation between equity and bond returns. It prevails in both strong and weak markets and in an asset/liability context as well. Sponsors whose risk tolerance admits substantial equity exposure can thus expand their range of bond duration choices by evaluating bond risk at the total fund level rather than the asset class level.

Chapter 13. Benchmark Departures and Total Fund Risk: A Second Dimension of Diversification uses the total fund effect in rethinking the role of benchmarks in fund management. The "secondary" benchmarks used to "manage the managers" are operational conveniences, unlike the primary benchmark, which represents the sponsor's fundamental objectives. The operational efficiency that the secondary benchmarks are intended to promote can interfere with economic efficiency by unduly constraining return-seeking departures. Such departures may be penalized merely for producing risk relative to the managers' assigned benchmarks, even if they add little or no risk to the total portfolio. This study examines both tactical and strategic departures from asset class benchmarks. *If they can credibly promise incremental expected returns,* even departures whose value appears marginal when viewed relative to the "local" benchmarks can show attractive reward/risk ratios for the overall fund. This line of reasoning also argues for granting increased latitude to any active managers in whom the fund has placed its confidence.

Chapter 14. The Hierarchy of Benchmarks: Structuring Retirement Fund Risk outlines a process of managing retirement (or other) funds through a series of benchmarks.

- The *policy benchmark* is a passive mix of standard asset class indexes that reflects the key objectives of the fund as articulated by senior management. These objectives may include goals for asset-only performance, surplus control, and performance relative to a peer group.

- The *strategic benchmark* refines the policy benchmark by reflecting long-term views about possible improvements relative to the standard market-weighted benchmarks, and by adding active management processes, such as tactical overlays, into the strategic allocation.

- The *assigned asset class/subclass benchmarks* are the components of the strategic benchmark that are assigned to the managers. Manager assignments can be passive or active, but active managers are encouraged to be aggressive in their return-seeking departures from the benchmarks, because of both the passive core and the total fund effect.

PART II—YIELD-CURVE POSITIONING

Chapter 15. A Shortfall Approach to Duration Management illustrates the use of shortfall risk to determine an acceptable range of durations in an all-bond portfolio. As in Chapter 2, we consider variations in the three elements of a shortfall threshold: a minimum level of return that the fund needs to attain, a required probability of achieving that level, and a measurement horizon. Corresponding to any specified shortfall threshold is a straight line in yield/duration space. The point at which this shortfall line intersects the yield curve indicates the maximum duration that achieves the targeted shortfall threshold. As the horizon lengthens, the shortfall line shifts, generally accommodating more aggressive portfolios.

Chapter 16. Statistical Duration: A Spread Model of Rate Sensitivity across Fixed-Income Sectors refines the duration risk measurement for domestic non-Treasuries—bonds other than Treasuries. Such "spread bonds" are exposed to both Treasury rate changes and spread changes, which are commonly treated as separate risk factors. However, to the extent that spread changes correlate with Treasury rate changes, the Treasury-related portion of the spread change risk can be combined with the direct Treasury risk in a measure that we label the "statistical duration." Statistical duration risk can be hedged in the Treasury market. The intrinsic risk of spread bonds is the residual—that component of spread changes that cannot be associated with changes in Treasury rates.

Chapter 17. The Spread Curve and the Risk/Return Decision: Structuring Fixed-Income Portfolios for Treasury Benchmarks employs the statistical duration concept in optimizing a fixed-income portfolio relative to a Treasury benchmark. (A simplified model uses a flat Treasury curve and limits yield-curve changes to parallel shifts.) The investor introduces a non-Treasury allocation to gain spread. This non-Treasury component has two types of risk relative to the benchmark: Treasury rate risk, measured by statistical duration, and residual risk, measured by "spread duration" (the non-Treasury percentage multiplied by its standard duration). By shifting the duration of the Treasury component, the investor can neutralize the Treasury risk, leaving only the residual risk. Given a maximum weight for the non-Treasury component, the optimization can then proceed by focusing *exclusively* on the spread curve. For a positively sloped spread curve, this simplified model endorses the longest non-Treasury duration that satisfies the shortfall constraint. Moreover, this non-Treasury portfolio turns out to be optimal for *any* Treasury benchmark in the context of the simplistic model.

Chapter 18. The Spread Curve and a Mixed-Sector Benchmark: Structuring Fixed-Income Portfolios for Relative Performance extends the methodology of the previous chapter to a benchmark that includes non-Treasury bonds as well as Treasuries. As before, the investor boosts the non-Treasury allocation to the maximum allowed, introducing spread-duration risk relative to the benchmark. Now, however, the presence of a non-Treasury component in the benchmark allows the investor to reduce the relative risk by shortening the non-Treasury duration, thus compensating for its increased size. Within the confines of a simplified model (parallel yield-curve shifts only and no credit risk), adjustments to the Treasury and non-Treasury duration can produce a new portfolio that has a positive spread and no risk relative to the mixed benchmark. The investor who is willing to accept some spread risk may be able to pick up even more return by further adjusting the non-Treasury duration within a region dictated by a shortfall constraint.

Chapter 19. Spread Immunization: Portfolio Improvements through Dollar-Duration Matching generalizes the optimization problem from a flat Treasury curve to a sloped curve. Again, the investor increases the non-Treasury component to gain yield spread. The heightened spread risk is offset by shortening the non-Treasury duration while lengthening the Treasury duration to preserve the overall duration risk of the portfolio. This process, called "spread immunization," protects the portfolio against parallel shifts in *both* the yield curve and/or the spread curve. With a sloped Treasury curve, however, the loss of yield from shortening the non-Treasury duration may partially or fully offset the benefit of the higher non-Treasury allocation. This effect depends on the relative slopes of the two curves and the magnitude of the spread. We present a geometric interpretation that offers an estimate of the potential gain and indicates an optimal positioning. In general, the best results occur for departures from the benchmark portfolio where the non-Treasury curve is relatively flat (the longer durations) and the Treasury curve is steep (the short end).

Chapter 20. Yield-Curve Positioning for Multisector Bond Portfolios refines the optimization process relative to a mixed benchmark to provide explicit geometric solutions. As indicated in the previous chapter, the intuitive approach is to (1) maximize the non-Treasury percentage; (2) match the dollar durations to eliminate Treasury and spread risk; and (3) extend the non-Treasury duration (while balancing by shortening the Treasury duration) to further increase portfolio spread, subject to a spread duration constraint. With a sloped Treasury curve, however, each of these steps can involve a loss of yield under some circumstances. It turns out that the correct solution may involve such counterintuitive measures as *minimizing* the non-Treasury duration, *decreasing* the non-Treasury weight, or using *intermediate* positions within the allowable range of non-Treasury weight or duration.

PART III—GLOBAL FIXED-INCOME INVESTMENTS

Chapter 21. Global Fixed-Income Investing: The Impact of the Currency Hedge illustrates how the returns on currency-hedged foreign bonds relate to the structure of both the domestic and foreign markets. We begin by reviewing the relationship between yields and expected returns within a one-country bond market. We then describe the key concepts of currency hedging, including the interest-rate parity that governs the relationship between spot and forward currency exchange rates. We show how to translate the foreign return curve into a domestic risk/return diagram, with the hedged foreign return curve intersecting the domestic return curve at the "hedge point." Finally, we develop a formula that identifies the precise segments of the domestic and foreign yield curves that determine the hedged return.

Chapter 22. Interest-Rate Risks in Currency-Hedged Bond Portfolios shows how yield-curve shifts in the domestic and foreign currencies determine the return fluctuations in currency-hedged foreign bonds. We demonstrate that an investment in a hedged foreign bond is equivalent to a long position in a domestic zero-coupon note with a maturity equal to the hedge length, *plus* a long position in the foreign bond, *plus* a short position in a foreign zero-coupon note with a maturity equal to the hedge length. This formulation illuminates the exposures to changes in domestic or foreign interest rates and intermarket spreads. We conclude by outlining how investors who anticipate specific types of yield-curve movements should alter their foreign holdings and their currency hedge point.

Chapter 23. The Volatility of Hedged Global Fixed-Income Investments analyzes the interaction of the various factors that determine the volatility of a hedged foreign bond. The hedge partitions the duration of the foreign bond between domestic and foreign interest-rate exposure. This partitioning has little significance if domestic and foreign rates correlate perfectly. With an imperfect intermarket correlation, however, the hedge has more potent influence in shaping portfolio volatility. A long-term hedge can reduce the volatility of long-duration foreign bonds by diversifying their interest-rate risks between the two currencies; it can *increase* the volatility of short-duration foreign bonds by transforming their short foreign duration into a long domestic duration *plus a negative foreign duration.*

Chapter 24. The Duration of Hedged Global Fixed-Income Investments unites the model developed in Part III with the duration framework delineated in Part II. Statistical duration describes the sensitivity to domestic rate changes, and spread duration expresses the sensitivity to intermarket spread changes. We have shown that the currency hedge partitions the foreign bond duration between domestic and foreign rate exposure. To the extent that foreign and domestic rate changes are correlated, however, a portion of the foreign rate risk can be combined with the domestic risk to establish a "statistical duration." Statistical duration risk in a global portfolio can be folded in with the risk of the domestic component. The residual foreign exposure, captured by the spread duration, must be balanced against the return outlook in the foreign markets.

Chapter 25. Global Fixed-Income Investments: The Persistence Effect explores the implications of alternative views about how well forward rates predict future yield-curve shapes and currency exchange rates. We define a *persistence factor* that reflects the tendency of spot rates to persist, as opposed to giving way to forward rates. A high yield-curve persistence factor (spot rates persist) rewards duration extension along a positively sloped yield curve. Similarly, a high level of persistence in currency exchange rates favors the acceptance of currency exposure when investing in high-yielding foreign bond markets. Zero persistence—that is, all forward rates are fully realized—equalizes *all* global fixed-income returns and eliminates any incentive for return-seeking activity. Thus, all fixed-income investment decisions rely on an assumption, perhaps implicit, about persistence, and the persistence model can aid investors in evaluating their prospects for improving returns.

Part I

Asset Allocation

Chapter 2

Asset Allocation under Shortfall Constraints

INTRODUCTION

Over the long term, equity investors have been richly rewarded for the risks that they have endured. For example, during the 1926–1987 period, the S&P provided an annual return advantage of 6.8%, compared with long-term corporate bonds. By contrast, over shorter periods, stocks actually underperformed cash on a surprisingly frequent basis. In particular, over the past 15 years, stocks have underperformed Treasury bills in almost 35% of 6- to 18-month time periods.[1] These shorter horizons are comparable to the periods over which the performance of money managers is monitored. Thus, although we may reasonably expect superior equity returns over long investment horizons, few professional investors are able to observe calmly and passively while high volatility buffets their portfolio's value over the short run.

Most fund sponsors control their overall risk by adjusting the extent of their equity position. By adding cash or bonds, and thereby lowering the equity exposure, fund sponsors reduce the volatility of their portfolio. At the same time, however, they give up a portion of the risk premium that equity offers. Thus, decreased exposure to equity leads to a reduction in expected returns.

---

[1] See *Investment Policy Weekly*, R. S. Salomon, Jr., Caroline H. Davenport, Maria A. Fiore, and Susan G. Brand, Salomon Brothers Inc, February 5, 1990.

In this chapter, we focus on the balance between risky and risk-free assets. Although we use equity as the proxy for *all* of the risky assets in a portfolio, the methodology of this chapter applies equally to any basket of risky assets. We offer a simple model of how risk tolerance can be quantified and then used to determine the maximal equity investment.

We measure downside risk by the "shortfall probability" relative to a minimum return threshold.[2] By specifying both this threshold and a shortfall probability, we can establish a "shortfall constraint" to determine the maximum allocation to risky assets. We also consider the sensitivity of the risky asset allocation to changes in volatility, equity risk premium, return threshold, and shortfall probability. Finally, we show how this methodology can be applied to multiyear investment horizons.

THE EFFICIENT FRONTIER FOR AN EQUITY/CASH PORTFOLIO

A portfolio manager with a well-established horizon always has a continuum of choices between risky and riskless assets. For example, over a one-year investment horizon, the one-year Treasury STRIP provides a riskless return equal to its yield, that is, this "cash" asset has no return volatility. However, modern theory suggests that a holder of risky assets should be compensated for the associated volatility ("risk") by means of a positive increment in expected return—the so-called risk premium. Current estimates of the equity risk premium for U.S. equities range from a 4% expected return advantage to a 6% expected return advantage. Because "cash" does not have any return volatility, the volatility in an equity/cash portfolio entirely reflects the proportion of equity in that portfolio. Thus, the portfolio manager can control volatility risk by adjusting the equity/cash balance. As the percentage of equity increases, so do both the portfolio risk and expected return. In Figure 2–1, we illustrate the linear relationship between the expected return and risk for the full spectrum of equity/cash portfolios over a one-year holding period.

In Figure 2–1 we assume that the riskless asset yields 8%, the equity risk premium is 5%, and the expected return is equal to the nominal yield. The risk measure is the standard deviation of returns, which we assume is 17% for equity. If "equity" is taken to represent the market portfolio of risky as-

---

[2] The "shortfall" approach is also discussed in Chapter 15.

Figure 2–1. The Efficient Frontier for an Equity/Cash Portfolio (One-Year Horizon)

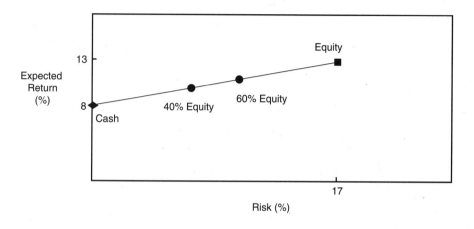

sets, the straight line in Figure 2–1 can be interpreted as the "efficient frontier" that represents portfolios that provide the maximal return for any given level of risk. The left endpoint of the efficient frontier represents a portfolio with 0% equity, while the right endpoint represents 100% equity. In addition, we have indicated the location of those portfolios that consist of 40% equity and 60% equity.

THE SHORTFALL LINE

The equity portfolio manager is faced with a critically important strategic decision regarding the appropriate extent of his or her equity position. The determination of the "right" equity/cash balance ultimately depends on the fund's risk tolerance. In this section, we quantify "risk tolerance" in a simple and intuitive manner by considering first the minimum return that can be tolerated over a given investment horizon. For purposes of exposition, we assume that the plan sponsor believes that it is worth risking a one-year return as low as 3% for the potential gain that can be achieved from equity investment.

Figure 2–2. Portfolios with a 50% Probability of Exceeding a 3% Return

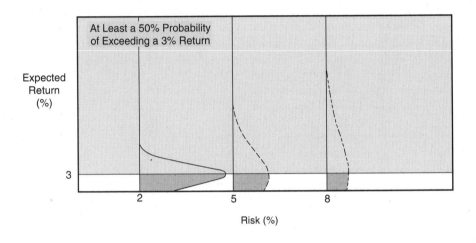

Unfortunately, although investment in a one-year 8% Treasury STRIP ensures an 8% return, there can be no minimum return guarantee with an equity investment. However, by adjusting the equity/cash balance, it is possible to lower the probability of failing to meet the 3% minimum return objective. In particular, we seek to fulfill the following "shortfall constraint" under the assumption that returns are normally distributed:

It is required that there be a probability of 10% or less that the return falls below a 3% threshold over the one-year horizon.[3]

This shortfall constraint will lead to a "shortfall line" in the return/risk diagram that divides the diagram into two regions. All portfolios that have return/risk characteristics that place them in the upper region will meet or

---

[3]The shortfall probability is an incomplete measure of risk, because it fails to provide any indication of how bad the shortfall will be in the event that one should occur. For a more fully developed theory of shortfall analysis that incorporates these broader considerations, see "Asset Pricing in a Generalized Mean-Lower Partial Moment Framework: Theory and Evidence," W. V. Harlow and R. Rao, in *Journal of Financial and Quantitative Analysis*, September 1989; and "Capital Market Equilibrium in a Mean, Lower Partial Moment Framework," V. Bawa and E. B. Lindenberg, in *Journal of Financial Economics*, November 1977.

exceed the shortfall constraint. Those portfolios that fall in the lower region will fail to satisfy the shortfall constraint. To understand how the shortfall line is constructed, we first consider all of the portfolios that have an expected return of 3%. Such portfolios are represented in Figure 2–2 by the horizontal line at the 3% return level. Each point on this line represents a different degree of volatility, with higher volatilities leading to more "spread-out" distributions. Thus, as illustrated, the distribution that corresponds to a standard deviation of 5% has a higher concentration of returns near 3% than the distribution that corresponds to a standard deviation of 8%. In all cases, however, 50% of the returns fall below the expected value of 3%; that is, there is a 50% shortfall probability. The lower tail of the distribution, which is shaded in Figure 2–2, is called the "shortfall region." The size of the shortfall region corresponds to the shortfall probability.

Now we focus our attention on the portfolio with a standard deviation of 5%. To reduce the size of the shortfall region to 10%, we must "push up" the distribution (that is, raise the expected return to 9.4%) so that only 10% of the returns fall below 3%. In a similar manner, by sufficiently raising the expected return at all risk levels, we create the 10% shortfall line in Figure 2–3.

It can be shown that, under a wide range of conditions, the shortfall constraint always leads to a straight line in the expected return/risk diagram.

Figure 2–3. Portfolios with a 90% Probability of Exceeding a 3% Return

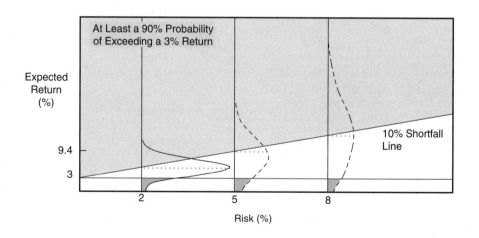

Comparing Figure 2–2 with Figure 2–3, we can see that both shortfall lines emanate from the threshold point of 3% on the vertical axis.

However, the 50% shortfall line of Figure 2–2 was horizontal (that is, it had a slope of 0), while the 10% shortfall line in Figure 2–3 had a much more positive slope. The general result is that more stringent shortfall probabilities require more steeply sloped shortfall lines. In Figure 2–4, we reproduce the "shortfall line" (note that we have changed the scale) and observe that all portfolios above the line have sufficiently large expected returns so that they offer at least a 90% probability of a 3% or greater return. Similarly, all portfolios below the line have less than a 90% probability of producing returns above 3%.

THE SHORTFALL CONSTRAINT AND THE EFFICIENT FRONTIER

Our goal of locating portfolios that meet or exceed the shortfall constraint in the previous section now can be achieved by superimposing the shortfall line on the efficient frontier in Figure 2–1. In Figure 2–5, we note that *all*

Figure 2–4. The Shortfall Line

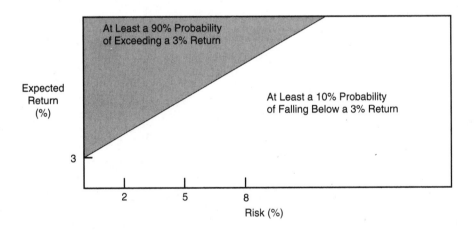

points on the efficient frontier that lie above the shortfall line will meet or exceed the requirement of at most a 10% probability of returns below the 3% threshold. The maximum equity holding that is consistent with this shortfall constraint is found at the intersection of the shortfall line and the efficient frontier. As indicated in the graph, this intersection point corresponds to a 30%/70% equity/cash portfolio. The expected return of this portfolio is 9.49%, and its standard deviation is 5.06%.

The low percentage of equity in the portfolio at first may seem counterintuitive. However, it actually reflects the powerful impact of the high volatility of equity over a one-year horizon. In a later section of this chapter, we will show how much larger equity percentages become feasible as we move to longer investment horizons.

Further insight into the equity allocation in Figure 2–5 may be gained by observing that the efficient frontier is itself a shortfall line that corresponds to an 8% minimum return threshold, because it emanates from the 8% point on the return axis. In fact, we can show that the slope of the efficient frontier corresponds to a 38% probability of shortfall (see Figure 2–6). Such a shortfall line implies that *all* portfolios with greater than 0% equity have a 38% probability of a one-year return below the risk-free rate of 8%. In this context, it is not surprising that the portfolio manager would want only a lim-

Figure 2–5. The Shortfall Constraint and the Efficient Frontier (One-Year Horizon)

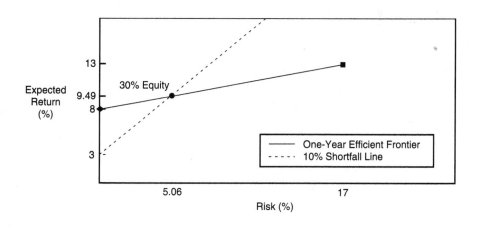

Figure 2–6. A Shortfall Interpretation of the Efficient Frontier

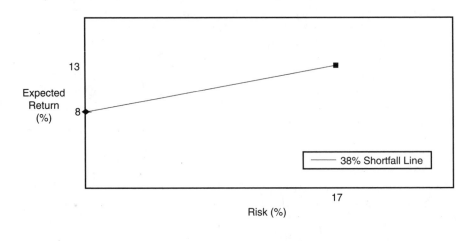

ited amount of equity in his portfolio as long as he had a *strictly* one-year horizon (and no market view other than that implied by the expected return estimates).

SENSITIVITY TO ALTERNATIVE VOLATILITY AND RISK PREMIUM ESTIMATES

In our example, we assume that equity volatility is 17% over a one-year period. Because volatility is, in fact, not constant but varies with changing market conditions, we must test the sensitivity of the equity allocation to variations in volatility. The impact of changes in volatility is illustrated in Figure 2–7, where we observe that the endpoint of the efficient frontier shifts horizontally as volatility varies. Observe that lower volatilities increase the slope of the efficient frontier. Consequently, with lower volatility, as we should expect, the maximum admissible equity allocation increases. This increase in equity allocation is evident in Figure 2–8, where we superimpose the shortfall line on the efficient frontiers from Figure 2–7.

Note that the effect of volatility on the allowable equity holding is asymmetric. A 3% increase in the volatility estimate lowers the equity percent-

Figure 2–7. The Efficient Frontier with Alternative Volatility Estimates

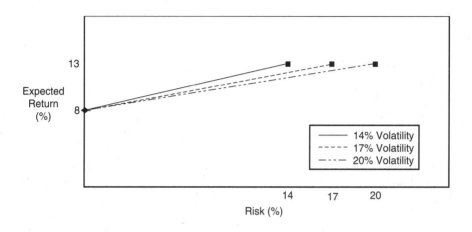

Figure 2–8. The Impact of Equity Volatility on the Maximum Equity Holding

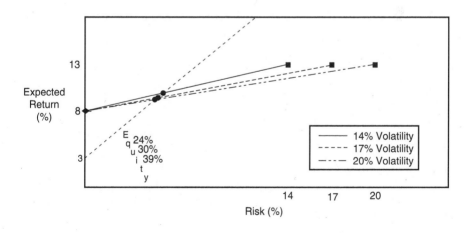

Figure 2–9. The Impact of Alternative Risk Premium Estimates

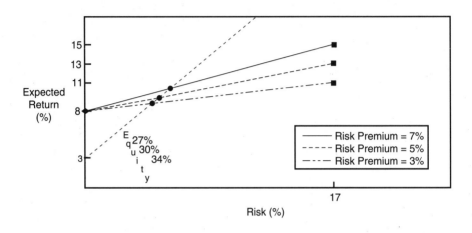

Figure 2–10. The Impact of the Minimum Return Threshold on the Maximum Equity Holding

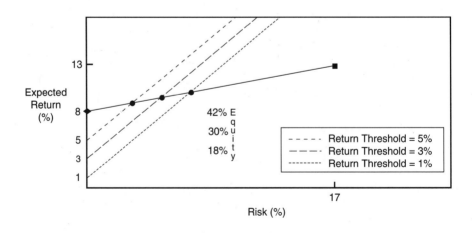

age by 6%, while a 3% decrease in volatility raises the equity percentage by 9%.

Next, we consider the impact of changes in estimates of the risk premium on the equity allocation. In Figure 2–9, we show both the shortfall line and the efficient frontiers for risk premiums of 3%, 5%, and 7%. Changing the risk premium moves the endpoint of the efficient frontier vertically, but its slope only undergoes a modest change. Consequently, for the one-year horizon, the equity allocation is fairly insensitive to the risk premium. In fact, it only varies from a low of 27% at a 3% risk premium to a high of 34% at a 7% risk premium.

In summary, over one-year horizons, we have found that the equity allocation is moderately sensitive to the volatility estimate and fairly insensitive to the risk premium estimate. This is fortuitous, because market estimates of the volatility tend to be more stable than estimates of the risk premium. Thus, for the one-year horizon, the shortfall constraint itself, rather than market estimates, most strongly influences the equity allocation.

SENSITIVITY TO VARIATIONS IN THE SHORTFALL CONSTRAINT

The shortfall constraint consists of both a minimum return threshold and a shortfall probability. In Figure 2–10, we illustrate the impact of changes in the minimum return threshold on the equity allocation.

Because the shortfall line always emanates from the threshold value on the vertical axis, the changing minimum return threshold simply results in a parallel shift of the shortfall line. Observe that a 2% change in the minimum return threshold results in a 12% change in the equity allocation. For example, a 1% minimum return threshold allows for an increase in the equity allocation from 30% to 42%.

In Figure 2–11, we illustrate the impact of changes in the shortfall probability. As noted earlier, the more stringent probabilities lead to steeper slopes for the shortfall lines and vice versa for more liberal probabilities. Thus, if we only require a 15% shortfall probability relative to a 3% return threshold, the lower slope leads to an increase in the maximum equity holding to 40%. However, if we demand a more stringent 5% shortfall probability, the slope is steeper and the maximum equity holding falls to 22%.

Figure 2–11. The Impact of Shortfall Probability

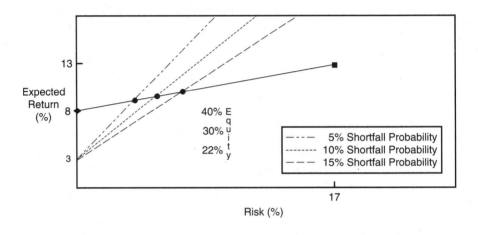

Figure 2–12. The Efficient Frontier for Multiyear Horizons

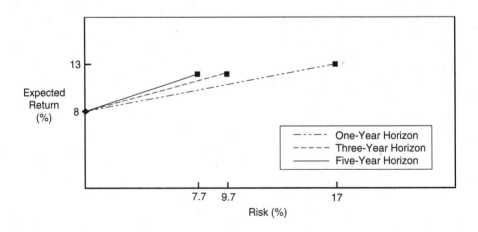

THE MULTIYEAR INVESTMENT HORIZON

In this section, we consider the impact of an extension in the investment horizon on the equity/cash mix. To this end, we use the expected annualized compound return as our return measure and the standard deviation of annualized returns as the risk measure. These choices of annualized return/risk measures enable us to use the same shortfall line as we did for a one-year horizon.

In Figure 2–12, we illustrate the efficient frontier for a one-, three-, and five-year horizon. Here, we assume that, for any horizon, there is a riskless asset with an 8% expected return, that is, one-year, three-year, and five-year STRIPs. Note that the efficient frontier steepens significantly as the horizon increases, because the *annualized* volatility of returns decreases dramatically from 17% to 7.7% as we lengthen the horizon from one year to five years.[4]

Proceeding with our analysis, now we superimpose the shortfall constraint on the efficient frontiers for the three different time periods (see Figure 2–13). The maximum equity allocation increases dramatically as the horizon increases. In particular, it extends from 30% over a one-year horizon to 60% for a three-year horizon and to 85% for a five-year horizon. For any horizon that is longer than about six years, our shortfall constraint allows a 100% equity allocation.

Of course, over a five-year horizon, the 3% threshold is probably too generous. A more realistic 6% threshold dramatically reduces the maximal equity allocation from 85% to only 34%, as shown in Figure 2–14.

Longer horizons offer a greater opportunity to capture more fully the benefits of high-risk premiums. Thus, we should expect the maximum equity allocation to become sensitive to the risk premium estimate. For a fixed three-year horizon, this sensitivity is illustrated in Figure 2–15. Here we observe that an increase in the risk premium from 5% to 7% leads to a rise in the maximum equity allocation from 60% to 80%. We also observe that the sensitivity to the risk premium is asymmetric. In particular, a 2% decrease in the risk premium only drops the maximum equity allocation from 60% to 48%.

---

[4]The decrease in annualized return volatility reflects the standard random walk model. In this model, the volatility of cumulative return increases with the square root of elapsed time. As a result, the volatility of the *annualized* returns over the investment horizon actually declines as the horizon period lengthens. We also can see from Figure 2–12 that, for the five-year horizon, the expected return on equity decreases from 13% to 12%. This drop is a result of what has been termed "volatility drag." For a detailed discussion of this concept, see "Equity Risk Premiums and the 'Volatility Drag,'" Martin L. Leibowitz, Stanley Kogelman, and Terence C. Langetieg, in *The Journal of International Securities Markets* 3, Summer 1989.

Figure 2–13. The Multiyear Shortfall Constraint with a 3% Return Threshold

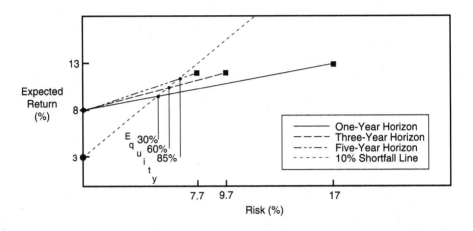

Figure 2–14. The Multiyear Shortfall Constraint with a 6% Return Threshold

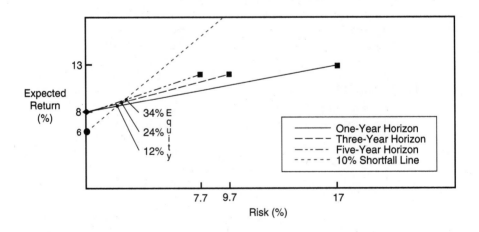

Figure 2–15. The Three-Year Shortfall Constraint with Alternative Risk Premium Estimates

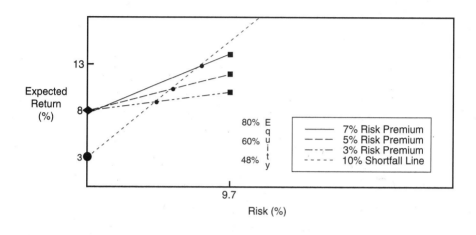

SUMMARY AND CONCLUSION

In this chapter, we have utilized a simple shortfall methodology to gain insight into the maximal allocation of risky assets. There are three critical ingredients to this analysis: (1) the investment horizon; (2) the minimum return threshold; and (3) the allowable probability that returns will fall below this threshold. Surprisingly, we found that with a 10% shortfall probability, a 3% return threshold, and a one-year horizon, only 30% of the portfolio should be in risky assets. Over the short term, the volatility of risky assets creates a high probability of poor returns. In effect, there is insufficient time to reliably capture the risk premium that these assets offer. As long as we focus on a one-year horizon, this result holds across a wide range of risk premiums.

By contrast, as the horizon increases, there is a marked decrease in annualized return volatility. As a result, the allowable equity allocation increases dramatically. We found, for our example, that over a five-year horizon, the risky asset allocation could be increased to 85% for a minimum return threshold of 3%. Moreover, the multiyear allocations are more sensitive to the risk premium, with higher risk premiums leading to substantially greater equity allocations.

The strength of our shortfall model lies in its ability to capture the allocation impact of a simply stated measure of risk tolerance across one or more investment horizons. Accordingly, this shortfall approach should help fund sponsors address the delicate problem of finding a balance between seeking long-term gains and defending against the risk of adverse performance.

Asset Performance and Surplus Control: A Dual-Shortfall Approach

INTRODUCTION

This chapter presents an asset allocation methodology for constructing port-folios that strike a balance between asset performance and maintenance of acceptable levels of downside risk in both asset and surplus contexts. In the real world, pension fund sponsors do not have the luxury of being able to pursue a single well-defined goal. Rather, they must contend with a complex set of multiple objectives. These include achieving market-related returns on assets when the market does well and attaining at least some minimum re-turn when the market does poorly. At the same time, sponsors are expected to maintain or improve their funding status relative to a variety of liability measures.

Even when the plan's funding status is not considered, the strategic as-set allocation decision is not easy. The fundamental issue is how to capture the risk premium of equity while avoiding excessively high levels of volatil-ity. Through a combination of mean-variance analysis and tradition, most funds have settled on a long-term strategic allocation target of a 50%–60% investment in equitylike assets, with the balance primarily in fixed-income securities. The fixed-income component tends to be regarded as a single as-set class whose characteristics reflect the bond market as a whole. This char-acterization leads to a duration that is representative of the investment-grade bond market—currently about 4.64 years.[1] In essence, when stripped of the (usually token) investments in other asset classes, many allocation studies really lead to a single decision: the percentage to be allocated to equity.

Unfortunately, the resulting 60% stock/40% bond portfolio has far less interest-rate sensitivity than a pension plan's accumulated benefit obligation (ABO), which typically has a duration of about 10 years. Thus, the standard allocation leads to a significant surplus volatility, because the pension fund is vulnerable both to poor equity returns when the stock market weakens, and to high liability returns when the bond market rallies. In recent years, particularly with the advent of the Financial Accounting Standards Board Statement 87 (FASB 87), there has been a growing interest in models that set the allocation problem in a liability framework.[2] However, these new asset/liability models generally have problems of their own.

At one extreme, an "immunized" portfolio minimizes surplus risk by matching the duration of a 100% bond portfolio to the duration of the liability. While "immunization" may be useful in the short-term management of the ABO under unusual circumstances, a dynamic ongoing fund has a far more complex liability structure than can be represented by the ABO alone. Thus, immunizing against the ABO (or indeed, against any single liability measure) tends to foreclose the growth opportunities and inflation protection needed for the long-term benefit of plan sponsors and participants alike.

However, there are more general surplus-based models that treat bonds as a "variable asset class" with duration/volatility values that range from Treasury bills up to risk levels that far exceed that of domestic equities. In contrast to asset-only models that essentially prescribe only an equity percentage, these generalized surplus-based models tend to characterize allocations in terms of an equity percentage and a duration target for the bond component. These models move beyond immunization and can accommodate significant equity holdings. However, surplus optimizations almost invariably push the duration to extremes by forcing the dollar-duration of the bond component to match the dollar-duration of the liabilities. The resulting bond durations of 15 years or longer may make sense from a narrowly defined surplus-only vantage point, but they entail extraordinary levels of asset volatility.[3]

---

[1]Over the past seven years, the effective duration of the Salomon Broad Investment-Grade (BIG) Bond Index has ranged from a low of 3.87 years to a high of 4.69 years. On April 1, 1991, the duration was 4.64 years.

[2]For example, see "A New Perspective on Asset Allocation," Martin L. Leibowitz, The Research Foundation of The Institute of Chartered Financial Analysts, December 1987.

[3]For one approach that avoids many of these problems, see "Liabilities—A New Approach," William F. Sharpe and Lawrence G. Tint, *The Journal of Portfolio Management*, Winter 1990.

Figure 3–1. Assumptions on Stock and Bond Returns (Stock/Bond Correlation = 0.35)

Asset	Expected Return	Standard Deviation
Equity	13.0%	17.0%
BIG Index	8.0	7.0
60% Stock/40% BIG Index (Benchmark)	11.0	11.5

For these reasons, surplus optimization models have not proven productive in generating allocations that most funds would find viable. To achieve a reasonable balance between asset and surplus risks, this chapter presents a methodology for applying simultaneous shortfall constraints on both the asset performance and the fund surplus. As an example of this methodology, we construct a new portfolio with the same asset-only shortfall risk as the 60/40 benchmark portfolio but with a more stringent limit on the surplus shortfall. One surprising finding is that modest adjustments to the bond duration and equity percentage are often sufficient to satisfy both constraints. This finding contrasts with surplus optimization approaches that tend to suggest unpalatably long durations. Thus, our dual-shortfall approach avoids the problem of extreme portfolios to which single-objective optimizations are notoriously prone. By design, this approach can develop allocations that are better crafted for the more realistic situation where the fund faces conflicting goals.

THE ASSET-ONLY FRAMEWORK

To analyze the risk/return characteristics of stock/bond portfolios with bonds of varying durations, we must make assumptions regarding expected returns, volatilities, and the stock/bond correlation (see Figure 3–1). We assume that the one-year expected return for the BIG Index is 8.0%, and that U.S. equity provides a 5% risk premium over bonds. The one-year volatility of U.S. equity is taken as 17%, interest-rate volatility is 1.5%, and the stock/bond correlation is 0.35. Under these assumptions, the bond asset class will have a volatility of approximately 7.0%.[4] For later reference, Figure 3–1 also shows the expected return and standard deviation of the benchmark portfolio.

---

[4]Because the duration of the BIG Index is fairly stable, we estimate the return volatility by multiplying the 4.64-year duration by the 1.5% interest-rate volatility. In this chapter, we make the simplifying assumption that the interest-rate volatility is the same at all points along the yield curve.

Figure 3–2. The Risk/Return Trade-Off for Stock/Bond Portfolios (Duration = 4.64 Years)

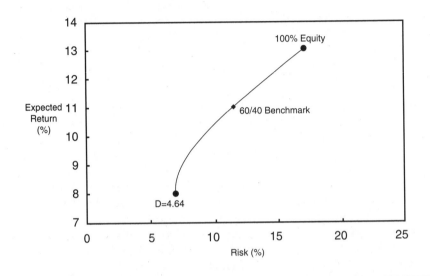

The volatilities and expected returns of portfolios consisting of varying proportions of stocks and the BIG Index plot along a curve in a risk/return diagram, as illustrated in Figure 3–2. As equity is added to the bond portfolio, the portfolio return increases proportionately. The volatility of the portfolio returns also changes with the additional equity. However, because the correlation is fairly low, diversification may initially lead to a decrease (or very gradual increase) in volatility.

We now broaden our discussion of asset allocation by varying the duration of the fixed-income component of the portfolio. To clarify the impact of duration, we use an artificial "flat yield curve" model that makes two assumptions: (1) bonds of all maturities provide the same 8% yield; and (2) the expected return is equal to the yield. The "cash" asset is taken to be one-year Treasury STRIPS that have an initial duration of 1 year and a zero volatility at the end of the 1-year holding period. As the duration of bonds increases, so does the return volatility. This is shown in Figure 3–3, where we have indicated a range of fixed-income portfolio durations along a horizontal line at an 8% expected return.

In Figure 3–4 we have drawn a diagonal line from the cash point to the 100%-equity point. This line represents the risk/return characteristics of the full range of cash/equity portfolios. These portfolios plot on a straight line

Figure 3–3. The Flat Yield Curve

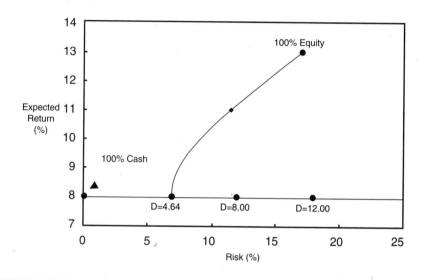

because all the portfolio risk is due to the proportion of equity. At any given level of risk, by moving vertically in the risk/return diagram, we see that the cash/equity portfolio provides a higher return than a portfolio of stocks and 4.64-year-duration bonds. This results from the zero volatility of cash, which permits a higher proportion of equity for a given portfolio volatility.

In Figure 3–4, we have also added the risk/return curve for portfolios containing 12-year-duration bonds. The "efficient" portfolios are located on the upper portion of this curve. The deep "bubble" to the left reflects the fact that the benefits of diversification are more pronounced for these long-duration, high-volatility bonds.

More generally, every point in the risk/return diagram represents a unique stock/bond portfolio that is characterized by the equity percentage and the duration of the fixed-income component. With our simplistic assumption of a flat yield curve and a positive stock/bond correlation, the portfolio that provides the highest return for a given level of risk will always be a cash/equity portfolio. In this sense, cash/equity portfolios dominate all other stock/bond portfolios.

If the yield curve is not flat, there may be mixes of cash, bonds, and equities that dominate the cash/equity portfolios. In addition, it should be noted that although the stock/bond correlation tends to be positive over long time

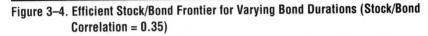

Figure 3–4. Efficient Stock/Bond Frontier for Varying Bond Durations (Stock/Bond Correlation = 0.35)

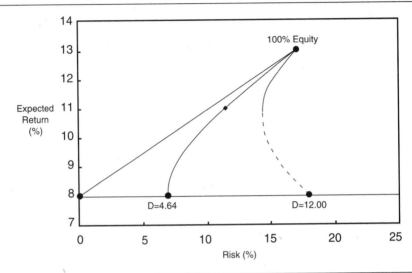

periods, there are occasional periods when the correlation is negative. During such periods, longer-duration bonds may provide significant diversification benefits even if the yield curve is flat.[5]

THE RETURN DISTRIBUTION FOR THE BENCHMARK PORTFOLIO

To gain some perspective on the expected performance of the benchmark portfolio, we assume that both stock and bond returns over a one-year horizon are normally distributed. In Figure 3–5, we illustrate the 60/40 benchmark portfolio return distribution. It can be shown that this 60% stock/40% bond portfolio has an expected return of 11% and a standard deviation of 11.5%. For any normal distribution, there is a 16% probability that returns will fall more than one standard deviation below the mean (that is, below −0.5% = 11.0% − 11.5%), and there is a 10% probability that returns will be

---

[5]See *Portfolio Optimization Utilizing the Full Yield Curve: An Improved Approach to Fixed Income as an Asset Class,* Martin L. Leibowitz, Roy D. Henriksson, William S. Krasker, Salomon Brothers Inc, October 1987.

Figure 3–5. The Return Distribution for the Benchmark Portfolio

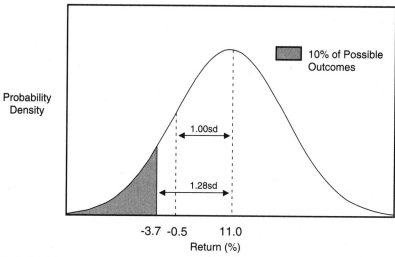

sd = Standard deviation.

more than 1.28 standard deviations below the mean (that is, below –3.7% = 11.0% – 1.28 × 11.5%). The region to the left of –3.7% is shaded and will be referred to as the 10% shortfall region. A return of –3.7% will be referred to as the threshold return.

The –3.7% threshold return represents the implicit shortfall risk inherent in the benchmark portfolio. We will assume that the plan sponsor is comfortable with this level of asset-only risk. Consequently, any new allocation that offers a higher expected return but the same shortfall risk as the benchmark portfolio will be viewed as a portfolio improvement.[6]

In Chapter 2, we have shown that all portfolios with equivalent shortfall risk plot along a straight line in a risk/return diagram. In Figure 3–6, we have constructed a 10% shortfall line through the benchmark portfolio point.

---

[6]We utilize the indicated measure of shortfall risk because it is intuitively appealing and easy to apply. However, the shortfall probability we have defined is an incomplete measure of risk. It fails to provide any indication of how bad the shortfall will be in the event that one should occur. For a more fully developed theory of shortfall analysis that incorporates these "higher" considerations, see "Asset Pricing in a Generalized Mean-Lower Partial Moment Framework: Theory and Evidence," W. V. Harlow and R. Rao, in *Journal of Financial and Quantitative Analysis*, September 1989; and "Capital Market Equilibrium in a Mean, Lower Partial Moment Framework," V. Bawa and E. B. Lindenberg, in *Journal of Financial Economics*, November 1977.

Figure 3–6. The Implicit Shortfall Constraint for the Benchmark Portfolio

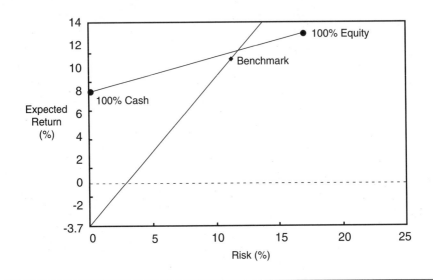

Note that this line intersects the (vertical) expected return axis at –3.7%—the threshold return point. All points along the shortfall line represent portfolios for which the expected return offsets the portfolio volatility sufficiently to ensure a 90% probability that the one-year return will exceed –3.7% (that is, there is only a 10% chance that returns will fall below the –3.7% threshold). Portfolios above the shortfall line have a higher expected return for a given shortfall risk than portfolios on the line. Consequently, all portfolios above the line have a greater than 90% probability that the one-year return will exceed –3.7%. Conversely, portfolios below the shortfall line have inferior shortfall performance.

The shortfall line in Figure 3–6 can be shown to intersect the cash/equity line at a point representing a portfolio with 70% stocks and 30% bonds. This portfolio has the same shortfall risk as the benchmark portfolio, but it has an expected return of 11.5%. Thus, by moving to the 70/30 portfolio, the fund manager can pick up 50 basis points in expected return while maintaining the same level of asset shortfall risk.

MODELING THE LIABILITY

Our analysis focuses on the relatively well-defined ABO. The ABO is the value of benefits earned to date by retirees, former employees with vested rights, and current employees. It approximates the termination liability of the plan. Thus, a comparison of the ABO with the current value of plan assets indicates the deficit or surplus that would exist if the plan were terminated.

The ABO is also the basis for a balance sheet liability under FASB 87, and a proxy for the "current liability" used under ERISA to determine whether plan contributions are currently required from the employer. Because the future events reflected in the ABO are primarily demographic (mortality, age at retirement), rather than economic (salary increases), the ABO benefit stream may be regarded as essentially fixed for investment purposes. Consequently, the ABO can be modeled as if it were a fixed-income security. The benefit payments associated with more comprehensive measures of liability, such as the projected benefit obligation (PBO), reflect future economic events and have a more complex structure.

The ABO duration is plan-specific, depending on the mix of active and retired plan participants, their ages, the assumed retirement ages of active employees, and the benefit formula. Most plans have ABO durations in the range of 9 to 12 years.

In computing the ABO, FASB 87 directs the use of a discount rate equivalent to that at which plan benefits could be "settled," for example, by an annuity purchase. The yield on high-quality fixed-income investments (8% in our examples) is suggested as a suitable guide for this settlement rate. This rate may also be interpreted as the expected "liability return." In other words, the ABO is expected to grow at 8%, apart from benefit payments and adjustments for the additional benefits that employees earn each year (that is, the "service cost").

In Figure 3–7, we illustrate the position of the ABO in the risk/return diagram of Figure 3–4. Note that the benchmark portfolio point and the liability point are quite far apart; that is, the risk/return characteristics of the benchmark portfolio differ markedly from those of the ABO liability. We should therefore expect considerable variations in the pension fund surplus over time.[7]

---

[7]Our approach can easily be extended so that a performance benchmark is viewed as a "liability" against which "surplus" returns are measured. Thus, the dual-shortfall approach can be viewed as simultaneously controlling both the absolute asset risk and the risk relative to a designated performance benchmark.

Figure 3–7. A Ten-Year-Duration ABO Liability

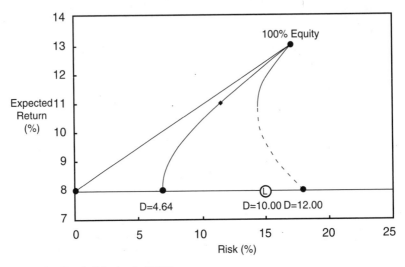

ABO = Accumulated Benefit Obligation. L = Liability.

THE SURPLUS RETURN

The pension fund surplus is the difference between the current value of the assets and the present value of the liability.[8] Over time, as the value of assets and liabilities changes, so will the surplus. There are a number of ways to define a "surplus return" measure. Since the surplus itself is commonly expressed as a percentage of the liability, we define our surplus return as follows:[9]

$$\text{Surplus Return} = \frac{\text{Change in Surplus}}{\text{Initial Value of Liabilities}}$$

[8]For a discussion of the application of the shortfall approach to managing an insurance company's surplus, see *Asset Allocation for Property/Casualty Insurance Companies: A Going-Concern Approach,* Alfred Weinberger and Vincent Kaminski, Salomon Brothers Inc, July 1991.

[9]The surplus could just as easily have been measured against the current value of assets. For example, see "Asset Allocation," William F. Sharpe, in *Managing Investment Portfolios,* 2nd ed., John L. Maginn and Donald L. Tuttle, eds., Waren, Gorham & Lamont, 1990. Our results can be converted to surplus returns relative to the current asset value by dividing by the funding ratio. Also, our results can be converted to dollar surplus changes by multiplying by the initial liability value.

Figure 3–8. A Liability-Based Surplus Return Example (Dollars in Millions)

Funding Ratio		Initial Value	Final Value	Liability or Asset Return	Surplus Return
	Liability	$100.0	$108.0	8.0%	
140%	Assets	140.0	155.4	11.0	
	Surplus	40.0	47.4		7.4%
100	Assets	100.0	111.0	11.0	
	Surplus	0.0	3.0		3.0
60	Assets	60.0	66.6	11.0	
	Surplus	(40.0)	(41.4)		(1.4)

For example (see Figure 3–8), suppose that the initial liability is $100 million and the initial assets are $140 million. Then the funding ratio is 140% ($140 million/$100 million) and the surplus is $40 million. If the liability increases by 8% to $108 million, and the assets increase by 11% to $155.4 million, the surplus will have increased by $7.4 million to $47.4 million ($155.4 million – $108 million). This surplus increase is 7.4% of the initial liability.

Figure 3–8 also shows how the value of the surplus return depends on the initial funding ratio. In general, if two pension plans have the same asset and liability returns, the plan with the greater funding ratio will have the greater surplus return. For example, if the funding ratio is 100%, the assets and liabilities are equal and the surplus is zero. In this case, 11% asset growth leads to a surplus return of 3%. If the funding ratio is less than 100%, the assets will be less than the liability, and the surplus may decrease even though the asset return is greater than the liability return. For a 60% funding ratio, for example, the surplus return is –1.4%, despite the 11% asset growth.

We will now focus on the distribution of surplus returns when the funding ratio is 140% and the assets are represented by our benchmark portfolio. Because both the asset and liability returns are assumed to be normally distributed, the surplus returns are normally distributed as well. Under our assumptions, the expected surplus return is 7.4% and the standard deviation of surplus returns is 14.7% (see the Appendix to this chapter for details). For any normal return distribution, there is a 10% probability that the return will be 1.28 or more standard deviations below the 7.4% mean. Thus, there is a 10% probability of a surplus decline of at least 11.5% ($-11.5\% = 7.4\% - 1.28 \times 14.7\%$). In Figure 3–9, we summarize the return and shortfall characteristics

---

Figure 3–9. Performance Summary for the Benchmark Portfolio

	Current Expected Return	Current Standard Deviation	Current 10th-Percentile Return	Target 10th-Percentile Return
Asset-Only Performance	11.0 %	11.5 %	(3.7) %	(3.7)%
Surplus Performance	7.4	14.7	(11.5)	(7.0)

from both asset and surplus perspectives. The last column in the figure shows target 10th-percentile returns that will be discussed in subsequent sections.

THE SHORTFALL CURVE FOR THE SURPLUS RETURN

Pension fund sponsors who wish to achieve stability in the plan's surplus can do so with a bond portfolio that matches the liability in present value, duration, and other volatility characteristics. Such an "immunized portfolio" will preserve the surplus within some reasonable range of interest-rate changes. Most sponsors, however, do not require this degree of safety. Typically, a sponsor with a 140% funding ratio might be willing to sustain some surplus risk provided that the portfolio had substantial upside potential. However, there usually will be some limit to the surplus loss that a sponsor can comfortably sustain. This loss limit will depend on a variety of factors, including the current funding ratio, the fund's performance over prior years, and the level of funding needed to avoid a balance-sheet liability or sustain a contribution holiday. To quantify surplus return risk, we focus on the 10th-percentile surplus return and somewhat arbitrarily impose the following **surplus shortfall condition:**

> **There should be no more than a 10% probability that the surplus return will be less than –7%. That is, we require 90% assurance of a surplus return in excess of –7%.**

In an earlier section of this chapter, we showed that an asset shortfall constraint that was similar to the above surplus constraint could be represented by a straight line in a risk/return diagram. The surplus constraint pattern is far more complicated, and it is represented by an "egg-shaped" convex curve (see the Appendix to this chapter for a theoretical discussion).

Figure 3–10. The Surplus Shortfall Curve (Funding Ratio = 140%)

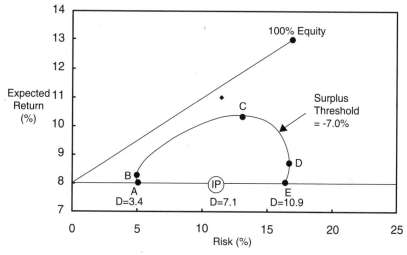

IP = Immunizing portfolio.

In Figure 3–10 we illustrate the surplus shortfall curve for a pension fund with a 140% funding ratio and a 10-year duration liability. Each point within the "egg" represents an asset portfolio that fulfills the surplus shortfall condition. We have also included the benchmark portfolio and the immunizing portfolio points for reference. The immunizing portfolio is an all-bond portfolio that has the same dollar sensitivity to interest-rate changes as the liability. The duration of the immunizing portfolio is 7.1 years (that is, the 10-year liability duration divided by the 140% funding ratio). To see why this is so, we first observe that if the liability is $100 million, the assets are $140 million. If interest rates decline by 1%, the liability, with its 10-year duration, will grow by approximately 10%, or $10 million (10% of $100 million). At the same time, the assets will increase by 7.1% (the 7.1-year duration multiplied by 1%). In dollar terms, this also represents a $10 million increase (7.1% of $140 million).

To develop an intuitive understanding of the shortfall curve, we first observe that point A in Figure 3–10 represents a 100% bond portfolio with a 3.4-year duration. This is the shortest duration all-bond portfolio for which there is at most a 10% probability that the surplus return will be –7% or less. For any all-bond portfolio with shorter duration, the gap between the bond duration and the immunizing portfolio is too large, and the shortfall probability will exceed 10%.

As we move to the right of portfolio A, we encounter all-bond portfolios with durations that are closer to the 7.1-year immunizing duration. Consequently, such portfolios will have better shortfall performance than portfolio A. Ultimately, we reach portfolio E, which has a 10.9-year duration. Because the durations of portfolios A and E are equidistant from the 7.1-year immunizing duration, both of these portfolios have the same duration gap and therefore the same −7% surplus shortfall threshold. Portfolios to the right of portfolio E have longer durations than E and will not meet the shortfall constraint.

We now consider the impact of adding equity to portfolio A. Since equity provides a 5% expected return premium over fixed income, the portfolio return will increase as the equity percentage increases. In addition, the low correlation between equity and the liability at first causes the surplus volatility to increase more slowly than the surplus return. Consequently, the initial additions of equity actually reduce the surplus shortfall probability, and the shortfall curve bubbles slightly to the left as we move upward from A. However, a point (B) is reached where further equity additions cause the surplus volatility to increase very rapidly. To compensate for this equity-related volatility, the bond duration must be increased so as to bring the asset portfolio duration closer to the immunizing duration.

Under the assumptions of our example, each point along the shortfall curve represents a unique portfolio characterized by the percentage of equity in the portfolio and the duration of the fixed-income component. Portfolio C is the maximum equity portfolio that fulfills the shortfall constraint. It consists of 47% stocks and 53% bonds. From a surplus perspective, portfolio C looks very attractive because of its high expected return. However, the long duration (close to 10 years) of the fixed-income portion of the portfolio leads to high volatility from an asset-only perspective.

Portfolios that lie on the portion of the shortfall curve from C to E can be understood by applying logic similar to that used for portfolios from A to C. It suffices to note that these points correspond to very long-duration portfolios consisting of a decreasing percentage of equity.

All portfolios that fall on or within the shortfall "egg" will meet or exceed the surplus shortfall condition. Because the benchmark portfolio "diamond" falls outside the shortfall curve, it fails to meet the surplus shortfall condition. The portion of the "egg" between portfolios B and C can be thought of as a "surplus-shortfall efficient frontier" because, among all portfolios meeting the surplus constraint, these portfolios offer the most favorable risk/return trade-off. However, from an asset-only perspective, some of these portfolios will have greater shortfall risk than the benchmark portfolio. In the next section, we show how the asset and surplus shortfall constraints can be jointly managed.

BALANCING ASSET AND SURPLUS SHORTFALL REQUIREMENTS

We have observed that the benchmark portfolio lies outside the surplus shortfall curve corresponding to a minimum surplus return of –7%. This is consistent with the earlier observation that the 10th percentile surplus return for the benchmark portfolio was –11.5%. Thus, meeting the surplus constraint will require restructuring the asset portfolio so that the new portfolio lies on or within the surplus shortfall curve. In choosing this new portfolio, we must be careful that the asset-only constraints are also maintained.

Under the assumption that the plan sponsor finds the asset-only risk of the benchmark portfolio to be acceptable (that is, a –3.7% asset-return threshold), we now construct a portfolio that maintains that level of asset-only shortfall and meets the surplus constraint. Earlier in this chapter, we observed that all portfolios that met the asset constraint were located on or above the shortfall line drawn through the benchmark portfolio (see Figure 3–6). In Figure 3–11, we superimpose this line on the surplus shortfall curve of Figure 3–10. The region above the line but inside the "egg" consists of all portfolios that meet both the asset and surplus shortfall requirements. The indicated point of intersection between the asset-only line and the surplus "egg" corresponds to the portfolio with the highest expected return that meets both shortfall requirements. This "dual-shortfall" portfolio consists of 44% stocks and 56% bonds with a 6.6-year duration.

In comparison to the benchmark portfolio, the reduced equity allocation in the dual-shortfall portfolio leads to an 82-basis-point reduction in expected return, from 11.00% to 10.18%. This reduction can be interpreted as the "cost" of bringing the surplus shortfall risk to an acceptable level. On the other hand, the dual-shortfall portfolio has a significantly higher expected return and about the same volatility as the immunizing portfolio.[10]

Thus, even in this simple case, the dual-shortfall solution provides for more acceptable return/risk characteristics than either the original 60/40

---

[10] See "Shortfall Risk and the Asset Allocation Decision: A Simulation Analysis of Stock and Bond Risk Profiles," Martin L. Leibowitz and Terence C. Langetieg, *The Journal of Portfolio Management,* Fall 1989, and Chapter 2.

Figure 3–11. A Portfolio That Meets Both Asset-Only and Surplus Shortfall Constraints

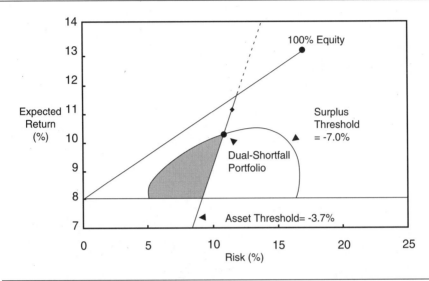

benchmark portfolio (which has too great a surplus risk) or the immunizing portfolio (which guarantees low asset return and high asset volatility).

It should be noted that these results strongly depend on the one-year investment horizon assumed in our analysis. The one-year time frame allows a relatively short period in which to reliably capture the equity risk premium. Over longer horizons, reasonable surplus shortfall constraints can be achieved with substantially higher equity allocations and with more moderate duration shifts.

THE IMPACT OF CHANGES IN THE SHORTFALL THRESHOLDS

In the previous sections, we arbitrarily imposed a –7% threshold on the surplus return and assumed that the –3.7% asset-only threshold should be maintained. More often, however, the problem is determining the appropriate balance between asset-only and surplus risks. After assessing the implicit shortfall risks in the portfolio, the plan sponsor may decide that the current

Figure 3–12. Implicit Shortfall Constraints in Asset-Only and Surplus Contexts

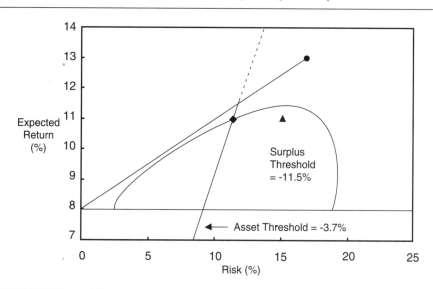

portfolio structure is satisfactory. If that is not the case, the sponsor must decide whether the current risk posture should be modified in either an asset-only context, a surplus context, or both. In contrast to our earlier example, this assessment might lead to a tightening of the asset constraint, while allowing for greater surplus variability.

In order to better understand the available options for portfolio restructuring, we first review the shortfall characteristics of our benchmark portfolio with a 140% funding ratio and 10-year duration liability. Recall that in Figure 3–6, we constructed an implicit shortfall constraint for the benchmark portfolio. To that figure, we now add the surplus shortfall curve corresponding to the benchmark portfolio's *implicit* –11.5% surplus return threshold. The benchmark portfolio with the shortfall line and the "–11.5% egg" are shown in Figure 3–12. Note that at a –11.5% threshold, the surplus shortfall requirement is so weak that it is met by almost all stock/bond portfolios. If we had set –14% as the surplus threshold, the "egg" would have been still larger and would have begun to merge with the cash/equity line.

Every portfolio on the "egg" in Figure 3–12 will have a 10% probability of a surplus decline of 11.5% or more. In addition, every portfolio on the asset shortfall line will have a 10% probability of an asset decline of 3.7% or

Figure 3–13. Changing the Asset Return Threshold

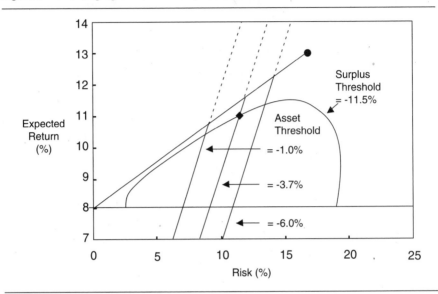

more. Both of these conditions are fulfilled at the point of intersection of the shortfall line and shortfall curve (the benchmark in this case).[11]

Changes in the asset threshold return requirement can be viewed as parallel shifts of the shortfall line. In Figure 3–13, we illustrate the effect of moving the asset threshold return to a less stringent –6% and to a more stringent –1%. As we increase the threshold return requirement, we move to the left along the "egg" and must accept a lower expected return in order to meet the same surplus shortfall condition. By contrast, as we lower the threshold return, we move to the right along the "egg" and can achieve higher expected returns with the same –11.5% surplus shortfall threshold.

Raising the surplus return threshold will shrink the "egg" and significantly reduce the range of acceptable asset portfolios. As an example, in Figure 3–14, we show the surplus "eggs" corresponding to 10th-percentile surplus returns of –7% (our example from the last section) and –3%.

In effect, we can think of the entire risk/return diagram as being covered

---

[11]For simplicity, we are treating the two shortfall conditions separately. We require that *each* shortfall probability be 10%; that is, we require a 90% assurance of satisfying the asset shortfall and a 90% probability of meeting the surplus requirement. Note that this is *not* equivalent to a 90% probability that all shortfall requirements are satisfied.

Figure 3–14. Changing the Surplus Return Threshold

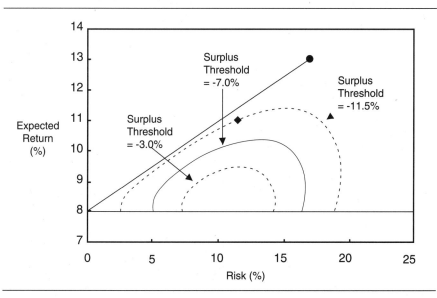

by a grid of shortfall lines and shortfall curves (see Figure 3–15). Within this grid, the portfolio manager must select an appropriate surplus shortfall curve and a suitable asset shortfall line. The highest intersection point of the line and the curve represents a balanced portfolio that meets the dual-shortfall condition. For example, the most stringent surplus threshold (–3%) would require a portfolio of only 26% stocks, with the balance invested in 6.9-year-duration bonds to meet the surplus requirement and still have the same asset shortfall characteristics as the benchmark (see the "square" in Figure 3–15). When no intersection point exists, either the asset or the surplus shortfall requirement (or both) must be relaxed before a suitable portfolio can be found.

THE IMPACT OF THE FUNDING RATIO

To this point, our examples have focused on pension funds for which the funding ratio is 140%. In actuality, individual funds may have very different goals in terms of surplus preservation. For example, even two funds having the same high funding ratio may set very different courses. One fund may desire to lock in the surplus and therefore adopt a more conservative surplus

Figure 3–15. The Shortfall Grid

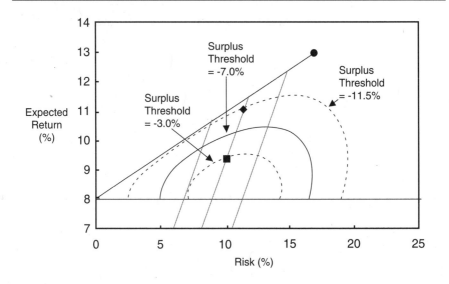

threshold. In contrast, a second fund may feel that its ample surplus allows room to sustain additional surplus risk in order to reach for higher returns.

Thus, funds with the same funding ratios may use different surplus constraints. If the funding ratios are different, we should not be surprised to encounter an even greater range of allocation choices. In fact, it turns out that the allocation trade-offs are radically altered at different funding ratios, even when the surplus constraints are kept the same.

To better understand this "funding ratio effect," we will maintain a –7% surplus threshold while varying the funding ratio.[12] In Figure 3–16, we compare the shortfall "eggs" for funding ratios of 140%, 110%, and 80%. At a 140% funding ratio, the shortfall "egg" covers a wide swath of portfolios having reasonable performance characteristics and also satisfying the asset-only shortfall constraint. As the funding ratio declines, the "eggs" move to the right and the duration of the fixed-income portfolio is forced to more closely approximate an even longer immunizing duration. At a funding ratio of 110%, the 9.1-year immunizing duration (10 years divided by 1.1) is

---

[12] The degree to which a plan is vulnerable to surplus shortfall risk can be analyzed in terms of changes in the funding ratio rather than surplus returns. See Chapter 10.

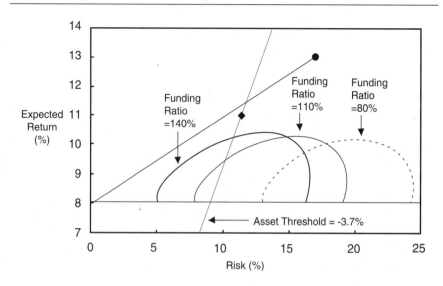

Figure 3–16. Changing the Funding Ratios (Surplus Threshold = –7%)

almost the same as the 10-year liability duration. The "egg" now has a less desirable location in terms of asset volatility. The asset-only shortfall line passes through the "egg," but the set of relatively low-return portfolios that satisfy both constraints is very restricted.

At a funding ratio of 80%, no portfolios meet the dual-shortfall conditions. In the case of such low funding ratios, there is no easy solution. An immunizing portfolio will simply lock in a negative surplus return by eliminating surplus volatility. Moreover, immunization would create a very volatile bond portfolio (duration = 12.5 years) from an asset-only perspective. As duration is decreased, asset risk decreases, but the surplus risk increases and the expected surplus return remains negative. Our methodology does not provide a solution to the underfunding problem, but it does offer a convenient process for assessing the trade-offs in this very difficult environment.

More generally, this analysis shows that a fund's initial funding ratio and its tolerance for surplus risk will significantly affect the optimal target duration. Consequently, one would expect the plan sponsor to find that a more customized fixed-income benchmark is better suited to the plan's goals than any broad market benchmark such as the BIG Index. Fortunately, the diversity of the fixed-income markets naturally allows for the construction of a wide range of such customized indexes.[13]

SUMMARY AND CONCLUSION

This chapter represents a blend of three themes: (1) surplus management, (2) shortfall constraints, and (3) the expansion of fixed income from a single asset class to a full continuum of available duration points. With our simple flat "return curve" assumption, cash/equity portfolios dominate all other bond/equity portfolios in terms of asset-only performance. In a surplus context, however, the picture changes dramatically. Cash/equity portfolios have considerable surplus volatility and will be inferior to portfolios where the bond component has a reasonable duration.

In a standard risk/return diagram, the asset-only shortfall constraint is represented by a simple diagonal line. In contrast, the surplus shortfall constraint requires a far more complex "egg-shaped" curve that is roughly centered on top of the immunizing portfolio point. By overlaying these two constraint patterns, it becomes clear how a relatively modest adjustment to the duration and equity percentage can bring the surplus shortfall to within reasonable limits. The trick is to do this without violating restrictions on the asset shortfall.

By extending the process, an asset and surplus shortfall grid can be created that enables the plan sponsor to quickly assess the trade-offs that must be made between asset-only performance and surplus control. The nature of this grid pattern is highly dependent on the initial funding ratio. Moreover, for two funds with the same funding ratio, the choice of an acceptable allocation will depend critically on the plan sponsor's risk tolerance, both in absolute and in relative terms. Consequently, one would expect the optimal portfolio duration target to vary markedly from plan to plan. It would be a rare plan that would find, by happenstance, that its duration target coincided with the duration of a broad market index. Thus, this dual-shortfall approach offers a promising technique for sponsors who are willing to break away from the traditional benchmarks and pursue allocations that are truly based on their own fund's needs and objectives.

---

[13] See *Salomon Brothers Fixed-Income Indexes,* Salomon Brothers Inc, July 1989.

APPENDIX

The Surplus Return Distribution

For any pension fund, the surplus is defined to be the excess of the market value of the assets over the present value of the liability. We will assume that the liability discount rate is the yield on high-quality fixed-income instruments.

Because the values of the assets and the liabilities change with changing market conditions, so will the value of the surplus. To model the surplus distribution, we assume that the values of the assets and liabilities are normally distributed. Symbols for the relevant variables are introduced in Figure 3–A1.

Figure 3–A1. Definition of Asset, Liability, and Surplus Variables

Variable	Initial Value	Random Value	One-Year Return	Mean Return	Standard Deviation of Returns	Correlation of Returns with Asset Return
Assets	A_0	$\tilde{A}$	$\tilde{r}_A$	μ_A	σ_A	1.0
Liabilities	L_0	$\tilde{L}$	$\tilde{r}_L$	μ_L	σ_L	ρ_{AL}
Surplus	S_0	$\tilde{S}$	$\tilde{r}_S$	μ_S	σ_S	—

The initial values of the surplus and funding ratio are

$$S_0 = A_0 - L_0 \tag{1}$$

$$F_0 = A_0 / L_0. \tag{2}$$

After one year the values of the assets, liabilities, and surplus will have changed to $\tilde{A}$, $\tilde{L}$, and $\tilde{S}$ according to the following:

$$\tilde{A} = (1 + \tilde{r}_A) A_0$$
$$\tilde{L} = (1 + \tilde{r}_L) L_0$$

$$\tilde{S} = \tilde{A} - \tilde{L}$$
$$\tilde{S} = (1 + \tilde{r}_A) A_0 - (1 + \tilde{r}_L) L_0$$
$$\tilde{S} = (A_0 - L_0) + \tilde{r}_A A_0 - \tilde{r}_L L_0.$$

In the above equation, the first term on the right is S_0. Hence,

$$\tilde{S} - S_0 = L_0 [\tilde{r}_A(A_0/L_0) - \tilde{r}_L]. \tag{3}$$

Because S_0 may be zero, it is necessary to define a convenient base against which surplus changes can be measured. The natural choice for this base is either A_0 or L_0. We find it convenient to choose L_0 because it is the base against which the surplus usually is measured. After dividing both sides of equation (3) by L_0 and replacing A_0/L_0 by F_0 (see equation [2]), the surplus return can be expressed as follows:

$$\tilde{r}_S \equiv \frac{\tilde{S} - S_0}{L_0}$$

$$\tilde{r}_S = F_0 \tilde{r}_A - \tilde{r}_L. \tag{4}$$

If we think of $F_0 \tilde{r}_A$ as an "adjusted-asset return," equation (4) states that the surplus return is the difference between the adjusted-asset return and the liability return.

The mean of the surplus return distribution can be found by calculating the expected value of both sides of (4).

$$\mu_S = E [\tilde{r}_S] = E [F_0 \tilde{r}_A - \tilde{r}_L]$$

$$\mu_S = F_0 \mu_A - \mu_L \tag{5}$$

By definition, the variance of the surplus return distribution is

$$\sigma_S^2 = E [(\tilde{r}_S - \mu_S)^2].$$

By using equations (4) and (5), we derive the following formula for the surplus variance:

$$\sigma_S^2 = E [\{F_0 (\tilde{r}_A - \mu_A) - (\tilde{r}_L - \mu_L)\}^2]$$
$$= (F_0 \sigma_A)^2 + (\sigma_L)^2 - 2 (F_0 \sigma_A) \sigma_L \rho_{AL}.$$

The standard deviation of the surplus return distribution is

$$\sigma_S = \sqrt{(F_0\sigma_A)^2 + \sigma_L^2 - 2\,(F_0\sigma_A)\,\sigma_L\,\rho_{AL}}. \tag{6}$$

Allocation Variables

In the previous section, we showed that the volatility of surplus returns depends on both the volatility of the portfolio and the asset/liability correlation. Both these variables depend on the composition of the asset portfolio. Thus, we must derive a formula for σ_A and ρ_{AL} in terms of the relevant asset variables and their respective allocation weights. A summary of symbols for the asset variables is provided in Figure 3–A2.

Figure 3–A2. Definition of Asset Variables

Asset	Percent of Portfolio	One-Year Return	Mean Return	Standard Deviation of Returns	Correlation of Returns with Equity Return	Correlation of Returns with Liability Return
Equity	w	$\tilde{r}_E$	μ_E	σ_E	1.0	ρ_{EL}
Bonds	$1-w$	$\tilde{r}_B$	μ_B	σ_B	ρ_{EB}	ρ_{BL}

Because the asset portfolio consists of only stocks and bonds, its return is the weighted average of the stock and bond returns. That is,

$$\tilde{r}_A = w\,\tilde{r}_E + (1-w)\,\tilde{r}_B. \tag{7}$$

Likewise,

$$\mu_A = w\,\mu_E + (1-w)\,\mu_B. \tag{8}$$

Also, from the definition of the standard deviation and the correlation coefficient, it follows that

$$\sigma_A = \sqrt{[w\,\sigma_E]^2 + [(1-w)\,\sigma_B]^2 + 2\,w\,(1-w)\,\sigma_E\sigma_B\rho_{EB}}. \tag{9}$$

To find ρ_{AL}, we must first find the asset/liability covariance, σ_{AL}. By definition,

$$\sigma_{AL} = E\,[(\tilde{r}_A - \mu_A)\,(\tilde{r}_L - \mu_L)]. \tag{10}$$

After utilizing (7) and (8) in (10), we find that

$$\sigma_{AL} = w\,E\,[(\tilde{r}_E - \mu_E)\,(\tilde{r}_L - \mu_L)] + (1-w)\,E\,[(\tilde{r}_B - \mu_B)\,(\tilde{r}_L - \mu_L)]. \tag{11}$$

The first expectation in (11) is the equity/liability covariance, σ_{EL}, and the second expectation is the bond/liability covariance, σ_{BL}. Thus, σ_{AL} is the weighted-average covariance,

$$\sigma_{AL} = w\,\sigma_{EL} + (1-w)\,\sigma_{BL}. \tag{12}$$

In general, the covariance between two random variables is the product of the correlation coefficient and the two standard deviations. Thus, (12) can be rewritten as follows:

$$\sigma_A\,\sigma_L\,\rho_{AL} = w\,\sigma_E\,\sigma_L\,\rho_{EL} + (1-w)\,\sigma_B\,\sigma_L\,\rho_{BL}, \quad \text{or}$$

$$\rho_{AL} = [w\,\sigma_E\,\rho_{EL} + (1-w)\,\sigma_B\,\rho_{BL}]\,/\sigma_A.$$

If we assume that $\rho_{BL} = 1$ and the return distributions are normal, then $\rho_{EL} = \rho_{EB}$ and

$$\rho_{AL} = [w\,\sigma_E\,\rho_{EB} + (1-w)\,\sigma_B]/\sigma_A. \tag{13}$$

As an example of the use of the formulas we have developed, we consider the assets and liabilities given in Figure 3–A3.

Figure 3–A3. A Pension Fund Example (Dollars in Millions)

Asset or Liability	Initial Value	Expected Return	Standard Deviation of Returns	Correlation with Bonds
Equity	$84.0	13.0%	17.00%	0.35
Bonds	56.0	8.0	6.96	1.00
Liability	100.0	8.0	15.00	1.00

We observe that the asset portfolio is 60% stocks/40% bonds and use equations (8) and (9) to find μ_A and σ_A.

$$\mu_A = 0.6 \times 13.0\% + 0.4 \times 8.0\% = 11.0\%$$

$$\sigma_A = \sqrt{(0.6 \times 0.17)^2 + (0.4 \times 0.0696)^2 + 2 \times (0.6 \times 0.4) \times (0.17 \times 0.0696) \times 0.35}$$

$$= 11.5\%$$

Turning our attention to the pension fund surplus, we first observe that the funding ratio is 140% ([84 + 56]/100). Then, according to equation (5),

$$\mu_S = (1.4 \times 11.0\%) - 8.0\% = 7.4\%.$$

We now use equation (13) to find ρ_{AL}, and equation (6) to compute σ_S:

$$\rho_{AL} = [(0.60 \times 0.17 \times 0.35) + (0.4 \times 0.0696)]/0.115 = 0.554, \text{ and}$$

$$\sigma_S = \sqrt{(1.4 \times 0.115)^2 + (0.15)^2 - 2 \times (1.4 \times 0.115) \times 0.15 \times 0.554}$$

$$= 14.7\%$$

The Surplus Shortfall Constraint

We wish to locate all stock/bond portfolios whose risk/return characteristics are such that there is a probability k that the surplus return $\tilde{r}_S$ will exceed some minimum threshold S_{MIN}. This requirement can be expressed as follows:

$$P[\tilde{r}_S \geq S_{MIN}] = k. \tag{14}$$

The above requirement is equivalent to

$$P[(\tilde{r}_S - \mu_S)/\sigma_S \geq (S_{MIN} - \mu_S)/\sigma_S] = k. \tag{15}$$

Because the quantity to the left of the inequality in (15) is a standard normal variate, there is a positive value z_k (assuming $k > 0.5$), such that the shortfall constraint (14) is satisfied when

$$(S_{MIN} - \mu_S)/\sigma_S = -z_k$$

or, equivalently, when

$$\mu_S = S_{MIN} + z_k \sigma_S. \tag{16}$$

As an example, we note that $z_k = 1.282$ when $k = 0.90$, because there is a 90% probability that a standard normal variable will exceed -1.282.

Equation (16) looks deceptively simple because it is expressed in surplus terms. To locate the asset portfolios that fulfill equation (16), we must express μ_S and σ_S in terms of asset variables by making use of the various equations in this Appendix.

Although the resulting mathematical relationship between μ_A and σ_A is complicated, the portfolios that fulfill that relationship can readily be graphed in a risk/return diagram. The "shape" of the relationship between μ_A and σ_A for portfolios that satisfy the surplus shortfall condition can best be described as "egglike." Examples of these surplus shortfall "eggs" are provided in the body of this chapter.

Chapter 4

Asset Allocation under Liability Uncertainty

INTRODUCTION

The simplest type of pension liability consists of known benefit amounts payable at known future dates. A pension sponsor wishing to preserve the pension plan surplus can do so with virtual certainty by purchasing an immunizing portfolio—that is, an all-bond portfolio with the same duration as the liability.

Of course, the sponsor may have objectives other than surplus preservation, particularly asset-only objectives such as maximizing asset value (subject to some asset risk constraint), matching a market benchmark, or attaining a satisfactory peer-group ranking. These objectives can lead to mismatching the durations of the bonds and the liabilities and to introducing equities or other asset classes such as real estate or nondollar investments into the portfolio. For pension plan sponsors with typical risk tolerance, traditional asset allocation studies have produced a portfolio comprising about 60% equity and 40% fixed-income securities. The fixed-income allocation commonly has a duration of four or five years, approximating that of the bond market as a whole.

Such a portfolio should, over time, produce substantially higher returns than an immunizing portfolio but at a considerable cost in terms of the volatility to which the surplus is exposed from year to year. Balancing surplus objectives and asset-only objectives is a demanding task, and several authors have developed methodologies for assessing the necessary trade-offs.[1]

These trade-offs are difficult to manage even when the liability payment schedules are known with certainty and their values are subject only to inter-est-rate risk. They become far more difficult when the payment schedules themselves are uncertain. Even the liability for a closed group of retirees is subject to mortality risk. More comprehensive liabilities can involve uncer-tainties about the ages at which employees will retire, their pay rates, changes in the demographics of the workforce, and other factors. These uncertainties in payment schedules, which we refer to as **liability noise,** can dramatically complicate the surplus management task. The immunizing portfolio no longer offers a safe harbor. The surplus risk of the 60% equity/40% bond portfolio also increases, though not as much as the risk of the immunizing portfolio. Once reconciled to the inherently greater risk of "noisy" liabilities, however, the plan sponsor will find a pleasant surprise: The trade-offs between asset-only objectives and surplus objectives are much improved. For example, an extra dose of equity may mean only a very small increment in surplus risk. In some situations involving noisy liabilities, adding equity may actually *reduce* the overall surplus risk.

THE SURPLUS SHORTFALL CONSTRAINT

This section recaps our earlier work on managing pension assets subject to a limitation on the risk to which the surplus may be exposed. As in our earlier work, the pension liability consists of known benefit amounts payable at known dates and will be modeled as a riskless bond. We use the capital mar-ket assumptions shown in Figure 4–1.

We begin by looking at a risk/return diagram of the possible portfolios. Figure 4–2 shows the 100% cash point (8% expected return and 0% volatil-ity), the 100% equity point (13% expected return and 17% volatility), and the line between them, representing all combinations of cash and equity. The dotted line depicts all possible bond holdings, with an expected return of 8% and volatilities ranging up from zero, depending on duration.[2]

Figure 4–2 also includes information about the current asset allocation. The diamond represents the current, or benchmark, 60/40 portfolio. This

---

[1]For example, see Chapter 3 and "Liabilities—A New Approach," William F. Sharpe and Lawrence G. Tint, *The Journal of Portfolio Management*, Winter 1990.

[2]As a first-order approximation, bond volatility is assumed to equal bond duration multiplied by interest-rate volatility (1.5% annually, by assumption).

Figure 4–1. Capital Market Assumptions

Assets = $100 Million

40% Bonds

- Expected Return = 8% for All Bonds

- Duration = 4.64 (Typical Market Duration Based on the Salomon Brothers Broad Investment-Grade Bond Index[SM])

60% Equity

- Risk Premium = 5% (Expected Return = 13%)

- Volatility = 17% Annually

Bond-Equity Correlation = 0.35

Expected Return = 40% of 8% + 60% of 13% = 11%

Figure 4–2. The Cash/Equity and Asset Shortfall Lines

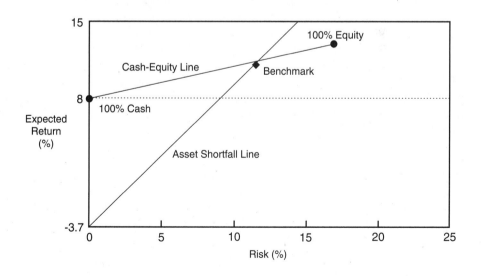

portfolio has an expected return of 11% and, from the volatilities and correlation of its components, a volatility (standard deviation) that can be calculated as 11.5%. (See the Appendix to this chapter for all formulas used in this chapter.) As a measure of risk, we have focused in previous chapters on the **shortfall threshold**—that is, the level of performance that a plan sponsor wishes to have a high probability (90%, for example) of exceeding.[3] Assuming that the equity and bond returns are normally distributed, there is a 10% probability that the actual return in any year will be more than 1.28 standard deviations below the mean—that is, below –3.7% (11% – 1.28 × 11.5%). This –3.7% return represents the shortfall risk of the current portfolio, so we assume that the plan sponsor can accept this level of risk in an asset-only framework. We have previously shown that all portfolios with equal levels of shortfall risk plot along a straight line,[4] and the line for the –3.7% threshold is shown in Figure 4–2; all portfolios on or to the left of this line meet the implied shortfall constraint.

We now consider the liability and surplus of the pension plan. We focus on the accumulated benefit obligation (ABO), which approximates the termination liability. The ABO is calculated by discounting the expected benefit payment schedule at a current bond market rate, which we have taken to be 8%, and we assume it has a duration of 10 years. Our illustrative plan has assets of $100 million and a liability of the same amount for a surplus of zero.

We use the term **liability return** to refer to the rate at which the liability grows (apart from benefit payments and the additional benefits that employees earn through additional service). In our example, the expected liability return is 8%, and the actual liability return will be 8% plus the effect of any change in the discount rate.

We define the **surplus return** as the change in surplus divided by the initial value of the liability. For example, suppose that the liability increases from $100 million to $108 million (a liability return of 8%), while the assets increase from $100 million to $111 million (an asset return of 11%). Then the surplus increases from zero to $3 million—a surplus return of 3% when measured against the $100-million starting liability.

---

[3]We recognize that the shortfall probability is an incomplete measure of risk, because it fails to indicate how bad the shortfall will be should one occur. For a more fully developed theory of shortfall analysis that incorporates these "higher" considerations, see "Asset Pricing in a Generalized Mean-Lower Partial Moment Framework: Theory and Evidence," W. V. Harlow and R. Rao, *Journal of Financial and Quantitative Analysis*, September 1989; and "Capital Market Equilibrium in a Mean, Lower Partial Moment Framework," V. Bawa and E. B. Lindenberg, *Journal of Financial Economics*, November 1977.

[4]See Chapter 2.

In this example, both the liability and asset returns—and, consequently, the surplus return—were equal to their expected values. Such results, of course, are not assured, and the surplus may decrease by a substantial amount. To measure the surplus risk, we again focus on the 10th-percentile return. We impose the following surplus shortfall constraint on the asset allocation:

There should be no more than a 10% probability that the surplus return will be less than –12%. In other words, we require a 90% assurance that the surplus return will exceed –12%.

For our illustration, the expected surplus return is 3%, as shown above, and the standard deviation is 12.9% (see the Appendix to this chapter). Therefore, the 10th-percentile surplus return is –13.5% (3.0% – 1.28 × 12.9%), and the benchmark portfolio fails to meet the surplus shortfall constraint.

Figure 4–3 shows the portfolios that do meet the surplus constraint. They lie in an egg-shaped pattern, roughly centered on the immunizing portfolio. This portfolio, marked IP, is a 100% bond portfolio with a duration of 10 years. It has an expected surplus return of zero and surplus volatility of zero, so the 10th-percentile surplus return is also zero. As we move left or right of

Figure 4–3. The Surplus Shortfall Curve (Surplus Return Threshold = –12%)

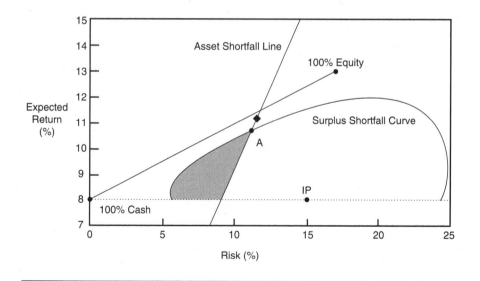

the immunizing portfolio, introducing a duration mismatch, the 10th-percentile surplus return falls until it reaches the –12% threshold at the outer edges of the bottom of the egg. The rest of the egg is formed by the addition of equity to the portfolio.

All portfolios with risk/return characteristics that place them within the "egg" will meet or exceed the surplus shortfall constraint. (Note that the 60/40 portfolio falls outside the egg, because its 10th-percentile surplus return is –13.5%.) Similarly, all portfolios that lie to the left of the asset shortfall line will meet the asset constraint. The shaded region represents portfolios that meet both the surplus and asset shortfall requirements.

The highest-return portfolio that meets both the –12% surplus shortfall condition and the –3.7% asset shortfall condition is found at the intersection of the asset shortfall line and the surplus shortfall curve (point A). This portfolio, which we refer to as the **optimal dual-shortfall portfolio,** has an expected return of 10.7% and a volatility of 11.2%. This risk/return profile corresponds to a portfolio with 53.6% equity and a bond duration of 6.0 years, sacrificing 32 basis points of expected return relative to the 60/40 portfolio.

Figure 4–4. Liability Return versus Change in Discount Rate

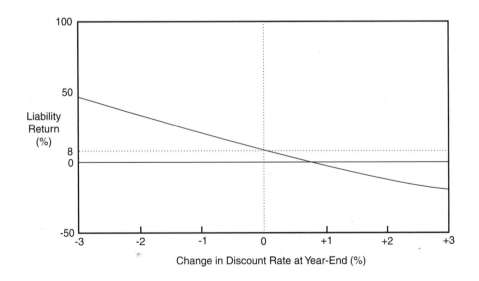

LIABILITY NOISE

Thus far, we have dealt with a liability that has known cash flows at known dates and therefore can be modeled as a bond. Suppose, for example, that a liability consists of the obligation to make a single payment of known amount at a fixed date such that the liability duration one year from now is 10 years. After one year, if the discount rate has not changed from the current 8%, the liability will have grown by 8%. If the rate has changed, however, the liability and the liability return will be altered by about 10% for each 1% change in the rate. The pattern of liability returns relative to changes in the discount rate is shown in Figure 4–4.

Now suppose that the future payment is uncertain. It can be estimated currently, but its ultimate size depends on the amount of benefits that a group of plan participants is eligible to receive. Survival rates, retirement rates, pay increases, and other factors will influence the total payment. During the year, the plan's demographic and economic experience may alter our estimate of the amount. We assume that the alteration in our estimate is normally distributed with a mean of zero and a standard deviation of N, which we refer to as a **noise factor.** We also assume that this noise is not correlated with the returns of any asset class, an assumption that we will relax later. The liability

Figure 4–5. Liability Return versus Change in Discount Rate with 7% Noise

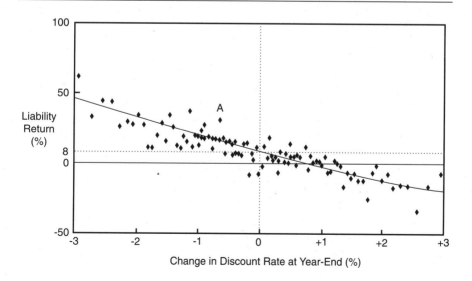

return distribution no longer consists simply of a curve for which the return is uniquely determined by the discount rate: It now is a scattergram, as shown in Figure 4–5, where the noise factor is 7%.

We produced Figure 4–5 using a simulation of liability returns. For example, the point marked A resulted from a 0.65% decline in the discount rate. By itself, the discount rate drop would have boosted the liability return from the expected 8% to 15.2%. In that particular simulation, however, the noise factor—or disturbance of the liability payment schedule—further increased the liability return to 31.5%.

How large might the noise level be for various pension liabilities? The simplest liability is for a closed group of retirees receiving fixed pensions for life; the only liability noise results from mortality fluctuations. If the underlying mortality probabilities are known with certainty, the potential liability fluctuations can be calculated by standard statistical methods. The volatility would range from 2% to 3% for a small group (a $10-million liability) to just a small fraction of 1% for a liability of $1 billion. More difficult to estimate is the **model risk**—the potential liability fluctuation from a change in the underlying mortality rates themselves (for example, from medical advances), which would undercut the statistical foundation on which our volatility calculations are based. By its nature, model risk cannot be precisely quantified, but as an indication of its possible magnitude, we note that a one-year increase in life expectancy would raise a typical retiree liability by 3% to 4%.

As we widen our focus to include more comprehensive measures of pension liability, bringing in active employees and perhaps even future hires, the uncertainties grow. The accumulated benefit obligation (ABO) measures the accrued benefits of all plan participants, both active and retired, and is subject to uncertainties regarding turnover and retirement patterns. The projected benefit obligation (PBO) is the ABO expanded to reflect expected future pay increases, and many pension investors regard it as a better measure of a plan sponsor's accrued liability. Because of the PBO's dependence on future pay increases, as well as the uncertainties present in the ABO, a model that treats the PBO as a bond will have a large noise factor: 7% is implied by one published study.[5] Some investors prefer to focus on liability measures that reflect the future service of current participants, sometimes referred to as a "total benefit obligation," or even on measures that encompass future hires, sometimes called the "ultimate benefit obligation"; both these mea-

---

[5]See "Asset Allocation by Surplus Optimization," D. Don Ezra, *Financial Analysts Journal,* January–February 1991. This article shows a monthly volatility for a typical projected benefit obligation of 5.02% and a correlation with long bonds of 0.77. We can calculate an annual volatility of 17.4% (5.02% $\times \sqrt{12}$), where interest rates (i.e., the bond correlation) explain 0.77^2, or 59.3%, of the volatility. This leaves a volatility unexplained by interest rates—a noise factor N—equal to 40.7% of 17.4%, or 7%.

Figure 4–6. Volatility of Uncertain Liabilities

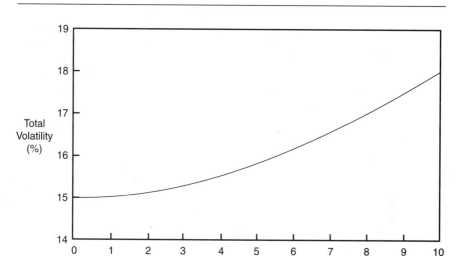

sures also may reflect future plan amendments, including those that are due to changing statutory requirements. For such liabilities, the noise levels would be very high and would strongly promote asset-only considerations over surplus considerations, leading to vastly different optimal allocations.[6]

Figure 4–6 shows the volatility of a 10-year-duration liability as the noise level varies. We are using an annual interest-rate volatility of 1.5%, so in the absence of noise, the standard deviation of the liability return can be approximated as 15% (the product of duration and interest-rate volatility), representing pure interest-rate risk. The standard deviation rises to 15.8% at a noise level of 5% and then, more steeply, to 18% when the noise level reaches 10%.[7] Because, by assumption, the mean value of the noise is zero regardless of its volatility, the expected liability return remains at 8%.

---

[6]As we shall see, a model with liability noise approaching or exceeding 10% offers little practical assistance in surplus management against our illustrative liability, because the model explains an unsatisfactorily low percentage of the liability variance. For very high noise levels that cannot be reduced by better modeling (that is, significant correlation with asset classes other than bonds), the potential surplus fluctuations are so large that most plan sponsors would simply focus on asset-only considerations.

[7]The variance of the liability (the volatility squared) is increased by N^2 over its level based purely on discount rate changes. At a noise level of 5%, the standard deviation of the liability return is $15\%^2 + 5\%^2$, or 15.8%. See the Appendix to this chapter for the liability variance formula.

SHORTFALL CONSTRAINTS FOR NOISY LIABILITIES

Liability noise makes surplus management much more difficult. Given our tentative assumption that noise is not correlated with any asset class, there is no zero-surplus-risk portfolio: The 100% bond, 10-year-duration immunizing portfolio that eliminated all surplus risk for the purely bondlike liability does not eliminate the risk of noise. Figure 4–7 graphs the 10th-percentile surplus return for the "immunizing portfolio" against the noise level N as defined above. The graph simply shows a straight line running from a zero return for the zero-noise liability (where the surplus can be truly immunized) to a –9% return at a 7% noise level and a –12.8% return at a 10% noise level. This pattern reflects the fact that, once interest-rate risk has been removed, the standard deviation of the surplus return is simply the standard deviation of the noise term, so the 10th-percentile surplus return is proportional to the noise term.

The poorer surplus performance of the immunizing portfolio suggests that meeting a specified surplus shortfall constraint will permit smaller deviations from the immunizing portfolio as the noise level grows. Figure 4–8 appears to bear this out, comparing the –12% surplus shortfall curves for noise levels of 0%, 7%, and 9%. As the noise level rises, fewer portfolios meet the –12% surplus shortfall condition, as evidenced by the shrinkage of the "eggs." For example, when 7% noise is introduced, the optimal dual shortfall portfolio—the highest-return portfolio that meets both the asset shortfall constraint of –3.7% and the surplus shortfall constraint of –12%—drops precipitously in expected return, with the equity percentage falling from 54% at point A to 33% at point B. For a noise level of 9%, no portfolio satisfies both the –3.7% asset shortfall constraint and the –12% surplus shortfall constraint. Point C on the curve shows the portfolio that meets the surplus shortfall condition and comes closest to meeting the asset condition; it has a 10th-percentile asset return of –6.3%.

Figure 4–8 suggests that liability noise requires an extremely constrained portfolio to achieve satisfactory surplus performance. Paradoxically, however, an opposite view is quite plausible. Liability uncertainty clearly increases the level of surplus risk. But, as we shall see, a small increase in surplus risk tolerance can lead to a disproportionate gain in the range of asset allocation choices.

As shown in Figure 4–7, when the noise level is zero, the immunizing portfolio has a 10th-percentile performance of 0%, meaning that the surplus does not change. In this case we can say that there is no "built-in" surplus risk. With a riskless strategy available, a –12% surplus shortfall constraint

Figure 4–7. The Immunizing Portfolio: 10th-Percentile Surplus Return versus Liability Noise

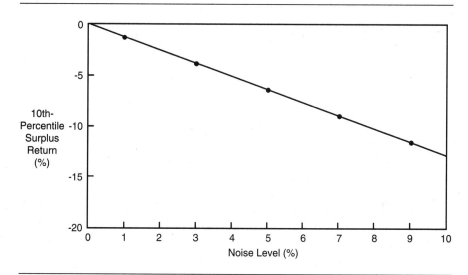

Figure 4–8. Surplus Shortfall Curves at Varying Noise Levels (Surplus Return Threshold = –12%)

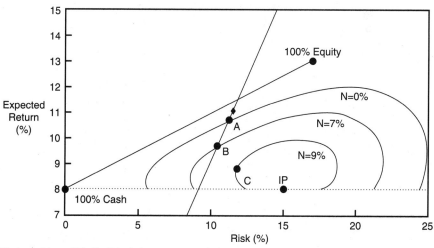

IP = Immunizing portfolio. N = Noise factor.

Figure 4–9A. Shifting the Shortfall Threshold with 7% Noise

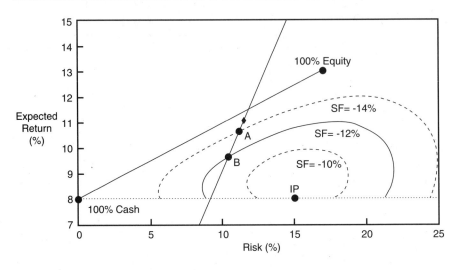

IP = Immunizing portfolio. SF = Shortfall threshhold.

gives considerable leeway in the selection of an asset portfolio. But when the
noise level is as high as 7%, the built-in surplus risk, as measured by the
10th-percentile surplus performance of the immunizing portfolio, shown in
Figure 4–7, stands at –9%. The small move from a –9% built-in risk to a –12%
surplus shortfall requirement would constrict the portfolio choice to a tiny
menu of unpalatably low-return selections.

If the plan sponsor focuses on what is possible instead of what is desirable, he or she might accept a –14% shortfall risk—just 5% worse than the
protection afforded by the immunizing portfolio. Figure 4–9A shows how
dramatically this relaxation of the surplus shortfall constraint expands the
portfolio choice, permitting an equity percentage of 50% (point A) instead of
the 33% limit (point B) imposed by the –12% surplus shortfall constraint.
Tightening the constraint to –10%, however, is so stringent a requirement as
to be incompatible with the asset shortfall condition.

In contrast, Figure 4–9B shows that when the noise level is zero, changes
in the surplus shortfall constraint are far less important. The reward for relaxing the constraint from –12% to –14% is to increase the equity percentage
only from 54% to 63%.

Figure 4–9B. Shifting the Shortfall Threshold with Zero Noise

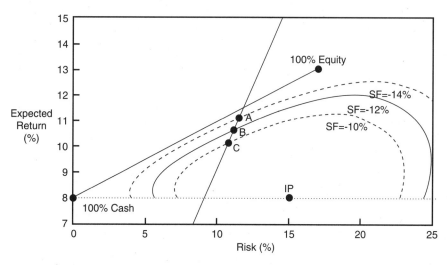

IP = Immunizing portfolio. SF = Shortfall threshhold.

The same effect is evident with regard to allowable bond duration gaps. The 100% bond portfolios that meet the shortfall constraint in Figure 4–9A (the outer points at the bottom of the "egg" curves) are closer to the immunizing portfolio than those in Figure 4–9B, implying a small permitted duration gap at a 7% noise level. But the permitted gap expands by 6.6 years when the shortfall threshold is loosened from –10% to –14%, as shown by the distance between the two curves in Figure 4–9A. At a zero noise level, as shown in Figure 4–9B, the permitted gap expands by only 4.2 years. A relaxation of the shortfall constraint against uncertain liabilities therefore permits a bond manager to take on the greater incremental risk associated with duration mismatches, sector spreads, or yield-curve positioning. As uncertainty about liabilities grows, small increments in risk tolerance are more richly rewarded, whether the incremental risks are taken in equities or bonds.

Figure 4–10 makes a similar point. On Figure 4–7, which showed the surplus shortfall performance of the immunizing portfolio at varying noise levels, we superimpose the surplus shortfall performance of the 60/40 benchmark portfolio. At a noise level of zero, the shortfall performance levels of the two portfolios are far apart: 0% for the immunizing portfolio versus

Figure 4–10. Surplus Shortfall Performance of Immunizing and Benchmark Portfolios at Varying Noise Levels

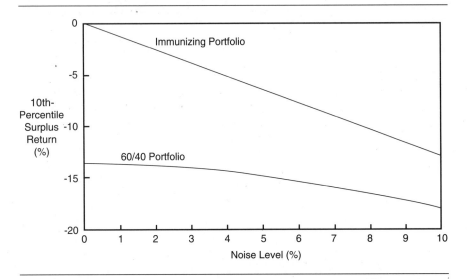

Figure 4–11. Adding Equity to the Immunizing Portfolio at Varying Noise Levels

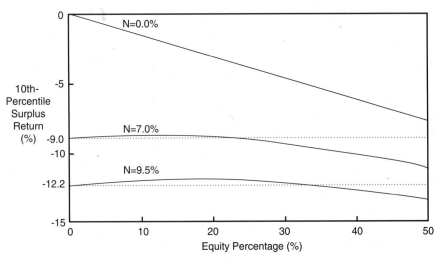

N = Noise level.

–13.5% for the benchmark. The performance disparity narrows markedly as the noise level rises: At a 7% noise level, the gap has halved: –9.0% for the immunizing portfolio versus –15.8% for the benchmark.

Thus the trade-off between asset performance and surplus performance is altered as liability noise increases, and portfolio shifts made for the sake of better asset performance may carry much less incremental surplus risk. Regardless of the noise level, the shift from the immunizing portfolio to the 60/40 benchmark raises the expected asset return from 8% to 11%, while lowering the asset volatility from 15% to 11.5% and improving the 10th-percentile asset return from –11.2% (8% – 1.28 × 15%) to –3.7%. But we have just seen that this portfolio shift lowers the 10th-percentile surplus performance by 13.5% at a zero noise level and by only 6.8% at a 7% noise level. Thus, the same gain in asset-only performance is accompanied by a much smaller loss in surplus control at the higher noise level.

Figure 4–11, which plots the effect of adding equity to the immunizing portfolio at varying noise levels, offers additional evidence of the improved trade-off between asset and surplus performance as liability noise increases. (The dollar duration of the total portfolio is preserved by lengthening the residual bond portfolio as equity is substituted for bonds.)

At a zero noise level, the plot is unsurprising: More equity means poorer tracking of the liability, more noninterest-related volatility, and more surplus risk. As liability noise is introduced, however, the trade-off changes in a surprising and dramatic way. Bonds can no longer track the liability perfectly, so removing them from the portfolio is less damaging to the surplus performance. The "cost" of substituting equity, with its poorer liability tracking, therefore declines and, in fact, is outweighed at some levels by its higher expected return. At a noise level of 9.5%, for example, the 100% bond immunizing portfolio has a 10th-percentile surplus return of –12.2%. A comparison of the dotted line at the –12.2% level and the 10th-percentile curve shows that the all-bond portfolio is *not* the minimum surplus risk portfolio. The minimum risk (highest 10th-percentile return) is found in a portfolio of the same total duration with 15% equity. Even a portfolio with 31% equity has no greater surplus shortfall risk than the all-bond immunizing portfolio, while its asset performance improves markedly: an expected return of 9.6% rather than 8%, and a 10th-percentile return of –10.7% versus –11.2%. In other words, we can add substantial amounts of equity to improve expected returns while *reducing* the downside risk to which the surplus is exposed.[8]

---

[8]A similar conclusion is reached in *Asset Allocation for Property/Casualty Insurance Companies*, Alfred Weinberger and Vincent Kaminski, Salomon Brothers Inc, July 1991. For the very noisy liabilities of property/casualty companies, this report shows that efficient portfolios designed to control surplus will contain sizable equity holdings in the absence of additional constraints.

Figure 4–12. Surplus Shortfall Curves at Varying Noise Levels (Surplus Return Threshold = –12%)

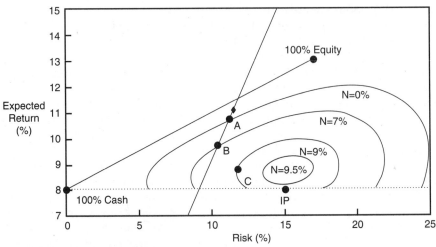

IP = Immunizing portfolio. N = Noise level.

This effect shows up again in Figure 4–12, where we add the surplus shortfall curve for a 9.5% noise level to the curves shown in Figure 4–8. Now the "egg" that defines the portfolios meeting the –12% surplus shortfall constraint has lifted off the 8% return line on which all 100% bond portfolios lie. This means that the immunizing portfolio (point IP) does not satisfy the surplus condition, but portfolios with similar durations and modest amounts of equity (up to 26%) do meet the condition. The equity/bond trade-off is now extremely favorable, with the additional expected return on equity outweighing the liability-tracking power of the bonds.

Another view of the shortfall "egg" at a 9.5% noise level also emphasizes the fund manager's ability to use equity. Figure 4–13 replots that contour from Figure 4–12 but in an equity percentage/bond duration diagram instead of a risk/return diagram. Rather than depicting the risk/return characteristics of those portfolios that satisfy the –12% shortfall constraint, Figure 4–13 shows the specific asset allocations of the portfolios: the equity weight and the duration of the bond component. The curve shows a moderate amount of freedom along the equity dimension, permitting a range from 4% to 26% equity. The bond component, however, is confined in what many managers would find an uncomfortable range of 9.6 to 12.9 years.

Figure 4–13. Surplus Shortfall Curve in an Equity Percentage/Bond Duration Diagram (Surplus Return Threshold = –12%; Noise Level = 9.5%)

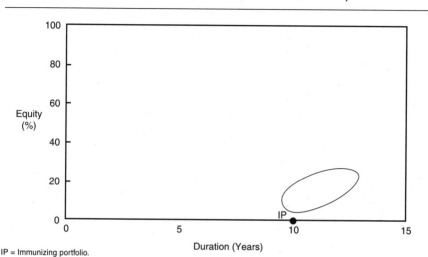

IP = Immunizing portfolio.

LIABILITY NOISE WITH EQUITY CORRELATION

We have defined liability noise as any change in the liability that cannot be statistically explained by interest-rate changes and therefore cannot be hedged by bonds. We also have made the tentative assumption that the noise is unrelated to equity returns as well. We now reconsider that assumption.

Noise may be due to both the demographic and economic experience of the pension plan. Several factors, such as retirements and turnover, may show some correlation with macroeconomic forces. Other factors, such as pay increases, future hiring, and inflation-related pension increases, may exhibit more significant correlations. Over the longer term, it is plausible that some of the forces that drive pay rates and hiring patterns for an individual firm will make their presence felt in the stock market.

Any correlation of the liability noise with equity returns clearly will favor the substitution of equity for bonds in the portfolio. We now introduce an equity/noise correlation and compare the results to some of our earlier graphs.[9] Figure 4–14 repeats Figure 4–10 with an overlay depicting the sur-

─────────

[9]For simplicity, we assume that the expected liability return remains at 8%. It could be argued, however, that such equity-correlated liabilities should carry higher expected returns.

Figure 4–14. Surplus Shortfall Performance of Immunizing and Benchmark Portfolios at Varying Noise Levels

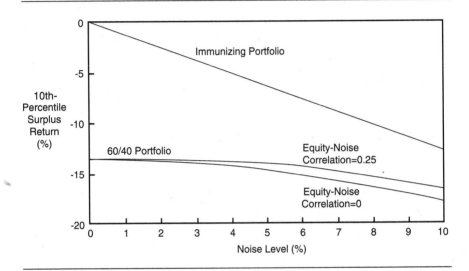

plus shortfall performance of the 60/40 portfolio under the assumption that the noise has a 0.25 correlation with equity returns.[10] The advantage of the immunizing portfolio over the 60/40 portfolio narrows more rapidly than before, and at a 10% noise level the advantage is only 3.9%, compared with a 13.5% advantage at a zero noise level.

Figure 4–15 compares shortfall curves at three different levels of noise/equity correlation—0, 0.25, and 0.50—using the –12% surplus shortfall threshold and the 9.5% noise level curve from Figure 4–12. The portfolio selection process becomes much more equity tolerant as the correlation rises. For example, the surplus shortfall constraint (though not the asset and surplus constraints together) can be met with an equity holding as high as 59% when the noise has a 0.25 correlation with equity but only 26% when the correlation is zero.

---

[10]At a zero noise level, the liability/bond correlation is 1.0, and the liability/equity correlation is 0.35 (equal to the assumed bond/equity correlation). At a noise level of 7%, with no equity correlation, the liability/bond correlation drops to 0.906, while the liability/equity correlation drops to 0.317. Keeping the noise level at 7% and introducing a 0.25 equity/noise correlation raises the liability/bond correlation to 0.913 and the liability/equity correlation to 0.409. The increase in the liability/bond correlation arises because the liability noise is now correlated with equity returns, which in turn are correlated with bond returns. See the Appendix to this chapter for details.

Figure 4–15. Surplus Shortfall Curves at Varying Noise/Equity Correlations (Surplus Return Threshold = –12%; Noise = 9.5%)

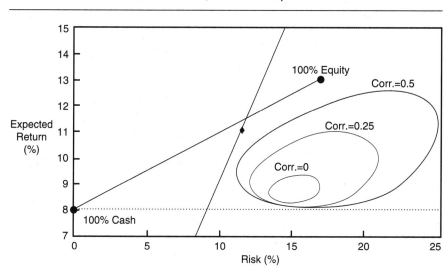

CONCLUSION

This chapter extends our asset/liability management methodology to liabilities whose uncertainties make them impossible to hedge with complete assurance. In a world of uncertain liabilities, surplus risk is higher and so are the potential rewards for investors willing to tolerate more than minimal surplus risk. Although the surplus risk is higher, small equity increments can actually reduce that risk. As liability uncertainty grows, quite substantial amounts of equity can be added to a portfolio without increasing the surplus risk. If significant equity/noise correlations appear, still greater equity allocations gain appeal.

In practice, pension fund assets are managed against various measures: pension liabilities of different types (ABO, PBO, and others), market indexes (standard or customized), a universe of funds, and other explicit or implied standards set by plan sponsors. All these measures and benchmarks can be viewed—and mathematically treated—as "liabilities" against which a manager must strive to produce favorable surplus returns. The methodology in this chapter facilitates the task of managing assets against these various "noisy" liabilities.

APPENDIX

The Surplus Return Distribution

In earlier chapters, we developed formulas for asset and surplus expected returns and standard deviations. We reproduce those formulas in this Appendix (without their derivations) and then extend them to incorporate "noisy" liabilities.

The surplus distribution is modeled under the assumption that both asset and liability returns are normally distributed. Symbols for the relevant variables are presented in Figure 4–A1.

Figure 4–A1. Definition of Asset, Liability, and Surplus Variables

Variable	Initial Value	Random Value	One-Year Return	Mean Return	Standard Deviation of Returns	Correlation of Returns with Asset Return
Assets	A_0	$\tilde{A}$	$\tilde{r}_A$	μ_A	σ_A	1.0
Liabilities	L_0	$\tilde{L}$	$\tilde{r}_L$	μ_L	σ_L	ρ_{AL}
Surplus	S_0	$\tilde{S}$	$\tilde{r}_S$	μ_S	σ_S	—

The initial values of the surplus and funding ratio are

$$S_0 = A_0 - L_0, \tag{1}$$

$$F_0 = A_0 / L_0. \tag{2}$$

Because S_0 may be zero, we choose L_0 as a convenient base against which surplus changes can be measured. The surplus return is defined as follows:

$$\tilde{r}_S \equiv \frac{\tilde{S} - S_0}{L_0},$$

$$\tilde{r}_S = F_0 \tilde{r}_A - \tilde{r}_L. \tag{3}$$

The mean, variance, and standard deviation of the surplus return distribution are

$$\mu_S = F_0 \mu_A - \mu_L, \tag{4}$$

$$\sigma_S^2 = (F_0 \sigma_A)^2 + (\sigma_L)^2 - 2(F_0 \sigma_A)\sigma_L \rho_{AL},$$

$$\sigma_S = \sqrt{(F_0 \sigma_A)^2 + \sigma_L^2 - 2(F_0 \sigma_A)\sigma_L \rho_{AL}}. \tag{5}$$

The Asset Return Distribution

Because the volatility of surplus returns depends on the volatility of the plan assets and liability, as well as the asset/liability correlation, we now include formulas for σ_A and ρ_{AL} in terms of the relevant asset variables and their respective allocation weights. A summary of symbols for the asset variables is provided in Figure 4–A2.

Figure 4–A2. Definition of Asset Variables

Asset	Percent of Portfolio	One-Year Return	Mean Return	Standard Deviation of Returns	Correlation of Returns with Equity Return	Correlation of Returns with Liability Return
Equity	w	$\tilde{r}_E$	μ_E	σ_E	1.0	ρ_{EL}
Bonds	$1 - w$	$\tilde{r}_B$	μ_B	σ_B	ρ_{EB}	ρ_{BL}

Because the asset portfolio consists only of stocks and bonds, its return is the weighted average of the stock and bond returns. That is,

$$\tilde{r}_A = w\tilde{r}_E + (1 - w)\tilde{r}_B. \tag{6}$$

Likewise,

$$\mu_A = w\mu_E + (1 - w)\mu_B. \tag{7}$$

Also,

$$\sigma_A = \sqrt{[w\sigma_E]^2 + [(1 - w)\sigma_B]^2 + 2w(1 - w)\sigma_E\sigma_B\rho_{EB}}, \tag{8}$$

and the asset/liability covariance is

$$\sigma_{AL} = wE[(\tilde{r}_E - \mu_E)(\tilde{r}_L - \mu_L)] + (1 - w)E[(\tilde{r}_B - \mu_B)(\tilde{r}_L - \mu_L)]. \tag{9}$$

From equation (9) it follows that σ_{AL} is the weighted average of the equity/liability covariance, σ_{EL}, and the bond/liability covariance, σ_{BL}:

$$\sigma_{AL} = w\sigma_{EL} + (1 - w)\sigma_{BL}. \tag{10}$$

From equation (10) and the fact that $\sigma_{AL} = \sigma_A\sigma_L\rho_{AL}$, it follows that the asset/liability correlation is

$$\rho_{AL} = [w\sigma_E\rho_{EL} + (1 - w)\sigma_B\rho_{BL}]/\sigma_A. \tag{11}$$

Thus it is apparent that to compute ρ_{AL}, we must know the correlation between the liability and both bonds and equity. Formulas for those correlations are developed in the following section.

The Liability Model

We now turn to the development of a generalized liability model that incorporates both interest-rate sensitivity and uncertainty in the schedule of liability payments. To do so we assume that pure interest-rate-related changes in the liability are perfectly correlated with bond returns. In addition, we allow for the possibility that uncertainty in the liability schedule is, to some extent, related to the overall level of returns in the equity market as modeled by S&P performance. These assumptions are incorporated in the following multiple linear regression equation:

$$\tilde{r}_L - \mu_L = a(\tilde{r}_B - \mu_B) + b(\tilde{r}_E - \mu_E) + \tilde{x}. \tag{12}$$

In equation (12), $\tilde{x}$ is an error term with a mean of zero and no correlation with either equity or bond returns. The values of the coefficients a and b are related to the correlations between equities, bonds, and the liability. The expected liability return, μ_L, is simply the accrual of interest with the passage of time.

We define $\tilde{r}_I$ as the portion of the liability return due solely to the change in interest (discount) rates, with the benefit schedule held constant. Thus,

$$\tilde{r}_I \equiv a(\tilde{r}_B - \mu_B). \tag{13}$$

The above defining relationship for $\tilde{r}_I$ implies that

$$\mu_I = 0.$$

Because

$$\sigma_I^2 = E[(\tilde{r}_I)^2] = a^2 E[(\tilde{r}_B - \mu_B)^2],$$

it follows that

$$a = \sigma_I / \sigma_B. \tag{14}$$

A few observations about the nature of σ_I and σ_B will clarify the meaning of the coefficient a. We assume that the interest-rate volatility of the given liability schedule is modeled by the product of the liability duration, D_L, and the volatility of interest rates, σ_i. In that case,

$$\sigma_I = D_L \sigma_i.$$

The volatility of bond returns is also modeled by the product of duration and rate volatility so that

$$\sigma_B = D_B \sigma_i.$$

By substituting for σ_I and σ_B in equation (14), we see that a is simply the ratio of the liability duration to bond duration.

Returning to our general liability model, equation (12), we define $\tilde{r}_N$ as the portion of the liability return due to "noise"—that is, any change in the benefit payment schedule itself. Thus,

$$\tilde{r}_N = b(\tilde{r}_E - \mu_E) + \tilde{x}. \tag{15}$$

The above relationship implies that

$$\mu_N = 0.$$

In addition, b can be determined by calculating the equity/noise covariance, σ_{EN}. We first multiply both sides of equation (15) by $\tilde{r}_E - \mu_E$ and then take expectations of the resulting equation:

$$\sigma_{EN} = E[\tilde{r}_N(\tilde{r}_E - \mu_E)] = E[b(\tilde{r}_E - \mu_E)^2] + E[\tilde{x}(\tilde{r}_E - \mu_E)].$$

Because the error term is uncorrelated with equity, the last term in the above equation is zero, and

$$\sigma_{EN} = b\sigma_E^2.$$

Substituting $\sigma_E \sigma_N \rho_{EN}$ for σ_{EN} and dividing by σ_E^2 gives the following:

$$b = \sigma_{EN}/\sigma_E^2 = \sigma_E \sigma_N \rho_{EN} / \sigma_E^2, \text{ or}$$

$$b = (\sigma_N / \sigma_E) \rho_{EN}. \tag{16}$$

With the above definitions of $\tilde{r}_I$, $\tilde{r}_N$, a, and b, we can compute σ_{IN} by multiplying equation (13) by equation (15) and taking expectations of the resulting equation.

$$\sigma_{IN} = E[\tilde{r}_I \tilde{r}_N] = abE[(\tilde{r}_B - \mu_B)(\tilde{r}_E - \mu_E)] + aE[\tilde{x}(\tilde{r}_B - \mu_B)].$$

Because the error term is uncorrelated with bonds,

$$\sigma_{IN} = ab\sigma_{EB} = ab\sigma_E \sigma_B \rho_{EB}.$$

Finally, by substituting for a and b as given in equations (14) and (16), we find that the covariance is

$$\sigma_{IN} = \sigma_I \sigma_N \rho_{EN} \rho_{EB}. \tag{17}$$

We now have developed the ingredients needed to compute the liability variance. To do so, we first rewrite equation (12) as follows:

$$\tilde{r}_L - \mu_L = \tilde{r}_I + \tilde{r}_N. \tag{18}$$

Then, we square both sides of equation (18) and take expectations of the resulting equation.

$$\sigma_L^2 = E[(\tilde{r}_L - \mu_L)^2] = E[\tilde{r}_I^2] + E[\tilde{r}_N^2] + 2E[\tilde{r}_I \tilde{r}_N] = \sigma_I^2 + \sigma_N^2 + 2\sigma_{IN}.$$

Using equation (17) to substitute for σ_{IN}, we find that

$$\sigma_L^2 = \sigma_I^2 + \sigma_N^2 + 2\sigma_I \sigma_N \rho_{EN} \rho_{EB}. \tag{19}$$

Equation (19) shows that the variance of the liability is the sum of the variance it would have if the benefit payment schedule were fixed (the "basic variance"), the variance due to noise, and, if the noise is correlated with equities (and therefore with bonds through the equity/bond correlation), a term reflecting the correlation between the basic variance and the noise.

We also need the correlations of the liability with both bond and equity returns. To compute σ_{BL}, we multiply both sides of equation (12) by $(\tilde{r}_B - \mu_B)$ and take expectations of the resulting equation.

$$\sigma_{BL} = E[(\tilde{r}_L - \mu_L)(\tilde{r}_B - \mu_B)]$$

$$= aE[(\tilde{r}_B - \mu_B)^2] + bE[(\tilde{r}_E - \mu_E)(\tilde{r}_B - \mu_B)] + E[\tilde{x}(\tilde{r}_B - \mu_B)].$$

Thus,

$$\sigma_{BL} = (\sigma_I / \sigma_B)\sigma_B^2 + (\sigma_N / \sigma_E)\, \rho_{EN}\, \sigma_{EB} + 0.$$

Substituting $\rho_{BL}\, \sigma_L\, \sigma_B$ for σ_{BL} and $\rho_{EB}\, \sigma_B\, \sigma_E$ for σ_{EB},

$$\rho_{BL}\, \sigma_L\, \sigma_B = \sigma_I\, \sigma_B + (\sigma_N / \sigma_E)\, \rho_{EN}\, \rho_{EB}\, \sigma_E\, \sigma_B,$$

and

$$\rho_{BL} = (\sigma_I / \sigma_L) + (\sigma_N / \sigma_L)\, \rho_{EN}\, \rho_{EB}. \qquad (20)$$

Similarly, we can derive the following formula for the equity/liability correlation:

$$\rho_{EL} = (\sigma_I / \sigma_L)\rho_{EB} + (\sigma_N / \sigma_L)\, \rho_{EN}. \qquad (21)$$

A Pension Fund Example

We have now developed all the ingredients needed to compute the surplus mean and standard deviation. As an example, we consider the assets and liabilities given in Figure 4-A3. We observe that the asset portfolio is 60% stocks/40% bonds and use equations (7) and (8) to find μ_A and σ_A.

$$\mu_A = 0.6 \times 13.0\% + 0.4 \times 8.0\% = 11.0\%$$

Figure 4–A3. A Pension Fund Example (Dollars in Millions)

Asset or Liability	Initial Value	Expected Return	Standard Deviation of Returns	Correlation with Bonds	Equity
Total Assets	$100.0	11.0%	11.50%		
Equity	60.0	13.0	17.00	0.35	1.00
Bonds	40.0	8.0	6.96	1.00	0.35
Liability	100.0				
Basic Schedule		8.0	15.00	1.00	
Noise		0.0	7.00		0.25

$$\sigma_A = \overline{(0.6 \times 0.17)^2 + (0.4 \times 0.0696)^2 + 2 \times (0.6 \times 0.4) \times (0.17 \times 0.0696) \times 0.35}$$

$$= 11.5\%$$

With regard to the liability, we note that $\mu_L = 8\%$, and we can determine the standard deviation by using equation (19):

$$\sigma_L = \overline{(0.15)^2 + (0.07)^2 + 2 \times 0.15 \times 0.07 \times 0.25 \times 0.35} = 17.1\%.$$

The correlations of the liability with bonds and equities can be found by using equations (20) and (21):

$$\rho_{BL} = (0.15 / 0.171) + (0.07 / 0.171) \times (0.25 \times 0.35) = 0.913$$

$$\rho_{EL} = (0.15 / 0.171) \times (0.35) + (0.07 / 0.171) \times (0.25) = 0.409.$$

(If the liability were perfectly correlated with bonds, the liability noise would be zero and ρ_{EL} would be 0.35.)

Turning our attention to the pension fund surplus, we observe that the funding ratio is 100% [(60 + 40)/100]. Then, according to equation (4),

$$\mu_S = (1.0 \times 11.0\%) - 8.0\% = 3.0\%.$$

To compute σ_S as defined in equation (5), we must first find the value of ρ_{AL} in accordance with equation (11). By substituting the computed values of σ_A, ρ_{BL}, and ρ_{EL} in equation (11), we find that

$$\rho_{AL} = [(0.60 \times 0.17 \times 0.409) + (0.40 \times 0.0696 \times 0.913)] / 0.115$$

$$= 0.584.$$

We now have all the information needed to compute σ_S:

$$\sigma_S = \sqrt{(1.0 \times 0.115)^2 + (0.171)^2 - 2 \times (1.0 \times 0.115) \times 0.171 \times 0.584}$$

$$= 13.9\%.$$

(For comparison, we note that with liability noise of zero, ρ_{AL} and σ_S would be 0.554 and 12.9%, respectively.)

Chapter 5

"Optimal" Portfolios Relative to Benchmark Allocations

INTRODUCTION

A fund manager's performance is generally evaluated relative to a predetermined benchmark. The benchmark itself and the expected relative performance may be self-imposed or externally specified, implied or explicit, vague or precise. In this chapter, we assume that the benchmark is an equity/bond portfolio for which the equity percentage and bond duration are specified. The manager must select an asset allocation that tracks the benchmark allocation with a specific level of precision.[1] We first examine portfolio performance relative to an all-bond benchmark with a duration that is representative of the investment-grade bond market. We then consider a series of benchmarks derived by adding equity or changing the duration of the initial benchmark. For each benchmark, we determine the composition of the asset portfolios that meet a specified tracking requirement.

Surprisingly simple rules govern the extent to which the bond duration and equity percentage of the asset portfolio may deviate from the benchmark. For example, we investigate how much equity a manager can hold beyond that in the benchmark, while meeting a fixed tracking constraint.

---

[1]The methodology of this chapter generalizes our previous work on surplus management. For example, see Chapter 3; *Risk-Adjusted Surplus*, Salomon Brothers Inc, August 1991; and Chapter 4. These focus on controlling the relationship of the assets of a pension fund to its liability, which also can be treated as a benchmark. This chapter generalizes our earlier work to cover asset allocation benchmarks; it does not explicitly treat benchmarks within individual asset classes.

The allowable "extra" equity turns out to be a *constant* amount, independent of the structure of the benchmark for all but extreme cases. We also find that holding the maximum allowable equity may hinder, rather than promote, effective management of the fund. By holding the maximum equity allocation, the manager maximizes the expected return but limits the allowable bond duration range to a single point. Holding slightly less equity creates a surprisingly broad range of duration choices, permitting an opportunistic— rather than rigid—approach to the duration management. Thus, one of our main findings is that a portfolio that is slightly suboptimal relative to a narrowly defined measure of benchmark performance in fact may be "optimal" in a broader context. We then observe that the benchmark-tracking problem is reduced to a straightforward asset-only problem when the benchmark becomes an all-cash portfolio.

In the concluding section, we show how the shortfall approach to managing against a benchmark can apply to the realities of asset allocation, which must deal with multiple objectives and constraints. We present an example of a pension plan sponsor whose objectives include satisfactory asset-only performance, surplus management against the pension liability, and reasonable performance in relation to a 50% equity/50% bond benchmark allocation. We cannot simply find the "optimal" portfolio that best meets any one

Figure 5–1. Benchmarks in a Risk-Return Diagram

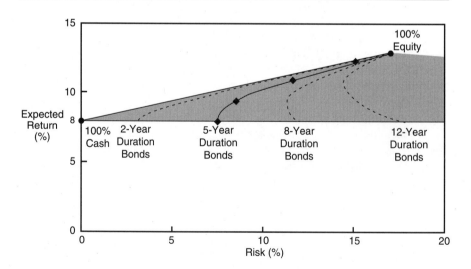

of these objectives to the exclusion of the others. Rather, for each of the three objectives, we use the benchmark tracking methodology to define a region or a set of portfolios that meets a shortfall constraint relative to the objective. The intersection of the three regions provides an area within which the portfolio can be managed, while simultaneously ensuring adequate levels of asset-only return, surplus control, and relative asset performance.

THE GENERALIZED BENCHMARK

In this chapter, we consider benchmarks for which the return distributions are equal to those of portfolios with specified percentages of equity and specified bond durations. Figure 5–1 portrays the risk/return space in which these benchmarks can be plotted.

The horizontal line represents all possible bond portfolios, which are assumed to have an 8% expected return, regardless of duration. We assume that the volatility of a bond portfolio is determined completely by its duration and the volatility of interest rates, which we take to be 1.5% annually; we ignore convexity, nonparallel yield-curve shifts, and other factors.[2]

We assume that both equity and bond returns are normally distributed. Equity carries a 5% risk premium over bonds, or a 13% expected return, and an annual volatility of 17%. The correlation of equity and bond returns is 0.35.

The cash-equity line represents all unleveraged combinations of cash and equity. The curves represent all unleveraged combinations of equity and bonds of selected durations. If those curves were drawn for *all* bond durations (including those available only through very long zero-coupon bonds), they would fill the shaded region, with each point in this region corresponding to a single portfolio.[3]

---

[2]For simplicity, we look at one-year returns and assume that volatility is governed by the duration at the one-year horizon. All mentions of duration in this chapter therefore should be interpreted as referring to durations at the one-year horizon. For example, the "cash" asset in Figure 5–1, represented by the zero-volatility point, actually is a portfolio of one-year Treasury bills, which have a zero duration and zero volatility at the one-year horizon.

[3]We are restricting our available portfolios to unleveraged long positions in equity and bonds; the bonds must have nonnegative durations at the one-year horizon. By relaxing these restrictions, we would expand the feasible region in several ways. We could extend the cash/equity line by allowing leveraged positions in equity, with expected returns greater than that of a 100% equity portfolio. We could move some distance to the left of the cash/equity line by allowing negative bond durations, which can be obtained with short positions in positive-duration bonds or long positions in exotic securities such as interest-only mortgage strips (IOs). Finally, points below the shaded region correspond to portfolios with short positions in equity. Permitting these positions would eliminate most of the flattening that appears in our graphs when theoretically feasible solutions are barred by the portfolio restrictions.

The solid curve in Figure 5–1 represents all unleveraged combinations of equity and five-year-duration bonds. We initially consider managing against four benchmarks consisting of the five-year-duration bonds and equity allocations of 0%, 30%, 60%, and 90% (the four points on the curve that are denoted by diamonds).

We use the term *relative return* to refer to the excess of the asset return over the benchmark return.[4] The riskiness of relative returns can be quantified in various ways. We focus on a surplus shortfall constraint, defined as follows: **The asset portfolio should have a 90% assurance of tracking the benchmark within 2% on the downside. That is, there should be only a 10% probability that the relative return will be less than –2%.**[5]

Figure 5–2 shows the asset portfolios that meet this shortfall constraint against a 100% bond benchmark with a five-year duration. The portfolios form an egg-shaped curve roughly centered over the benchmark. All points on the curve represent portfolios that have a 10th-percentile relative return of –2%; all points inside the curve have better 10th-percentile relative returns. To help explain the shape, we note that deploying the assets to replicate the benchmark ensures a relative return of zero. Because the shortfall constraint allows for a 2% underperformance, the manager has the freedom to hold an all-bond portfolio whose duration (and therefore volatility) deviates in either direction from the benchmark. The extent of that freedom is indicated by the two points at which the "egg" curve intersects the 8% bond return line.

Starting at each of these two points, equity can be added, initially with little incremental asset risk (or even a reduction in risk) because of diversification benefits. The addition of equity affects the relative return shortfall in several ways. First, because the equity has a different sensitivity to interest-rate changes than bonds, the interest-rate risk of the relative return is altered. Specifically, the bond/equity correlation and volatility

---

[4]In the special case where the benchmark is a pension liability, *surplus return* refers to the change in surplus divided by the initial liability. This can be shown to equal the excess of the asset return over the benchmark liability return but with the asset return multiplied by the pension plan funding ratio. See Chapter 3 and *Risk-Adjusted Surplus*, Salomon Brothers Inc, August 1991. The definition of relative return that we use in this chapter implicitly defines the funding ratio as 100%, but it can be generalized to cover other funding ratios.

[5]We recognize that the shortfall probability is an incomplete measure of risk, because it fails to indicate how severe the shortfall will be should one occur. For a more fully developed theory of shortfall analysis that incorporates these "higher" considerations, see "Asset Pricing in a Generalized Mean-Lower Partial Moment Framework: Theory and Evidence," W. V. Harlow and R. Rao, *Journal of Financial and Quantitative Analysis*, September 1989; and "Capital Market Equilibrium in a Mean, Lower Partial Moment Framework," V. Bawa and E. B. Lindenberg, *Journal of Financial Economics*, November 1977.

Figure 5–2. The Relative Return Shortfall Curve against a 100% Bond Benchmark

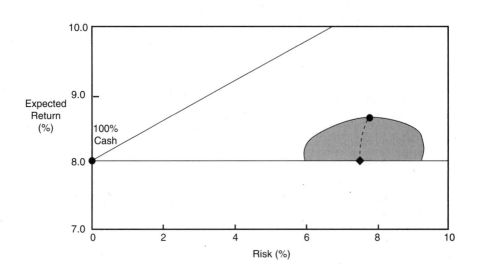

assumptions that we use in this chapter imply an equity duration of 4.0 years.[6]

A second effect of equity additions is that the relative return is exposed to the residual (noninterest-related) volatility of equity. As the equity percentage and the associated residual volatility rise, interest-rate risk becomes less affordable and eventually must be eliminated.

Finally, the equity has a higher expected return than the bonds and increases the *expected* relative return, creating a cushion that allows a higher relative return volatility, while still meeting the shortfall constraint.

The dashed line shows the portfolios that eliminate interest-rate risk by matching the duration of the asset portfolio to that of the benchmark. All of these portfolios have a *total* duration of 5.0 years, and the bond duration is adjusted to balance the 4.0-year duration of the equity.[7] Duration risk can be

---

[6]See *Total Portfolio Duration,* Salomon Brothers Inc, February 1986. Note that interest-rate risk can be eliminated by adjusting the bond duration, without altering the expected asset or relative return. This is possible because we are assuming that all bonds have the same 8% expected return, regardless of duration.

[7]For example, a portfolio consisting of 10% equity with a 4.0-year duration and 90% bonds with a 5.1-year duration would have the same total portfolio duration as the five-year bond benchmark: 10% × 4.0-year equity duration + 90% × 5.1-year bond duration = 5.0-year portfolio duration.

taken in either direction against these duration-matched portfolios, until the equity percentage rises to its maximum. At that point, the residual equity volatility alone fills the allowance provided by the relative return shortfall constraint. The maximum equity point is found at the intersection of the shortfall curve and the duration-matched portfolio line, where the equity percentage is 13.0% and the bond duration is 5.2 years.[8]

BENCHMARKS WITH EQUITY ALLOCATIONS

We now consider the benchmarks that contain substantial equity allocations. We maintain the duration of the benchmark bond component at five years. Figure 5–3 shows the –2% relative return shortfall curve against a benchmark of 30% equity and 70% five-year-duration bonds. The shortfall curve for Figure 5–2's all-bond benchmark appears as a dotted line for comparative purposes. This new "egg" has lifted off the 8% bond return line, meaning that an all-bond portfolio cannot provide sufficient return and correlation with the benchmark to track within a 2% tolerance. Again, the shortfall curve can be thought of as pairs of points positioned on both sides of the duration-matched portfolio line, representing opposite duration mismatches, for any given level of expected return (or equity percentage).

The lift-off enables us to see the full shape of the shortfall curve, which is cut off for the all-bond benchmark by the 8% bond return line. Note that the minimum equity holding represents a smaller deviation from the benchmark than the maximum equity holding because of the positive relative return that equity additions are expected to contribute. The relative return *volatility* associated with a specific equity percentage gap between the assets and the benchmark is the same, regardless of whether the gap is positive or negative. However, the shortfall measure recognizes not only volatility but expected return. It *rewards* the positive expected return associated with equity increments by permitting a larger volatility (equity percentage gap), while it *penalizes* the negative return of equity decrements by reducing the permitted equity percentage gap.

---

[8]The equity percentage is based on an expected return of 8.65% at the high point of the curve. A portfolio's equity percentage can be determined from its expected return by using the following relationship: Equity Percentage = (Expected Portfolio Return – Expected Bond Return)/(Expected Equity Return – Expected Bond Return). Here, the equity percentage is (8.65% – 8%)/(13% – 8%) = 13%. The 5.2-year bond duration is required to match the total portfolio duration to the benchmark duration: 13% × 4.0-year equity duration + 87% × 5.2-year bond duration = 5.0-year portfolio duration.

Figure 5–3. The Shortfall Curve against a 30% / 70% Benchmark

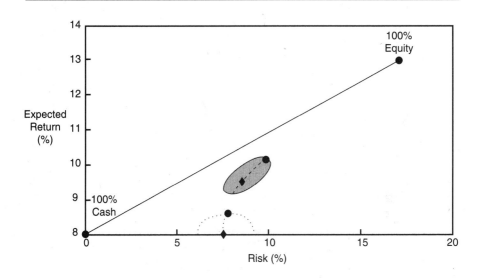

In Figure 5–4, the benchmark has been moved up to 60% equity and 40% bonds. The shape of the shortfall "egg" continues to change in a way that we will examine shortly.

In Figure 5–5, we have moved the benchmark up to 90% equity and 10% bonds. Now the left side of the shortfall curve has flattened against the cash-equity line. The flattening tells us that the –2% shortfall constraint can be met—with room to spare—if the bond portfolio is held in "cash" (that is, one-year Treasuries, which have zero volatility for the one-year time frame). The flattening at the top tells us that an all-equity portfolio also will meet the constraint.

Figures 5–2 to 5–5 show the risk/return characteristics of the portfolios that meet a relative return shortfall constraint against a series of benchmarks. As mentioned earlier, each point on the risk/return diagram corresponds to a single portfolio that is defined by its equity percentage and bond duration. Figure 5–6 replots the shortfall curves for 0%, 30%, 60%, and 90% equity benchmarks in an equity percentage/bond duration diagram. From this diagram, we can read directly the composition of the portfolios that meet the –2% shortfall constraint.

The increasing breadth of the curves as the benchmark equity percentage increases is striking. It conveys the simple fact that when bonds consti-

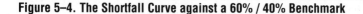

Figure 5–4. The Shortfall Curve against a 60% / 40% Benchmark

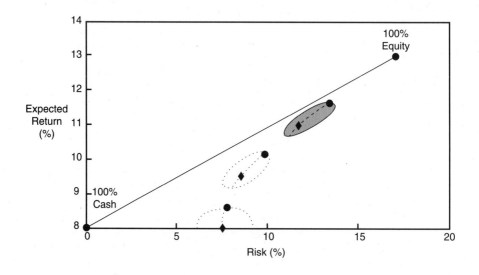

tute a smaller portion of the asset portfolio, their duration can depart further from the benchmark duration without increasing the overall shortfall risk. This concept can be understood by considering the width of the shortfall curves at the point where the asset portfolio has the same equity percentage as the benchmark. At this point, there is no equity risk relative to the benchmark, and all relative risk arises from the bond-duration mismatch. We analyze the benchmarks as follows:

- **Benchmark = 0% equity/100% bonds.** An all-bond asset portfolio can meet the shortfall constraint with a 1.04-year duration on mismatch in either direction, compared with the five-year duration of the bonds in the benchmark.[9] This mismatch corresponds to a duration range of 3.96–6.04 years.

- **Benchmark = 30% equity/70% bonds.** An asset portfolio can meet the shortfall constraint with a 1.49-year duration mismatch against the benchmark bonds. A 1.49-year duration mismatch on 70% of the

[9]See the Appendix to this chapter for formulas. The symmetry of the duration mismatches arises because we use simplified assumptions about bond returns; it is not fundamental to our conclusions.

Figure 5–5. The Shortfall Curve against a 90% / 10% Benchmark

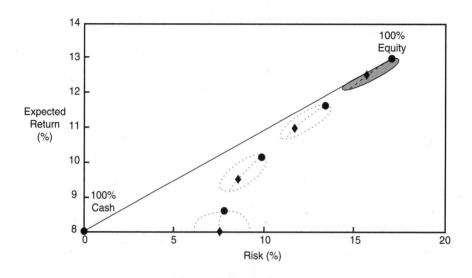

Figure 5–6. The Shortfall Curves in an Equity Percentage/Bond Duration Diagram

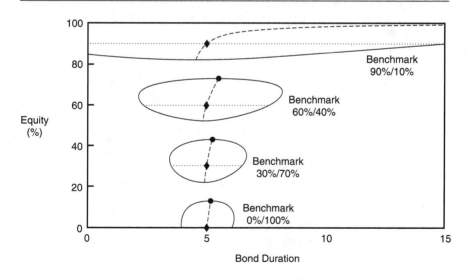

portfolio has the same effect as a 1.04-year mismatch on 100% of the portfolio (70% × 1.49 = 1.04). Therefore, the bond duration can range from 3.51 years to 6.49 years.

- **Benchmark = 60% equity/40% bonds.** The permitted duration gap is now up to 2.60 years on a 40% bond portfolio (40% × 2.60 = 1.04); thus, the bond duration can be 2.40–7.60 years.

- **Benchmark = 90% equity/10% bonds.** Almost anything goes in this case. The permitted duration gap is now 10.40 years (10% × 10.40 = 1.04). The duration for a 10% bond portfolio can be as high as 15.40 years (just off the scale to the right) and is confined on the downside to zero.

We now examine the 60%/40% benchmark curve more closely. As the asset portfolio begins to add equity beyond the 60% benchmark level, the maximum allowable bond duration in the asset portfolio rises, as evidenced by the bubbling out of the right side of the shortfall curve. The decreasing bond percentage permits a correspondingly larger duration gap, because the duration gap contributes less to the total volatility.

However, as the equity percentage of the asset portfolio moves far beyond that of the benchmark, the incremental equity risk absorbs some of the risk-taking allowance. This equity risk *reduces* the allowable duration gap, particularly as the equity additions approach their upper limit, when all nonequity risk must be eliminated. We can see this effect clearly in Figure 5–7, where we move in for a closer view of the top portion of the 60%/40% benchmark curve.

Figure 5–7 shows that an asset portfolio that meets the relative return shortfall constraint can have an equity allocation of up to 73.0%, 13% more equity than the benchmark itself. With that 73.0% maximum equity holding, there is no room for interest-rate risk. Therefore, the total portfolio duration of the assets must be matched to that of the benchmark, requiring a bond duration of exactly 5.5 years. Lowering the equity allocation by 0.5% to 72.5% removes enough equity risk to permit a bond duration range of 4.3–6.6 years— that is, a sacrifice of only 2.5 basis points of expected return (0.5% of the 5% equity risk premium) provides a reasonable duration range within which to manage the bond allocation. Lowering the equity allocation to 70.5%—giving up 12.5 basis points of expected return—widens the allowable bond duration range to 3.0–7.7 years. Thus, by backing away slightly from the "optimal" or maximum permitted equity allocation and corresponding maximum expected return, a fund manager gains substantial freedom for the bond duration. Then the manager can use a relatively low duration to reduce asset

Figure 5–7. Allowable Duration Gap as Equity Percentage Changes

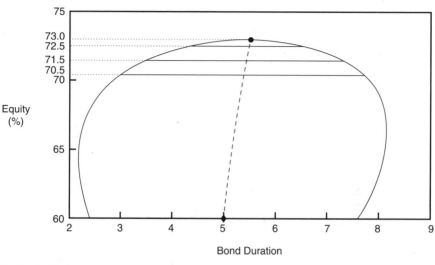

Benchmark = 60%/40%.

volatility, a high one to better match a long-duration liability, or the full range to take tactical positions on interest rates. We now see why maximization of equity holdings under a relative return shortfall constraint denies the fund access to a range of strategies that may offer significant upside potential. Figure 5–7 illustrates the danger of optimizing an allocation on excessively narrow criteria and forgoing the flexibility that slightly "suboptimal" allocations may offer.

THE MAXIMUM EQUITY INCREMENT

We now return to all-bond benchmarks. Figure 5–8 shows the shortfall curve against a 100% bond benchmark with a horizon duration of two years, compared with the shortfall curve for the five-year-duration benchmark that appears in Figure 5–2.

The new curve is shifted to the left, as would be expected; it is centered on the new benchmark (3% volatility, corresponding to a two-year horizon duration). The maximum expected return on the shortfall curve is 8.65%, the same as that for the five-year benchmark, and therefore, so is the corresponding maximum equity percentage, 13.0%.

Figure 5–8. The Shorfall Curve against a Benchmark with a Two-Year Horizon Duration

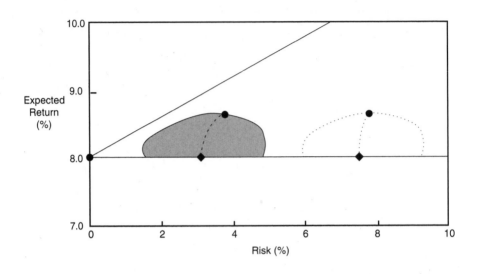

Pursuing this equality, we find that this same 13.0% maximum equity percentage holds for 100% bond benchmarks of all but the shortest durations. To see why this is the case, note that for any specified equity percentage in the asset portfolio, the manager can adjust the duration of the bond allocation so that the total duration of the asset portfolio equals the benchmark duration.[10] Then the relative return is immunized against changes in interest rates and is at risk only with respect to the noninterest-related volatility of the equity. We can calculate that an equity allocation of 13.0% will generate exactly the amount of volatility that is permitted by the –2% shortfall constraint, independent of the benchmark bond duration (see the Appendix to this chapter).

This reasoning is quite robust and can be extended to cover a benchmark with *any* equity percentage. The total duration of the asset portfolio again can be matched to that of the benchmark by adjusting the duration of the bond allocation. The relative return then will depend solely on the performance of the "extra" equity in the asset portfolio. The maximum amount of extra equity that can be held within the –2% shortfall constraint must be the

---

[10]Benchmark durations shorter than 0.5 year cannot be duration-matched by an asset portfolio with 13.0% equity, because the equity duration of 4.0 years would require a negative bond duration.

same 13.0% figure that applies for the all-bond benchmarks. This conclusion can be verified by a close observation of Figure 5–6, in which the maximum equity point for each benchmark is 13.0% above the benchmark point (with the exception of the 90% equity benchmark, for which the 100% limit caps the incremental equity).

Thus, we find that the "extra" equity that a manager can hold while managing with a shortfall constraint against a benchmark is limited to a constant percentage that depends on the constraint and the capital market assumptions but is independent of the structure of the benchmark.[11] The formula for this limit is derived in the Appendix to this chapter.

Figure 5–9 shows how the 13.0% equity allowance varies as some of the underlying assumptions change. For example, suppose that the relative return shortfall constraint is tightened from –2% to –1%, while the correlation and the risk premium remain at 0.35 and 5%, respectively (last column). At that point, the extra equity that a manager can hold against any benchmark is cut in half, from 13.0% to 6.5%.

Figure 5–9 shows that a decrease in the equity risk premium naturally would lower the extra equity that can be held. The same is true for a decrease in the bond/equity correlation because more of the equity volatility is non-interest-related and cannot be hedged by adjusting the bond duration.

Figure 5–9. Maximum Extra Equity under Varying Assumptions

Shortfall Constraint	Bond/Equity Correlation = 0 Equity Risk Premium		Bond/Equity Correlation = 0.35 Equity Risk Premium	
	3%	5%	3%	5%
–1%	5.3%	6.0%	5.7%	6.5%
–2%	10.6	11.9	11.5	13.0
–3%	16.0	17.9	17.2	19.5
–4%	21.3	23.8	23.0	25.9

Changes in the shortfall constraint result in a proportionate change in the extra equity allowance: Each 1% decrement in the shortfall constraint permits a constant increment of equity, as shown in Figure 5–10, which portrays shortfall curves for constraints of –1% through –6% against a 60%/40% bench-

[11]A decision by the manager to hold *less* equity than the benchmark is similarly limited, although by a different percentage because he or she is sacrificing, rather than gaining, risk premium.

Figure 5–10. Varying Shortfall Constraints against a 60% / 40% Benchmark

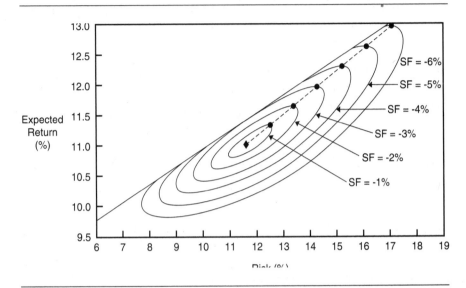

mark. The maximum equity points appear where the shortfall curves inter-sect the dashed duration-matching line. This duration-matching line can be regarded as an efficient frontier in this context, providing the maximum ex-pected return for a given level of shortfall risk. Duration-matched portfolios are efficient in that our model compensates investors for equity risk (with a 5% risk premium) but not for interest-rate risk (because expected bond re-turns are equal for all durations). In this model, therefore, the only risk that an "efficient" portfolio takes is equity risk. As we saw in Figure 5–7, how-ever, a less rigid view of risk may lead to a preference for slightly "ineffi-cient" portfolios.

Note that this "benchmark-tracking efficient frontier" always lies on or below the asset-only efficient frontier (the cash/equity line), given our as-sumption that expected returns are the same for all bonds: Our basic frame-work is an asset-only diagram in which the asset-only efficient frontier *must*

[12]For other illustrations of absolute and relative efficient frontiers, see *Portfolio Optimization Relative to a Benchmark*, Vilas Gadkari, Mark Spindel, and Chee Thum, Salomon Brothers Inc, October 1988; and *An Asset Allocation Framework for Central Bank Reserve Fund Management*, Vilas Gadkari, Henrik J. Neuhaus, and Mark Spindel, Salomon Brothers Inc, September 1989.

Figure 5–11. The Shortfall Curve against a Benchmark with a One-Year Horizon Duration

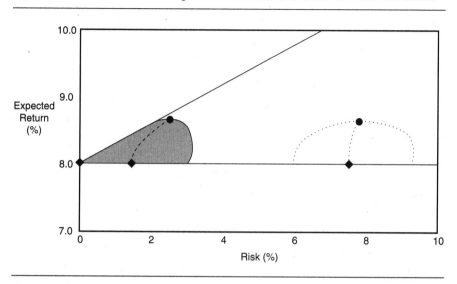

dominate all other portfolios. The two frontiers converge as the tracking constraint is relaxed. At tight constraints, the two frontiers diverge more widely. This divergence is typical of managing against multiple objectives: One cannot be tightly tethered to widely separated hitching posts.[12]

CONVERGENCE TO THE ASSET-ONLY SHORTFALL LINE

We now return to 100% bond benchmarks with lower durations. In Figure 5–11, the horizon duration is down to one year (we also show the five-year benchmark). The shortfall curve continues to shift to the left and has flattened slightly against the cash/equity line.

In Figure 5–12, we have lowered the horizon duration of the benchmark to zero. (This duration can be achieved with one-year Treasury bills, which is the "cash" or riskless asset for a one-year holding period.) The left side of the shortfall curve has flattened entirely onto the cash/equity line, and the right side also has become a straight line, leaving a triangular region of feasible asset portfolios with a tracking performance that meets or exceeds the –2% constraint.

To understand why the right-hand boundary is a straight line, we should consider what it means to manage an investment portfolio against a zero-

Figure 5–12. The Shortfall Curve against a Benchmark with a Horizon Duration of Zero

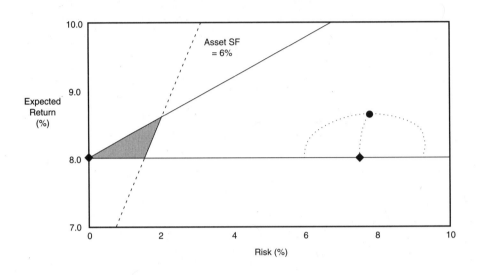

duration bond benchmark, subject to a –2% shortfall constraint. The benchmark has a fixed return of 8%. Therefore, the shortfall constraint is equivalent to a requirement that the asset return exceed 6% (the 8% benchmark less
the 2% shortfall allowance) with 90% assurance. **Thus, we have reduced the
relative-return problem to an asset-only problem**, not a true benchmark
problem; in effect, we are simply managing against an asset shortfall constraint. (More precisely, we now can see the asset-only shortfall problem as a
special case of this more general benchmark shortfall formulation.) In previous chapters, we have shown that the solution set for an asset shortfall constraint is the area to the left of an "asset shortfall line"—a straight line that
forms the right-hand boundary in Figure 5–12 (which would extend down
to intersect the expected return axis at 6%).[13]

---

[13]See Chapter 2. Briefly, to meet a shortfall constraint that requires the asset return to exceed 6% with
90% probability, a portfolio must meet the following condition: expected return –1.28 × standard
deviation of return = 6%. (The 10th percentile of a normal variable is 1.28 standard deviations below
the mean.) This condition establishes a linear relationship between the expected return and the volatility of an acceptable portfolio.

Figure 5–13. Multiple Benchmarks

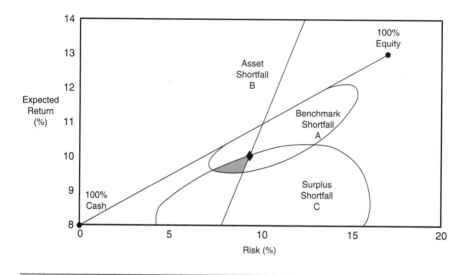

MANAGING AGAINST MULTIPLE BENCHMARKS

We began this chapter by observing that the investment performance of a
fund is generally evaluated in relation to a benchmark. The benchmark can
be a market index, a peer group, a liability to pay pension benefits or another
obligation, or some other type of standard. In practice, a fund likely will
operate in an environment of multiple objectives and constraints, each of
which may serve as a benchmark. The methodology in this chapter permits
consideration of multiple benchmarks and a determination of whether they
all can be met simultaneously, or whether trade-offs and compromises are
necessary. For example, Figure 5–13 shows the situation faced by a pension
plan sponsor with $150 million in assets and $100 million in liabilities who
wishes to manage within the following constraints, each with 90% assurance
each year:

1. **Relative return shortfall constraint.** Produce a relative return that
   exceeds –5% against a benchmark that consists of 50% equity and
   50% five-year-duration bonds (the area within curve A).

2. **Asset shortfall constraint.** Produce an asset return above –2% (the area to the left of line B—note that this represents a –10% relative return shortfall against a Treasury bill portfolio).

3. **Surplus shortfall constraint.** Do not lose more than $7 million of the pension fund surplus (the area below curve C).

The feasible region is shaded in Figure 5–13 at the intersection of the three benchmark areas. Within this region, the highest-return portfolio (marked by a diamond) consists of 41% equity and 59% bonds of 4.9-year duration. This portfolio may not satisfy other, more positive objectives of the plan sponsor, such as achieving a sufficiently high return over the long term; thus, some of the constraints may have to be loosened.

The graph illustrates, however, a view of the pension fund management task as remaining within an area bounded by a series of "electric fences," each of which can be penetrated only at the risk of violating one of the many constraints that may limit a fiduciary.

CONCLUSION

In this chapter, we have extended our earlier research on asset/liability management to encompass management against a generalized "liability" that can be any benchmark that can be replicated by a portfolio of securities. Typically, a manager is expected to track a benchmark within a particular tolerance, and he or she may use that tolerance to pursue perceived investment opportunities relative to the benchmark. Although it may be tempting to use the entire allowed deviation in the single dimension that promises the greatest reward, slightly "suboptimal" allocations may permit a more flexible and opportunistic approach. The structure that we set forth in this chapter enables a fund manager to balance the risk and return trade-offs available within the limits imposed by a benchmark tracking requirement.

APPENDIX

The Relative Return Distribution

The relative return distribution is modeled under the assumption that both bond and equity returns are normally distributed. We also assume that bonds of all durations have the same expected returns and that their actual returns are perfectly correlated. We will derive the mean and variance of the relative return, using the symbols in Figure 5–A1.

Figure 5–A1. Definition of Asset, Benchmark, and Relative Return Variables

	Percentage of Portfolio	One-Year Return	Mean Return	Standard Deviation of Returns	Correlation with Bonds in Portfolio
Asset Portfolio	—	$\tilde{r}_A$	μ_A	—	—
Equity	W	$\tilde{r}_E$	μ_E	σ_E	ρ_{EB}
Bonds	$1 - W$	$\tilde{r}_B$	μ_B	σ_B	1.0
Benchmark Portfolio	—	$\tilde{r}_a$	μ_a	—	—
Equity	w	$\tilde{r}_E$	μ_E	σ_E	ρ_{Eb}
Bonds	$1 - w$	$\tilde{r}_b$	μ_b	σ_b	1.0
Relative Return (Differential)	—	$\tilde{r}_D$	μ_D	σ_D	—

The one-year returns on the asset and benchmark portfolio and the relative return can be expressed in terms of the equity and bond components:

$$\tilde{r}_A = W \tilde{r}_E + (1 - W) \tilde{r}_B$$

$$\tilde{r}_a = w \tilde{r}_E + (1 - w) \tilde{r}_b$$

$$\tilde{r}_D = \tilde{r}_A - \tilde{r}_a = (W - w) \tilde{r}_E + (1 - W) \tilde{r}_B - (1 - w) \tilde{r}_b. \qquad (1)$$

It follows from equation (1) that

$$\mu_D = (W - w) \mu_E + (1 - W) \mu_B - (1 - w) \mu_b.$$

By assumption, $\mu_B = \mu_b$, so

$$\mu_D = (W - w)\,\mu_E + (1 - W - 1 + w)\,\mu_B$$

$$= (W - w)(\mu_E - \mu_B). \tag{2}$$

Equation (2) states that the expected relative return is simply the excess equity held in the asset portfolio multiplied by the equity risk premium.

The following relationship defines the relative return variance:

$$\sigma^2{}_D = E\,[(\tilde{r}_D - \mu_D)^2].$$

Utilizing equations (1) and (2), we find that

$$\sigma_D^2 = E[\{(W - w)\,(\tilde{r}_E - \mu_E) + (1 - W)\,(\tilde{r}_B - \mu_B) - (1 - w)\,(\tilde{r}_b - \mu_b)\}^2]$$

$$= (W - w)^2\,\sigma_E^2 + (1 - W)^2\,\sigma_B^2 + (1 - w)^2\,\sigma_b^2 + 2\,(W - w)\,(1 - W)\,\sigma_{EB}$$

$$- 2\,(W - w)(1 - w)\,\sigma_{Eb} - 2\,(1 - W)(1 - w)\,\sigma_{Bb}. \tag{3}$$

By assumption, $\rho_{Bb} = 1$. Because we assume that the equity and bond returns are normally distributed, it follows that $\rho_{EB} = \rho_{Eb}$. In addition, $\sigma_{EB} = \sigma_E\sigma_B\,\rho_{EB}$, and similar relationships hold for σ_{Eb} and σ_{Bb}. Thus, equation (3) becomes

$$\sigma_D^2 = (W - w)^2\,\sigma_E^2 + (1 - W)^2\,\sigma_B^2 + (1 - w)^2\,\sigma_b^2$$

$$+ 2\,(W - w)\,(1 - W)\,\sigma_E\sigma_B\,\rho_{EB} - 2\,(W - w)(1 - w)\,\sigma_E\sigma_b\,\rho_{EB}$$

$$- 2\,(1 - W)(1 - w)\,\sigma_B\sigma_b.$$

We simplify this equation by subtracting and adding $(W - w)^2\,\sigma_E{}^2\rho_{EB}{}^2$:

$$\sigma_D^2 = [(W - w)^2\,\sigma_E^2 - (W - w)^2\,\sigma_E^2\rho_{EB}^2] + [(W - w)^2\,\sigma_E^2\rho_{EB}^2$$

$$+ (1 - W)^2\,\sigma_B^2 + (1 - w)^2\sigma_b^2 + 2\,(W - w)(1 - W)\,\sigma_E\sigma_B\,\rho_{EB}$$

$$- 2\,(W - w)(1 - w)\,\sigma_E\sigma_b\,\rho_{EB} - 2\,(1 - W)(1 - w)\,\sigma_B\,\sigma_b]$$

$$= (W - w)^2\,\sigma_E^2\,(1 - \rho_{EB}^2)$$

$$+ [(W - w)\,\sigma_E\,\rho_{EB} + (1 - W)\,\sigma_B - (1 - w)\,\sigma_b]^2. \tag{4}$$

Equation (4) gives a usable formula for σ_D and enables us to find portfolios that meet the shortfall constraint. Further simplification can be achieved by using the bond and equity durations:

(a) We model bond returns by $\tilde{r}_B = \mu_B - D_B \tilde{\delta}_i$, where

D_B = Duration of bonds in asset portfolio, and

$\tilde{\delta}_i$ = Actual interest-rate change over one year.

We assume that $E[\tilde{\delta}_i] = 0$ and denote $E[\tilde{\delta}_i^2]$ by σ_i^2.

Because $\sigma_B^2 = E[(-D_B\,\tilde{\delta}_i)^2]$,

$$\sigma_B = D_B\sigma_i. \tag{5}$$

(Similarly, $\sigma_b = D_b\sigma_i$, where D_b is the duration of the bonds in the benchmark, and σ_b is the bond volatility of the benchmark.)

(b) In a previous paper[14] in which equity returns were regressed against interest-rate changes, D_E, the duration of equity, was found to be

$$D_E = \rho_{EB}\sigma_E/\sigma_i. \tag{6}$$

The total portfolio duration is the weighted average of the equity and bond durations of the assets and the benchmark as follows:

$$D_A = WD_E + (1 - W)\,D_B, \quad \text{and}$$

$$D_a = wD_E + (1 - w)\,D_b. \tag{7}$$

We now rewrite equation (4) by multiplying the bracketed term by σ_i^2/σ_i^2 and rearranging as follows:

$$\sigma_D^2 = (W - w)^2\,\sigma_E^2\,(1 - \rho_{EB}^2)$$

$$+ \left[W\frac{\sigma_E\,\rho_{EB}}{\sigma_i} + (1 - W)\frac{\sigma_B}{\sigma_i} - \left(w\frac{\sigma_E\,\rho_{EB}}{\sigma_i} + \{1 - w\}\frac{\sigma_b}{\sigma_i} \right) \right]^2 \sigma_i^2.$$

---

[14]See *Total Portfolio Duration*, Salomon Brothers Inc, February 1986.

Substituting the duration equations (5), (6), and (7) gives

$$\sigma_D^2 = (W - w)^2\, \sigma_E^2\, (1 - \rho_{EB}^2) + (D_A - D_a)^2\, \sigma_i^2, \qquad (8)$$

which can be understood as the sum of the following:

- Equity differential squared multiplied by the noninterest-related equity variance; and
- Duration differential squared multiplied by the interest-rate variance.

The Relative Return Shortfall Constraint

We wish to identify all asset portfolios whose risk/return characteristics are such that $\tilde{r}_D$ exceeds a minimum threshold S_{min} with probability k. This requirement can be expressed as

$$Prob\ [\tilde{r}_D \geq S_{min}] = k. \qquad (9)$$

This is equivalent to

$$Prob\ [(\tilde{r}_D - \mu_D)\ /\ \sigma_D \geq (S_{min} - \mu_D)\ /\ \sigma_D] = k. \qquad (10)$$

Because the quantity to the left of the inequality sign in equation (10) is a standard normal variate, there is a positive value z_k (assuming $k > 0.5$), such that the shortfall constraint (9) is satisfied when

$$(S_{min} - \mu_D)\ /\ \sigma_D = -z_k, \quad \text{or}$$

$$\sigma_D = (\mu_D - S_{min})\ /\ z_k. \qquad (11)$$

For example, we note that $z_k = 1.282$ when $k = 0.90$, because there is a 90% probability that a standard normal variable will exceed -1.282.

Other Useful Formulas

- **Duration-matched portfolio.** To find the bond duration D_B needed to match the total portfolio duration of the assets to that of the benchmark, we write

$$W D_E + (1 - W) D_B = w D_E + (1 - w) D_b, \quad \text{so that}$$

$$D_B = \frac{D_E(w - W) + (1 - w)D_b}{1 - W}. \tag{12}$$

- **Allowable duration mismatch.** Suppose that we wish to find the allowable bond duration mismatch when the equity differential is zero and it is necessary to meet a shortfall constraint. We note that $\mu_D = 0$, based on equation (2), and equation (8) reduces to

$$\sigma_D^2 = (D_A - D_a)^2 \, \sigma_i^2.$$

Using equation (7) with $w = W$, we get

$$\sigma_D = (1 - W) M \, \sigma_i,$$

where M is the duration mismatch $|D_B - D_b|$.

Based on equation (11), we also can write

$$\sigma_D = -S_{min}/z_k, \quad \text{so that}$$

$$(1 - W) M \, \sigma_i = -S_{min}/z_k, \quad \text{and}$$

$$M = \frac{-S_{min}}{z_k (1 - W)\sigma_i}.$$

For example, suppose that the benchmark is 60% equity and 40% five-year-duration bonds, and we require a 90% assurance that the relative return of an asset portfolio with 60% equity exceeds –2%. What are the duration boundaries on the bonds in the asset portfolio?

$$M = 2\% / (1.282 \times 40\% \times 1.5\%) = 2.6,$$

so that the bond duration can range from 2.4 years to 7.6 years (5.0 ± 2.6).

- **Allowable equity differential.** Suppose that we wish to find the allowable equity differential when the total portfolio durations of the assets and benchmark are matched, and it is necessary to meet a shortfall constraint. Under these conditions, equation (8) reduces to its first term:

$$\sigma_D = |W - w| \, \sigma_E \sqrt{1 - \rho_{EB}^2}.$$

Substituting this expression and equation (2) in equation (11) gives

$$|W - w| \, \sigma_E \sqrt{1 - \rho_{EB}^2} = \frac{(W - w)(\mu_E - \mu_B) - S_{min}}{z_k}.$$

Solving for $(W{-}w)$, we can write

$$(W - w) = \frac{S_{min}}{(\mu_E - \mu_B) \pm z_k \, \sigma_E \sqrt{1 - \rho_{EB}^2}},$$

where the negative sign in the denominator gives the maximum equity addition, and the positive sign gives the maximum subtraction. For example, under the assumptions used in this chapter,

$$W - w = \frac{-2\%}{(13\% - 8\%) \pm 1.282 \times 17\% \times \sqrt{1 - 0.35^2}}$$

$$= \frac{-0.02}{0.05 \pm 0.2179 \times \sqrt{0.8775}} = \frac{-0.02}{0.05 \pm 0.204} = -7.9\%, +13.0\%,$$

so that the asset portfolio can have 7.9% less equity than the benchmark or 13.0% more.

Chapter 6

Total Portfolio Duration and Relative Returns

INTRODUCTION

The effective duration of a bond portfolio is a well-understood concept that describes the sensitivity of the portfolio value to changes in interest rates. A portfolio with an effective duration of five years—typical of the investment-grade market—will gain (or lose) about 5% of its value if interest rates fall (or rise) by 1%. Effective duration also is a valuable tool in measuring the risk of a bond portfolio relative to a benchmark, such as a pension liability or a market index, against which the portfolio may be managed.

The concept of effective duration enables us to explain virtually all of a bond portfolio's return in terms of interest-rate changes. Other types of securities—for example, equity, real estate, and nondollar bonds—are more strongly influenced by factors other than U.S. interest rates. However, these securities do carry interest-rate risk as well, and an investor should take that risk into account when measuring or controlling the *total* interest-rate risk of a portfolio. In other studies, we have developed the concept of duration for securities other than bonds and for portfolios comprising multiple asset classes.[1] Duration for securities other than fixed-income instruments has been

---

[1] See "Total Portfolio Duration," Martin L. Leibowitz, in *Financial Analysts Journal*, September/October 1986; "A Total Differential Approach to Equity Duration," Martin L. Leibowitz, Eric Sorensen, Robert D. Arnott, and H. Nicholas Hanson, in *Financial Analysts Journal*, September/October 1989; and *A Look at Real Estate Duration*, Martin L. Leibowitz, David Hartzell, David Shulman, and Terence Langetieg, Salomon Brothers Inc, December 1987.

a source of controversy and confusion, partly for semantic reasons. The first type of security for which interest-rate sensitivity was measured was a bond whose cash flows were known with certainty; the interest-rate sensitivity for such a security relates to the average length of time required for the investor to collect those cash flows, which was, reasonably enough, labeled the "duration" of the bond.[2] Thus, duration came to refer to both the interest-rate sensitivity of a security and the average length of time necessary for an investor to collect the security's cash flows—two quantities that are identical for bonds whose cash flows are certain, but generally are quite different for other securities.

For practical application, the duration definition that matters is the one that relates to interest-rate sensitivity. In this chapter, we evaluate interest-rate sensitivity by observing market responses to changes in interest rates, rather than by using theoretical models of value. This chapter updates our work on duration, with particular reference to equities, and shows how duration can be used to control investment performance in relation to equity/bond benchmark allocations.

For most funds, performance is evaluated relative to predetermined benchmarks. Investment risk relative to a benchmark can be measured in various ways; we consider volatility, shortfall risk, and tracking error. Focusing on tracking error, we show that the concept of total portfolio duration simplifies portfolio design by analyzing the risk relative to the benchmark into two components: (1) the duration or interest-rate risk; and (2) the noninterest-related volatility. This approach greatly facilitates the investor's assessment of the relative return trade-offs inherent in any asset allocation decision.

STATISTICAL DURATION

The mathematics of bond duration is well developed, but it does not lend itself readily to finding the interest sensitivity of securities whose cash flows are not reasonably well defined. Instead, we use a statistical approach to examine how changes in interest rates affected returns in the equity markets during the January 1985–February 1992 period. To demonstrate the statistical approach, we show first how it would apply to bond returns if the traditional duration calculation were unavailable.

---

[2]See *Pros & Cons of Immunization,* edited by Martin L. Leibowitz, Salomon Brothers Inc, May 1980, which includes a historical discussion of Macaulay duration in "An Introduction to Bond Immunization," as well as an excerpt from Frederick R. Macaulay's 1938 paper, *The Movements of Interest Rates, Bond Yields and Stock Prices in the United States since 1856.*

Figure 6–1. Excess Five-Year Treasury Returns versus Change in Yield, Jan. 85–Feb. 92

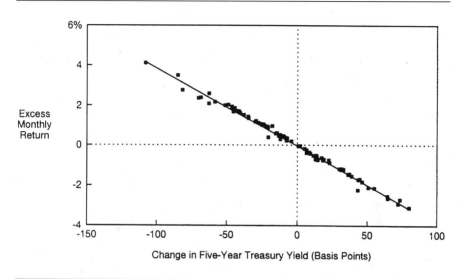

We can model the return on a Treasury bond as follows:

Actual Return = Expected Return − (Duration × Yield Change) + Error,   (1)

where the expected return can be taken as the yield at the start of the period (for short measurement periods). Then, we can estimate the "unexpected" or excess portion of the return (generally, the price change) as the duration multiplied by the yield change during the measurement period.

In Figure 6–1, we examine the validity of this estimate for five-year U.S. Treasury notes during the January 1985–February 1992 time frame. Figure 6–1 plots the excess portion of the monthly returns against the changes in yield during the month. (Throughout this section, we use the term "excess Treasury return" to refer to the monthly return on five-year Treasuries in excess of the yield at the start of the month.) The returns plot in nearly a straight line and have a −0.996 correlation with the yield changes.[3] We show the statistical relationships in Figure 6–2.

---

[3]The negative correlation reflects the fact that returns rise as yields fall. There are several reasons for the departure from a straight line, which would imply a correlation of −1.0. The average yield during the period studied was 8.25%, but the starting points for the individual one-month measurement periods ranged from 5.9% to 11.9%, which implies slightly different durations for the individual

---

Figure 6–2. Excess Five-Year Treasury Returns versus Change in Yield— Statistical Relationships, Jan. 85–Feb. 92

Slope	–3.90
Statistical Duration	3.90
Correlation of Excess Returns with Treasury Yield Changes	–0.996
Portion of Excess Returns Explained by Treasury Yield Changes	99.2%
Portion of Excess Returns Not Explained by Treasury Yield Changes	0.8%

The slope of the regression line is –3.90, which indicates a statistical duration of 3.90 years. That is, a 1% decrease in the yield implies a 3.90% "excess" return (over the expected return). For comparative purposes, we can calculate directly the duration of the "average" five-year Treasury note during the observation period—an 8.25% five-year note—at 4.03 years.

The –0.996 correlation tells us that the statistical duration has high explanatory power. If the expected return is estimated as the yield at the start of the month, the durational estimate of the effect of the yield change explains 99.2% (0.996^2) of the deviation of the actual return from the expected return, and the error averages only 0.8% of the deviation. The usefulness of the statistical approach depends on a reasonable stability of the statistical duration, a condition that in general is satisfied for Treasury notes but will require closer examination for equities.

As a second example, Figure 6–3 plots the excess monthly returns of the Salomon Brothers Broad Investment-Grade (BIG) Bond Index[SM] (relative to the yield on five-year Treasury notes at the start of the month) versus the change in the five-year Treasury yield during the month. We show the statistical relationships in Figure 6–4.

The plot is fairly close to a straight line, with a –0.974 correlation between the excess returns and the Treasury yield changes. This correlation indicates that a statistical duration model explains 94.9% (0.974^2) of the variability of excess returns. The statistical duration of the BIG Index, as determined by the slope of the regression line, is 3.74 years.[4] (This duration reflects the sen-

---

months. In addition, even if we were to confine our observations to months with the same starting yield curve, convexity would introduce a slight curvature into the plot and would prevent a perfect linear correlation. Finally, Figure 6–1 is not based on a single security; a new five-year note is substituted each quarter to maintain a constant maturity.

[4]In "Total Portfolio Duration," we derive the formula for the statistical duration D of a security relative to Treasury rates: $D = -\rho_{si}(\sigma_s / \sigma_i)$, where ρ_{si} is the correlation of returns on the security (in excess of the Treasury yield) with Treasury yield changes, and σ_s and σ_i are the standard deviations of the excess security returns and Treasury rates, respectively.

Figure 6–3. Excess Salomon Brothers Broad Investment-Grade Bond Index Returns versus Change in Treasury Yield, Jan. 85–Feb. 92

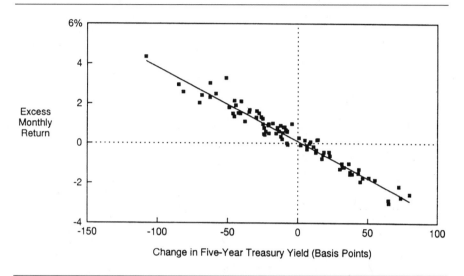

Figure 6–4. Excess Salomon Brothers Broad Investment-Grade Bond Index Returns versus Change in Treasury Yield—Statistical Relationships, Jan. 85–Feb. 92

Slope	–3.74
Statistical Duration	3.74
Correlation of Excess Returns with Treasury Yield Changes	–0.974
Portion of Excess Returns Explained by Treasury Yield Changes	94.9%
Portion of Excess Returns Not Explained by Treasury Yield Changes	5.1%

sitivity of BIG Index returns to Treasury rates, rather than to the overall BIG Index rate, for which the effective duration averaged 4.37 years.) Because the BIG Index is not a riskless portfolio, the expected return that we use in the model is the five-year Treasury yield plus a "risk premium," or spread, over Treasury rates.[5] (During the observation period, the risk premium realized

---

[5]The BIG Index return also can be modeled in relation to its own yield, rather than that of Treasuries. Then the correlation and duration would be higher (–0.99 and 4.37 years, respectively, during the observation period, reducing the error term to 1.9% of the variability), because the BIG Index reflects yield *spreads,* which do not appear in the Treasury yield series. We use the Treasury yield as a base in this chapter to model all security returns in terms of a single independent variable.

averaged 0.3% annually.) Thus, our model for the BIG Index return is as
follows:

BIG Index Return = 5-Year Treasury Yield + Risk Premium
$$- (\text{Duration} \times \text{Treasury Yield Change}) + \text{Error}, \qquad (2)$$

where the error term now accounts for 5.1% of the variability in returns (the
part not explained by Treasury yield changes).

Figure 6–5 extends the statistical duration methodology to equities, plotting excess monthly returns on the Standard & Poor's (S&P) 500 Stock Index
(relative to the yield on five-year Treasury notes at the start of the month)
versus the change in the five-year Treasury yield during the month. At a
yield change of zero, the excess *annual* return is 6.7%, implying a 6.7% equity
risk premium.

We have enlarged the scale in Figure 6–5 to accommodate the greater
variability of equity returns, and the fit of the regression line is much poorer.
The slope indicates a duration of 2.95 years and the correlation is only –0.232
(see Figure 6–6). Because excess Treasury returns have an almost perfect negative correlation with Treasury yield changes, the correlation sign reverses
when equity returns are regressed against Treasury returns, rather than

Figure 6–5. Excess S&P 500 Returns versus Change in Treasury Yield, Jan. 85–Feb. 92

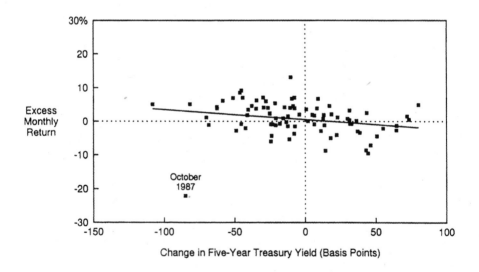

Change in Five-Year Treasury Yield (Basis Points)

Figure 6–6. Excess S&P 500 Returns versus Change in Treasury Yield—Statistical Relationships, Jan. 85–Feb. 92

	Including October 1987	Excluding October 1987
Slope	−2.95	−4.62
Statistical Duration	2.95	4.62
Correlation of Excess Returns with Treasury Yield Changes	−0.232	−0.411
Portion of Excess Returns Explained by Treasury Yield Changes	5.4%	16.9%
Portion of Excess Returns Not Explained by Treasury Yield Changes	94.6%	83.1%

against yield changes. Thus, equity returns are positively correlated with bond returns (0.232) and negatively correlated with interest rates (−0.232). Because of the weak correlation, duration explains only 5.4% of the excess returns (0.232^2), leaving 94.6% "pure" equity volatility.[6]

The correlation indicates little explanatory power in the duration model for equities and is somewhat weaker than the 0.30–0.40 equity/bond correlation commonly used in asset allocation models. The explanation is that the observation period includes October 1987, during which time the S&P 500 fell by 21.6% (while the bond market rallied); the point appears deep in the lower left-hand quadrant of Figure 6–5 and greatly affects the correlation and duration calculations. If we exclude this one extraordinary month, the calculations produce a correlation of −0.411 and a duration of 4.62 years (see Figure 6–6).[7]

STABILITY OF EQUITY DURATION OVER TIME

The usefulness of the statistical approach to determining equity duration depends on the stability of the duration over time. Figure 6–7 shows a rolling 36-month equity duration, calculated both with and without October 1987. The three-year average equity duration settled in a rather narrow

---

[6]An important implication of these percentages, as explained later in this chapter, is that in managing an investment portfolio against a benchmark, a manager can hedge away 5.4% of the equity volatility in the portfolio by adjusting the duration of the bonds in the portfolio.

[7]Even with an equity/bond correlation of −0.411, interest-rate movements explain only 16.9% (0.4112^2) of the equity volatility, leaving 83.1% in noninterest-related volatility. This high noninterest-related volatility makes equity duration difficult to observe empirically, the more so because of its instability over time as a result of variation in the underlying volatilities and correlation.

2¹/₂-to-3¹/₂-year range for periods beginning after the extraordinarily high interest rates of the early 1980s, until the October 1987 crash. The crash had a dramatic effect on the equity duration. If we exclude that month, we see that the equity duration climbs rapidly to settle in a range of 4¹/₂–6¹/₂ years, averaging 3.87 years for the observation period (January 1985 through February 1992). As we shall see, this increased duration primarily results from a decline in the volatility of interest rates. By contrast, when we include October 1987, the 36-month average duration declines to a zero to two-year range until the crash drops out of the averaging period in 1990; then, the duration shoots up to the 4¹/₂-to-6¹/₂-year range. Including October 1987, the equity duration averages 2.58 years during the observation period.

The rationale for excluding October 1987 is that the equity market plunge during that month was about five standard deviations below the mean, less than a one-in-a-million event under an assumption of normally distributed returns. Such a low-probability event can distort attempts to estimate the underlying volatility and correlations using periods of a few years. However, it can be argued that in the preceding months, the equity market had pushed far ahead of the bond market, making a correction inevitable, and that we should not ignore that correction simply because it took place within one month, rather than over several months.

Figure 6–7. Rolling 36-Month Equity Duration, Jan. 83–Feb. 92

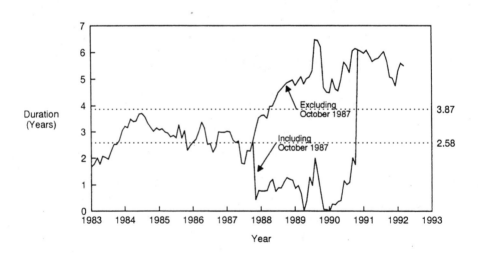

The following figures provide additional insight into the equity duration pattern during recent years, showing 36-month rolling averages for the three variables that determine the equity duration: (1) the correlation between excess equity returns and Treasury yield changes; (2) the standard deviation of excess equity returns; and (3) the standard deviation of Treasury yield changes.

Figure 6–8 shows the equity return/Treasury yield change correlation (with the sign reversed), almost always in a range of 0.3–0.6, if we omit October 1987. When we include October 1987, the 36-month average drops temporarily to a range of 0.0–0.1.

Figure 6–9 shows the rolling 36-month average of the annual equity volatility, mostly in a range of 13%–17% excluding October 1987. If we include the crash, volatility is driven temporarily to about 20%.

Figure 6–10 shows the annual absolute volatility of five-year Treasury yields, which falls steadily from an extraordinary 3.2% for the 1980–82 period to about 1.5%, with October 1987 having a less dramatic effect.

The steady drop in absolute volatility accompanied a marked decline in the five-year rates themselves, from more than 16% in the summer of 1981 to less than 10% a year and a half later and to about 6% by 1992. This accompanying decline suggests that a common measure of volatility, based on the

Figure 6–8. Rolling 36-Month Treasury/Equity Correlation, Jan. 83–Feb. 92

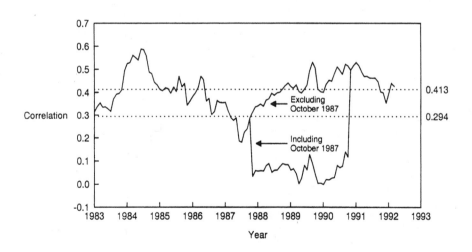

Figure 6–9. Rolling 36-Month Equity Volatility, Jan. 83–Feb. 92

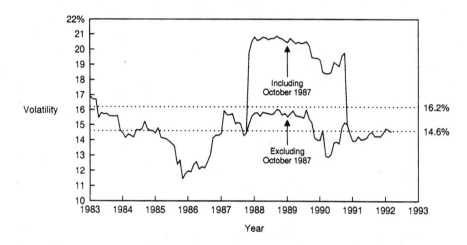

Figure 6–10. Rolling 36-Month Absolute Treasury Volatility, Jan. 83–Feb. 92

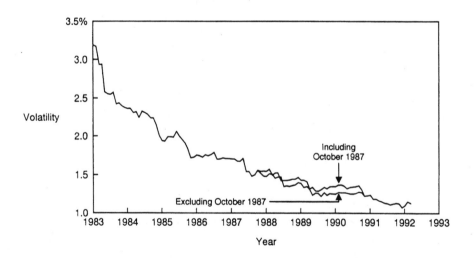

Figure 6–11. Rolling 36-Month Relative Treasury Volatility, Jan. 83–Feb. 92

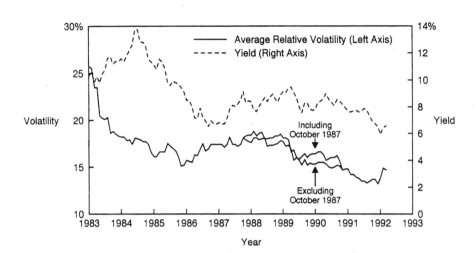

change in yield divided by the yield itself, rather than on the absolute change, might show more stability. Figure 6–11 shows this relative volatility measure,[8] together with a history of the yields.

Even by this measure, the volatility of the 1980–82 period was extraordinary and the drop from that level very rapid. Thereafter, the pattern differs somewhat from that of Figure 6–10, but it does not show markedly greater stability. Therefore, we conclude that the increased equity duration of recent years is caused primarily by the decline in the volatility of interest rates.

THE ROLE OF EQUITY DURATION IN CONTROLLING RISK

To explore the applications of equity duration, we now suppose that we have selected a specific equity/bond allocation percentage for a pension fund, and we wish to select a duration for the bond allocation that minimizes the risk to the surplus. Figure 6–12 shows possible portfolios in a traditional asset-only risk/return diagram.

---

[8]The volatilities in Figure 6–11 actually are computed from the time series of the natural logarithm of the monthly ratio of end-of-month yield to beginning-of-month yield.

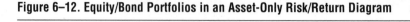

Figure 6–12. Equity/Bond Portfolios in an Asset-Only Risk/Return Diagram

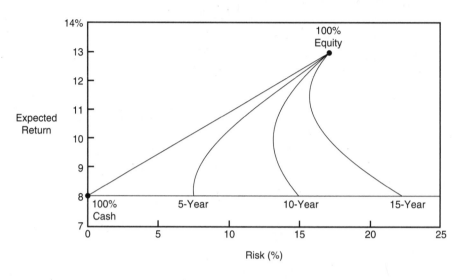

The horizontal line represents all possible bond portfolios, which we assume have an 8% expected return, regardless of duration. We assume that the volatility of a bond portfolio is completely determined by its duration and the volatility of interest rates, which we take to be 1.5% annually;[9] we ignore convexity, nonparallel yield-curve shifts, and other factors.

We also assume that both equity and bond returns are normally distributed. Equity carries a 5% risk premium over bonds, or a 13% expected return, and an annual volatility of 17%. The correlation of equity and bond returns in our illustrations is 0.35. The 0.35 correlation lies between the 0.232 and 0.411 correlations that we obtained for our observation period (depending on whether we include or exclude October 1987). Based on footnote 4, the duration of equity is 4.0 years ($0.35 \times 17\% / 1.5\%$), and duration explains 12.25% ($1 - 0.35^2$) of equity volatility.

The cash/equity line represents all unleveraged combinations of cash and equity. The curves represent all unleveraged combinations of equity and bonds of selected durations. If these curves were drawn for *all* bond durations (including those available only through very long zero-coupon bonds),

_____

[9]We define the volatility of interest rates as the standard deviation of year-to-year changes in yield.

they would fill the region to the right of the cash/equity line, with each point in this region corresponding to a single portfolio.

With our simplistic assumption of a uniform expected return for all bond durations and a positive equity/bond correlation, the portfolio that provides the highest return for a given level of risk always will be a cash/equity portfolio. In this sense, cash/equity portfolios dominate all other equity/bond portfolios and define the efficient frontier.

We now shift from asset-only considerations to a surplus view. Suppose that the assets are funding a pension liability of the same size as the assets, discounted at 8% and with a duration of 10 years. We use the term *liability return* to refer to the rate at which the liability grows (apart from benefit payments and the additional benefit credit that employees earn through additional service). In our example, the expected liability return is 8%, and the actual liability return will be 8%, plus the effect of any change in the discount rate.

We define the *surplus return* as the change in surplus divided by the initial value of the liability.[10] Because the funding ratio in our example is 100%, the surplus return becomes simply the asset return minus the liability return. Now, in Figure 6–13, we can view the pension fund in a risk/return diagram based on surplus return, rather than on asset return.

In Figure 6–13, we have changed the expected return scale. Expected *asset* returns range from 8% for all-bond portfolios to 13% for all-equity portfolios. Because the expected liability return is 8%, however, expected *surplus* returns range from 0% for all-bond portfolios (which are not expected to outgrow the liability) to 5% (the equity risk premium) for a 100%-equity portfolio. The riskless portfolio is no longer cash but 10-year-duration bonds, compared with Figure 6–12. Equity also has become somewhat riskier, because the interest-rate risk of the liability now combines with the volatility of the equity. It appears that the line that represents combinations of 10-year-duration bonds and equity defines the efficient frontier in surplus space, as the cash/equity line does in asset-only space. Figure 6–14, however, puts the problem in a different light, showing longer-duration bond portfolios—durations of 10 years and more, rather than 10 years or less, as in Figure 6–13.

An all-bond portfolio with a 15-year duration has the same 5-year-duration mismatch with the liability as a 5-year-duration portfolio has and, therefore, occupies the same risk/return point in a surplus diagram. This identity is well recognized. A less familiar fact, however, is that portfolios that combine equity with 15-year-duration bonds behave quite differently in surplus

---

[10]See Chapter 3.

Figure 6–13. Equity/Bond Portfolios in a Surplus Risk/Return Diagram

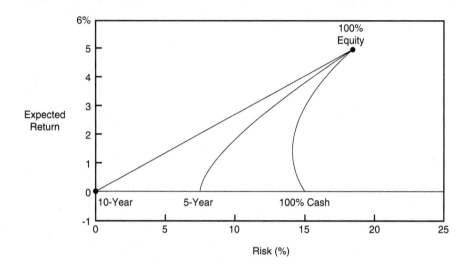

terms from combinations of equity and 5-year-duration bonds. Five-year-duration bonds already are too short to match the liability, and the substitution of equity for the bonds only *heightens* the mismatch. The 15-year-duration bonds, however, are too long, and the substitution of equity *lessens* the mismatch, causing the curve to bubble out over the line that represents combinations of equity with 10-year-duration bonds because of the reduced surplus volatility.[11] The same effect appears with the longer durations, and a straight line (dashed in Figure 6–14) can be drawn tangent to all of the long-duration bond/equity curves, representing the efficient frontier in surplus space.

This efficient frontier contains the answer to the question that we posed at the beginning of this section: For a given equity percentage (or expected return), what bond duration minimizes the surplus risk? When we solve algebraically for the condition that must be met by the portfolios on the efficient frontier, we find that the weighted average of the bond duration and

---

[11]The bubble indicates a negative correlation between the surplus returns produced by 15-year-duration bonds and those produced by equity. That is, the bonds have a longer duration than the liability; thus, their return will exceed the liability return when interest rates fall sharply; equity returns likely will lag the liability return under those conditions.

Figure 6–14. Equity/Long-Duration Bond Portfolios in a Surplus Risk/Return Diagram

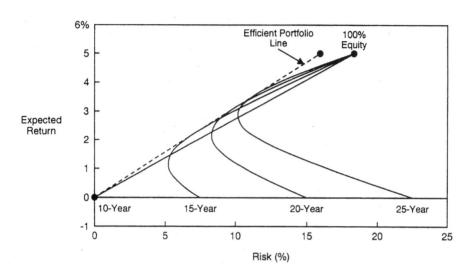

equity duration (weighted by the bond and equity percentages in the portfolio) must equal the liability duration. Thus, the bond duration must satisfy the following condition (see the Appendix to this chapter for derivation):

$$\text{Liability Duration} = \text{Bond Percentage} \times \text{Bond Duration} \\ + \text{Equity Percentage} \times \text{Equity Duration}, \qquad (3)$$

where the equity duration is defined as in footnote 4. We refer to the right side of equation (3) as the **total portfolio duration,** and we characterize the efficient portfolios as those for which the total portfolio duration matches the liability duration.

For example, suppose that we wish to identify the efficient (the lowest surplus risk) portfolio with 60% equity. We can substitute the equity duration of 4.0 in equation (3) and solve for the bond duration, which equals 19.0 years. Because 40% × 19.0 years + 60% × 4.0 years = 10 years, the total portfolio duration equals the liability duration.

Before we leave Figure 6–14, it is interesting to consider the endpoints of the efficient portfolio line. The bottom point—the riskless portfolio in a surplus context—is, of course, an immunizing portfolio of 10-year-duration bonds, but what is the top point? Each point on the line represents a certain percentage of equity, combined with fixed-income holdings of a duration that eliminates all interest-rate risk in the surplus return. In such a matched-duration portfolio, the surplus return is subject only to the *noninterest-related equity risk*, 87.75% of total equity risk under our assumptions; the surplus return is not subject to any interest-rate risk, including the interest-rate-related portion of equity risk.

As the equity percentage rises, the diminishing fixed-income allocation is forced to an ever-lengthening duration to achieve the necessary total duration match, eventually requiring a position in bond futures. The top point then can be thought of as a portfolio with 100% equity, combined with enough bond futures for the total portfolio duration to equal the 10-year duration of the liability. The expected return of this portfolio is the same as that of a conventional all-equity portfolio. The conventional all-equity portfolio has a higher surplus risk, which can be analyzed into two parts: (1) the noninterest-related equity risk (87.75% of the total equity risk); and (2) the interest-rate risk resulting from the mismatch between the liability duration and the total portfolio duration (that is, the equity duration). The duration-matched all-equity portfolio eliminates the second risk element, leaving only the 87.75% of equity volatility that is not the result of interest-rate volatility.

MEASURING TRACKING PERFORMANCE AGAINST A GENERAL BENCHMARK

In general, investment performance is measured in relation to specific benchmarks, which may be pension liabilities or other obligations that the fund is expected to meet, market indexes, or peer group performance. In this section, we consider benchmarks consisting of specified percentages of equity and specified bond durations. Our illustrative benchmark consists of 60% equity and 40% five-year-duration bonds. Its expected return is 11% (60% × 13% expected return on equity + 40% × 8% expected return on bonds).

We use the term **relative return** to refer to the excess of the return on the invested assets over the return on the benchmark. (This is the same as the surplus return defined earlier for a pension fund, if the assets equal the liability.) Because we have assumed that bond and equity returns are normally distributed, relative returns also are normally distributed. We assume that all bonds have the same 8% expected return, regardless of duration. Therefore, any portfolio with a 60% equity allocation has the same expected return as the benchmark, regardless of its bond duration, and an expected relative return of zero. To the extent that the equity percentage of the portfolio exceeds the 60% benchmark, the expected relative return is positive, reflecting the 5% risk premium that we assign to equity. For example, suppose that the asset portfolio holds 70% equity, compared with the 60% benchmark. The expected relative return would be 0.5% (the 10% increment of equity multiplied by the 5% risk premium).

Although the 10% incremental equity relative to the benchmark gives us a positive expected relative return, it also introduces relative return risk: If equities underperform, the asset portfolio may trail the benchmark. A manager also may try to surpass the benchmark by establishing a duration mismatch, reflecting a view on the direction of interest rates; again, such a stance introduces relative return risk.

Relative return risk can be measured and constrained in several ways. We will look at three: (1) volatility, (2) tracking error, and (3) shortfall.

The traditional measure of general investment risk is **volatility,** expressed by the standard deviation of returns. This measure captures the full range of the relative return distribution, reflecting not only the downside deviations that investors think of as risk, but also upside deviations, relative to the expected relative return. Reflecting both upside and downside deviations is not a problem, as long as the returns have a reasonably symmetrical distribution; in that case, the risk rankings of a series of asset allocations would be much the same whether they were based on a downside-only or downside-and-upside measure.

Because this measure is independent of the level of expected return, it fails to reward a positive relative return or to penalize a negative one. By itself, therefore, the standard deviation is an insufficient guide to benchmark-tracking performance in situations that include the possibility of a nonzero expected relative return. For example, most investors would prefer an allocation that has an expected relative return of 3% with a standard deviation of 1% to an allocation that always matches the benchmark precisely (expected relative return and standard deviation = 0%), although the first portfolio is riskier according to the standard deviation measure.

An alternative measure is **tracking error,** which reflects the deviations of the relative return not from its expected value, but from zero. This measure is quite similar to volatility, except that where the volatility measure neither rewards a positive mean relative return nor penalizes a negative return, tracking error penalizes both. This penalty is appropriate in situations in which *any* deviation from the benchmark is because of chance, and a tracking-error constraint may be imposed on a manager whose assignment is to match a representative index. Tracking error alone is *not* a useful measure or constraint in situations that allow for a systematically higher-return strategy (which could represent either skill or simply a higher-risk strategy, such as a greater equity holding than that represented by the benchmark), because the higher returns themselves will increase the tracking error.

In a previous paper on managing against a benchmark, we used a **short-fall constraint** to focus exclusively on downside risk by setting a threshold loss level below which the relative return should rarely drop.[12] For example, a fund sponsor might want a 90% assurance that the fund will not have a return worse than 2% below the benchmark return, a −2% shortfall constraint. This type of constraint does reward a positive expected relative return by permitting a higher volatility, and it similarly penalizes a negative one, as we will see. An objection to the shortfall constraint is that it gives no indication of how bad the shortfall might be if one does occur.[13]

In Figure 6–15, we summarize the mathematical relationships among these different approaches to measuring risk relative to a benchmark. To illustrate, we continue to use the 60%/40% benchmark and both a 70%/30% and a 50%/50% asset portfolio, all with five-year bond durations.

The expected relative return for the 70%/30% portfolio, as calculated previously, is 0.5%. The standard deviation measures deviations from this 0.5% level and can be calculated at 1.60%.[14] The relative return for the portfolio of 50% equity instead of 70% also would carry a standard deviation of 1.60% (against a mean relative return of −0.5%), so that both would appear to be equally risky on that basis.[15]

The tracking error measures the deviations not from the 0.5% mean incremental or decremental return, but from zero. The tracking error is related to the standard deviation as follows:[16]

$$(\text{Tracking Error})^2 = (\text{Standard Deviation})^2 + (\text{Mean Relative Return})^2. \tag{4}$$

For both the 70% equity/30% five-year-duration bond portfolio and the

---

[12]See Chapter 5.

[13]For an approach that addresses some of the shortcomings of these measures, see "Asset Pricing in a Generalized Mean-Lower Partial Moment Framework: Theory and Evidence," W. V. Harlow and R. Rao, *Journal of Financial and Quantitative Analysis*, September 1989; and "Capital Market Equilibrium in a Mean, Lower Partial Moment Framework," V. Bawa and E. B. Lindenberg, *Journal of Financial Economics*, November 1977.

[14]For a derivation of the formula, see the Appendix of Chapter 5.

[15]The symmetry of the 70%/30% and 50%/50% relative returns follows from the fact that each portfolio differs from the benchmark by the exchange of 10% equity for 10% five-year-duration bonds.

[16]Equation (4) is derived as follows: We let $\tilde{r}$ = relative return; thus, the tracking error $T = \sqrt{E[\tilde{r}^2]}$. Letting σ = standard deviation of relative return, and μ = mean relative return, we can write

$$\sigma^2 = E[(\tilde{r} - \mu)^2] = E[\tilde{r}^2] - E[2\tilde{r}\mu] + E[\mu^2] = T^2 - 2\mu^2 + \mu^2, \quad \text{so } T^2 = \sigma^2 + \mu^2.$$

Portfolio	Expected Relative Return	Standard Deviation	Tracking Error	Shortfall
70%/30%	0.5%	1.60%	1.68%	−1.55%
50%/50%	−0.5	1.60	1.68	−2.55

50%/50% portfolio, the tracking error against the 60%/40% benchmark would be 1.68% ($\sqrt{0.016^2 + 0.005^2}$), compared with the volatility of 1.60%.

The shortfall constraint described previously is equivalent to a requirement that the 10th-percentile relative return equal a specified threshold level (–2% in the earlier example). To determine the 10th-percentile relative return for a given portfolio, we use the following relationship, which will hold for normally distributed returns:

$$\frac{\text{10th-Percentile}}{\text{Relative Return}} = \frac{\text{Expected Relative Return} - (1.28 \times \text{Standard}}{\text{Deviation of Relative Return})}. \qquad (5)$$

For the 70%/30% portfolio with its expected relative return of 0.5%, the 10th-percentile return is –1.55% (0.5% – 1.28 × 1.60%). Thus, the 10th-percentile return of the 70%/30% portfolio exceeds –2%, and it handily satisfies the shortfall constraint. The 50%/50% portfolio has an expected relative return of –0.5%; thus, its 10th-percentile return is –2.55% (–0.5% – 1.28 × 1.60%), which fails to meet the shortfall constraint. This relationship illustrates our earlier statement that a shortfall constraint, unlike a volatility or tracking error constraint, rewards a positive expected relative return and penalizes a negative one.

MEETING A TRACKING CONSTRAINT

We now examine the asset portfolios that meet a tracking constraint of the type discussed in the preceding section. We use a series of four benchmark portfolios: (1) a 100% bond portfolio with a five-year duration; (2) 30% equity/70% five-year-duration bonds; (3) 60% equity/40% five-year-duration bonds; and (4) 90% equity/10% five-year-duration bonds. We focus on a tracking error constraint. (A standard deviation constraint produces virtually identical results; a shortfall constraint produces similar results that require somewhat more complicated explication.) For each of the four benchmarks, we consider the set of portfolios whose tracking error does not exceed 2%.

In an earlier chapter, we plotted the equity percentage and bond duration of portfolios that meet benchmark tracking constraints.[17] It is more instructive, however, to view the portfolios in terms of their equity percentage and *total* portfolio duration. This plot is shown in Figure 6–16 for the four benchmarks (denoted by diamonds) and the portfolios that meet a 2% tracking error against each benchmark.

The cash/equity line now runs from zero duration and zero equity percentage to the 4.0-year equity duration and 100% equity. The benchmarks drift to the left as the equity percentage rises and the total portfolio duration moves toward 4.0. The all-bond benchmark appears, of course, at a total portfolio duration of 5 years and an equity percentage of zero. As the equity allocation rises and its 4.0-year duration displaces the 5-year duration of the bonds, the total portfolio duration decreases. For example, the 60%/40% benchmark appears at an equity percentage of 60% and a total portfolio duration of 4.4 years (60% × 4.0-year equity duration + 40% × 5.0-year bond duration).

A region of portfolios that meet the 2% tracking error constraint surrounds each benchmark. These regions are circles of equal size, except where they are cut off by the boundaries that define the acceptable portfolios (the cash/equity line to the left and the 100% equity and zero equity percentage lines at the top and bottom). A portfolio on one of the circles will have exactly a 2% tracking error relative to the benchmark; a portfolio within the circle will track more closely. The perfect circular shape depends on the relative scales that we use for the equity percentage and the portfolio duration. Although equity percentage and portfolio duration obviously measure different things, they both can be translated into *risk units*. We define one risk unit as the tracking error introduced by a one-year departure from the benchmark in total portfolio duration, or 1.5% under our interest-rate volatility assumption. For example, as we noted earlier, the 60%/40% benchmark has a total portfolio duration of 4.4 years. A 60%/40% portfolio with the bond duration lengthened from 5 years to 7.5 years would have a total portfolio duration of 5.4 years, for a one-year mismatch against the benchmark—one risk unit—and a 1.5% tracking error.

If instead of mismatching the benchmark duration, we mismatch the benchmark equity percentage, we also introduce tracking error. As shown in the Appendix to this chapter, to create a 1.5% tracking error, we would mis-

---

[17]See Chapter 5.

Figure 6–16. Meeting a Tracking Error Constraint

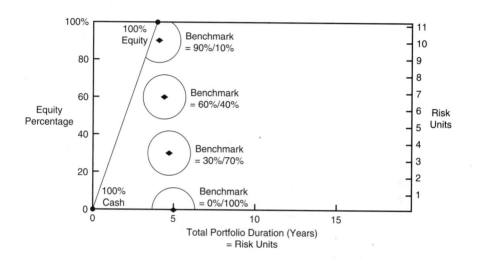

match the equity percentage by 8.99%.[18] Thus, an 8.99% equity percentage mismatch introduces the same tracking error as a one-year mismatch in total portfolio duration (a somewhat surprising relationship—most investors would intuitively attach a higher risk to the equity mismatch than to the duration mismatch). The 8.99% equity mismatch and the one-year duration mismatch each may be regarded as carrying one unit of relative return risk, and thus, each is assigned the same length in Figure 6–16. With a 2% tracking error constraint, we are permitted 1.33 risk units (2%/1.5%).

Figure 6–16 and its underlying formula provide us with a useful way of thinking about the departures that an asset portfolio can take from a benchmark, while meeting a tracking error constraint. The departures can be taken in equity percentage and in total portfolio duration and are limited by the following equation (derived in the Appendix to this chapter):

$$\frac{(\text{Equity Differential})^2}{8.99\%^2} + (\text{Total Portfolio Duration Differential})^2 = (1.33)^2, (6)$$

---

[18]That is, raising the equity percentage from 60% to 68.99% or lowering it to 51.01%, while adjusting the bond duration to maintain a matched total portfolio duration of 4.4 years, would introduce a 1.5% tracking error.

where the 8.99% and the 1.33 will vary, depending on the capital market assumptions and the specified tracking error limit.[19] With equation (6), a manager can readily assess the trade-off between taking on equity risk and interest-rate risk relative to the benchmark. To illustrate, we focus on the 60%/40% benchmark. A manager who decides to take all of the allowable risk by adding equity may increase the equity percentage to 71.99% equity (adding 11.99%/8.99% = 1.33 risk units), while maintaining a total portfolio duration match by adjusting the bond duration.[20] Alternatively, a manager who anticipates a bond rally may take all of the risk in the duration dimension by keeping the 60% equity allocation and lengthening the total portfolio duration by 1.33 years (1.33 risk units). This total portfolio duration corresponds to a 3.3-year lengthening of the 40% bond allocation.

CONCLUSION

In this chapter, we have focused on the use of total portfolio duration in managing assets against a liability or a market benchmark. The determination of total portfolio duration depends on equity duration, which we have estimated statistically, rather than theoretically, by observing the historical response of equity returns to changes in interest rates.

When asset performance is measured against a liability, the efficient frontier consists of portfolios whose total portfolio duration matches that of the liability.[21] This result follows from the flat expected return curve that we have used in modeling bond portfolios, which implies that the market does not reward interest-rate risk, only equity risk. Because expected returns do not vary significantly over the range of bond durations that most funds use, under normal conditions, this result provides reliable guidance about portfolio efficiency.

We conclude by showing how total portfolio duration can be useful in evaluating risk relative to a benchmark allocation by splitting the total risk into its interest-rate risk and noninterest-related equity risk components. A manager can use the total portfolio duration measure to allocate the total risk tolerance between these components in a way that reflects both tactical and strategic views.

---

[19]The 8.99% is a scaling factor to convert the equity differential percentage to risk units, and 1.33 is the number of risk units permitted by the tracking error constraint. Equation (6) states that the sum of the squares of the equity risk units and the duration risk units is limited to 1.33^2.

[20]The adjusted bond duration would be 5.4 years. Then, the total portfolio duration would be (71.99% × 4.0-year equity duration) + (28.01% × 5.4-year bond duration) = 4.4 years. The benchmark duration also would be (60% × 4.0 years) + (40% × 5 years) = 4.4 years.

[21]We developed the same result for measuring performance against a generalized asset allocation benchmark in Chapter 5.

APPENDIX

The Efficient Frontier in Surplus Space

We first derive an expression for the surplus return, using the symbols in Figure 6–A1.

In an earlier chapter,[22] we defined the surplus return, $\tilde{r}_S$, as the change in surplus (assets less liability) divided by the liability at the beginning of the period. We showed that

$$\tilde{r}_S = F\tilde{r}_A - \tilde{r}_L,$$

where F = the funding ratio (assets divided by liability) at the beginning of the period. Because we assume that bond (and liability) returns are completely determined by their expected return, duration, and the one-year change in interest rates (which we denote by $\tilde{\delta}_i$, with a mean of zero and a standard deviation of σ_i), we can write

$$\tilde{r}_S = F(W\tilde{r}_E + (1-W)\tilde{r}_B) - \tilde{r}_L$$

$$= F(W\tilde{r}_E + (1-W)(\mu_B - D_B\tilde{\delta}_i)) - (\mu_L - D_L\tilde{\delta}_i).$$

Figure 6–A1. Definition of Asset, Liability, and Surplus Return Variables

	Percentage of Portfolio	One-Year Return	Duration	Expected Return	Standard Deviation of Return	Correlation with Bond Returns
Asset Portfolio						
Equity	W	$\tilde{r}_E$	D_E	μ_E	σ_E	ρ_{EB}
Bonds	$1-W$	$\tilde{r}_B$	D_B	μ_B	σ_B	1.0
Total	—	$\tilde{r}_A$	—	—	—	—
Liability		$\tilde{r}_L$	D_L	μ_L	σ_L	1.0
Surplus	—	$\tilde{r}_S$	—	μ_S	σ_S	—

---

[22] See Chapter 3.

It follows that

$$\mu_S = F (W\mu_E + (1 - W) \mu_B) - \mu_L, \quad \text{and}$$

$$\tilde{r}_S - \mu_S = F (W (\tilde{r}_E - \mu_E) - (1 - W) D_B \tilde{\delta}_i) + D_L \tilde{\delta}_i$$

$$= F W (\tilde{r}_E - \mu_E) + \tilde{\delta}_i [D_L - F (1 - W) D_B]. \tag{1}$$

By definition,

$$\sigma_S^2 = E [(\tilde{r}_S - \mu_S)^2],$$

thus,

$$\sigma_S^2 = (F W)^2 E [(\tilde{r}_E - \mu_E)^2] + E [\tilde{\delta}_i^2] (D_L - F (1 - W) D_B)^2$$

$$+ 2 F W (D_L - F (1 - W) D_B) E [(\tilde{r}_E - \mu_E) \tilde{\delta}_i]$$

$$= (F W)^2 \sigma_E^2 + \sigma_i^2 (D_L - F (1 - W) D_B)^2$$

$$+ 2 F W (D_L - F (1 - W) D_B) \sigma_{Ei}.$$

σ_{Ei}, the covariance of equity returns and interest-rate changes, is by definition $\rho_{Ei}\sigma_E\sigma_i$. In addition, $\rho_{Ei} = -\rho_{EB}$, because bond returns have a -1.0 correlation with interest-rate changes. Therefore, $\sigma_{Ei} = -\rho_{EB}\sigma_E\sigma_i$; thus,

$$\sigma_S^2 = (F W)^2 \sigma_E^2 + \sigma_i^2 (D_L - F (1 - W) D_B)^2$$

$$- 2 F W (D_L - F (1 - W) D_B) \rho_{EB} \sigma_E \sigma_i. \tag{2}$$

We wish to find the bond duration that minimizes σ_S^2 for a given equity percentage (which is equivalent to a given expected surplus return). Therefore, we take the derivative of σ_S^2 with respect to D_B and set it equal to zero:

$$\frac{d\sigma_S^2}{dD_B} = -2 \sigma_i^2 F (1 - W) D_L + 2\sigma_i^2 F^2 (1 - W)^2 D_B$$

$$+ 2 F^2 W (1 - W) \rho_{EB} \sigma_E \sigma_i$$

$$= 0. \tag{3}$$

We can rewrite equation (3) as

$$D_L = \frac{\sigma_i^2 \, F^2 \, (1 - W)^2 \, D_B + F^2 \, W \, (1 - W) \, \rho_{EB} \, \sigma_E \, \sigma_i}{\sigma_i^2 \, F \, (1 - W)}$$

$$= F \, [(1 - W) \, D_B + W \, \rho_{EB} \, (\sigma_E \, / \, \sigma_i)]. \tag{4}$$

Thus, the duration of the liability equals the total portfolio duration, defined as the weighted average of the bond duration and equity duration, $\rho_{EB} \, (\sigma_E \, / \, \sigma_i)$, and multiplied by the funding ratio to equate the *dollar* durations of the assets and the liability.

Meeting a Tracking Error Constraint

In a previous chapter,[23] we derived the following expression:

$$\sigma_D^2 = (W - w)^2 \, \sigma_E^2 \, (1 - \rho_{EB}^2) + (D_A - D_a)^2 \, \sigma_i^2 \tag{5}$$

where

σ_D = standard deviation of return on an asset portfolio relative to a benchmark;

W and w = percentages of equity in the asset portfolio and benchmark, respectively; and

D_A and D_a = total portfolio durations of the asset portfolio and benchmark, respectively.

In this chapter, we showed that the tracking error, T, is related to the standard deviation by

$$T^2 = \mu_D^2 + \sigma_D^2 , \tag{6}$$

where μ_D = expected relative return, which is $(W - w) \, (\mu_E - \mu_B)$, the equity differential multiplied by the equity risk premium.

---

[23] See the Appendix to Chapter 5.

Combining equations (5) and (6), we get

$$T^2 = (W - w)^2 \left[(\mu_E - \mu_B)^2 + \sigma_E^2 (1 - \rho_{EB}^2) \right] + (D_A - D_a)^2 \, \sigma_i^2, \quad \text{or}$$

$$\frac{T^2}{\sigma_i^2} = \frac{(W - w)^2}{\sigma_i^2 / \left[(\mu_E - \mu_B)^2 + \sigma_E^2 (1 - \rho_{EB}^2) \right]} + (D_A - D_a)^2. \tag{7}$$

If we wish to hold the tracking error constant at 2%, equation (7) above becomes equivalent to equation (6) in the text, with the scaling factor

$$\sqrt{ \sigma_i^2 / \left[(\mu_E - \mu_B)^2 + \sigma_E^2 (1 - \rho_{EB}^2) \right] } = 8.99\%,$$

and the permitted risk units $T / \sigma_i = 1.33$.

Chapter 7

Return Targets, Shortfall Risks, and Market Realities

INTRODUCTION

The recent decline in interest rates has taken U.S. Treasury yields to their lowest levels of the past two decades (see Figure 7–1). Investor responses to lower rates generally have fallen into two camps: **stand pat** and **reach for return.** Those investors reaching for return include many pension plan sponsors, insurance companies, banks, money managers, and even households. The entire investor hierarchy—from the highest-level global asset allocator to the narrowest specialist focusing on a single fixed-income sector—has felt the pressure. Government bond portfolios have been pushed further up the yield curve; high-grade bond managers have relaxed their overall credit standards, and high-grade allocations have been redirected into high-yield bonds and emerging market debt; investors have sought higher returns overseas, sometimes with attendant currency exposures. The surge of funds into equities has been well documented, especially the massive retail purchases of equity mutual funds.

Increased Volatility for Investors Who Reach for Return

There should be no quarrel with the active pursuit of investment opportunities or the periodic revision of a fund's risk posture; these activities lie at the heart of active management. The important issue is whether this strategic risk expansion reflects a thoughtful reassessment of investors' objectives or simply a compulsive pursuit of goals that have been outdated by changing

Figure 7–1. U.S. Treasury Rates, Jan. 64–June 93, and Expected Long-Term Rate of Return of Fortune 500 Industrials, 1987–92

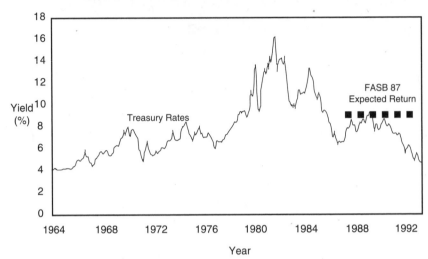

Source: U.S. Treasury Rates—Salomon Brothers Inc—Average Yield of the Treasury Component of Salomon Brothers Broad Investment-Grade Bond Index (estimated for periods before 1980).

Expected Long-Term Rate of Return on Plan Assets of Fortune 500 Industrials—Hewitt Associates—Pension Plan Disclosure under FASB Statement No. 87. (The 1992 figure is preliminary.)

markets. In either case, the increased risk levels associated with these overt tilts toward higher returns are clear to all.

Increased Shortfall Risk Even for Investors Who Stand Pat

A more subtle problem confronts investors who have made no asset allocation changes whatsoever. Even investors who have remained steadfast in their allocations throughout the interest-rate decline will find that significant additional risk has crept into their portfolios! The added risk is a type not recognized by asset allocation models that measure risk through a symmetric calculation of volatility. Rather, it is **shortfall risk**—the danger of failing to earn some prescribed minimum level of return. For example, a shortfall risk constraint could take the form of a requirement to earn a positive return each year, with 90% assurance. The interest-rate decline has made any such fixed threshold more difficult to achieve, even if volatility has remained constant.

Outdated Investment Return Targets

Shortfall risk is particularly critical for pension funds. Plan sponsors base their pension contributions and financial reporting on specific investment return assumptions. A shortfall between the assumption and the actual performance can lead directly to an increase in contributions and unfunded liabilities. Because the investment return assumptions commonly change only at intervals of several years, they can become quickly outdated when markets move.

Most pension plan sponsors face this situation today, because their investment return assumptions have not declined as market rates have fallen. Figure 7–1 shows that the return assumptions used by the Fortune 500 Industrials for reporting pension cost have remained virtually constant, within 15 basis points of 9.25%, since Financial Accounting Standards Board (FASB) Statement No. 87 became effective in 1987. These assumptions now greatly exceed not only Treasury rates, but also most yields throughout the investment-grade bond market.

Given the increased difficulty of meeting previously fixed targets, the sponsors of well-funded plans may be concerned about maintaining their surplus and, for many in the private sector, their contribution holidays. Less fortunate sponsors must consider whether their existing investment strategies and contribution schedules will suffice to meet their obligations.

This chapter addresses the implications of this interest-rate decline for investors in general, with particular attention to defined-benefit pension plans, both public and private. We first consider how plan sponsors can address the unprecedented gap between *the returns that they are counting on and those truly available* in the fixed-income and equity markets. We consider the possibilities of: (1) leaving the asset allocation unchanged; or (2) restructuring it, either aggressively to recapture the expected return that existed before the rate decline or conservatively to reduce the shortfall risk to its previous level. The restructurings can be implemented by specific adjustments to the bond duration and the commitment to risky assets. Figure 7–2 summarizes these possible responses and their implications for expected returns and shortfall risks, from both an asset-only perspective and a surplus perspective.[1] The consequences are shown relative to the return/risk levels that existed before the rate decline, for sponsors with no special views on the future direction of interest rates or the adequacy of risk premiums.

---

[1]In Figure 7–2, we use "equity percentage" as a shorthand reference to risky assets generally, including, for example, the allocation to lower-grade credits within the bond portfolio. The "surplus shortfall risk" column is based on a typical pension liability, which is equivalent to a long-duration fixed-income benchmark, but a similar column could be developed for risk relative to any performance benchmark.

Figure 7–2. Plan Sponsor Issues and Implications (Neutral Market Views)

	Adjustment to		Consequences		
Objective	Bond Duration	Equity Allocation	Expected Return	Asset Shortfall Risk	Surplus Shortfall Risk
Maintain Prior Asset Allocation	None	None	Lower	Higher	Higher
Maintain Prior Expected Return	Lengthen None	None Increase	Unchanged Unchanged	Much Higher Much Higher	Lower Much Higher
Maintain Prior Shortfall Risk— In Asset Terms	Shorten None	None Decrease	Much Lower Much Lower	Unchanged Unchanged	Much Higher Approx. Unchanged
Maintain Prior Shortfall Risk— In Surplus Terms	Lengthen None	None Decrease	Somewhat Lower Much Lower	Much Higher Apoprox. Unchanged	Unchanged Unchanged

Irreconcilable Demands Created by Outdated Targets

Figure 7–2 shows that there are no comfortable responses to the interest-rate decline. The first row depicts a plan sponsor who does not adjust the bond duration or equity (risky asset) structure. Even such a "stand-pat" investor must absorb not only a lower expected return, but also increased levels of risk, both in asset and surplus terms.

The second row shows portfolio changes aimed at recapturing the original expected return. These changes, however, generally pile further shortfall risks on those that are passively accepted by the stand-pat investor.

Even the cautious investor who seeks to restore the original risk level faces the painful choices shown in the remainder of Figure 7–2. A lower equity allocation reduces both the asset and surplus shortfall risks by approximately equal amounts, but it further penalizes the expected return that has already been battered by the interest-rate decline. Changing the bond duration has opposite effects on asset risk and surplus risk, so any duration adjustment that reduces one of these risks will increase the other.[2]

Incorporating Market Views in the Asset Allocation

Finally, we explore how a sponsor's views on the direction of interest rates and the adequacy of risk premiums can dictate changes in investment strategy apart from actuarial considerations. Market views justify reaching for return only for investors who see continued low interest rates and attractive risk premiums. However, many investors are concerned that the widespread

---

[2]An asset allocation model that accommodates multiple risk constraints is described in Chapter 3.

search for yield may itself be narrowing spreads and risk premiums to unrealistic levels.

Plan sponsors face a serious dilemma when they target their investment policies toward obsolete return assumptions. Persistence in their prior investment policies means a sharply heightened prospect of failing to meet these "artificial" targets. However, striving for the needed above-market return necessarily involves incremental risk that may well lie outside the boundaries set by the fund's risk tolerance. This strategic problem has no universal solution. Rather, plan sponsors must choose their own trade-offs after reassessing the relative importance of the return target and each risk factor in the new interest-rate environment.

ACTUARIAL IMPLICATIONS

Traditionally, investors have measured risk in terms of asset returns, and analysis of asset-only risk remains critical to many market participants. Particularly since the advent of FASB Statement No. 87, however, pension plan sponsors have become increasingly concerned about *surplus risk*—the risk that asset returns will fail to keep pace with liability increases. When discount rates drop, fixed pension plan liabilities rise substantially. Because of their extended payout period, pension liabilities generally have a substantially greater duration, or sensitivity to interest-rate changes, than a typical bond portfolio. (As we discuss below, however, *inflation-sensitive* benefits can have durations as short as zero.) A rate decline, therefore, typically drives up liabilities more than assets, eroding surplus (or increasing deficits). This surplus erosion is not just an actuarial artifact: Assets do lose future benefit-paying power when prospective investment returns fall, and more assets are required to service a given benefit stream. To protect against this danger, many plan sponsors have established dedicated or immunized portfolios: long-duration portfolios that are designed to track the movements of some or all of the liabilities. Many of these portfolios were established a decade ago, when an investment motivation to lock in high interest rates joined with an actuarial motivation to protect against the liability increase that would occur if rates dropped.

Public and private pension plans are subject to quite different rules regarding the reporting and funding of their obligations. FASB 87 requires private plan sponsors to report their surplus on a mark-to-market basis, so current financial reports already reflect the consequences of the interest-rate decline. The calculation of the pension cost that is charged against earnings, however, can involve the use of a relatively stable "long-term" rate of return assumption that need not closely reflect current market conditions.

The financial reports of public pension funds are regulated by Governmental Accounting Standards Board Statement No. 5 (GASB 5). GASB has decided that a mark-to-market pension standard would create volatility inappropriate for public plans, given their very long life and the fact that their sponsors are not valued and traded daily in public markets. Under these conditions, a stable long-term investment return assumption is satisfactory because it avoids giving undue prominence to short-term fluctuations. Thus, unlike their private sector counterparts, public entities do not measure their pension liabilities with a discount rate that reflects current market conditions.

Contributions to pension funds also are controlled by rules and practices that vary between private plans (regulated by the Employee Retirement Income Security Act of 1974 [ERISA]) and public plans (regulated by the laws of their state or municipality). In general, however, pension contributions are determined by using a relatively stable long-term investment return assumption.

Thus, return assumptions that are not related to current market rates can be used by public plans generally and by private plans for certain purposes. Although the use of noncurrent assumptions can deflect pressure to deal with short-term rate movements, persistent low rates ultimately must be addressed by public and private plan sponsors alike, regardless of the rule books. Over time, market realities override actuarial and accounting conventions, and the actual—not assumed—returns will determine pension costs.

Lower interest rates have not come about in a vacuum; they are accompanied by, and in large measure due to, lower inflation expectations. While lower interest rates lead to higher contributions to make up for diminished earning power, lower inflation expectations can have a variety of effects:

1. Lower pay raises may produce reduced benefits at retirement.

2. Lower pay raises decrease the payrolls upon which employer and employee contributions are based, requiring a higher *percentage* contribution rate to meet a specified obligation. (Constrained growth or actual shrinkage of the workforce—another reality of the current environment—may exacerbate this situation. Poorly funded plans, where the active employee base supports the amortization of a large unfunded liability, are particularly vulnerable in this regard.)

3. Lower Consumer Price Index increases mean smaller pension increases subsequent to retirement for the many public plans that pay CPI-linked pensions, as well as for those plans without automatic indexing that periodically grant ad hoc pension increases.

Most pension plans base their benefit formulas on pay, either at the date of retirement or else averaged over a brief period immediately preceding retirement. A number of public plans also pay benefits that are fully indexed for CPI increases after retirement. These public plans may find that an equal decrease in investment returns and inflation has little or no net effect on the required contributions.[3]

Even the most generous public plans, however, are unlikely to be *fully* inflation-sensitive (for example, because of "stickiness" in pay raises or caps on CPI-linked increases). In addition, many sponsors may feel that interest rates have come down more than inflation expectations (that is, real rates have dropped). Thus, although lower inflation may mitigate the effect of lower rates, the overall effect is adverse for virtually all plans.

POSSIBLE RESPONSES

Return targets can be of two broad types. For some investors, return targets and performance relative to these targets have immediate significance. As market conditions change, fixed targets could lead such investors to erratic changes in their investment policies, and they probably would be better advised to adjust their targets as necessary to reflect current market conditions.

For pension funds, however, the actuarially assumed investment returns are a type of long-term target, subject to correction over time. Few plan sponsors wish to alter their contribution schedules or overall investment policies in response to every market movement. They generally can afford to wait several years for the market to return to the levels contemplated when the targets were set. Meanwhile, they can keep the targets in place but temporarily relax the pressure to meet them.

Sponsors who decide to retain their previously fixed investment return targets have various ways of addressing the gap between those targets and the current market return opportunities. Three possibilities are maintaining the prior asset allocation, maintaining the prior expected return, and maintaining the prior shortfall risk. We consider these choices in the context of a plan sponsor who has neutral market views, believing that the positive yield curve offers expected returns on bonds that rise with duration and that equities provide a fair risk premium over bonds.

---

[3]It can be shown that an inflation-driven change in *nominal* rates, without a change in real rates, does not affect the cost of a fully indexed benefit.

Figure 7–3. Bond/Equity Portfolios—Old Expected Returns

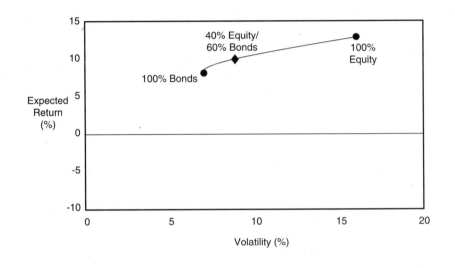

Maintaining the Prior Asset Allocation

Most sponsors think of their investment return assumption as a long-term view of "average conditions," expecting that market rates and investment returns will sometimes be higher and sometimes lower than the assumption. These sponsors may feel that they now face merely a temporary shortfall in investment opportunities or results. They also may feel that the gap is small enough to be bridged by the risk premiums that their current asset allocation can capture in other sectors of the bond market, as well as in equities and other more risky investments. These sponsors are inclined to maintain their assumptions, investment strategies, and contribution schedules until the current conditions have shown enough staying power—at least through a market cycle—to establish a new long-term norm for interest-rate levels, well below the level that they need to meet their obligations.

One consequence of this *laissez-faire* policy is a diminished expected return, at least temporarily. A more subtle consequence is the acceptance of greater shortfall risk—the potential downside performance relative to a fixed investment return target. Figures 7–3 to 7–6 illustrate this effect.

Figure 7–3 shows the expected one-year returns and volatilities (standard deviation of return) of various combinations of bonds and equity. The returns are based on the following assumptions, which typified the market two years ago and which we refer to as the "old expected returns":

Bonds: Expected Return = 8%
             Standard Deviation = 7%

Equity: Risk Premium = 5%
             (Expected Return = 8% + 5% = 13%)
             Standard Deviation = 16%

Bond/Equity Correlation = 0.35

Figure 7–3 highlights a moderately risk-averse 40% equity/60% bond portfolio, which has an expected return of 10% (40% × 13% expected equity return + 60% × 8% expected bond return). Assuming that the equity and bond returns are distributed normally, we can calculate that the standard deviation is 8.8%.

In previous chapters, we developed a risk measure known as the *shortfall threshold*—that is, the level of performance that a plan sponsor wishes to have a high probability (90%, for example) of exceeding.[4] For example, a sponsor may want 90% certainty that his asset return in a particular year is not less than some prescribed minimum value. The minimum may be specified directly (for example, zero) or indirectly (for example, 10% below the investment return assumption).[5]

We now evaluate the risk of this portfolio under the shortfall approach. In any year, the probability is 10% that the actual return will be more than 1.28 standard deviations below the mean—that is, below –1.3% (10% – 1.28 × 8.8%). This –1.3% return represents the shortfall risk implicit in the current portfolio, so we assume that the plan sponsor can accept this level of risk in an asset-only framework. We previously have shown that all portfolios with equal levels of shortfall risk plot along a straight line that intersects the vertical axis at the shortfall threshold.[6] Figure 7–4 shows the line for the –1.3%

---

[4]We recognize that the shortfall probability is an incomplete measure of risk, because it fails to indicate how bad the shortfall will be should one occur. For a more fully developed theory of shortfall analysis that incorporates these "higher" considerations, see "Asset Pricing in a Generalized Mean-Lower Partial Moment Framework: Theory and Evidence," W. V. Harlow and R. Rao, *Journal of Financial and Quantitative Analysis*, September 1989; and "Capital Market Equilibrium in a Mean, Lower Partial Moment Framework," V. Bawa and E. B. Lindenberg, *Journal of Financial Economics*, November 1977.

[5]A sponsor might wish to constrain not only the potential asset loss, but also the potential loss of surplus. See Chapter 3.

[6]See Chapter 2.

Figure 7–4. Bond/Equity Portfolios—Shortfall Line (–1.3% Threshold)

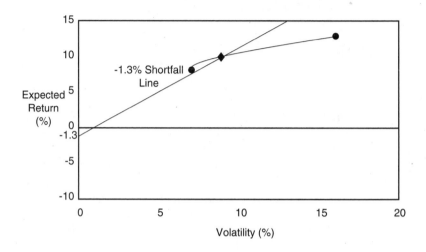

Figure 7–5. Bond/Equity Portfolios—Old and New Expected Returns

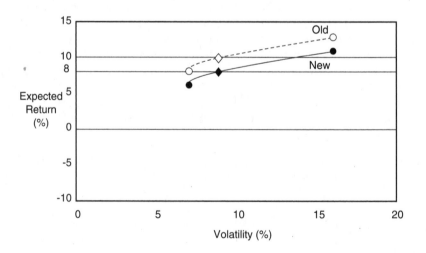

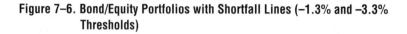

Figure 7–6. Bond/Equity Portfolios with Shortfall Lines (–1.3% and –3.3% Thresholds)

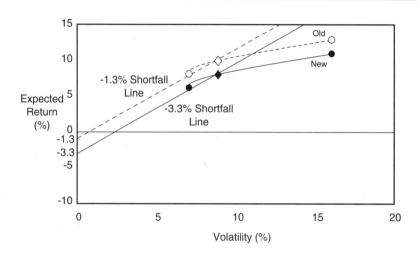

threshold; all portfolios on or to the left of this line, including the 40%/60% portfolio, meet the implied shortfall constraint.

Now we lower the expected bond return by 2%,[7] holding the equity risk premium constant and therefore lowering the expected equity return by 2%. We refer to these results as the "new expected returns"; all other assumptions are held constant. Figure 7–5 shows the entire risk/return curve shifted down by 2%, decreasing the expected return of the 40%/60% portfolio from 10% to 8%.

As Figure 7–6 shows, the new market conditions not only lower the expected return, but also make the portfolio riskier in shortfall terms. That is, the threshold annual return that the plan sponsor can exceed with 90% confidence drops from –1.3% to –3.3%. We also can determine that the probability of failing to achieve a return of at least –1.3% increases from 10% to 15%. *Thus, even with an unchanged investment structure, the rate decline imposes higher levels of risk relative to fixed return targets.*

---

[7]For comparison to our 8% old and 6% new bond return assumptions, the yield of the BIG Index averaged 8.1% during 1991; it stood at 6% on June 1, 1993.

Figure 7–7. Bond Sector Spreads to Government Bonds—Jan. 85–June 93

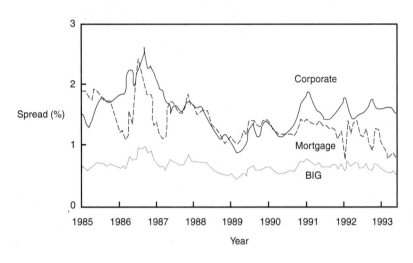

Source: Salomon Brothers Inc

Maintaining the Prior Expected Return

Other public or private plan sponsors may face questions about the gap between investment return assumptions and market realities from stakeholders such as plan participants, shareholders, government officials, or taxpay-
ers. These stakeholders may question whether the investment structure can
produce the needed returns, and demand a restructuring, in lieu of the more
painful alternative, a contribution increase.

Figure 7–7 indicates the potential gains that can be obtained by accepting more risks within the bond market. It shows the yield advantage over
government securities offered by the corporate and mortgage-backed sectors and by the bond market as a whole, as represented by the Salomon Brothers Broad Investment-Grade (BIG) Bond Index.[SM]

From Figure 7–7, it appears that a gap as large as 100 basis points between government yields and the investment return assumption might be
eliminated or reduced to insignificance with a conventional bond portfolio
allocated among the government, corporate, and mortgage-backed sectors.
This strategy, however, will be successful only if most of the yield advantage
is in fact realized as a risk premium. For example, if concerns about credit or

Figure 7–8. Preserving 10% Expected Return with 80% Equity/20% Bond Portfolio

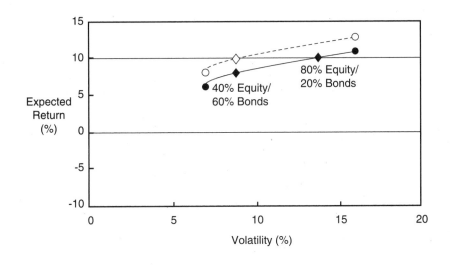

mortgage prepayment rates cause corporate and mortgage-backed spreads to widen, or if credit losses actually occur, the yield advantage may be dissipated by capital losses. Under any conditions, a gap approaching 200 basis points would require at least a moderate exposure to equities or other relatively risky investments before it could plausibly be expected to be covered by the capture of risk premiums. *Risk premiums imply risk as well as premiums.* Despite the benign experience of recent years, stretching for higher returns does heighten the possibility of serious losses. Funds that choose to step up to a higher risk level should be certain that they do not ignore the risk dimension, which is illustrated in the next set of charts.

We return to the plan sponsor whose situation was set forth in Figures 7–3 to 7–6. Suppose that the plan sponsor decides to revise the asset allocation to recapture the 10% expected return at which the investment policy originally aimed. The lower expected return levels require an increase from 40% equity to 80% (80% × 11% expected equity return + 20% × 6% expected bond return = 10%). Figure 7–8 shows this change.

The additional risk accepted by the fund is substantial. Under the old market conditions, the shortfall threshold (10th-percentile return) was –1.3%; the new market conditions lowered it to –3.3%. By moving to an 80% equity

Figure 7–9. Shortfall Consequences of 80% Equity/20% Bond Portfolio

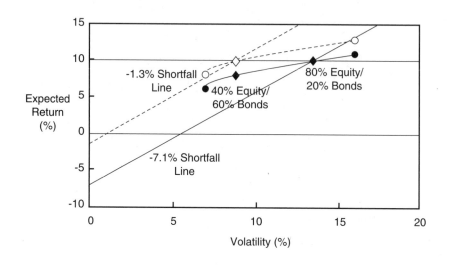

allocation, however, the fund now significantly elevates its risk. As Figure 7–9 illustrates, the shortfall threshold is now –7.1%. That is, the fund now faces a 10% probability that its one-year return will be –7.1% or lower—nearly 6% worse than the old threshold. (As another way of viewing the increased risk, we can calculate that the 80%/20% portfolio has a 20% probability of returning –1.3% or less. In other words, the –1.3% return that was previously a once-in-10-years event is now one in five.)

These increased risks are substantial, and sponsors that accept them must have a higher tolerance for financial and other consequences than they had before. If all goes well, the prior contribution schedule can be maintained; if not, very large increases could be needed. Furthermore, these sponsors should be comfortable that risk premiums remain at adequate levels; as we will discuss, some investors feel that current market conditions also have depressed risk premiums below their equilibrium levels. *Funds whose overall objectives and concerns are unchanged should not casually increase their risk levels to meet return targets that were set when rates were much higher than they are today— especially in view of the increased shortfall risks in the existing portfolio that have already been created by the rate decline.*

Figure 7–10. Maintaining the Shortfall Threshold

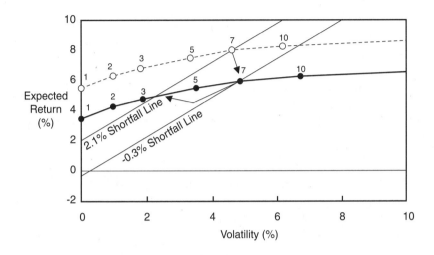

Maintaining the Prior Shortfall Risk

The third response, which a risk-averse sponsor might adopt, is to maintain the prior shortfall threshold. Whether the sponsor is concerned with asset-only risk or surplus risk, reducing the equity allocation can restore some or all of the threshold reduction brought about by lower rates, at a cost of reducing the expected return. Note, however, that *no* point on the new return curve in Figure 7–9 satisfies the old –1.3% shortfall constraint; that is, no point on the new curve lies on or left of the old shortfall line. Reducing the equity allocation does bring the shortfall threshold closer to the –1.3% line, however.

Adjusting the bond duration can also help to improve shortfall risk. Figure 7–10 illustrates how shortening duration can restore the asset-return shortfall threshold that was lowered by a drop in rates. It shows a hypothetical yield curve, on which the seven-year bond has an expected return of 8% and a shortfall threshold (10th-percentile return) of 2.1%. (The one-year expected returns are assumed to equal the yields.) The curve then undergoes a parallel shift of –2% (to the heavy line), lowering the expected return on the seven-year bond to 6% and the shortfall threshold to –0.3%. To restore the 2.1% shortfall threshold on the new curve, we must drop to the three-year bond, with an expected return of only 4.75% but with a volatility low enough to give the necessary downside protection.

The bond duration shortening, however, is a double-edged sword: Shortening duration reduces asset risk (and expected return) but increases surplus risk. A risk-averse sponsor who is concerned more about surplus than asset performance actually would lengthen duration to avoid compounding the risk of mismatched asset and liability durations with the market-imposed loss of yield.

The sponsor who chooses to maintain the prior risk level can do so by adjusting either the bond duration or the equity allocation (or both). *Reductions in the equity allocation affect asset and surplus risk similarly.*[8] *Changes in the bond duration pull the asset and surplus risk in opposite directions.*

INCORPORATING MARKET VIEWS IN THE ASSET ALLOCATION

We have reviewed a range of policy responses to lower interest rates, including the summary in Figure 7–2. This review is based on a neutral strategic viewpoint—in other words, we have assumed that the sponsor believes that all markets are currently fairly priced, with no special short-term opportunities or risks. Now we suppose that the asset allocation policy or norm has been reset (if necessary) to reflect the sponsor's choice regarding the possibilities set forth in the preceding section and consider further adjustments relative to this norm to reflect specific market views. These views can be grouped around two key questions:

- Whether we are near the bottom of a downward spike in rates or at (or on the path toward) a new normal level; and
- Whether equity risk premiums currently offer fair compensation for the risk of equity investments.

Expected Rate Direction

A sponsor with strong views about the direction of rates can make the obvious adjustments to the bond duration, moving to the long end of his allowable range if he expects a continued rally and the short end if he anticipates

---

[8]Reducing the equity allocation (while maintaining the total portfolio duration) has identical effects on the asset and surplus *variance*. The effects on asset and surplus *volatility*, however, may differ somewhat because of the arithmetic of square roots. Maintaining the asset shortfall risk, therefore, may require a slightly smaller or larger equity adjustment than maintaining the surplus shortfall risk.

a backup in rates. Whether he should also adjust the equity allocation in response to a rate forecast is a more difficult issue for two reasons:

1. A rate prediction typically is embedded in a more comprehensive economic forecast, which may contain an implied or explicit equity forecast.

   For example, falling rates tend to help the equity markets—but not if the rate decline is part of a recessionary scenario. Rising rates similarly can appear in a variety of contexts—for example, economic expansion, monetary contraction, or a resurgence of inflation—with quite different consequences for the equity markets.

2. Given an unchanged risk tolerance, a sponsor who alters a plan's risk level by changing the bond duration may want to compensate by adjusting the equity allocation.

For example, shortening duration in response to bearish rate expectations reduces the asset risk and permits a compensating increase in equity risk. On the other hand, that same duration shortening generally *increases* surplus risk because of the long liability duration. If the sponsor is concerned primarily with surplus risk, the duration shortening represents an increased risk that calls for a compensating *decrease* in equity risk. The risk consequences of a duration adjustment, therefore, depend on whether the sponsor is more concerned about asset risk or surplus risk.

Assessment of Risk Premiums

A judgment about the adequacy of risk premiums is particularly critical to those considering stepping up their risk levels to bridge the gap between their return targets and what their existing portfolios offer. Many investors have already increased their dependence on risky assets to produce higher returns. Within the bond market, investors dissatisfied with government yields are increasing their allocations to corporate and mortgage-backed securities and pushing higher-grade corporate bond allocations into higher yields. Others are turning to equities. Many, however, fear that this widespread reach for incremental yield is making these sectors too rich. For example, the *yield* premiums on corporate bonds may not be realized as *return* premiums, because the potential for credit problems is being inadequately priced in the quest for higher yields. Similarly, the flow of money into the equity market may have driven equity risk premiums below the levels justified by the underlying economics.

A sponsor who believes that equity risk premiums are higher or lower than equilibrium levels will want to increase or decrease the equity allocation accordingly. The resulting alteration in the risk profile of the fund may call for a compensating adjustment in the bond duration.

With an unchanged risk tolerance, a sponsor who accepts increased risk by adding equities may make an offsetting risk reduction in the bond duration. The duration adjustment depends on which of the risk measures is more binding—asset risk or surplus risk. A sponsor who is concerned primarily with asset risk would reduce that risk by shortening duration, while one concerned with surplus risk would lengthen duration to match her liabilities more closely.

Decreasing equity risk because of a perceived inadequacy of risk premiums loosens the constraints on the bond duration that may have been imposed by the need to control asset or surplus risk. This loosening frees the sponsor to act more vigorously on her rate forecast or duration preference.

At interest-rate levels that many investors have not previously seen during their careers, few can be very confident of either their mathematical models or their intuitions. Under these circumstances, some plan sponsors shun risk; others feel that in such times of uncertainty, risks are well compensated. A middle ground is to maintain or even step up their allocations to risky asset *classes* but to favor the low-risk segment of each such class—accepting more credit risk in the bond market, for example, but at short maturities, or looking for value rather than growth in the equity market.[9]

CONCLUSION

For funds with unchanged allocation policies, the interest-rate decline has caused expected returns to plummet. It is less well known that the rate decline has escalated risk, as measured by the potential shortfall against fixed return targets. Pressure to meet those targets points toward a longer duration and an increased commitment to equities. However, those changes would further increase risk at a time when many sponsors may see low rates as temporary and risk premiums as inadequate. The only genuine resolution of this conflict lies in recognizing the artificiality of a fixed return target. Sponsors should pursue such targets in the face of market realities only if their risk tolerance has greatly increased and/or they feel that equities and other risky assets now offer unusually positive opportunities.

---

[9]See *Portfolio Tilts for a Dreary Equity Market*, Eric H. Sorensen, Berry W. Cox, and Rommel T. Nacino, Salomon Brothers Inc, May 18, 1993.

Chapter 8

Interest-Rate Sensitive Asset Allocation: A New Approach to Strategic Asset Allocation

INTRODUCTION

Traditional procedures for strategic asset allocation begin with estimates of the return premiums, volatilities, and correlations among various asset classes. Then, with overall portfolio volatility as a risk measure, optimal percentage allocations are determined for the available asset classes. This allocation result is taken as the fixed strategic norm until the next formal allocation study. While tactical departures may be allowed, the strategic target serves as the neutral posture, regardless of any market movements that occur prior to the next study.

Many investors, however, have concerns that are not fully addressed by the traditional risk measure of volatility. Some investors focus on various forms of "shortfall risk"—the probability that returns may fall below a prescribed threshold. For example, requiring a 90% assurance of achieving positive returns is tantamount to setting a return threshold at zero. Because allocation studies typically determine the expected equity returns by adding a risk premium to a specified interest rate (or expected bond return), the potential for penetrating a fixed shortfall threshold rises as interest rates fall. Consequently, when a fixed shortfall threshold is added to the traditional risk/return objectives, the result is surprising: The optimal strategic allocation no longer consists of a *fixed* set of percentages, but rather it becomes a *prescription for changing* the allocation percentages as a function of interest-rate levels.

157

This chapter presents an Interest-Rate Sensitive Asset Allocation (IRSA) approach that provides a methodology for modifying the allocation targets to maintain a prescribed level for shortfall risk. Specifically, the IRSA approach calls for greater commitments to equities and other risky assets at higher interest rates, and to lower risky asset allocations and shorter bond durations at lower interest rates.

In a changing market environment, the interval between asset allocation studies may be characterized not only by changing interest rates, but also by fluctuations in volatilities, correlations, and equity risk premiums.[1] Thus, portfolio managers also may need to update their estimates of these factors. When volatility and equity risk premium adjustments are combined with changes in the level of interest rates, the impact of IRSA adjustments may be softened (or even reversed). However, the standard procedures for *strategic* asset allocation generally treat equity risk premiums and volatilities as long-term estimates and keep them constant over the investment horizon. We follow this convention in our examples and focus exclusively on the effects of changing interest rates.

It should be noted that the IRSA technique is based on *strategic*, rather than on *tactical* considerations. Even though the allocation percentages change in a prescribed fashion, IRSA is quite distinct from tactical asset allocation.[2] IRSA does not involve any judgments about the direction of interest rates or about the cheapness or richness of various markets. IRSA is also quite different from portfolio insurance in that the allocation of equities is driven by interest rates, rather than by the movement of the equity market.

SHORTFALL RISK AND EQUITY ALLOCATIONS

The risk/return trade-offs available from various stock/bond portfolios over a one-year investment horizon form the starting point for our analysis. For illustration (see Figure 8–1), we consider portfolios that combine five-year-duration bonds (which are expected to return 7%) with equity (which is expected to return 12%, reflecting a 500-basis-point equity risk premium). We assume that the investor has neutral market views, in that he or she regards equity risk premiums as fair and stable and foresees no specific changes in

---

[1] For a detailed analysis of the time series properties of expected returns, see "Business Conditions and Expected Returns on Stocks and Bonds," Eugene F. Fama and Kenneth R. French, *Journal of Financial Economics* 25 1989.

[2] For an overview of tactical asset allocation and portfolio insurance, see *Active Asset Allocation*, Robert D. Arnott and Frank J. Fabozzi, eds., Chapter 7 (by William F. Sharpe), Probus, 1992.

Figure 8–1. Bond/Equity Portfolios

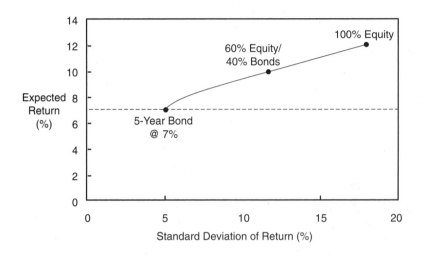

interest rates. Figure 8–1 highlights a typical portfolio consisting of 60% equity and 40% bonds that has a 10% expected return.[3]

In previous chapters, we developed a risk measure known as the "shortfall threshold," which is a minimum level of performance that an investor wishes to ensure with a high probability.[4] For example, an investor may want 90% assurance of a positive return in any given year. More generally, investors may specify any minimum return level as their risk threshold. Alternatively, we can examine the current portfolio structure and determine the implied shortfall risks. For example, the 60/40 portfolio can be shown to carry

---

[3]We have assumed that equity and bond returns are normally distributed with an 18% equity volatility, a 1% interest-rate volatility, and a 0.35 equity/bond correlation. These assumptions lead to an 11.7% volatility for the return of the 60%/40% portfolio. The expected return of this portfolio is 60% × 12% equity return + 40% × 7% bond return, or 10%.

[4]We recognize that the shortfall probability is an incomplete measure of risk, because it fails to indicate how bad the shortfall will be if one should occur. Nevertheless, we believe that the use of more complex shortfall measures would generally lead to the same result as depicted in this development. For a more fully developed theory of shortfall analysis that incorporates these "higher" considerations, see "Asset Pricing in a Generalized Mean, Lower Partial Moment Framework: Theory and Evidence," W. V. Harlow and R. Rao, *Journal of Financial and Quantitative Analysis*, September 1989; and "Capital Market Equilibrium in a Mean, Lower Partial Moment Framework," V. Bawa and E. B. Lindenberg, *Journal of Financial Economics*, November 1977.

a 10% probability of generating one-year returns that fall below –5%.[5] Therefore, an investor holding a 60/40 portfolio may be viewed as implicitly accepting this –5% shortfall threshold level. For purposes of illustration, the
–5% minimum return will be taken as a *fixed* threshold that retains its significance for the investor as market conditions change.[6]

We previously showed that all portfolios with equal shortfall risk plot
along a straight line that intersects the vertical axis at the shortfall threshold.[7] Figure 8–2 shows the shortfall line for the –5% threshold: All portfolios
on this line, including the 60/40 portfolio, meet the implied shortfall constraint exactly—they provide a 90% assurance of exceeding the –5% return
threshold. This constraint will be met by all portfolios with return/risk combinations that fall in the shaded region above the shortfall line. All portfolios
that fall below the shortfall line fail to meet the shortfall constraint and, hence,
are unacceptable.

Now we assume that interest rates fall by 200 basis points, while the
equity risk premium, stock and bond volatilities, and stock/bond correlation remain constant. Figure 8–3 shows that the entire risk/return curve then
shifts down by 200 basis points, decreasing the expected return of the 60/40
portfolio from 10% to 8%. By leaving the shortfall line unchanged, the new
market conditions make the 60/40 portfolio riskier in shortfall terms; thus,
the portfolio drops out of the shaded area, which implies that it no longer
meets the shortfall constraint.[8] In fact, there is now a 10% probability that the
one-year return of the 60/40 portfolio will fall below –7%. *Thus, with an unchanged investment structure, a rate decline imposes higher levels of risk relative to
a fixed return target.*

---

[5]For any normal return distribution, the probability is 10% that in any year, the realized return will be
more than 1.28 standard deviations below the mean. Thus, there is a 10% chance that the benchmark
return will fall below –5% (= 10% – 1.28 × 11.7%).

[6]Certain types of shortfall thresholds automatically "float" with the market—for example, those related to market indexes or peer group performance. Other shortfall thresholds may float through a
deliberate decision—for example, the adjustment of a pension plan's investment return assumption
to reflect a substantial rate movement. Some thresholds, however, remain fixed, or at least "sticky,"
despite market changes—the discount rates or investment return assumptions of many pension plans,
for example, or a specific return threshold such as zero or –5% that the investor regards as critical.

[7]For a derivation of the shortfall line, see Chapter 15. Other aspects of shortfall and "risk-of-loss" are
discussed in *Active Asset Allocation*, Chapter 7; *Determining a Performance Benchmark for Central Banks*,
Thomas E. Klaffky and Robin Grieves, Salomon Brothers Inc, July 1993; and "Benchmark Management," in *Asset and Liability Management: Concepts and Strategies for Monetary Authorities*, Salomon
Brothers Inc, 1989.

[8]If, with the 200-basis-point decline in interest rates, equity return volatility had decreased to 15.4%,
the entire asset allocation curve (with five-year bonds at 5%) would have shifted to the left. As a
result, the 60/40 portfolio would have still met the –5% shortfall constraint. Alternately, the 60/40
portfolio would have been acceptable if volatility had remained unchanged but the equity risk premium had increased to 8.2%.

Figure 8–2. Stock/Bond Portfolios and the Shortfall Line (–5% Return Threshold)

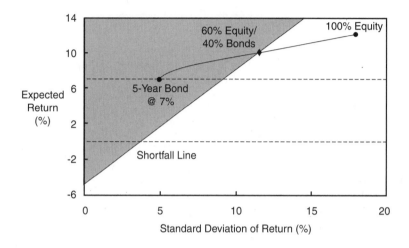

Figure 8–3. Old and New Expected Returns for Stock/Bond Portfolios

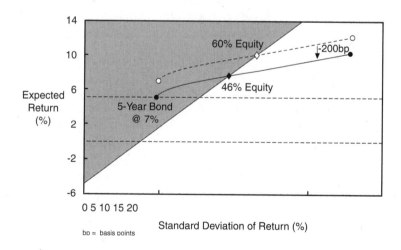

bp = basis points.

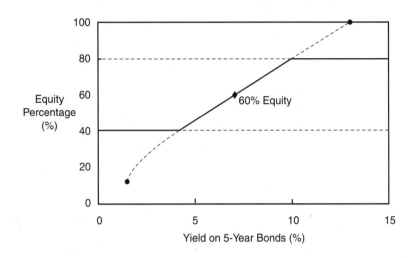

Figure 8–4. Maximum Equity Allocation with Shortfall Threshold Maintained at –5%

The intersection of the shortfall line with the new, lower expected return curve in Figure 8–3 shows that only portfolios with less than 46% equity will return a satisfactory shortfall performance. Thus, lower rates combined with a fixed minimum acceptable return compel a reduction in the equity allocation. Conversely, higher rates enable an investor to increase the equity commitment without endangering a fixed shortfall threshold.

Figure 8–4 shows the allowable equity percentage as a function of changing interest rates. When the five-year bond yield drops below 1.33%, the expected equity return falls below 6.33%, and *no* stock/bond portfolio can provide the required 90% assurance of exceeding a –5% return. In contrast, when the five-year bond yield exceeds 13.08%, the expected equity return rises above 18.08%, providing a sufficiently large return "cushion" so that even a 100% equity portfolio can meet the shortfall constraint. In practice, investors are unlikely to take such extreme levels of equity exposure. Figure 8–4 illustrates this "range constraint" with horizontal lines that limit the equity percentage to a range of 40%–80%.

INTEREST-RATE SENSITIVE EQUITY ALLOCATIONS

We now contrast the expected return, volatility, and shortfall threshold of an IRSA policy and a fixed 60/40 allocation policy.

The expected returns that result from both policies are the same when the five-year bond is at 7% (see Figure 8–5). For the 60/40 portfolio, each 1% decline (or rise) in rates leads to a 1% decrease (or increase) in expected return. In contrast, the equity allocation in the IRSA portfolio decreases as rates fall, resulting in a magnified expected return reduction. Thus, falling rates deal a "double hit" to the expected returns of the IRSA portfolio. In Figure 8–5, we can see that with the IRSA policy, each 1% drop in interest rates brings about a significantly greater decrease in the portfolio's expected return—the cost of preserving shortfall risk. When the minimum 40% equity percentage is reached, the allocation is not lowered, even if rates fall further. From that point, lower rates lead to a direct basis point–for–basis point drop in expected return.

At the other extreme, when interest rates are at 10%, the 80% equity maximum is reached and the IRSA expected return is 100 basis points greater

Figure 8–5. Expected Returns of the IRSA and Benchmark Portfolios

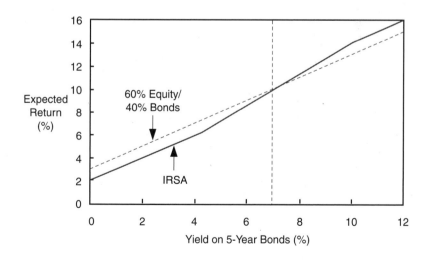

Figure 8–6. Volatility of the IRSA and Benchmark Portfolios

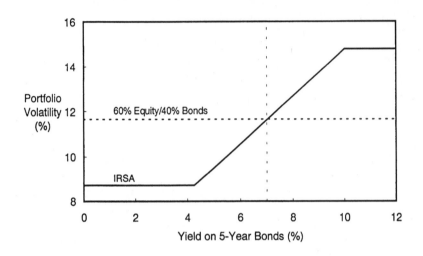

than that of the 60/40 portfolio. At higher rates, the IRSA and 60/40 expected returns move up in parallel, preserving the 100-basis-point IRSA advantage.

Figure 8–6 compares the return volatilities of the IRSA and the 60/40 portfolios. For purposes of clarity, we have made the (heroic) assumption that changes in the level of interest rates do not change the volatility of either interest rates or equities. Consequently, the 60/40 portfolio's volatility is independent of rates. In contrast, as rates fall, the IRSA policy reduces volatility by limiting equity exposure to fit the narrowing margin between the lower expected returns and the fixed shortfall threshold. At higher rates, the IRSA policy takes advantage of the wider return-to-shortfall margin by adding equity and, thus, volatility.

As indicated above, the IRSA policy maintains a constant –5% shortfall threshold—its fundamental objective—as long as the "implied" equity percentage does not fall outside the allowable 40%–80% range (see Figure 8–7). In contrast, the 60/40 portfolio precisely meets the shortfall constraint only when interest rates are at 7%. Any decrease or increase in rates produces an equal change in the implied shortfall threshold.

Figure 8–7. Shortfall Thresholds of the IRSA and Benchmark Portfolios

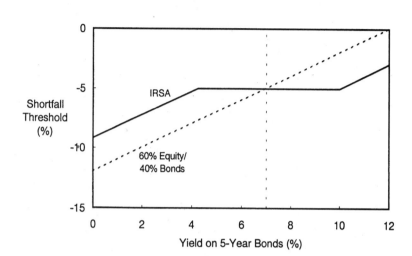

BOND PORTFOLIOS UNDER IRSA

We now turn from bond/equity combinations to 100% bond portfolios and explore how an IRSA policy affects the duration choice. Figure 8–8 displays a positively sloped yield curve that includes the five-year bond at its original yield rate of 7%. We assume that the yield curve can be taken as a return/risk diagram, and we set the shortfall threshold at a 0% return so that our constraint becomes a 90% assurance of positive *nominal* returns.[9] As shown in Figure 8–8, the resulting shortfall line intersects the yield curve at a duration of 5.6 years. All shorter-duration bonds will satisfy this positive return constraint, while all longer-duration bonds will violate it. The five-year-duration bond thus represents an acceptable level of portfolio risk at the 7% rate level.

Figure 8–9 shows the effect of a 200-basis-point downward shift in the yield curve. Because the shortfall line now intersects the yield curve at a duration of 3.7 years, the 5-year bond is no longer a feasible investment.

---

[9]For a detailed discussion of the relationships between yield curves and expected return curves, see Chapter 21. In addition, it is interesting to note that when interest rates are driven solely by inflation, a fixed real return target will act as a floating target within an IRSA context.

Figure 8–8. A Rising Expected Return Curve for Fixed-Income Investments

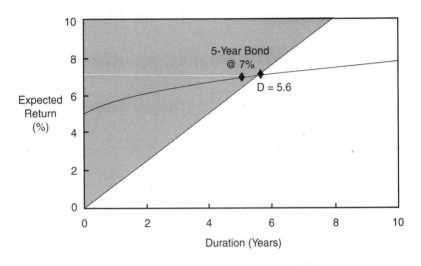

D = duration.

Figure 8–9. Bond Selection when Interest Rates Fall by 200 Basis Points

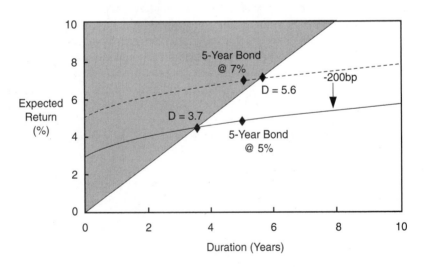

bp = basis points; D = duration.

To maintain a 0% shortfall threshold in lower-interest-rate environments, the manager must move toward ever lower durations. In contrast, when bond yields are very high, the investor has an almost unlimited choice of bond durations.

We have used the context of a 100% bond portfolio to explore the impact of an IRSA policy on the duration decision. As we might anticipate, this duration effect is also present when dealing with mixed equity/bond portfolios. For such portfolios, risk reduction can also be achieved by shortening duration, as well as by lowering the equity percentage. In general, a combination of both factors leads to the highest return portfolio that satisfies a given shortfall constraint.

SHORTFALL RISKS AND LIABILITY CONSTRAINTS

In this section, we address the dilemma of a pension plan sponsor who is concerned with maintaining both an absolute return threshold and a given level of surplus relative to his liabilities. For example, assume that the sponsor must maintain a –5% asset shortfall threshold, while limiting potential surplus losses to –8%.[10] Within these constraints, the sponsor's asset allocation decision involves the simultaneous choice of equity percentage and bond duration.

First, we address the problem of finding all stock/bond combinations that meet the –5% "asset-only" shortfall constraint. Figure 8–10 displays these portfolios in terms of their equity percentage (the vertical axis) and bond duration (the horizontal axis). The curve represents all equity percentage/ bond duration combinations that *exactly meet* the –5% threshold. The market context for this shortfall curve is the yield curve in Figure 8–8, with the five-year bond at 7%.

The shortfall curve originates at a point on the vertical axis that corresponds to a portfolio with 62% equity and 38% bonds with zero duration (that is, cash securities). Such an equity/cash portfolio eliminates the effect of bond volatility and therefore allows for a maximal exposure to equity. The bond duration can be increased moderately with little effect on the allowable equity percentage. As the duration grows beyond seven years, the higher bond volatility starts seriously to increase the overall portfolio volatility, forcing sharp reductions in the allowed equity allocation. At the bottom of the

---

[10]We define the surplus return as the change in surplus *divided by* the initial liability. For a detailed discussion of the surplus return, see Chapter 3.

Figure 8–10. Equity Percentage and Bond Duration of Portfolios That Meet a –5% Asset-Only Shortfall Constraint (With 5-Year Bond Yielding 7%)

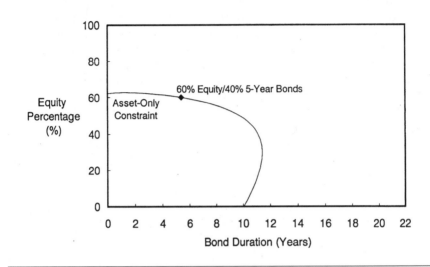

---

shortfall curve, when the equity percentage is reduced to zero, the all-bond portfolio with a duration of 10.05 years will just satisfy the –5% threshold. Note that the shortfall curve defines two regions: The region within the curve represents portfolios that meet the shortfall requirement, while the region outside the curve represents portfolios that violate the shortfall requirement.

If asset performance were the only consideration, the investor could choose the highest expected return portfolio along the curve, regardless of the bond duration. In our example, the optimal portfolio is close to the 60/40 portfolio.[11]

Now consider the very different shortfall problem associated with the pension fund's liability. Suppose that the funding ratio is 100% and the liability has a 10-year duration. To plot the portfolios that satisfy the –8% surplus shortfall condition, we recall our earlier work on liability shortfalls, in which we showed that these portfolios form an egg-shaped curve approximately centered over the 10-year liability duration point (see Figure 8–11). All

---

[11]If the expected return curve for bonds is flat, the maximum return portfolio will have the highest equity percentage. With a positively sloped curve, the optimization problem becomes more complex.

Figure 8–11. Portfolios Meeting Both Asset and Surplus Shortfall Constraints

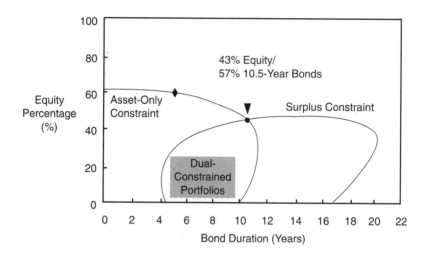

portfolios that provide at least 90% assurance that the surplus will fall by no more than 8% of the liability lie on or within the egg.[12]

Now suppose that the pension sponsor simultaneously wants to satisfy both constraints—the –5% minimum return and the –8% limit on surplus loss, each with 90% assurance. Portfolios that meet both of these shortfall constraints fall within the intersection area of the two eggs. Within this feasible set, the maximum return portfolio will be located at or near the intersection of the two curves. In our example, the highest expected return portfolio will contain 43% equity and 57% 10.5-year-duration bonds. This dual-constrained portfolio has an expected return of 9.65%, significantly lower than the 10% expected return of the singly constrained 60/40 portfolio. This return reduction can be viewed as the "cost" of having to satisfy the liability constraint.

Figure 8–11 is based on a 7% interest-rate environment. If all specifications of the problem are kept constant but the five-year yield drops to 5%, we obtain the situation depicted in Figure 8–12. The asset-only shortfall region

---

[12]We assume equal initial values of the assets and liabilities, a 10-year liability duration, and a liability discount rate equal to the yield on a 10-year-duration bond. The reasoning behind the surplus shortfall egg is developed in Chapter 5.

Figure 8–12. Dual Shortfall Portfolios at Lower Rates

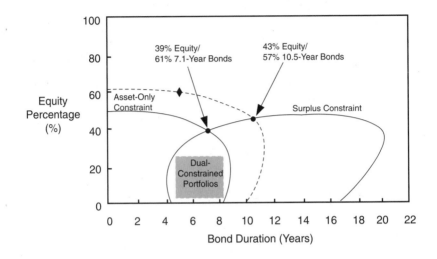

constricts because reduced equity percentages and lower bond durations are needed, given the smaller return cushion afforded by the lower interest rate. In contrast, if we assume that the actuarial discount rate floats with the market, the acceptable surplus shortfall portfolio set will be unaffected by rate changes.[13] Consequently, the liability "egg" will remain unchanged. As we can see, the intersection set of the two curves is now greatly reduced. The optimal dual-constrained portfolio now turns out to have only 39% equity and a bond duration of 7.1 years, providing an expected return of 8.0%.

This example provides a useful illustration of how an IRSA *strategic* target can be combined with *tactical* tilts based on market views. Even when liabilities are a source of serious concern, sponsors may be reluctant to maintain long-duration bond portfolios in a low-interest-rate environment. Suppose that the sponsor believed that rates were at a cyclic trough and not likely to fall much further. He or she might then have a natural inclination to shorten the duration far more than prescribed by the strategic IRSA target. Any such duration shortening would be based on his or her tactical view that rates are more likely to head higher, rather than lower. In contrast, we

---

[13]With funding ratios other than 100%, the surplus shortfall egg will be affected in a more complex way by changes in interest rates.

must remember that the IRSA target duration is based on an assumed neutral prospect for the direction of rates.

CONCLUSION

The traditional asset allocation approach produces a fixed asset allocation intended to preserve an appropriate risk/return trade-off through normal market cycles. By using volatility as the sole measure of risk, however, this approach neglects some investors' concerns about achieving a critical threshold return that remains fixed as markets vary. We have shown that an Interest-Rate Sensitive Asset Allocation (IRSA) policy can enable these investors to maintain a constant shortfall risk posture at varying levels of interest rates. An IRSA policy calls for increased equity percentages and/or longer bond durations at higher interest rates, and decreased equity exposure and/or shorter bond duration at lower rates. The IRSA portfolio shifts are independent of any market views. However, short-term tactical views on the level of risk premiums and volatilities may be used as an overlay on the strategic norms set by IRSA. For example, in a disinflation environment, low interest rates may be viewed as highly beneficial for financial assets. This view could result in a strong tactical bias, leading to increased equity allocations, even in the face of lower IRSA-based targets for equity.

Chapter 9

Strategic Allocation under Changing Market Conditions

INTRODUCTION

Traditionally, many investors accept volatility as the measure of risk. Others, however, focus on "shortfall risk," the probability that returns may fall below a prescribed threshold. These investors may require, for example, a 90% assurance of achieving positive returns, effectively setting a return threshold of zero. Such a threshold may retain its significance even as market conditions change dramatically, making the threshold a far more difficult—or easier—hurdle and calling for a restructured portfolio.

In an earlier chapter,[1] we observed that traditional fixed strategic asset allocations may not meet the shortfall risk constraints of many investors when market conditions change. Addressing the concerns of investors with fixed shortfall constraints, we presented an Interest-Rate Sensitive Asset Allocation (IRSA) methodology that periodically modifies the allocation targets in order to maintain a prescribed level of shortfall risk.

Under the IRSA approach, lower interest rates demand lower risky asset allocations and shorter bond durations, while higher rates permit greater commitments to equities and other risky assets—all other factors (such as volatility) being equal. Interest rates, however, do not change in isolation: Stock and bond volatilities, correlations, and equity risk premiums also vary, though the changes are more difficult to observe and measure. In this chap-

---

[1]See Chapter 8.

Figure 9–1. A Rising Expected Return Curve for Fixed-Income Investments

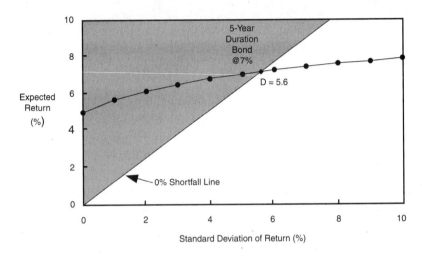

D = duration.

ter, we consider the asset allocation consequences of these changes. For example, we show that if volatilities move in tandem with interest rates, the reallocations called for by IRSA may be softened or even reversed; other types of capital market changes can exacerbate the need for reallocation.

Our principal message is that all investors should be alert to changing conditions that could undermine their existing asset allocation strategy—even investors who do not engage in tactical asset allocation or other forms of market timing. Periodic formal asset allocation studies do not exempt conscientious investors from a continuing review of conditions that may depart from those on which their studies were based.

BOND PORTFOLIOS UNDER IRSA

We initially examine how a modified IRSA policy affects the duration choice for a 100% bond portfolio. Figure 9–1 displays an illustrative yield curve, with the markers representing durations of zero, one year, two years, and so forth. The curve is positively sloped, with the five-year-duration bond yielding 7%; we take the yield to be the expected return over a one-year investment horizon.[2] We consider only parallel yield-curve shifts and approximate the return volatility as the bond duration multiplied by interest-rate volatility. Interest-rate changes are normally distributed with an absolute annual volatility (standard deviation) of 1%.[3]

In previous chapters, we have developed a risk-control measure known as the "shortfall constraint." The shortfall constraint is the minimum level of performance that an investor wishes to ensure with a high probability. For example, an investor may want 90% assurance of a positive return in any given year. In this case, we call 0% the shortfall threshold, and we use the term "shortfall risk" to describe the probability that the actual return in any measurement period will fail to reach the shortfall threshold. In practice, investors may specify any minimum return level as their risk threshold.

We have shown that all portfolios with equal shortfall risk plot along a straight line that intersects the vertical axis at the shortfall threshold.[4] Figure 9–1 shows the shortfall line for the 0% threshold. It intersects the yield curve at a duration of 5.6 years. All portfolios in the shaded region above the short-fall line, including bond portfolios with durations of 5.6 years or less, satisfy the shortfall constraint by providing at least 90% assurance of a positive one-year return. Portfolios with longer durations fail to meet the shortfall constraint and thus fall below the shortfall line.

Figure 9–2 shows the effect of a 200-basis-point downward shift in the yield curve, assuming that absolute annual interest-rate volatility remains unchanged at 1%. If the investor's shortfall risk tolerance remains fixed at 0%, the shortfall line does not change.[5] Thus, at lower rates, all bonds become riskier in shortfall terms. Specifically, the 5.6-year bond drops out of the shaded area because it offers less assurance of a positive return and no longer meets the shortfall constraint. As the intersection of the shortfall line with the new curve demonstrates, the maximum allowable duration short-

---

[2]For a detailed discussion of the relationships between yield curves and expected return curves, see Chapter 21.

[3]Later in this chapter, we will consider interest-rate changes as having a fixed *relative* volatility. For example, a relative volatility of 14.3% at a rate level of 7% equals an absolute volatility of 1% (14.3% × 7% = 1%).

[4]See Chapter 15.

[5]Certain types of shortfall thresholds automatically "float" with the market—for example, those related to market indexes or peer group performance. Other shortfall thresholds may float through a deliberate decision—for example, the adjustment of a pension plan's investment return assumption to reflect a substantial rate movement. Some thresholds, however, remain fixed, or at least "sticky," despite market changes—for example, the investment return assumptions of many pension plans or a specific return threshold, such as 0% or –5%, that the investor regards as critical.

Figure 9–2. Bond Selection when Interest Rates Fall by 200 Basis Points: Constant Absolute Interest Rate Volatility

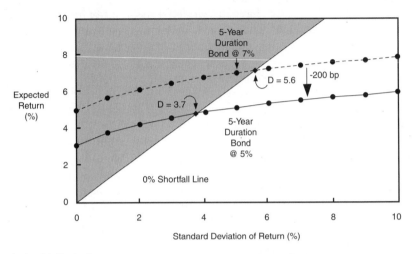

bp = basis points; D = duration.

ens from 5.6 years to 3.7 years. To maintain a constant shortfall risk posture, the investor who uses IRSA must shorten duration in lower interest-rate environments (assuming constant absolute rate volatility). In contrast, when bond yields are unusually high, the IRSA investor may enjoy an almost unlimited choice of bond durations.

THE EFFECT OF CHANGING VOLATILITY ON IRSA BOND PORTFOLIOS

Thus far, we have assumed that absolute interest-rate volatility remained constant as rates fell. Many investors, however, believe that interest-rate volatility is related to rate levels. This belief is suggested by data such as Figure 9–3 presents, plotting one-year realized interest-rate volatility (based on monthly changes) against the beginning-of-year five-year Treasury yield for the period 1980–1992 (excluding October 1987).

The squares in Figure 9–3 reflect the 1980–1992 data, and the dotted regression line is a modest fit, with a correlation of 0.62. The turbulent 1980–1981 period is represented by the two hollow squares. Excluding those two

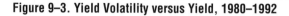

Figure 9–3. Yield Volatility versus Yield, 1980–1992

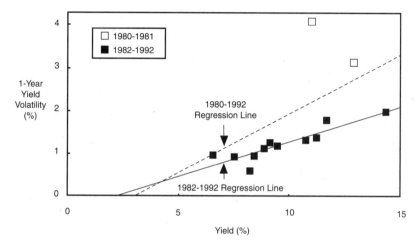

Source: Salomon Brothers Broad Investment-Grade Bond Index, Government-Corporate Sector.

years, we see that the solid regression line fits the 1982–1992 data extraordinarily well, passing reasonably close to the origin, with a correlation of 0.90. This data strongly supports the common practice of quoting rate volatility as a percentage of the rate level, rather than an absolute amount.

To illustrate how changing volatility affects the IRSA duration selection, we adopt the assumption that rate volatility is proportional to the five-year-duration bond yield, an assumption that has served well during the past decade. Specifically, because we have been using a 1% volatility with a five-year bond yield of 7%, we assume that rate volatility is 14.3% (1%/7%) of the five-year yield. When rates decline by 200 basis points, the absolute rate volatility drops to 0.71% (14.3% of the 5% five-year bond yield). Figure 9–4 displays the result.

As the yield curve falls, the decline in volatility causes a leftward contraction. As a result, shortfall thresholds in our illustration change only modestly, and 5.6 years continues to be the maximum feasible duration that meets the 0% shortfall constraint. In this special case—a zero shortfall threshold and volatility proportional to yields—IRSA imposes no duration adjustment. Dropping either of these conditions would lead to a duration change, as Figure 9–5 illustrates for the curves used in Figure 9–4.

The dashed +2% and –2% shortfall lines in Figure 9–5 show the effect of other shortfall constraints. With volatility dropping proportionately, as rates

Figure 9–4. Bond Selection when Interest Rates Fall by 200 Basis Points: Constant Relative Interest-Rate Volatility

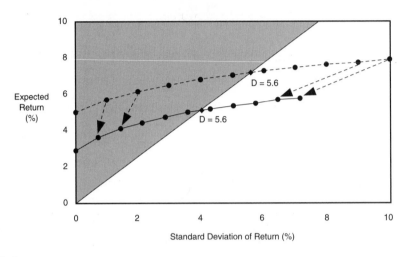

D = duration.

Figure 9–5. Constant Relative Interest-Rate Volatility with Alternative Shortfall Thresholds

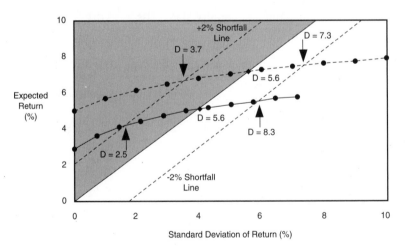

D = duration.

Figure 9–6. Yield Volatility versus Yield

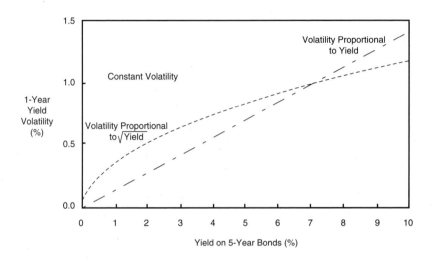

Yield on 5-Year Bonds (%)

decline from 7% to 5%, the duration limit *falls* from 3.7 years to 2.5 years for the +2% shortfall, while it *rises* from 7.3 years to 8.3 years for the –2% shortfall.

As we have indicated, the relationship between interest-rate volatility and rate level is uncertain. Illustrating a range of possibilities, Figure 9–6 shows three different volatility assumptions:

1. The rate volatility remains constant at 1%, as in Figure 9–2;

2. The rate volatility is 14.3% of the five-year yield, as in Figures 9–4 and 9–5; and

3. The rate volatility is proportional to the square root of the five-year yield, following a model commonly used in interest-rate theory that lies between assumptions 1 and 2.[6]

---

[6]The constant of proportionality used is 3.78%, so that the volatility at a 7% rate level is 1% for all three assumptions. For a model that uses this relationship, see "A Theory of the Term Structure of Interest Rates," John C. Cox, Jonathan E. Ingersoll, Jr., and Stephen A. Ross, *Econometrica* 53, no. 2 (March 1985).

Figure 9–7. IRSA Duration Choices under Differing Volatility Assumptions

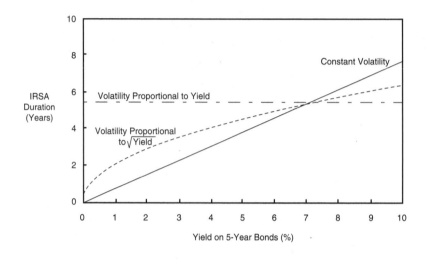

Figure 9–7 compares the effects of an IRSA policy on bond duration se-lection under the three assumptions shown in Figure 9–6. Under the con-stant volatility assumption, the maximum allowable duration changes con-tinuously and substantially as rates change. Under the proportional volatil-ity assumption, the duration can remain virtually fixed and continue to meet the shortfall constraint. The curve of the third assumption lies between the maximum duration lines given by the constant and proportional volatility assumptions.

Figure 9–7 shows that if volatility is proportional to yield, an investor can maintain a 0% shortfall threshold without changing duration. As noted earlier, this result is specific to the 0% shortfall threshold and will not hold for other constraints. Nevertheless, it indicates that for all-bond portfolios, IRSA adjustments would be somewhat muted if the recent volatility/yield relationship endures.

EQUITY ALLOCATIONS UNDER IRSA

We now consider the risk/return trade-off of various equity/bond portfo-lios over a one-year investment horizon. For illustration (see Figure 9–8), we

Figure 9–8. Equity/Bond Portfolios

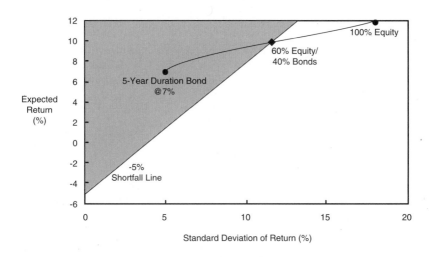

consider portfolios that combine five-year-duration bonds with equity. The five-year-duration bond is expected to return 7% and the equity is expected to return 12%, reflecting a 500-basis-point risk premium. Figure 9–8 highlights a typical 60% equity/40% bond portfolio, with a 10% expected return.[7]

For this mixed-asset portfolio, we assume that the investor has a –5% shortfall constraint, requiring 90% assurance that the one-year return will not fall below –5%. In Figure 9–8, the –5% shortfall line intersects the portfolio curve exactly at the 60/40 point. This 60/40 portfolio is therefore the most aggressive that the investor can hold.

The Effect of Lower Interest Rates

We next assume that interest rates fall by 200 basis points, while the equity risk premium, equity and bond volatilities, and equity/bond correlation all remain constant. Figure 9–9 shows that the entire risk/return curve shifts

---

[7]We assume that equity and bond returns are normally distributed with an 18% equity volatility, a 1% interest-rate volatility, and a 0.35 equity/bond correlation. These assumptions lead to an 11.7% volatility for the return of the 60/40 portfolio. The expected return of the portfolio is 60% × 12% equity return + 40% × 7% bond return, or 10%.

Figure 9–9. Old and New Expected Returns for Equity/Bond Portfolios

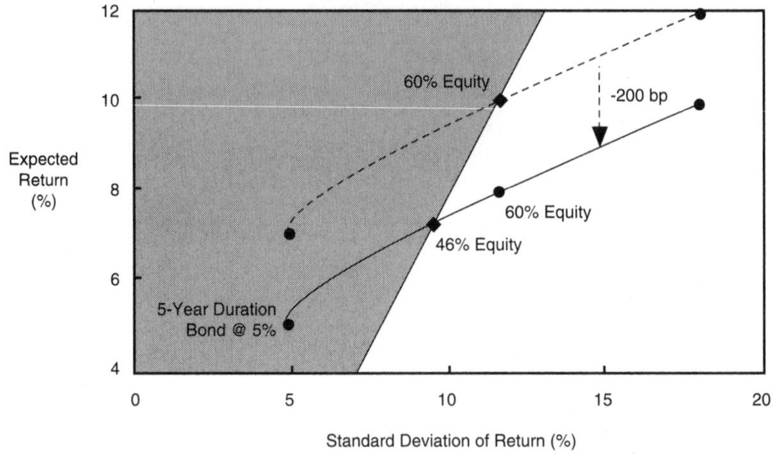

bp = basis points.

down by 200 basis points, decreasing the expected return of the 60/40 portfolio from 10% to 8%. (We have rescaled the next several graphs to show more clearly the effects of this decrease.)

The intersection of the shortfall line with the new, lower expected return curve in Figure 9–9 shows that only portfolios with less than 46% equity will offer satisfactory shortfall performance. Thus, all other things being equal, lower rates combined with a fixed minimum acceptable return compel a reduction in the equity allocation. Conversely, higher rates enable an investor to increase the equity commitment without endangering a fixed shortfall threshold.

The change in allowable equity holdings from 60% to 46%, under the IRSA policy in our example, was founded on a 200-basis-point interest-rate decline, with volatilities, correlation, and risk premium held constant. We now consider how changes in those factors would affect our conclusions.

The Effect of Changing Volatilities

First, we consider the impact of changing volatilities—for equity as well as interest rates. While several theories link interest-rate volatilities to rate lev-

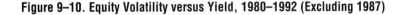

Figure 9–10. Equity Volatility versus Yield, 1980–1992 (Excluding 1987)

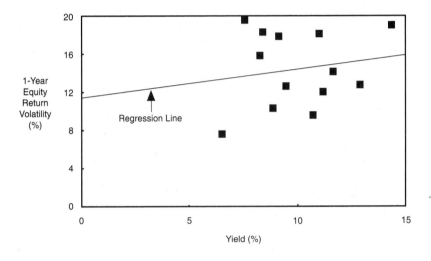

els, the theoretical or empirical support relating equity volatilities to interest rates is far more tenuous. Figure 9–10 shows the recent data, plotting one-year realized equity volatility for 1980–1992 (excluding October 1987) against the beginning-of-year five-year Treasury yield. The relationship is very weak, with a correlation of only 0.18. In the absence of a well-defined connection between equity volatility and interest rates, we consider two alternative equity volatility assumptions: the 18% used thus far and a more modest 16%.

In Figure 9–11, the dashed line repeats the new expected return line of Figure 9–9, with constant volatility. To illustrate the effect of changing equity and bond volatilities, we choose two possible combinations.

The first is the change in interest-rate volatility that we previously considered—from 1% to 0.71%, with no change in equity volatility. The all-equity point remains at an expected return of 10% and volatility of 18%, while the all-bond point shifts left to reflect its lower volatility. As a result, the equity/bond curve stretches to the left, raising the equity allocation percentage at the shortfall line intersection to 50%.

The second volatility alternative combines the same decreased interest-rate volatility with a reduction in equity volatility from 18% to 16%. This

Figure 9–11. Old and New Expected Returns for Equity/Bond Portfolios with Varying Volatilities

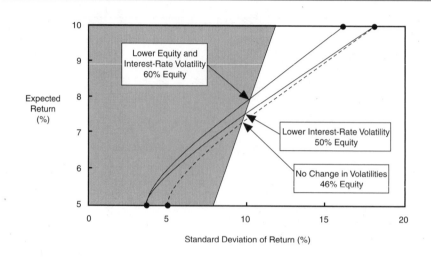

volatility decline shifts the entire dashed return curve to the left, allowing the equity holding to remain at the original 60%.[8]

Thus, we see that volatility changes can moderate or even reverse the reallocations that an IRSA policy would use to respond to changes in interest rates alone. Unfortunately, it is difficult to estimate reliably the one-year volatility of interest rates or equity returns. Option prices imply a market forecast of volatility, but their predictive power is unimpressive. Many investors prefer to use long-term historical averages for their strategic asset allocations. These obviously do not change as rapidly as interest rates.

---

[8]We have simplified this discussion by treating equity as a single asset—unlike bonds, for which we assume that volatility can be controlled by adjusting duration. The investor's ability to lower the volatility of the equity portfolio (at some loss of expected return) may offer a worthwhile alternative to simply reducing the equity weighting.

Of course, it is extremely unlikely that a combination of interest-rate and volatility changes would leave the shortfall threshold unchanged. For example, we have supposed that the investor's shortfall constraint demanded 90% assurance of exceeding a –5% return. Suppose instead that the constraint required 80% assurance of a *positive* return—a condition that can be shown to be precisely met by the 60/40 portfolio under our initial return and volatility assumptions. To preserve that zero threshold while staying with a 60/40 portfolio in the face of a 200-basis-point rate drop, the equity volatility would need to fall all the way to 14%.

Figure 9–12. Old and New Expected Returns for Equity/Bond Portfolios with Varying Correlations

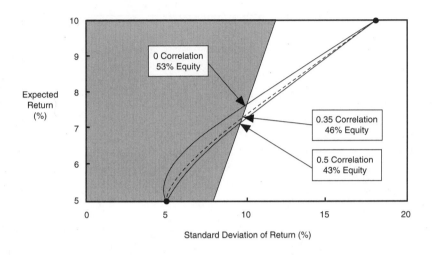

The Effect of Changing Equity/Bond Correlations

Determining prospective equity/bond correlations is even more difficult than determining volatilities, and there is little agreement on how they might relate to interest-rate levels. Most asset allocators use long-term historical relationships to project correlations, so the projections change quite slowly. Figure 9–12 illustrates the effect of a change in the assumed correlation that accompanies the interest-rate decline. Along with our "base" assumption of a 0.35 correlation, Figure 9–12 portrays correlations of 0 and 0.5 at the lower rate level.

The "bowing out" of the equity/bond return curves reflects the diversification benefits of low correlations. With a zero correlation, the riskiness of equity is mitigated by its diversification benefits, and a portfolio with 53% equity meets the –5% shortfall constraint. In other words, with the correlation unchanged, a 200-basis-point interest-rate drop would have compelled a decrease in the equity percentage from 60% to 46%. The decrease in the equity/bond correlation from 0.35 to 0 brings the allowable equity holding back up from 46% to 53%. An increase in the correlation to 0.5, however, would diminish the diversification effect and reduce the allowable equity even further, to 43%.

Figure 9–13. Old and New Expected Returns for Equity/Bond Portfolios with Varying Risk Premiums

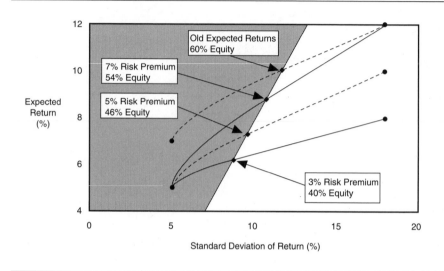

The Effect of Changing Risk Premiums

Figure 9–13 shows how a changing equity risk premium affects the IRSA reallocation. The upper dashed curve reflects the "old" expected returns of 7% for bonds and 12% for equities—conditions that enable the investor to meet the shortfall constraint with 60% equity. The lower dashed curve reflects the 200-basis-point rate decline with the same 500-basis-point risk premium. For the two solid curves, we allow the risk premium to rise to 700 basis points or fall to 300 basis points, while holding the correlation and volatilities constant. (Our remarks about the difficulties of determining volatilities and correlations apply with even greater force to risk premiums. Other than tactical asset allocators, most investors assume an unchanging risk premium, although there is some evidence suggesting that risk premiums are higher at the bottom of economic cycles, when rates are low.)

Of course, the lower risk premium of 300 basis points makes equity less attractive, pivoting the return curve downward and driving the allowable allocation down to 40%. This 40% compares to 60% before the rate decline and to 46% after the rate decline but before the risk premium change.

The 700-basis-point risk premium restores equity to the full 12% expected return that it offered before the decline. Equity thus has the same risk/return

Figure 9–14. Interest Rate/Equity Volatility Combinations Providing a –5% Shortfall Threshold for Various Portfolios

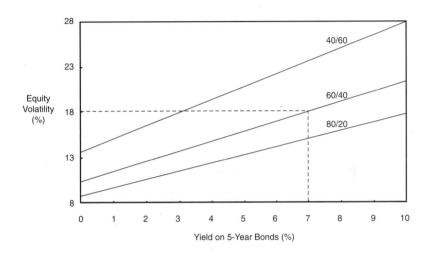

characteristics with which it began and has greatly increased appeal relative to bonds. It is therefore surprising that the equity holding is still limited to 54%—better than the 46% permitted with an unchanged risk premium but well below the original 60%. The explanation is that the rate decline has twisted the bond/equity curve, thereby lowering the expected return and increasing the shortfall risk of the entire curve (except for the excessively risky all-equity point). The investor who must preserve a –5% shortfall threshold has no choice but to move to a more conservative allocation.

Market Changes That Maintain a Constant Shortfall Threshold

Of the factors that we have examined, equity volatility is the most potent in its ability to offset (or intensify) the allocation changes that interest-rate movements can produce under an IRSA policy. Figure 9–14 shows the combinations of interest-rate level and equity volatility that maintain a –5% shortfall threshold for the 60/40 portfolio. An IRSA policy would hold the asset allocation constant at 60/40 as conditions in the capital markets remain unchanged on this curve. (We assume that the risk premium and correlation are unchanged, and that interest-rate volatility is 14.3% of the five-year rate—that is, 1% when the five-year rate is 7%, and 0.71% when the rate is 5%.) We also show the constant shortfall condi-

Figure 9–15. Allocations to Meet a –5% Shortfall Constraint

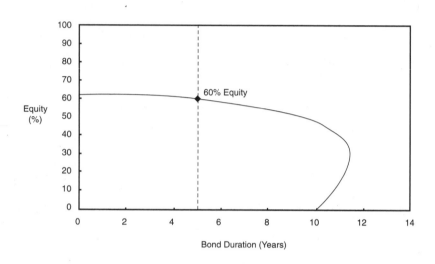

tions for portfolios with 80% and 40% equity holdings. An investor who accepts the assumptions underlying Figure 9–14 thus could locate the correct allocation by plotting the current equity volatility and bond yield and determining which portfolio curve the plot falls on.

Portfolio Changes That Maintain a Constant Shortfall Threshold

Thus far, we have dealt with bond duration and the equity/bond split as separate allocation issues. In practice, investors must combine these decisions to meet their objectives optimally. For example, asset risk can be lowered by reducing the bond duration or the equity allocation, as illustrated in Figure 9–15.

The curve in Figure 9–15 shows the asset allocations that meet a –5% shortfall constraint under our baseline assumptions, including a 7% yield on the five-year bond, 18% equity volatility, and 1% interest-rate volatility. On this curve, we highlight the 60% equity/40% five-year bond portfolio. Extreme allocations of 62% equity/38% cash and 100% 10-year bonds also satisfy the –5% shortfall constraint. The investor may tilt toward one of these extremes based on other goals, such as surplus control.

Figure 9–16. Allocations to Meet a –5% Shortfall Constraint under Varying Rate Levels and Volatilities

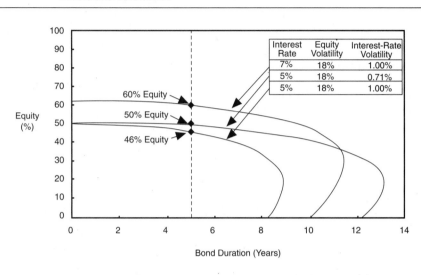

Figure 9–16 adds additional curves for alternative assumptions. Lowering the five-year rate to 5% with unchanged volatilities produces the bottom curve, which includes a 46% equity/54% five-year bond portfolio, as shown in Figure 9–11. If the interest-rate volatility falls to 0.71%, the middle curve results, including the 50% equity/50% five-year bond portfolio. Again, we can see the variety of portfolios that meet the –5% shortfall constraint, from 50% equity/50% cash to a long-duration, all-bond portfolio.

CONCLUSION

The traditional asset allocation approach produces a fixed allocation intended to preserve an appropriate risk/return trade-off through normal market cycles. By using volatility as the sole measure of risk, however, this approach neglects some investors' concerns about achieving a critical threshold return that remains fixed as markets vary. As we have shown, an Interest-Rate Sensitive Asset Allocation policy can provide these investors a constant shortfall risk posture at varying levels of interest rates.

In this chapter, we have extended the IRSA methodology to encompass changes in other capital market conditions besides interest rates. Among these conditions, volatility has the greatest effect. Some theoretical and empirical evidence points to a relationship between interest-rate volatility and interest-rate levels that would moderate the bond portfolio changes called for by the rate changes alone. Unfortunately, equity volatility, bond/equity correlations, and risk premiums are more difficult to establish, and there is no widely recognized relationship between those factors and interest-rate levels. Nonetheless, investors must continually review their strategic asset allocation norms to ensure that they remain appropriate as fundamental market conditions change.

Chapter 10

Funding Ratio Return: A More "Universal" Measure for Asset/ Liability Management

INTRODUCTION

The interest-rate downtrend that prevailed during 1991 through 1993 adversely affected the funding status of most corporate pension funds (see Figure 10–1). In 1991, pension fund liabilities soared as rates declined, but exceptional equity market performance (a 30.5% total return on the Standard & Poor's 500 Index [S&P]) provided sufficient asset growth to maintain prevailing funding levels. In 1992 and 1993, liabilities continued their rapid growth, but equities provided only moderate returns. Fixed-income investments also could not keep pace with liability growth in a declining rate environment because bond portfolios generally have much shorter durations than liabilities. The total returns of the Salomon Brothers Broad Investment-Grade (BIG) Bond Index and the S&P were almost equal in both 1992 (7.58% BIG return; 7.63% S&P return) and 1993 (9.90% BIG return; 10.08% S&P return). In contrast, based on our recently developed Pension Liability Index, we estimate that the typical pension fund liability grew by about 11.5% in 1992 and 22.8% in 1993.[1]

A plan's funding ratio is the market value of assets divided by the present value of future liabilities. For corporate plans, the funding ratios are usually calculated for both the Accumulated Benefit Obligation (ABO) and the

---

[1]See *Introducing the Salomon Brothers Pension Discount Curve^SM and the Salomon Brothers Pension Liability Index^SM : Discounting Pension Liabilities and Retiree Medical Liabilities Under the New SEC Interpretation*, Lawrence N. Bader and Y. Y. Ma, Salomon Brothers Inc, March 1994.

191

Figure 10–1. Average Year-End Funding Ratios, 1988–93E

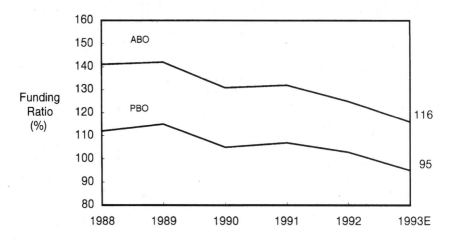

ABO = accumulated benefit obligation; E = Salomon Brothers Inc estimate; PBO = projected benefit obligation.

Source: *Pension Plan Disclosure Under FASB Statement No. 87*, Hewitt Associates, 1993.

somewhat larger Projected Benefit Obligation (PBO). With the favorable markets of the 1980s, most plans ended the decade with funding ratios so comfortable that they were not required (or allowed) to make annual contributions. However, during 1990 through 1993, the excess of liability growth over investment returns, together with prolonged "contribution holidays," brought many funding ratios well below their "comfort range." As a result, the contribution holidays of well-funded plans may soon end. Less fortunate sponsors may face substantial increases in contributions and in the premiums payable to the Pension Benefit Guaranty Corporation. Many sponsors will also experience troublesome "hits" to their earnings and/or their balance sheets. In this environment, as plan sponsors review their strategic asset allocations, they have naturally begun to pay more attention to liability considerations. To help address these concerns, this chapter proposes a "funding ratio return" (FRR) approach that can be readily integrated into the traditional asset allocation analysis.

The FRR is the percentage change in the funding ratio over a one-year investment horizon. When the liability structure remains stable, the FRR depends on only the asset and liability returns. In other words, a specific combination of asset and liability returns will always result in the same FRR—regardless of the initial funding level. This independence enables the FRR to serve as a kind of "universal" measure in developing strategic allocations. Every combination of assets has associated values for the expected FRR and the FRR volatility. These FRR values can be used to construct return/risk diagrams and efficient frontiers. Because of their independence from the initial funding ratio, the FRR return/risk plots will apply to *all* funds (given the same characterizations of liability and asset class behavior).

The individual fund's risk tolerance will determine the range of acceptable portfolios. Although the FRR does not depend on the initial funding ratio, the starting level of funding will be one factor that influences the level of risk tolerance. For example, at a 100% funding ratio, when the market value of assets is exactly the same as the present value of the liability, a sponsor may be very risk-averse. On the other hand, at funding ratios greater than 100%, a surplus exists that can provide a reserve cushion against market volatility. This cushion enables the sponsor to consider asset allocations that include riskier investments with higher expected returns.

One way of expressing a fund's risk tolerance is to require that the funding ratio stay above some minimum acceptable level. In this chapter, we express this form of risk tolerance as a shortfall constraint. For example, a sponsor may demand a 90% assurance that the funding ratio will remain above 110% over a one-year horizon. If the initial funding ratio is 120%, this shortfall condition can be restated as requiring an FRR of no worse than –8.3%.

The sponsor's shortfall risk tolerance determines the range of duration choices and the maximum equity allocation. High risk tolerance leads to high equity allocations and a wide range of duration choices. More moderate risk tolerance constrains the equity allocation and narrows the band of duration choices. When even modest declines in the funding ratio are potentially dangerous, the plan sponsor must move toward "virtual immunization"—a minimal equity allocation and a highly restricted range of durations.

A SURPLUS-ORIENTED VIEW OF THE 1993 EXPERIENCE

In 1993, the total returns of the bond and stock markets, as measured by the BIG Index (9.9%) and the S&P (10.1%), were so close that any blend of stocks and bonds would have returned about 10%. Because about 90% of U.S. pension fund assets are invested in U.S. stocks and bonds, we can use this 10% figure as a reasonable proxy for the 1993 return on pension fund assets. In contrast, the Salomon Brothers Pension Liability Index suggests that a typical PBO liability increased by 22.8% in 1993. The wide duration gap between the BIG Index (4.8 years) and the liability (14 years) at the end of 1993 accounts for most of the difference between their returns.

Figure 10–2. Surplus and Funding Ratio Changes (Dollars in Millions)

	Assets	Liability	Surplus	Funding Ratio
Initial Value	$1,400	$1,000	$400	140%
Final Value	1,540	1,228	312	125
Return	10.0%	22.8%	–6.3%	–10.4

Note: Surplus return = change in surplus ÷ initial asset value. FRR = change in funding ratio ÷ initial funding ratio.

Figure 10–2 shows the effect of the asset and liability returns on the surplus and funding ratio of a pension plan that began 1993 with a $1,000-million liability and a $1,400-million asset portfolio.[2] The liability growth over 1993 reduced the $400-million surplus to $312 million, an $88-million drop. In terms of the initial asset base of $1,400 million, this $88-million decline can be expressed as a "surplus return" of –6.3%.[3] The funding ratio also declined to 125% from 140%. This decrease in the funding ratio, when expressed as a percentage of the initial 140% ratio, corresponds to an FRR of –10.4% (= –15%/140%).

The surplus return depends on the dollar value of both the initial surplus and the initial assets. Thus, funds with different initial funding ratios will generally not have the same surplus return. To illustrate this, consider a fund with a 100% funding ratio that experienced the asset and liability returns depicted in Figure 10–2. In this case, $1,000 million in assets would grow by 10% to $1,100 million. The liability, as before, ends up at $1,228 million. The "surplus" moves from zero to a deficit of $128 million, representing a –12.8% surplus return—quite a different value from the –6.3% surplus return experienced by the fund with a 140% ratio.

In funding ratio terms, the fund with the 100% initial ratio will experience a funding ratio drop to 89.6% at year-end (= $1,100/$1,228). This change corresponds to an FRR of –10.4% (= [89.6 – 100.0]/100.0)—the same FRR value that was obtained in Figure 10–2 for the case of a fund with an initial ratio of 140%. As shown in Figure 10–3, this FRR constancy holds quite generally: For given asset and liability returns, all funds will have the same FRR, no matter what their initial funding ratios.

---

[2]Throughout this chapter, we assume that all exogenous asset and liability flows net out to zero. Material net flows would alter calculation of the FRR.

[3]We measure the change in the surplus against the initial value of assets. For a discussion of this surplus return measure see "Asset Allocation," William F. Sharpe, in *Managing Investment Portfolios*, 2d ed., John L. Maginn and Donald L. Tuttle, eds., Warren, Gorham & Lamont, 1990. Our results can also be converted to dollar surplus changes by multiplying by the initial asset value. In fact, the surplus return can be measured against any convenient base, such as the initial value of the liability. See Chapter 3.

Figure 10–3. Surplus and FRRs, 1993 (Asset Return = 10%; Liability Return = 22.8%)

Initial Funding Ratio	Realized Surplus Return	New Funding Ratios	FRR
140%	−6.3%	125.4%	−10.4%
120	−9.0	107.5	−10.4
100	−12.8	89.6	−10.4
80	−18.5	71.7	−10.4

FRR = funding ratio return.

Note: Surplus return = change in surplus ÷ initial asset value. FRR = change in funding ratio ÷ initial funding ratio.

At first, it seems surprising that all FRRs are equal at −10.4%. This result becomes more plausible when we recognize that the ending funding ratio is *always* proportional to the beginning funding ratio. When we divide the change in funding ratios by the initial ratio, the initial ratio drops out of the expression.[4]

Figure 10–3 shows that the 1993 FRR decrement was difficult for all funds. For those with high funding ratios, the −10.4% FRR would have led to a sizable funding ratio decline. For funds that started with a low funding ratio, the funding ratio decline would have been more moderate, but it would have left the sponsor with an even more fragile funded status.

THE FUNDING RATIO RETURN DISTRIBUTION

The FRR's independence of the initial funding ratio makes it a valuable "universal measure" for asset/liability management. On a prospective basis, a given asset allocation will result in the *same* distribution of funding ratio returns, regardless of the initial funding ratio. This allows for a focused

---

[4]Initial Funding Ratio = $\dfrac{\text{Initial Assets}}{\text{Initial Liability}}$. In our example, Final Funding Ratio

$= \dfrac{1.10 \times \text{Initial Assets}}{1.228 \times \text{Initial Liability}} = \dfrac{1.10}{1.228} \times \text{Initial Funding Ratio}$. Thus, for all initial funding ratios, FRR

$= \%$ Change in Funding Ratio $= \dfrac{\text{Final Funding Ratio}}{\text{Initial Funding Ratio}} - 1 = \dfrac{1.10}{1.228} - 1 = -10.4\%$. From the definition

of FRR, it can also be shown that FRR $= \dfrac{\text{Asset Return} - \text{Liability Return}}{1 + \text{Liability Return}}$.

Figure 10–4. Return and Volatility Assumptions

	Bonds	Stocks	Liability
Duration	5 Yrs.	5.6 Yrs.[a]	12 Yrs.
Expected Return	8%	13%	8%
Volatility	5%	16%	12%
Correlation with Bonds	1.00	0.35	1.00

[a]The equity duration is computed from the stated volatility and correlation assumptions. See "Total Portfolio Duration: A New Perspective on Asset Allocation," *Financial Analysts Journal*, Martin L. Leibowitz, September/October 1986.

analysis of the allocation decision that can be applied to a wide range of funds.

Figure 10–4 illustrates an ABO liability with a 12-year duration and an 8% discount rate. Based on an assumed 1% interest-rate volatility at all points along the yield curve, the volatility of liability returns will be 12% (the 12-year duration multiplied by the 1% rate volatility). Even with such long-duration liabilities, most pension funds choose a market-type duration target for their fixed-income investments. We will use five-year-duration bonds for our example, reflecting the duration of the BIG index. We further assume that all long- and intermediate-duration bonds have the same 8% expected return. Finally, stocks are assumed to offer a 5% risk premium over bonds, bringing the expected return for equity to 13%.

With bonds and stocks in this example having duration values in the 5- to 6-year range, any portfolio combination will have a substantial duration gap relative to the 12-year liabilities. For our first example, consider a "typical" U.S. pension fund, with an allocation of 60% equity/40% five-year bonds. From an asset-only perspective, 60/40 portfolios with intermediate-duration bonds offer a reasonable balance between risk and return. From a liability perspective, however, the duration gap and high equity allocation lead to substantial funding ratio risk.

We assume that stock, bond, and liability returns are lognormally distributed. The asset mix is maintained by continually rebalancing to a 60/40 allocation. Under these assumptions, the portfolio distribution is lognormal. The FRR distribution is also lognormal because FRR is based on the ratio of two lognormal distributions.[5] As is typical for lognormal distributions (see Figure 10–5), there is a slight rightward skew and a fairly long tail, repre-

---

[5]The lognormality assumption is important but not critical. With lognormal distributions it is easier to arrive at analytical solutions. With other distributions, similar results can be obtained by simulation.

Figure 10–5. One-Year FRR Distribution (60% Equity/40% 5-Year-Duration Bonds; 12-Year-Duration Liability)

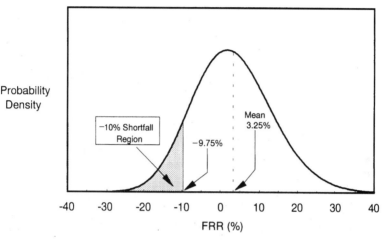

FRR = funding ratio return.

senting the possibility (but low probability) of very high FRRs. Such high FRR returns would likely coincide with extraordinary returns of the equity market or with very poor returns for the bond market.[6]

This FRR distribution for the 60/40 portfolio carries a wealth of information about year-end funding ratios. We can calculate that there is a 62% probability of a positive FRR—the final funding ratio is likely to be greater than the starting value. On the downside, Figure 10–5 highlights a "shortfall region" representing the lower 10% of the distribution. There is a 10% probability that the FRR will fall below –9.75%. In that case, a 120% funding ratio would fall to less than 108.3% over one year.

The same return and probability statements apply to all funds with the same 60/40 asset allocation, regardless of the initial funding ratio. However, the likelihood of a particular year-end funding ratio occurring will depend on the starting value. For example, a plan with a funding ratio of 130% has a 97% chance of staying above 110% because a decline from 130% to 110% represents a very unlikely –15.4% FRR. In contrast, if the initial funding ratio is

---

[6]The mean FRR is 3.25%. However, because of the skewed distribution, the probability of exceeding the mean is only 48%. The skewness also explains why the mean falls to the right of the mode (the peak probability).

Figure 10–6. FRR versus Risk (With 5-, 12-, and 19-Year-Duration Bonds)

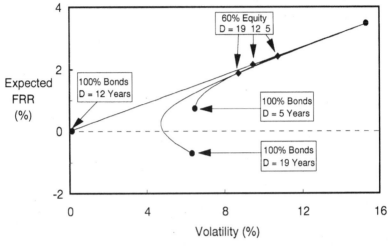

D = duration; FRR = funding ratio return.

120%, it takes only a –8.3% FRR to reduce the ratio to 110%. This –8.3% return corresponds to the 13th percentile of the FRR distribution. Thus, there is an 87% chance of staying above 110%. These observations suggest that the plan sponsor's risk tolerance should depend—at least in part—on the initial funding ratio.

VARYING BOND DURATIONS

In the next two sections, we show how different equity allocations and bond durations affect the FRR. For a 100% bond portfolio that is duration-matched to the 12-year liability, the asset and liability returns move together and there is no funding ratio risk—the expected FRR and the FRR volatility are both zero (see Figure 10–6). This extremal allocation represents the ultimate assurance that the funding ratio will be preserved. For the special case of a 100% funding ratio, the duration-matched allocation corresponds to an "immunization solution."[7]

---

[7]Some funds focus on preserving the dollar value of the surplus rather than the funding ratio. When stability of the dollar surplus is the goal, the immunizing portfolio is 100% bonds, with the dollar-duration matched to the dollar-duration of the liability.

From a liability management perspective, the duration-matched portfolio is the riskless investment. However, when portfolio performance is viewed in asset-only terms, the high volatility of long-duration investments approaches the volatility of equity. Under our rate volatility assumptions, for example, the volatility of 12-year bonds is 12%, approaching the assumed 16% volatility of equity, but with no risk premium. Thus, from the asset-only perspective, this duration-matched, all-bond portfolio would generally be quite unattractive.

As equity is added to the portfolio, more equity premium is expected but it is naturally accompanied by greater equity risk. Consequently, the expected FRR and the FRR volatility both increase with the level of equity investment.

Figure 10–6 also illustrates the risk/return trade-off for portfolios that include bond components with durations of 5 years and 19 years. Both of these values represent a 7-year-duration mismatch relative to the 12-year liability. The FRR volatility of the 100% bond portfolios is close to 7%, reflecting the seven-year-duration mismatch and the 1% interest-rate volatility. The slight curvature that results when equity is added to five-year bonds reflects the diversification benefit arising from the low correlation between equity and bonds. In contrast, equity mixed with 19-year-duration bonds leads to greater diversification benefits than with 5-year bonds. The resulting volatility reduction is reflected in the pronounced "bubbling back" of the 19-year bond curve.

Intuitively, one might have anticipated that with a *flat* expected return curve and an equal duration gap, both expected returns would be equal at the starting point corresponding to a 100% bond portfolio. In the five-year-duration case, the positive expected value results because, although equal upward or downward rate movements have precisely opposite effects on surplus, they do *not* have the same effect on the funding ratio. Figure 10–7 shows that initial assets (or liabilities) of $92.6 million are expected to grow by 8% to $100 million at year-end. If year-end rates are 100 basis points below their starting value, the liability increases by more than the assets, resulting in a $7-million loss of surplus and a funding ratio decline of –6%. However, with rising rates, the funding ratio increases (+8%) by more than it fell, because the same (absolute) asset change is measured against a smaller liability base. On average, this differential response to rate changes results in a +0.7% expected FRR for the 100% five-year bond portfolio. For the 19-year bond portfolio, the duration mismatch is in the opposite direction, leading to a –0.7% expected FRR.

Figure 10–8 shows the FRR expected value and volatility for all-bond portfolios with durations ranging from 0 to 24 years. The pattern exhibited

Figure 10–7. The FRR Paradox with 5-Year Asset Duration; 12-Year Liability Duration; Asset and Liability Expected Return = 8% (Dollars in Millions)

	Initial Value	Year-End Value (Rates Unchanged)	Year-End Value (Rates *Down* 100 bp)	Year-End Value (Rates *Up* 100 bp)
Liability	$92.6	$100	$112	$88
Assets (Bonds)	92.6	100	105	95
Surplus	0.0	0	–7	+7
Funding Ratio	100%	100%	94%	108%
FRR	–	0	–6	+8

bp = basis points; FRR = funding ratio return.

Figure 10–8. Expected Value and Volatility of FRR for All-Bond Portfolios

	0% Equity/100% Bonds	
Bond Duration (Yrs.)	Expected Value of FRR	Volatility of FRR
0	1.2%	11.2%
5	0.7	6.5
8	0.4	3.7
12	**0.0%**	**0.0%**
16	–0.4	3.6
19	–0.7	6.3
24	–1.2	10.8

FRR = funding ratio return.

now becomes clear from the preceding discussion. As the duration lengthens, the FRR "paradox" leads to ever lower expected FRR returns.[8]

With all-bond portfolios, volatility considerations would probably dominate the modest FRR return increments derived from the paradox. Thus, if one were restricted to all-bond portfolios, the duration would probably lie close to the liability duration (apart from asset-only considerations). However, more interesting trade-offs arise when one allows increasing levels of equity exposure.

---

[8]The FRR volatility of all-bond portfolios depends primarily on the duration gap relative to the 12-year liability. Thus, 5-year and 19-year bonds have the same 7-year gap and exhibit similar volatility. Likewise, cash and 24-year bonds share a 12-year gap and also have similar volatility. (It should be noted that our example assumes a flat yield curve. A positive yield curve—and a positive expected return curve—would offset the "paradoxical returns," thereby flattening the funding ratio return curves for all-bond portfolios.)

Figure 10–9. Expected Value and Volatility of FRR for Portfolios with 30%, 60%, or 90% Equity

Bond Duration (Yrs.)	30% Equity/70% Bonds		60% Equity/40% Bonds		90% Equity/10% Bonds	
	Expected Value of FRR	Volatility of FRR	Expected Value of FRR	Volatility of FRR	Expected Value of FRR	Volatility of FRR
0	2.2%	10.6%	3.4%	11.8%	4.8%	14.3%
5	1.9	7.6	3.3	10.5	4.8	14.1
8	1.7	6.0	3.1	9.8	4.8	14.0
12	1.3%	4.4%	2.9%	9.0%	4.7%	13.8%
16	1.0	4.1	2.7	8.5	4.6	13.6
19	0.7	4.8	2.5	8.2	4.6	13.5
24	0.5	5.6	2.3	8.1	4.5	13.4

FRR = funding ratio return.

VARYING EQUITY ALLOCATIONS

We now consider the interaction between the equity allocation and the choice of the bond component's duration. As a general principle, with long-duration bonds, equity/bond portfolios tend to be more strongly correlated with the liability, thereby reducing FRR risk.[9] The magnitude of this effect depends critically on the equity percentage level (see Figure 10–9). For the extreme case of 90% equity there is very little sensitivity to duration of the minimal 10% bond component. As one moves toward a more standard 60% equity percentage, the allocation is seen to be somewhat riskier for short-duration bonds than it is for long-duration bonds. However, for the 60% case, this variation in volatility remains low for durations beyond five years.

The duration choice becomes more critical as the equity allocation decreases further (see Figure 10–9 for 30% equity portfolios and Figure 10–8 for 0% equity portfolios). At these low equity allocations, the diversification benefits of equity decrease and FRR risk is *primarily* controlled through the choice of the bond duration.

In essence, the level of volatility that the plan can accept determines the significance of the bond duration choice. When high volatility levels are ac-

---

[9]In this asset/liability context, portfolios with 12-year bonds and equity behave similarly to cash/equity portfolios in an asset-only environment. Such "cash/equity" portfolios tend to dominate portfolios with other bond durations, if the expected return curve is flat across *all* bond durations. See Chapter 2.

ceptable, the allocation naturally moves toward a high equity percentage. From an FRR perspective, there is then a broad latitude in the choice of bond duration. (The duration choice can then be more freely targeted to address concerns that fall outside the FRR framework.)

At more moderate levels of acceptable FRR volatility, one must move toward reduced equity percentages *and* to a more limited duration range. This effect can be seen in the 30% equity column in Figure 10–9. For FRR volatilities below 6.0%, durations of eight years and beyond are required. However, at these lower equity percentages, there is a more complex interaction between FRR return and risk. To evaluate these lower risk choices, we must explore how a specific fund might be willing to balance the prospective risk/return trade-off. The "shortfall approach" addresses this fundamental question.

SHORTFALL RISK

In this section, we show how plan sponsors can use a "shortfall constraint" to select portfolios that provide a required level of funding protection. As a first example, consider a standard allocation of 60% equity/40% five-year-duration bonds. With the return and volatility assumptions shown in Figure 10–4, this portfolio has a 3.3% expected FRR and 10.5% FRR volatility (see Figure 10–9).

Because the characteristics of the FRR distribution are known, the probability of any particular return level can be calculated. For example, there is a 90% probability that the FRR return (over one year) will be greater than –9.75% (see Figure 10–5). In other words, there is only a 10% chance that the return will fall below –9.75%.

If this probability of loss is acceptable, the sponsor will have many portfolios from which to choose. In this context, we regard –9.75% as the "shortfall threshold," and we call the requirement of exceeding that threshold the "shortfall constraint."

In our previous work, we showed that portfolios that meet a shortfall constraint lie along a straight line in risk/return space, provided the underlying return distributions are normal.[10] Portfolios with risk/return characteristics that place them above the shortfall line will exceed the shortfall constraint. For the lognormal distributions used in this paper, the analysis is more complicated: The "shortfall line" will have some curvature. However,

---

[10]See Chapter 2.

Figure 10–10. Implicit Shortfall Constraint for 60% Equity/40% 5-Year Bond Portfolio

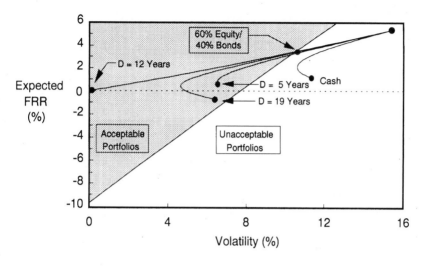

D = duration; FRR = funding ratio return.

for values in the relevant range, this curvature is slight and the basic results are quite similar. Figure 10–10 superimposes this shortfall "line" on the funding ratio risk/return curves for equity/bond portfolios, using durations of 0, 5, 12, and 19 years. The 0-duration curve corresponds to an equity/cash portfolio.

The shortfall line emanates from the shortfall threshold point on the vertical return axis. Any portfolio lying on or above this line will satisfy the shortfall constraint. Portfolios lying below the line are therefore unacceptable. Thus, all equity/cash combinations must be removed from consideration. On the other hand, some portfolios on the lower-equity portions of the 5-, 12-, and 19-year duration curves lie within the acceptable shortfall region. The point of intersection of the shortfall line and each FRR curve represents the portfolio with the maximum permissible equity allocation.

Figure 10–11 shows the relationship that exists between bond duration, maximum equity, and expected FRR. As the duration of bonds increases, so does the allowable equity. However, with a liberal shortfall tolerance of –9.75%, the equity allocation can remain high over a wide range of bond durations, and there is little change in the expected FRR. Thus, with high FRR shortfall tolerance, the sponsor has the latitude to essentially view the allocation decision from the asset-only perspective.

Figure 10–11. Maximum Equity Allocation with –9.75% Funding Ratio Return Shortfall Constraint

Bond Duration (Yrs.)	Maximum Equity	Expected FRR
0	–	–
5	60%	3.3%
8	66	3.4
12	71%	3.5%
16	74	3.5
19	74	3.4
24	75	3.1

FRR = funding ratio return.

Note: The dashes reflect situations in which there are no feasible mixtures of equity and bonds.

We now turn to more stringent funding ratio constraints. For example, a –7% funding ratio shortfall constraint would mean that a plan sponsor with a 120% funding ratio required 90% assurance that the year-end funding ratio would be greater than 111.6% (93% of 120%). The new –7% shortfall line is parallel to the –9.75% line but emanates from the –7% point on the vertical axis (see Figure 10–12).[11] Note that all portfolios with five-year (or shorter) bonds now fall outside the new, smaller shortfall region.

Figure 10–13 highlights how the level of shortfall tolerance limits the equity allocation and the range of acceptable durations. With a reduced shortfall tolerance (exemplified by the –7% FRR constraint), the equity allocation becomes more narrowly constrained and the duration choice is more restricted. Although all combinations of five-year bonds and equities will fail to pass the –7% shortfall test, by increasing the bond duration to eight years, the portfolio can accept up to 41% equity. A significantly higher equity percentage can be obtained by moving the bond duration out further to 12 years. On the other hand, duration extensions beyond the 12-year liability duration provide relatively little additional FRR benefit. Thus, a relatively modest duration extension beyond the standard five years captures most of the available FRR advantages. There is no need to proceed to the very long durations that would radically distort the fund's asset-only performance.[12]

----

[11]Parallel shifts of the shortfall line reflect changing shortfall thresholds, assuming the same 10% shortfall probability. Different shortfall probabilities are represented by shortfall lines with differing slopes. More stringent shortfall probabilities (with less than 10% probability of shortfall) lead to greater slopes. For a more complete discussion, see Chapter 2.

[12]At first this finding may appear to conflict with the view that the least risky strategy is to match the total portfolio duration of the assets to the duration of the liability. As mentioned earlier, with the

Figure 10–12. A –7% Funding Ratio Return Shortfall Constraint

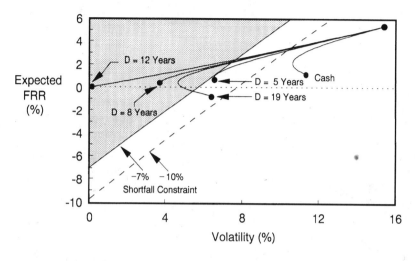

D = duration; FRR = funding ratio return.

Figure 10–13. Effects of Changing Funding Ratio Return Risk Tolerance

Bond Duration (Yrs.)	–10% Funding Ratio Shortfall Constraint		–7% Funding Ratio Shortfall Constraint		–2% Funding Ratio Shortfall Constraint	
	Maximum Equity	Expected FRR	Maximum Equity	Expected FRR	Maximum Equity	Expected FRR
0	–	–	–	–	–	–
5	60%	3.3%	–	–	–	–
8	66	3.4	41%	2.2%	–	–
12	71%	3.5%	50%	2.4%	14%	0.6%
16	74	3.5	53	2.3	–	–
19	74	3.4	54	2.1	–	–
24	75	3.1	–	–	–	–

FRR = funding ratio return. Note: The dashes reflect situations in which there are no feasible mixtures of equity and bonds.

FRR there is a complex interaction between asset and liability returns. For example, the long durations required for a total portfolio duration match cause a give-up in the FRR, resulting in a suboptimal performance. Another consideration is the problem of balancing between two frameworks—the asset/liability and the asset-only. Strictly optimal solutions in one framework may convey only marginal advantages over other allocations that represent a far more comfortable balance within both frameworks. For a discussion of balancing *surplus* risk against asset performance, see Chapter 3.

At minimal shortfall tolerance (–2% funding ratio shortfall constraint), the plan sponsor's choices are much more limited. Only a very small infusion of equity is permitted and the duration must be kept close to the 12-year liability duration. Thus, low shortfall tolerance implies a "virtual immunization"—minimal equity with asset and liability duration that are essentially matched.

CONCLUSION

The funding ratio of a pension plan is an important measure of a plan's ability to meet its liabilities. When the ratio is far in excess of 100%, sponsors tend to build their strategic asset allocation by considering only asset performance. Asset/liability considerations typically become more important when the funding ratio is closer to 100%. However, apart from low initial ratios, many other factors can increase a fund's sensitivity to deterioration in its funding ratio.

In this chapter, we show how pension fund sponsors can use a measure called the "funding ratio return" (FRR) to make funding ratio preservation part of the traditional asset allocation analysis. The FRR has broad applicability because it depends only on the asset return and the liability return. For a given set of market assumptions, a specific allocation is associated with a single well-defined FRR distribution. Thus, the same FRR analysis can apply to *all* funds, regardless of their initial funding ratio.

Shortfall analysis confirms that plans with high risk tolerance have broad latitude in their asset allocation. High equity allocations are unlikely to endanger the funding status, and there is low sensitivity to the duration of the fixed-income component. Alternatively, sponsors with only a moderate risk tolerance may need to reduce equities below the standard 60% and to extend the bond duration somewhat beyond the standard five years.

Finally, a sponsor with very low risk tolerance may wish to preserve the current funding ratio at virtually any (opportunity) cost. In such cases, the sponsor must move toward "virtual immunization"—minimal equity and a narrow range of bond durations that center on the liability duration.

Chapter 11

Pension Fund Risk Capacity: Surplus and Time-Horizon Effects on Asset Allocation

INTRODUCTION

A pension plan's ability to accept investment risk depends on a variety of factors—the investment horizon, the surplus, the anticipated rewards of risky investments, and a host of legal, institutional, and psychological factors that fall under the heading of "risk tolerance." The conventional wisdom holds that greater amounts of surplus and longer time horizons permit greater commitments to high-risk/high-return asset classes.[1]

In this chapter, we begin by expressing risk tolerance as the desired probability that assets will suffice to meet liabilities at a specified horizon. We use a 90% *assurance of full funding* to express a generic risk tolerance level—that is, the plan sponsor requires a 90% probability that the assets will equal or exceed the liability. In other words, the sponsor can tolerate a 10% probability of needing to tap some other source to meet the shortfall. Under this definition, we show that for a specified time horizon, the capacity to hold risky assets is *proportional to surplus*. Using equity as a proxy for risky assets, we define this capacity in terms of the maximum equity percentage that a plan sponsor can hold while giving the required assurance of full funding.

---

[1]Although the belief in the risk-reducing power of time remains influential in the pension community, many financial economists who have studied the issue in an asset-only context hold a different position. See "What Practitioners Need to Know About Time Diversification," Mark Kritzman, *Financial Analysts Journal,* Jan.–Feb. 1994. Citing Paul Samuelson among others, Kritzman argues, on the basis of utility theory, that risk preferences generally should be independent of the time horizon.

We then show that this risk tolerance criterion is a special case of a short-fall constraint based on the *funding ratio return (FRR)*, a more flexible measure for asset/liability analysis.[2] Using FRR constraints, we can generalize to a broader range of risk tolerance measures, and we show that the *maximum allowable equity is also proportional to the allowable FRR loss.*

Another key finding of this chapter is that the effect of the time horizon on the maximum allowable equity departs significantly from the conventional wisdom: As a multiple of surplus, equity capacity is high for *short* horizons, declines as the horizon extends, and turns upward rather modestly at a distant horizon. Under our basic assumptions, investors with moderately well-funded plans who can focus solely on their long-horizon results can hold as much equity as they wish. On the other hand, investors with slender surplus margins, higher required assurance levels, or conservative views of the equity risk premium must constrain their appetites for equity, *even over very long time horizons.* For such investors, the basic message is that equity, despite its potentially substantial benefits, poses funding risks that time is slow to erase.

A PENSION PLAN ASSET ALLOCATION MODEL

This chapter focuses on a simple pension plan model. We examine the cumulative performance of this model plan over a specified period, beginning with a one-year horizon and then considering more distant horizons.

The liability of our model plan is the discounted value of a benefit payment stream that begins at the measurement horizon. Of course, pension plans face benefit payments before their long-term measurement horizon is reached. Such plans, however, may regard certain assets or incoming cash flows as dedicated to meeting their benefit payment obligations over a limited horizon such as five years, while the balance of the fund is invested more aggressively. The model in this chapter applies directly to that balance.

The horizon liability is discounted at a market rate, which we assume to be 8% initially, representing the expected growth rate or liability return. The annual volatility of the horizon liability for our model is 10%, the volatility of the Salomon Brothers Pension Liability Index during the period January 1989–June 1994.[3]

---

[2]See Chapter 10. The FRR is the percentage change in the funding ratio: FRR = (Terminal Funding Ratio − Initial Funding Ratio)/Initial Funding Ratio. (In this simple definition, we do not consider any effects of cash flow or demographic changes.) An example of an FRR constraint would be to require a 90% probability that the FRR is better than −5%.

[3]This volatility resulted from interest-rate volatility of 0.8% and a liability duration that averaged about 12.5 years.

The assets are buy-and-hold portfolios that mix two asset classes:

1. A riskless asset—a dedicated bond portfolio that matches the liability cash flow and is initially priced to yield 8% annually; and

2. A risky asset—equity, which has annual returns that are distributed lognormally. The lognormal distribution reflects an expected return of 13% (a 5% risk premium), a volatility of 16%, and a 0.35 correlation with the liability return.

Although most funds use more sophisticated rebalancing strategies, the simple buy-and-hold policy provides useful insights into the effects of time and surplus on risk.

ONE-YEAR HORIZON

First, we assume that the liability stream begins in one year. We also assume that the fund is fully invested in equity and exactly covers the initial liability; that is, the *initial funding ratio* (assets divided by liability) is 100%. Figure 11–1 then shows the distribution of the *terminal funding ratio*—the ratio of the assets to the liability at the one-year horizon.

Figure 11–1. Terminal Funding Ratio (One-Year Horizon; 100% Initial Funding Ratio; 100% Equity)

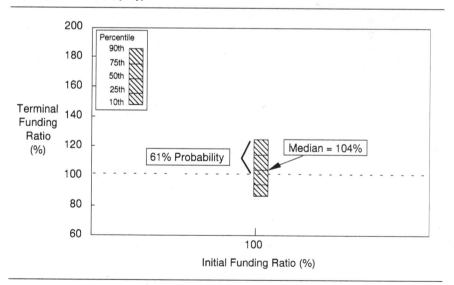

Figure 11–2. Terminal Funding Ratio for Varying Initial Funding Ratios (One-Year Horizon; 100% Equity)

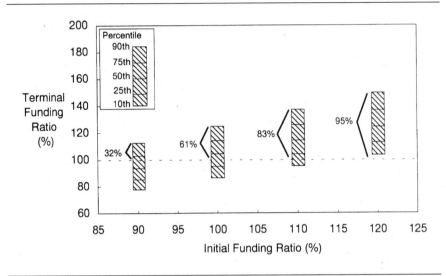

The shaded bar in Figure 11–1 represents 80% of the possible year-end outcomes, as indicated by the key in the upper left-hand corner. A total of 10% of the outcomes would be below the bottom of the bar (the 10th percentile), which represents an 87% terminal funding ratio. An additional 10% would be above the top (the 90th percentile), a 124% terminal funding ratio. The 50th percentile or median is 104%, and the 25th and 75th percentiles are also shown. The dotted line, representing a 100% terminal funding ratio, cuts the bar at the 39th percentile, implying a 61% probability that the assets will cover the liability. The assets will provide full coverage if they earn at least as much as the liability; thus, Figure 11–1 shows a 61% probability that equity earns at least as much as a liability-matching bond portfolio over the one-year period.

Varying Initial Funding Ratios

In Figure 11–2, we illustrate the effect of varying the initial funding ratio over the range of 90%–120%, while keeping the assets fully invested in equity. The relationship is simple: The bars rise and lengthen in proportion to the initial funding ratio. For example, the median terminal funding ratio for

Figure 11-3. Maximum Equity Percentage for 90% Probability of Full Funding (One-Year Horizon)

Initial Funding Ratio	Maximum Equity Percentage
100.0%	0.0%
105.0 %	36.9
110.0	70.4
114.8%	**100.0%**
115.0	100.0
120.0	100.0

a 100% initial ratio is 104%; for a 120% initial ratio, the median terminal ratio is 125%, or 120% of 104%.

Figure 11-2 also shows the probabilities that the assets will cover the liability at year-end. The probability that the terminal funding ratio will be at least 100% is only 32% at a 90% initial funding ratio. As we have seen, it reaches 61% at a 100% initial funding ratio, and it rises to 95% at a 120% initial funding ratio. In fact, an all-equity investor with a funding ratio of at least 114.8% can remain 90% confident of covering the liability at the one-year horizon.

Varying Equity Percentages

Thus far we have limited the investment to equity. The plan sponsor is, however, able to adjust the risk level of the assets by introducing (riskless) liability-matching bonds. We now turn to the question of risk capacity: How much equity can the plan hold while remaining 90% certain that the assets will cover the liability at year-end?[4] Figure 11-3 illustrates the answer for a range of initial funding ratios.

Figure 11-3 shows the permissible equity percentage rising from zero at a 100% (or lower) initial funding ratio to 100% at a 114.8% ratio. We had previously observed that an initial ratio that exceeds 114.8% permits the entire fund to be invested in equity, but the fact that a 100% initial ratio permits *no equity whatsoever* may be surprising. For a fund with no surplus, the total

---

[4]This "sufficiency test" (or the FRR constraint that we will introduce later in this chapter) is an all-or-nothing test that does not reflect how large the shortfall will be, should one occur. This shortcoming can be eliminated by a semivariance measure of risk, but our simple test permits a reasonable ranking of nondynamic strategies.

assets must match the liability return to sustain a 100% funding ratio. The risk-free assets do this automatically, so the overall requirement is met if the equity held by the fund matches the liability return; otherwise it is violated. Because equity has only a 61% probability of keeping pace with the liability, rather than the required 90% probability, the fund has no room for equity.

THE RELATIONSHIP BETWEEN SURPLUS AND RISK CAPACITY

We can obtain an enlightening transformation of Figure 11–3 by comparing the allowable equity percentage with the *surplus percentage,* rather than with the funding ratio. We define the surplus percentage as the surplus divided by the assets.[5] Figure 11–4 sets forth this relationship.

Figure 11–4 reveals a linear relationship: The maximum equity is uniformly 7.75 times the surplus, until the equity reaches the saturation point at a 114.8% funding ratio.[6] Thus, within our model, an investor requiring 90% assurance of full funding at year-end can simply measure the surplus and invest 7.75 times that amount in equity.[7] For example, as explained above, a plan with an initial funding ratio of 110% would have a 9.1% surplus percentage. This plan could hold up to 70.5% of its assets in equity ($7.75 \times 9.1\%$). The 7.75 multiple also applies in dollar terms: A plan with a $10-million surplus can hold $77.5 million of equity.

An intuitive understanding of this result may be fostered by supposing that the plan sponsor requires a 100% assurance of full funding. In this case, an amount of assets equal to the liability must be invested risklessly, and all the surplus may be invested in equity—a multiple of 1.0. This plan is protected even if the equity loses *all* its value—a very conservative position.

Now we suppose that the sponsor does not demand protection against a 100% drop in the equity value but is satisfied with protection against a 50% decline. (In this simplified example, we assume that the 50% decline is in-

---

[5]Some analysts may prefer to define the surplus percentage in relation to the liability, so that a plan with a 110% funding ratio would have a surplus percentage of 10%. We use the assets rather than the liability as the denominator, so that the equity percentage and surplus percentage have the same base. Thus, a plan with a 110% funding ratio has a 9.1% surplus percentage, computed as (110% − 100%)/110%.

[6]The 7.75 multiple continues to apply at richer funding levels if leverage can be used to raise the equity exposure above 100% of the assets.

[7]The constant would be different for different capital market assumptions, liability structures, required probabilities of sufficiency or, as we show later in this chapter, different horizons. See the Appendix to this chapter for details.

Figure 11–4. Maximum Equity Percentage versus Surplus Percentage (One-Year Horizon)

Initial Funding Ratio	Maximum Equity Percentage	Surplus Percentage	Maximum Equity Percentage Divided by Surplus Percentage
100.0%	0.0%	0.0%	–
105.0	36.9	4.8	7.75
110.0	70.4	9.1	7.75
114.8%	**100.0%**	**12.9%**	**7.75**
115.0	100.0	13.0	7.69
120.0	100.0	16.7	6.00

stantaneous, in order to avoid the complexity of accounting for the liability change.) Then the equity investment can be twice the surplus. For example, a surplus of $10 million permits a $20-million investment in equity; a 50% decline could then wipe out $10 million of value, leaving the fund exactly equal to the liability. Similarly, a $15-million surplus would permit a $30-million equity investment. The probability of failure would correspond to the probability that the equity return is worse than –50%.

Of course a 50% decline in equity value is still a highly improbable event; a sponsor satisfied with protection against a lesser decline (for example, one that represents a 10% probability) could invest a higher multiple of surplus in equity.[8] Thus, a sponsor who is willing to accept some risk of failure in pursuit of superior returns can allocate far more of the assets to equity than one who insists on a risk-free asset pool dedicated to the liability, with only the surplus available for equity investment.

FRR Constraints

The result obtained in Figure 11–4 can be generalized to a broader class of risk tolerances—those expressed by FRR constraints. A requirement to maintain full funding is a special case of an FRR constraint, and all such conditions can be stated in terms of FRRs. For example, requiring a fund with an initial funding ratio of 120% to remain fully funded is equivalent to requir-

---

[8]A precise calculation of the allowable multiple must reflect not only the equity decline but the change in liability, which has an expected growth rate of 8% annually. Even an equity return of zero represents a negative return relative to a growing liability and will likely erode surplus over time. See the Appendix to this chapter for details.

ing its terminal funding ratio to be at least 100%; therefore, the FRR must be no worse than –16.7% (120% – 16.7% × 120% = 100%). The sponsor, however, may not be willing to see the entire surplus dissipated in one year and may instead require 90% assurance that the year-end funding ratio will be at least 110%. This restriction is equivalent to an FRR constraint of –8.3% (120% – 8.3% × 120% = 110%). An FRR constraint may also be more useful for a weaker fund: The sponsor may be willing to accept a possible deficit (or a modest widening of an existing deficit) over a one-year period. We can re-state our previous result as follows:

For a 90% assurance of achieving a specified minimum one-year FRR,

Maximum Allowable Equity = 7.75 × Allowable FRR Loss.[9]

For example, a sponsor who can tolerate seeing a 120% funding ratio drop to 110% is prepared to accept a –8.3% FRR. This sponsor can hold up to 64% equity (7.75 × 8.3%).

This formulation also applies for funding ratios below 100%. For example, suppose that a sponsor with a funding ratio of only 60% decides to invest aggressively in an effort to improve the ratio but wants 90% assurance that the ratio will not fall below 55%. This condition is again a –8.3% FRR; there-fore, this sponsor can also hold 64% equity.

MULTIYEAR HORIZONS

We now consider time horizons greater than one year. Using lines rather than shaded bars to represent the key percentiles, Figure 11–5 portrays the distribution of terminal funding ratios for all-equity portfolios with five dif-ferent liability structures: benefit payments commencing after one, two, three, four, or five years. We use the same capital market assumptions for the multiyear case as for one year, without mean reversion of equity returns.[10]

---

[9]This equation assumes a negative FRR constraint. Note that the problem can be translated into the one already solved in this chapter by redefining a "target liability" that equals 110% of the true liability. The "surplus" then corresponds to the cushion over this 110% target. Allowing this notional "surplus" to fall to zero is equivalent to allowing the true funding ratio to fall to 110%; thus, we can apply the same 7.75 multiple to the "notional surplus."

[10]A mean reversion assumption would posit a negative correlation between the equity return for a given year and the returns for prior years. As a result, the cumulative return would tend toward the mean, and the range of possible outcomes would narrow.

Figure 11–5. Terminal Funding Ratios for Varying Liability Horizons (100% Initial Funding Ratio; 100% Equity)

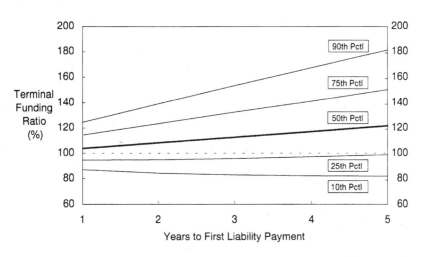

Pctl = percentile.

Distribution of Terminal Funding Ratio

Long-term equity investors generally focus on the sizable upside potential. Figure 11–5 illustrates that ever-higher funding ratios are possible over longer horizons; the 90th-percentile terminal funding ratio rises from 124% for the 1-year horizon liability to 181% for the 5-year horizon liability. It may be disturbing to long-term investors, however, to observe the *worsening* of the 10th-percentile results, from 87% at one year to 82% at five years.[11]

Figure 11–6 depicts the terminal funding ratios for a greater range of horizons with an expanded scale. The right-hand scale shows the percentiles in terms of cumulative FRRs. We can generalize the results by using these cumulative FRRs: They can be applied to *any* initial funding ratio to obtain the distribution of the terminal funding ratio. Although the higher percentile curves reach extraordinary levels, the 10th-percentile curve remains rather

---

[11]These ratios represent the potential size of an equity portfolio relative to the liability-matching bond portfolio. See "The Persistence of Risk: Shortfall Probabilities Over the Long Term," Martin L. Leibowitz and William S. Krasker, *Financial Analysts Journal*, Nov.–Dec. 1988; and "Shortfall Risks and the Asset Allocation Decision: A Simulation Analysis of Stock and Bond Risk Profiles," Martin L. Leibowitz and Terence C. Langetieg, *The Journal of Portfolio Management*, Fall 1989.

Figure 11–6. Terminal Funding Ratios and Cumulative FRRs for Varying Liability Horizons (100% Initial Funding Ratio; 100% Equity)

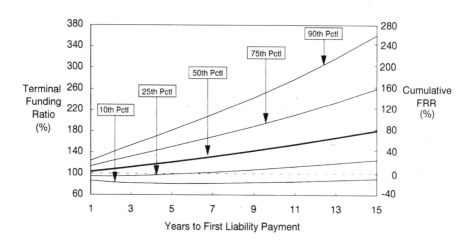

FRR = funding ratio return; Pctl = percentile.

Figure 11–7. Maximum Equity Percentage for Varying Horizons

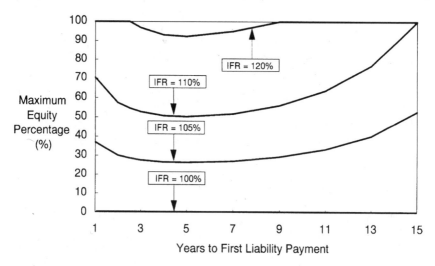

IFR = initial funding ratio.

discouraging; the decline reverses at 5 years but recovers quite slowly thereafter, not reattaining its 1-year level until 12 years.

We now generalize the findings that we reported for a one-year horizon and consider the broad issue set forth in the Introduction of this chapter: How do the factors of time horizon and surplus affect a pension fund's maximum equity allocation?

Figure 11–7 displays the maximum allowable equity percentages for 90% assurance of full funding over liability horizons of up to 15 years. The line for a 100% initial funding ratio lies on the horizontal axis—that is, no equity is allowed. As we observed earlier, for equity to be admitted into such a portfolio, it must have at least 90% assurance of surpassing the liability return over the investment period. Under our assumptions, this level of assurance is not attained for 20 years.

The curves for the higher funding ratios show a surprising pattern: relatively high for the one-year horizon, then declining rapidly, bottoming out at five years, and rising slowly thereafter. With a 110% initial funding ratio and a 1-year horizon, for example, the plan can hold 70% equity; the allowable equity allocation plunges to 57% for a 2-year horizon, reaches its nadir of 50% at 5 years, and rises slowly for several years thereafter, until shooting up to 100% at 15 years.

The initial drop in the allowable equity is understandable, although perhaps counterintuitive: The surplus of a well-funded plan is unlikely to vanish quickly but could be wiped out by a prolonged bear market. A plan with a 110% funding ratio invested entirely in equity can almost surely meet its liability if it matures in a week; the assurance drops considerably if the liability is due in a year. It is more surprising, however, that the decline in the maximum equity holding continues out to a 5-year horizon, and even a 10-year horizon conveys no more equity capacity than a 2-year horizon.

A plan with a 105% ratio has about one-half as high an equity allowance as the 110% plan, following the same pattern over time. We can assess the trade-off between surplus and time horizon as contributing to equity capacity by comparing the two curves. The 110% plan enjoys a 50% equity allowance at the five-year horizon. The 105% plan does not rise to this level until the horizon reaches 15 years.

The results are dramatic for a 120% funding ratio: This plan can hold 100% equity for all but the intermediate (three-to-nine-year) horizons. (In practice, a sponsor may prefer a more conservative stance that sacrifices expected return but reduces the risk inherent in the all-equity portfolio.)

Figure 11–8 extends our earlier transformation to the multiyear case, expressing the maximum allowable equity as a multiple of either the surplus (for a full-funding constraint) or the allowable FRR loss (for an FRR constraint).

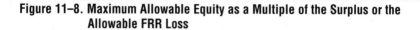

Figure 11–8. Maximum Allowable Equity as a Multiple of the Surplus or the Allowable FRR Loss

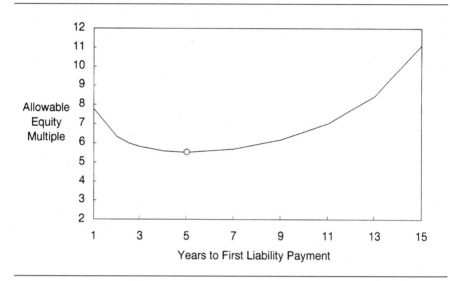

For example, with a five-year liability horizon, the multiple is 5.53. A plan sponsor with a 110% initial ratio who seeks 90% assurance of full funding has an FRR constraint of –9.1% (110% – 9.1% × 110% = 100%).[12] The plan can thus hold 50% equity (9.1% × 5.53). (Note that the plan also has a 9.1% surplus percentage, (110% – 100%)/110%, so the 5.53 can be applied to the surplus percentage as well.) If the sponsor can risk a 95% terminal ratio (with 10% probability), the FRR constraint is –13.6%, and the plan can hold 75% equity.

Sensitivity to Capital Market Assumptions

We observed earlier that different risk/return profiles for equity would produce different multiples. We now consider whether alternative assumptions would substantially alter the effects of time. Figure 11–9 compares the equity multiples of Figure 11–8 with those produced by different equity risk premium assumptions.

The heavy line in Figure 11–9 repeats the "base assumptions" of Figure

---

[12]Note that this –9.1% FRR is a nonannualized cumulative five-year return.

Figure 11–9. Maximum Allowable Equity Multiple under Varying Equity Risk/Return Assumptions

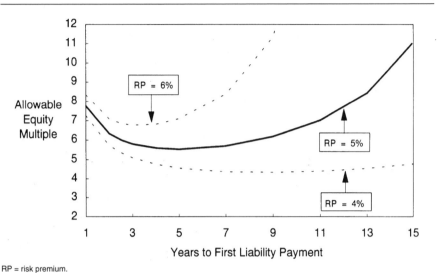

RP = risk premium.

11–8—a 5% risk premium for a 13% expected equity return. Increasing the risk premium from 5% to 6% increases the fund's equity capacity. The higher risk premium makes little difference initially, begins to tell in the two-to-five-year range, and then rapidly exceeds our scale.

Lowering the risk premium to 4% also has little effect in the short run, but after bottoming out, the maximum equity allocation does not recover within the 15-year time span. The curves suggest that investors can think in terms of three time periods: short horizons of one to two years, intermediate horizons of three–eight years, and long horizons. For the short horizons, the maximum equity allocation shows little sensitivity to the assumptions and declines rapidly as the horizon lengthens. The ability to hold equity stabilizes in the intermediate range. For the longer horizons, the allowable equity holding becomes increasingly responsive to the investor's view of equity's risk/return profile, and time horizon can once again become critical. For an investor with a conservative view of the equity risk premium, however, time offers no benefit within any meaningful horizon.

The effect of a higher risk premium can be neutralized by a tighter risk constraint. Figure 11–10 shows the 5% and 6% risk premium curves with a 95% rather than 90% required assurance. This constraint is quite restrictive, and again, time is no panacea. Lowering the required assurance level would,

Figure 11–10. Maximum Allowable Equity Multiple under Varying Risk Premiums with 95% Assurance

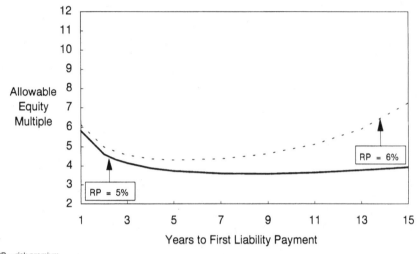

RP = risk premium.

of course, have the opposite effect: Plan sponsors with long horizons and other resources would be free to indulge their appetites for equities.

Moderate-to-high risk premium assumptions, then, offer considerable encouragement to long-term investors, particularly those with relatively loose constraints who can tolerate a modest chance of a poor result. For those holding a more cautious stance regarding the equity risk premium or the risk of failure, however, the lower curves in Figures 11–9 and 11–10 may be sobering. These curves counsel against having blind faith in the power of time to eliminate risk for a buy-and-hold equity strategy. Pension plan sponsors are often criticized for focusing on short-term horizons and therefore investing too protectively. Under some conditions, the truth may be quite the opposite. A sponsor with a comfortable surplus and a short-term view may see his funding position as impregnable; he may not look beyond the near term, assuming that time works for his benefit. In fact, a longer-term look may reveal a more precarious position. Of course, the opportunity for outsized returns grows substantially over time, but a small probability of failure persists. The real protection that long horizons can give to these investors is not the elimination of poor equity returns but the ability to change allocations (or liability accruals or funding patterns) in response to threatened failure— a type of "soft" portfolio insurance that can accept probabilistic rather than absolute protection and does not require continuous trading in difficult markets.[13]

At this point, it is useful to mention the effects of two other possible alternatives to our model assumptions. We have not reflected any possible mean reversion of equity returns; to the extent that equity returns tend toward some mean over time, the probability of prolonged equity weakness lessens and higher equity percentages become acceptable. The use of a rebalancing rather than buy-and-hold strategy, on the other hand, increases downside risk. A rebalancing strategy tends to outperform buy-and-hold in "average" markets but underperforms in strongly trending markets, because it calls for selling the better-performing security and buying the weaker. (Rebalancers are effectively sellers of portfolio insurance.) Therefore, the rebalancing equity allowances would be lower than the buy-and-hold allowances developed in this chapter.

CONCLUSION

Although they are not completely sheltered from the interim consequences of adverse market fluctuations, pension funds are unusually well suited to invest for the long term. Many plan sponsors enjoy the luxuries of time *and* comfortable surplus levels. They may believe that this combination permits them to harvest high investment returns from risky investment strategies, without endangering their ability to meet the pension obligations. In this chapter, we present a more complex picture. If the mainstream views about equity risk premiums are correct, the long-term risks that these investors face are indeed small. In contrast, for those with narrow surplus margins or less-hopeful views of equity returns, the risks loom much larger and time is not a panacea. Thus, asset allocations cannot rest on the assumption that if the short-term risks are acceptable, the medium- and long-term risks cannot be troublesome. Plan sponsors must understand and control these risks; they cannot rely on the benevolence of time.

---

[13]For a dynamic strategy based on similar principles, see the discussion of constant-proportion strategies in "Dynamic Strategies for Asset Allocation," André F. Perold and William F. Sharpe, *Financial Analysts Journal*, Jan.–Feb. 1988.

APPENDIX

In this Appendix, we demonstrate that the maximum allowable equity is a constant multiple of the allowable FRR loss.

We use the following definitions:

$\tilde{R}_E$ = 1 + Compounded Equity Return to the Horizon.

$\tilde{R}_L$ = 1 + Compounded Liability Return to the Horizon (and Return of the Matching Bond Portfolio).

A_0 = Initial Assets.

L_0 = Initial Liability.

FR_0 = Initial Funding Ratio = A_0/L_0.

A_T = Terminal Assets.

L_T = Terminal Liability.

FR_T = Terminal Funding Ratio = A_T/L_T.

FRR = Funding Ratio Return = $\dfrac{FR_T - FR_0}{FR_0}$.

w = Equity as a Percentage of Initial Assets.

From the definitions,

$$L_T = L_0 \tilde{R}_L,$$

$$A_T = A_0\,[(w\tilde{R}_E + (1 - w)\,\tilde{R}_L)], \quad \text{and}$$

$$FR_T = \frac{A_0\,[w\tilde{R}_E + (1 - w)\,\tilde{R}_L]}{L_0 \tilde{R}_L} .$$

Therefore,

$$FR_T = FR_0 \left[w\tilde{R}_E / \tilde{R}_L + (1-w) \right], \quad \text{so}$$

$$\frac{FR_T}{FR_0} = w\,\frac{\tilde{R}_E}{\tilde{R}_L} + 1 - w, \quad \text{and}$$

$$\frac{FR_T - FR_0}{FR_0} = w\left(\frac{\tilde{R}_E}{\tilde{R}_L}\right).$$

Based on the definition of FRR, then,

$$FRR = w\,(\tilde{R}_E / \tilde{R}_L - 1). \tag{1}$$

Assume that the plan sponsor has a funding ratio return constraint FRR_C that requires a 90% probability that $FRR \geq FRR_C$; that is, the 10th-percentile $FRR = FRR_C$.
Thus we have

$$FRR_C = \text{10th Percentile of } FRR$$

$$= \text{10th Percentile of } \left[w(\tilde{R}_E / \tilde{R}_L - 1) \right]$$

$$= w\,\left[\text{10th Percentile of } (\tilde{R}_E / \tilde{R}_L) - 1 \right]. \tag{2}$$

It is useful to define

$$k = \frac{1}{1 - \text{10th Percentile of } (\tilde{R}_E / \tilde{R}_L)}.$$

We can assume that the 10th percentile of $(\tilde{R}_E / \tilde{R}_L)$ is less than 1; otherwise, the fund could hold 100% equity without risk at the 10th percentile. Therefore, k is positive and $FRR_c = -w/k$ is negative.
Equation (2) shows that the FRR constraint is satisfied if

$$w = k\,(-FRR_c). \tag{3}$$

We now show that the same constant k can be applied to the surplus percentage when the objective is full funding at the 10th percentile. We demonstrate that a requirement to stay fully funded is equivalent to setting FRR_c equal to the negative of the surplus percentage.

By definition,

$$FRR = \frac{FR_T - FR_0}{FR_0}.$$

The plan is fully funded if $FR_T = 1$. Therefore, the FRR constraint that produces full funding is:

$$FRR_C = \frac{1 - FR_0}{FR_0} = \frac{1 - A_0/L_0}{A_0/L_0} = \frac{L_0 - A_0}{A_0}, \quad \text{so}$$

$$-FRR_C = \frac{A_0 - L_0}{A_0}, \tag{4}$$

which is our definition of surplus percentage. Thus, combining (3) and (4), we also have

$$w = k \times \text{Surplus Percentage.} \tag{5}$$

The Opportunity for Greater Flexibility in the Bond Component: The Total Fund Effect

INTRODUCTION

Investors have generally accepted the paramount importance of asset allocation in determining investment performance. They first determine their overall allocation, committing as much to equities and other risky assets as their risk tolerance permits; the balance of the fund is generally invested in bonds as a "buffering" asset. The bond portfolio typically is managed with a strict duration target—a market duration of four to five years if the investor is concerned primarily with performance relative to a market peer group; a shorter duration if the concern is with asset-only risk; and a longer duration if the objective is the management of surplus relative to a long-duration liability. Tight credit constraints also commonly apply, either explicitly in the form of quality constraints or implicitly via the benchmark specification.

In this chapter, we show that *for most pension plans and other equity-oriented funds, the severe constraints placed on the management of the bond portfolio are not only unnecessary but counterproductive.* We begin by reviewing the performance of Treasury bond portfolios spanning a range of durations, by themselves and mixed with 60% equity. The past 10 years rewarded longer durations in the all-bond portfolios quite generously; as we would expect, the returns of the 60/40 portfolios reflected about 40% of those rewards. Of course, the longer durations also carried higher volatilities, but only 23% of the higher volatility showed up in the longer-duration 60/40 portfolios. The 40% pass-through of returns, contrasted with the 23% pass-through of volatility, substantially improved the risk/return trade-off of duration extension.

After reviewing the historical results, we use a simple model to illuminate the mechanics and implications of this relationship. Bond portfolio risks that loom large relative to a bond benchmark can be nearly invisible in the overall risk level of the fund. For example, the risk/return trade-off of pursuing credit spreads or acting on interest-rate or yield-curve views may appear unfavorable when the bond portfolio is measured in isolation. That same trade-off can appear quite different when measured for the entire fund, where the bond risk is swamped by the equity volatility. *For a fund with an equity allocation of 60%, bond duration adjustments of several years have little effect on either asset risk or surplus risk*—although sponsors often constrain their bond managers within a range of one year or less.

Our findings indicate that, with little risk to their total performance, equity-oriented investors can pursue bond return increments over a remarkably broad range of durations. They should be prepared to ease their duration control in favor of strategies that they believe may produce incremental returns, including the following:

- Investing at durations that offer broad opportunities for security selection.
- Giving their managers wider duration ranges (perhaps with dynamic benchmarks) within which to maneuver.
- Using managers with particular expertise at durations outside the normal range for the fund.
- Investing in securities with complex (for example, optional) duration characteristics that are less amenable to strict duration management.
- Investing in currency-hedged nondollar bonds.

Although we focus on the diminished pass-through of *duration* risk to the total portfolio, similar arguments apply to other types of bond risk. Investors need not adhere rigidly to traditional market-weighted benchmarks that may be "Treasury-rich." They may, with very modest overall risk implications, accept limited risks in other dimensions. For example, they may seek to capture credit spreads in a diversified portfolio of corporate securities with suitable quality constraints.

MARKET EXPERIENCE DURING 1984–94

Figure 12–1 shows the performance of several portfolios during the January 1984 through October 1994 time period. The figure covers four all-Treasury portfolios, with constant durations of two, four, six, and eight years; and four equity/bond portfolios, each of which combines 40% of one of the constant-duration Treasury portfolios with 60% invested in the S&P 500.

The markets were strong during this period: The S&P 500 returned an average of 14.1% annually, while medium- and long-duration Treasuries produced double-digit returns. Under these conditions, the four-year duration Treasury portfolio outperformed the two-year portfolio by a substantial margin, 142 basis points annually (10.39% – 8.97%). The 60/40 portfolio with four-year duration Treasuries outdistanced the 60/40 two-year portfolio by 58 basis points annually (12.90% – 12.32%), which is 40.8% of the all-bond portfolio difference, as shown by the next-to-last column of Figure 12–1. While 40.8% of the incremental bond return passed through to the 60/40 portfolio, however, only 19.2% of the incremental bond volatility did so, as shown by the last column.

The pattern is similar for the further duration increments. For a two-to-eight-year duration extension, 41% of the additional bond return and only 23% of the additional bond volatility passed through to the 60/40 portfolio. Of course, the bond return increment (or decrement) depends on the interest-rate trend and was unusually large during that period; the markets do not commonly give a 50-basis-point reward for each year of duration extension. Although we cannot project the absolute rewards for duration, we will show that the 41% return and 23% volatility pass-through *percentages* are not trend-sensitive and offer a reasonable basis for projection.

Figure 12–1. All-Bond Portfolios versus 60/40 Portfolios, Jan. 84–Oct. 94

Bond Duration	100% Treasuries		60% S&P 500/ 40% Treasuries		Percent Pass-Through of Increases in Annual Return and Volatility		
	Annual Return	Annual Volatility	Annual Return	Annual Volatility	Duration Increment	Return	Volatility
2 Years	8.97%	2.72%	12.32%	9.45%	2 to 4 yrs.	40.8%	19.2%
4 Years	10.39	5.37	12.90	9.96	4 to 6	41.6	24.8
6 Years	11.28	7.71	13.27	10.54	6 to 8	41.5	25.5
8 Years	12.22	9.71	13.66	11.05	2 to 8	41.2	22.9

RISK AND RETURN IN ALL-BOND PORTFOLIOS

We now use a simple model to evaluate the bond risk/reward trade-off changes in an all-bond portfolio. Figure 12–2 illustrates the "base-case" bond risk/return profile that we use in this chapter. It shows the expected returns for a one-year holding period. The duration is measured at the end of the year, so the zero-duration bond, our risk-free "cash" investment, is a one-year security held to maturity, with a yield of 6.5%. The positive slope of the curve reflects a modest "term premium," raising the expected return to 7.75% for a 10-year duration bond.[1] The annual interest-rate volatility (standard deviation of absolute yield change) is 100 basis points.[2] Return volatility is proportional to duration, the only risk factor in our simple model that assumes normally distributed parallel rate movements and ignores convexity.

Figure 12–2 shows that an increase in duration from zero to one year offers a significant reward for the additional risk; further increases in duration risk are less rewarding. Figure 12–3 illuminates the trade-off by showing the Sharpe Ratio for increasing duration.[3] We calculate the Sharpe Ratio as the incremental expected return divided by the incremental volatility. This ratio equals the slope of the curve shown in Figure 12–2. For example, increasing the duration from one year to two gains 20 basis points of expected return (7.00% to 7.20%), while adding 100 basis points of volatility, for a Sharpe Ratio averaging about 0.20 (20/80) in the one-to-two-year range.

Figure 12–3 illustrates the decreasing marginal returns obtained for successive risk increments and helps to identify where the risk/return trade-off becomes unattractive to a particular investor. We also need a way of determining the point at which the *accumulated* duration risk, apart from possible return gains, reaches an unacceptable level. To help address this issue, we look at "shortfall risk." Shortfall risk is an appropriate measure for an investor who requires a high degree of assurance that the one-year return will not fall below some critical threshold. For example, the investor may require a 90% probability that the one-year return exceeds 0%; we can then speak of 0% as the investor's required "shortfall threshold." Figure 12–4 shows the

---

[1]Figure 12–2 displays an investor's expected return curve, not the yield curve. For a discussion of the relationship between expected return curves and yield curves, see Chapter 25. A steeper or flatter expected return curve would not alter the risk effects that we are studying but would affect the rewards that enter into the duration decision.

[2]Lower rate volatility would, of course, lower the return volatility of higher-duration bond portfolios. Duration risk would also be reduced if we refined our model to reflect the decline in rate volatility as duration increases—for example, during 1984–94, the annual yield volatility was 15 basis points lower for the eight-year-duration Treasuries than for the two-year Treasuries.

[3]See "The Sharpe Ratio," William F. Sharpe, *The Journal of Portfolio Management*, Fall 1994.

Figure 12–2. Expected Return versus Volatility of All-Bond Portfolios

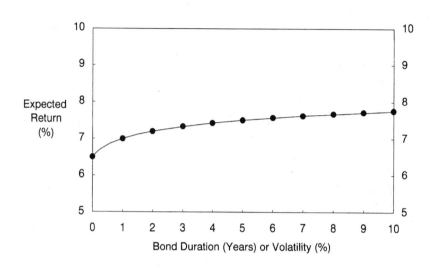

Figure 12–3. Sharpe Ratio versus Bond Duration for All-Bond Portfolios

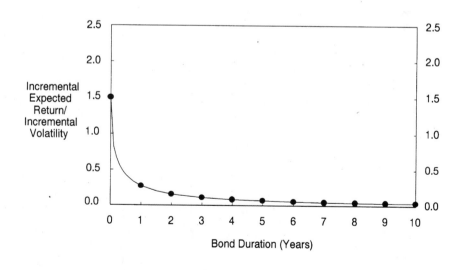

Figure 12–4. Asset Return Shortfall Threshold versus Bond Duration for All-Bond Portfolios

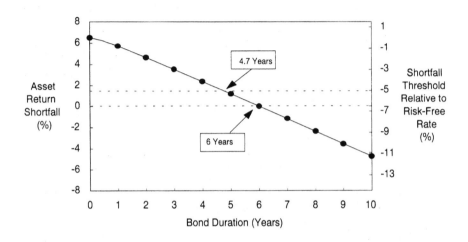

Figure 12–5. Expected Return versus Bond Duration for All-Bond and 60/40 Portfolios

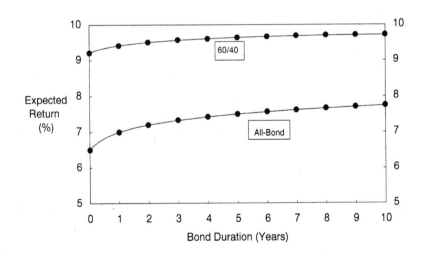

shortfall thresholds for bond portfolios with varying durations, and we can see that any portfolio with a duration of six years or less meets this constraint—that is, a six-year-duration portfolio has a 90% probability of a positive one-year return and only a 10% chance of a negative return.[4]

An investor may also view shortfall risk relative to the risk-free rate (6.5%), a more relevant measure of the potential loss associated with risk. The right-hand scale of Figure 12–4 shows this measure. We can see that a portfolio with a 4.7-year duration has a 10% chance of losing 5% or more relative to the risk-free one-year rate.

VARYING BOND DURATIONS IN 60% EQUITY/40% BOND PORTFOLIOS

Thus far, we have modeled only all-bond portfolios. We now consider allocations that include 60% equity, and we see that the risk/return trade-off for increasing bond duration becomes much more favorable. We assume that equity carries an expected return of 11.5%, representing a 5% risk premium over cash; its annual volatility is 16%, and the equity/bond correlation is 0.35.[5]

Figure 12–5 compares the expected returns of the 60/40 portfolios with those of the all-bond portfolios. The equity risk premium raises the initial level of the curve; the 60% equity allocation flattens it, as only 40% of the bond term premium passes through to the total return.

Figure 12–5 shows that the expected return curve flattens to 40% of its original slope when the bond allocation is reduced to 40%. The volatility curve, however, undergoes a far more dramatic reduction in slope, because the duration risk is swamped by the volatility of the 60% equity allocation, as Figure 12–6 illustrates.

Combining Volatilities

A brief explanation of the difference between how expected returns and volatilities combine may be helpful.[6] When two or more asset classes are

---

[4]The shortfall threshold of a portfolio is its 10th-percentile return. See Chapter 2.

[5]We assume that both equity and bond returns are distributed lognormally; with continuous rebalancing, the total portfolio returns are also lognormal.

[6]The explanation is couched in terms of normal distributions, which are easier to analyze than the lognormal distributions used in the rest of this chapter. (We use lognormal distributions to facilitate the calculation of funding ratio returns and multiyear returns.)

Figure 12–6. Volatility versus Bond Duration of All-Bond and 60/40 Portfolios

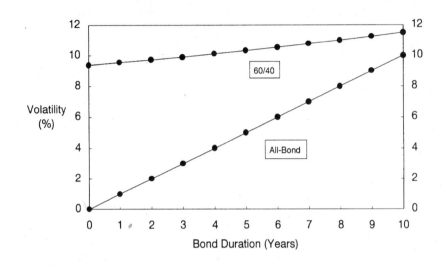

combined, the expected return of the combination is simply an arithmetic average of the individual expected returns. (The expected return of each asset class is weighted in proportion to its allocation percentage.) Volatilities combine in a more complex way, which produces risk-reducing diversification benefits when the portfolio components are imperfectly correlated. The combination sharply diminishes the impact of "small" risks that are not perfectly correlated with larger risks. In Figure 12–7, the equity allocation has a volatility of 16% and accounts for 60% of the portfolio; equity thus has a potential volatility contribution of 0.6 x 16% = 9.6%. Figure 12–7 also reflects a 40% allocation to five-year-duration bonds, with a potential volatility contribution of $0.4 \times 5\% = 2.0.\%$.

The top diagram in Figure 12–7 illustrates the combination of the two risks if they are perfectly correlated (correlation = 1.0). In that case, the risks add and the total volatility is 9.6% + 2.0% = 11.6%.

The second diagram assumes a correlation of zero. In that case, the two volatilities can be joined in a right angle, and the hypotenuse of the triangle represents the total volatility, 9.8% ($0.098^2 = 0.096^2 + 0.020^2$). The incremental portfolio volatility added by the bond risk is negligible.

The third diagram in Figure 12–7 assumes a correlation of 0.35, as we used in the previous figures. The bond volatility is now added at an angle

Figure 12–7. Total Volatility of All-Bond and 60/40 Portfolios

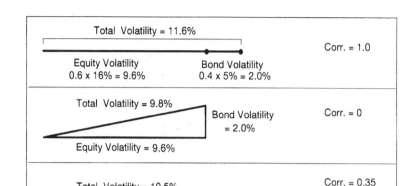

between those used in the two previous diagrams, and a modest portion of it passes through to the total volatility.[7]

Figure 12–8 compares the risk/return profile of the 60/40 portfolios with the all-bond portfolios; curves for portfolios with 30% equity and 90% equity are included to add perspective. (These curves differ from the traditional equity/bond efficient frontier in that each covers a range of bond durations with a fixed equity percentage, rather than a range of equity percentages with a fixed bond duration.) The choice of bond duration creates a broad range of risk/return possibilities for all-bond portfolios. The range diminishes as equity is added, and the bond duration has practically no effect on a 90% equity portfolio. (The 100% equity efficient frontier collapses into a single point.)

Compared with the all-bond curve, the 60/40 efficient frontier spans a somewhat reduced range of expected returns and a dramatically shrunken

---

[7]The formula for the total volatility is $(V_e^2 + V_b^2 + 2 \times \text{Bond/Equity Correlation} \times V_e \times V_b)^{1/2}$, where V_e is the product of the equity percentage and the equity volatility and V_b is the product of the bond percentage and the bond volatility. In the diagrams, the angle formed by the bond volatility leg and an extension of the equity leg is equal to the arc-cosine of the correlation (even for zero or negative correlation). As the diagrams indicate, a higher equity/bond correlation or a lower ratio of equity volatility to bond volatility would increase the total portfolio risk impact of duration risk.

Figure 12–8. Expected Return versus Volatility for Varying Equity Percentages

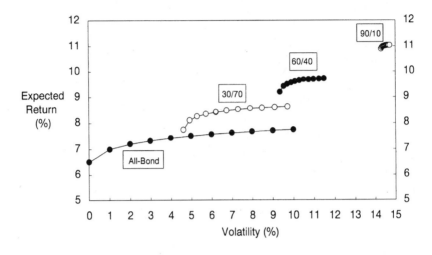

Figure 12–9. Sharpe Ratio versus Bond Duration for All-Bond and 60/40 Portfolios

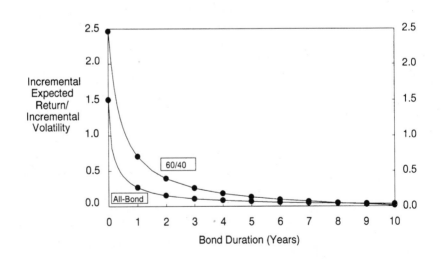

range of volatilities. In fact, the volatility range of the entire 60/40 frontier falls between the volatilities of a 9-year and a 12-year all-bond portfolio—graphically demonstrating how little the bond-duration risk matters in a 60% equity portfolio, compared with its impact on an all-bond portfolio. Because the equity allocation dilutes the volatility of the bond portfolio more than its return, the 60/40 return/risk curve is much steeper than the all-bond curve, indicating a more attractive return gain for each increment of duration risk.

Figure 12–9 compares the 60/40 and all-bond risk/return trade-offs explicitly, through the Sharpe Ratio. We previously observed that increasing the bond duration from one year to two in an all-bond portfolio adds 20 basis points of expected return and 100 basis points of volatility, for a Sharpe Ratio of 0.20. In a 60/40 portfolio, that trade-off is much more favorable—9 basis points of expected return and 18 of volatility, for a ratio of 0.50. The 60/40 Sharpe Ratios remain more than twice as high as those for the all-bond portfolios, until the bond duration approaches seven years. Thus, a "reach for yield" that appears to carry excessive risk for the bond portfolio by itself may be quite justifiable in a broader total portfolio context. When the bond duration reaches 10 years, the Sharpe Ratios in Figure 12–9 (the slopes in Figure 12–8) are quite flat and essentially equal, and duration extension is no longer a bargain (in terms of risk) for the equity-oriented investor.[8]

Figure 12–10 contrasts the effects of duration risk on the all-bond and 60/40 portfolios. In the all-bond portfolios, the shortfall threshold falls inexorably, by about 1% per year as duration increases. With 60% equity, however, duration extension is far more benign in its effect on shortfall risk. The shortfall threshold curve is relatively flat, remaining between –2.5% and –3.5% for durations up to six years, giving the investor a relatively free hand to engage in yield-curve or duration tilts within a broad range of durations.[9]

ASSET/LIABILITY RISK

Thus far, we have confined our investigation to an asset-only context, without considering liabilities. Many investors, such as insurance companies, need to tightly constrain their asset performance to match the performance of fixed-

---

[8]We have not compared the Sharpe Ratios for increasing equity with those for extending duration. At low equity percentages and high durations, equity increases are likely to provide the more favorable risk/return trade-offs. The comparison is very sensitive to the notoriously difficult assumptions concerning the equity risk premium and bond term premium.

[9]For an approach to maximizing expected return at specified durations, see Chapter 20.

Figure 12–10. Asset Return Shortfall Threshold versus Bond Duration for All-Bond and 60/40 Portfolios

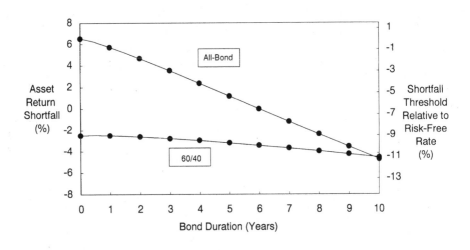

dollar liabilities. These investors, who may include a small minority of pension funds, have little appetite for equity and must be very sensitive to duration risk. Other investors with liability concerns, however, such as most pension funds, may have long horizons, uncertain liabilities, and relatively loose constraints, leading them to substantial equity allocations. We now show that for these investors, duration risk is likely to have very modest effects even in relation to their long-duration, fixed-dollar liabilities.

To measure asset/liability risk, we use the concept of a "funding ratio return" (FRR).[10] The FRR is the percentage change in the funding ratio (assets divided by liabilities) over the investment horizon. For example, a pension plan that begins a measurement period with a funding ratio of 120% and ends with a ratio of 110% has experienced an FRR of (110% – 120%)/120%, or –8.3%. The FRR depends only on the asset and liability returns, not on the initial funding ratios; that is, all funds with the same asset allocation and the same liability structures will experience identical FRRs regardless of their deficit or surplus level, permitting the FRR to serve as a "universal" measure of asset/liability risk.

---

[10]See Chapter 10.

Figure 12–11. FRR Shortfall Threshold for All-Bond and 60/40 Portfolios

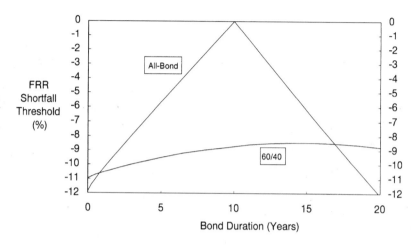

FRR = funding ratio return.

An investor who wishes to control the chance that the funding ratio will fall below a specified critical level can evaluate asset allocation decisions in terms of their FRR shortfall thresholds. Figure 12–11 plots the FRR shortfall thresholds for all-bond and 60/40 portfolios versus a 10-year duration liability.

For the all-bond portfolio, FRR shortfall risk is highly sensitive to bond duration. An investor holding a zero-duration bond portfolio runs a 10% chance of seeing the funding ratio drop by 12% or more. A 10-year-duration portfolio, on the other hand, matches the liability duration, immunizing the funding status and locking in a 0% FRR. As the bond duration extends *beyond* 10 years, a mismatch reappears and the all-bond line reverses its climb, forming an inverted "V."

With 60% equity, however, the bond duration again becomes a negligible factor. The high equity allocation prevents the FRR shortfall risk from improving beyond the –8.5% level for *any* bond duration. But once that equity risk is accepted, incremental bond risk becomes minor: Lowering the bond duration from the optimal 15 years[11] to 5 years adds only 1% to the

---

[11]The best FRR shortfall threshold is attained at a bond duration of about 15 years, when the total portfolio duration approximately matches the 10-year liability duration. See Chapter 6.

Figure 12–12. Asset and FRR Shortfalls for 60/40 Bond Portfolios

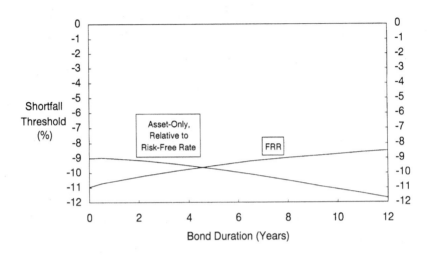

FRR = funding ratio return.

---

shortfall risk, and even a 1-year-duration bond portfolio bears only 2% more shortfall risk than the minimum-risk duration.

Similar consequences flow from poorly defined liabilities, such as those that depend heavily on future employment and compensation. Like high equity exposure, liability uncertainty creates "noise" that can drown out modest bond risk. Whatever their liability concerns, investors should not forgo return opportunities by trying to eliminate bond risk that adds insignificantly to the overall surplus risk. The less certain a fund's liabilities are, the less benefit there is in trying to closely match those liabilities and the more freedom is justified in pursuing high-return bond strategies.

Figure 12–12 illustrates how an investor might balance asset-only shortfall risk and surplus shortfall risk for the 60/40 portfolios.[12]

- In asset-only terms, relative to the risk-free rate, the shortfall threshold is at its maximum of –9% at a bond duration near zero; that is, a 60% equity/40% cash portfolio has a 10% chance of returning less than –2.5% absolute, or –9% relative to the risk-free 6.5% rate. The shortfall threshold falls to –12% at a bond duration of 12 years.

---

[12]Also see Chapter 3.

- In FRR terms, the absolute shortfall threshold is –11% at a bond duration of zero and peaks at –8.5% at about 15 years.

The two shortfall thresholds are quite stable over a broad range of durations. The asset-only threshold remains within 2% of its maximum level until the duration reaches 10 years; the FRR threshold remains within 2% of its maximum level until the duration *shortens* to 1.5 years. Thus, *both* thresholds remain within 2% of their maximum levels for durations ranging from 1.5 to 10 years; both stay within 1.5% for a three-to-eight-year duration range. *With 60% equity, then, anything reasonably close to an "intermediate" bond duration will not be far from optimal on both an asset-only and a surplus basis* (as well as for peer group comparisons). Conversely, an all-out commitment to optimizing in one of those dimensions brings only minor improvement, while doing serious damage in the other dimension. Duration shifts within a broad intermediate range can be justified by quite modest return increments; extremism in pursuit of one-dimensional optimization is no virtue.

CONCLUSION

In this chapter, we place bond portfolio risk in a total portfolio context. Viewed myopically, bond risk can deter an investor from pursuing return-enhancing strategies that substantially increase the risk of the bond portfolio *in isolation*. However, because bond risk is diluted more than bond return by diversified asset allocation, these strategies may offer attractive risk/return trade-offs for an equity-oriented portfolio as a whole.

Our findings apply when investors evaluate moderate increments of duration or credit risk to portfolios that already have *substantial* nonduration risks, such as equity exposure or liability uncertainty. These investors should be prepared to ease their duration control and credit limits in favor of strategies that they believe may produce incremental return.

In contrast, an insurance company or pension fund that is closely matching its well-defined, fixed-dollar liabilities must fine-tune its bond duration and lacks the flexibility that this chapter suggests. Also, our findings do not apply to a bond manager who is being measured against a well-defined fixed benchmark. We do, however, counsel a change in the thinking of a fund sponsor who severely constrains the bond manager. The key decision for a fund sponsor is the size of the allocation to risky assets. If this allocation is large, the bond managers should be measured against duration and quality targets or ranges that promise the highest returns and meet the sponsor's *overall* risk constraints.

Chapter 13

Benchmark Departures and Total Fund Risk: A Second Dimension of Diversification

INTRODUCTION

Benchmarks serve a number of purposes. On the one hand, a benchmark can articulate a fund's key objectives. For example, the performance of a fund whose exclusive purpose is to meet a well-defined liability should be measured relative to a benchmark that expresses the funding costs of that liability. In other instances, benchmarks may simply be tools used by the fund sponsor to control and measure the performance of individual managers or portions of the portfolio. There is a danger that such benchmarks, once they are set forth as performance standards, may take on a life of their own. They can then promote operational efficiency at the expense of economic efficiency, constraining investment flexibility in ways that are not congruent with the fund's overall objectives. In this chapter, we show how the excessively rigid use of benchmarks for controlling individual asset class or subclass management may deny investors access to superior strategies that fall well within their overall risk constraints.

The potential problem lies in a narrow focus on risk as measured by tracking error relative to an asset class benchmark. This focus can overstate risk in two ways:

Relative Risk versus Absolute Risk

1. If the benchmark is not in itself a critical one for the fund, the sponsor should be fundamentally concerned with absolute rather than rela-

241

tive risk. For example, constraining the risk relative to the benchmark can disallow a strategy that is rather different from the benchmark but promises a higher return, with acceptable risk, that would improve long-term performance.

Asset Class Risk versus Total Portfolio Risk

2. The allowable tracking error also may be constrained too tightly by failing to recognize that risks that loom large in isolation may be minor in the larger context of portfolio diversification. Diversification traditionally focuses on the allocation among asset classes, but a "second dimension of diversification" is its application to tactical and strategic tilts *within* asset classes. In a previous chapter, we showed how the reward/risk profile of an asset class investment strategy can improve when it is viewed in a total portfolio context.[1]

A Hierarchy of Risk

In this chapter, we distinguish the following hierarchy of risk levels: (1) *benchmark* tracking error, (2) incremental volatility at the *asset class level*, and (3) incremental volatility at the *total fund level*. We illustrate a hypothetical active bond investment strategy that increases the expected bond return by 80 basis points but has a 5% tracking error relative to the benchmark. The strategy thus appears to have a poor risk/return trade-off. In terms of its incremental volatility, however, the strategy sounds more promising: the volatility of the bond returns is only 2.03% higher than that of the assumed benchmark. Finally, quite a different picture emerges when we shift from the asset class level to a total fund that consists of 60% equity and 40% bonds. The same strategy adds 32 basis points of total portfolio return (40% × 80 basis points), while increasing the total fund volatility by only 0.18%.

In this chapter, we examine these three levels of risk as they apply to both tactical and strategic departures from a benchmark. To illustrate tactical departures, we use strategies based on an assumed ability to forecast interest-rate changes.[2] As an example of a strategic departure, we consider the much simpler decision to increase the *normal* allocation to corporate securities at the expense of Treasuries.

---

[1]See Chapter 12.

[2]We do not underestimate the difficulty either of forecasting rate movements successfully or of identifying successful forecasters. For example, see *Modern Portfolio Theory and Investment Analysis*, Edwin

A Hierarchy of Benchmarks

Our research suggests that a fund can be most successfully managed by using a hierarchy of benchmarks. The primary benchmark is set by the senior management of the sponsoring institution. For example, the critical objective for a corporate pension fund might be to keep pace with its liability, or to match the performance of the funds of an industry peer group with whom the sponsor competes for capital, labor, and profits. The primary benchmark could be expressed as a standard policy allocation that is highly correlated with the objective—for example, the average allocation of the industry peer group, which might be 60% Standard & Poor's (S&P) 500 Stock Index and 40% of a broad bond market index.

The pension officer is responsible for performance vis-à-vis this primary benchmark. He or she might decide that the best way to outperform it with acceptable risk is through a strategic tilt toward equities; the strategic norm for equities could be raised to 65% and diversified both internationally and in terms of capitalization size. The strategic bond allocation could similarly be adjusted, perhaps to overweight higher-yielding corporate or mortgage securities. The pension officer may then allocate portions of the fund to investment managers. Each manager would be evaluated according to a performance benchmark appropriate to the style and the universe of securities within which he or she will be operating. The measurement and constraints around the benchmark would reflect the impact of the manager's performance on *the return and volatility of the fund as a whole.*

Within this hierarchical structure, productive risk-taking initiatives by individual managers generally will have a much higher reward/risk ratio at the total fund level than at the asset class level. This result argues for granting increased latitude to those active managers in whom the fund has placed its confidence.

THE MODEL FOR TACTICAL DURATION TILTS

We begin at the lowest level of the risk and benchmark hierarchy by considering the manager of the fund's allocation of Treasury bonds. We use an expected return curve that is flat at 7.5% and subject only to parallel shifts. We

J. Elton and Martin J. Gruber, John Wiley & Sons, 1991, pp. 561–62; and *When Do Bond Markets Reward Investors for Interest Rate Risk?* Antti Ilmanen, proceedings from the Salomon Brothers 1994 Central Bank Seminar, May 1994. A survey of the literature can be found in *Investments*, William F. Sharpe and Gordon J. Alexander, Prentice-Hall, 1990, pp. 379–80. In this chapter, we merely explore the implications of assuming that these tasks can be done.

assume that annual rate changes are normally distributed, with an expected change of zero and a standard deviation of 100 basis points. The manager's benchmark is a five-year-duration portfolio, with an expected return of 7.5% and an annual return volatility of 5%. The manager has been chosen for his or her ability to forecast rate changes and is prepared to shift the duration anywhere in the 0-to-10-year range.

Innumerable types of forecasts are possible. A forecast may give a one-point prediction ("rates will rise to 8.5%"); it may include multiple scenarios ("if A occurs, then rates will rise to 8.5%, and if B occurs, rates will fall to 7%"), perhaps with probabilities specified; or it may present a full probability distribution of all potential rate changes. In this chapter, we assume a simple directional rate forecast—a prediction either of higher or lower rates one year hence—with a known likelihood of being correct.

We have chosen this simple type of forecasting model both for its computational clarity and because it is a type that is implicit in many statements that investors make about the markets. Even investors who are extremely reluctant to engage in tactical duration shifts will, from time to time, express the opinion that rates are quite high or quite low, implying that a correction is likely. More heroically, we assume that we can attach a specific reliability to the directional forecast; that is, we know the probability that the rate change will actually be drawn from the forecasted (positive or negative) half of the distribution.

TACTICAL DURATION TILTS IN ALL-BOND PORTFOLIOS

The Reward for Forecasting

First we suppose that the manager acts on the annual forecast simply by tilting the portfolio duration by five years in the appropriate direction. If the forecast calls for a rise in rates, the manager holds cash for the year; if the forecast calls for a drop, the manager holds 10-year-duration bonds.[3] Figure 13–1 displays the expected return of this strategy for levels of forecasting reliability that range from 50% to 100%; the left-hand scale indicates the expected return relative to the fixed five-year-duration benchmark, and the right-hand scale shows the absolute expected return.

---

[3]All references are to durations at year-end. The riskless security for a one-year holding period is a one-year note, which has a (year-end) duration of zero and which we refer to as cash. As a first-order approximation, we assume that bond volatility equals bond duration multiplied by the absolute volatility of interest-rate changes. The five-year-duration portfolio therefore has a return volatility of 5%. See the Appendix to this chapter for details of the forecasting model.

Figure 13–1. Reward for Rate Forecasting in an All-Bond Portfolio

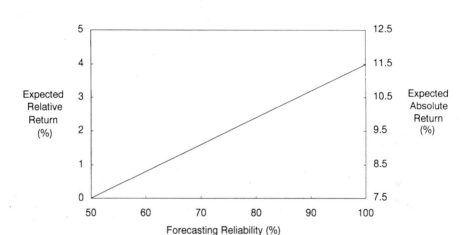

For a 50% forecaster, the one-year expected return is the 7.5% market rate; the manager neither gains nor loses expected return relative to the five-year benchmark. The expected return increases linearly to 11.5% for an omniscient forecaster, who earns 7.5% in cash when rates rise, and an average of 15.5% in 10-year-duration bonds when rates fall.[4]

Based on the sponsor's risk tolerance, the manager may decide to embark on a strategy of benchmark departures only if a specific amount of additional return is expected for each increment of risk—that is, the ratio of the expected incremental return to the incremental standard deviation of return must exceed a specified level.[5] Figure 13–2 sets forth the calculation for a 60% forecaster, whose incremental return for five-year-duration tilts is 80

---

[4]When rates fall, the average fall is about 80 basis points. The 80-basis-point figure is based on the fact that the mean of the top half of the standard normal distribution is $\sqrt{2/\pi}$, or 0.7979. With a 10-year duration, the investor earns appreciation averaging 8% (ignoring convexity). See the Appendix to this chapter for details.

[5]The Sharpe Ratio is the expected relative return divided by its standard deviation, which is given in the second row of numbers in Figure 13–2. See "The Sharpe Ratio," William F. Sharpe, *The Journal of Portfolio Management*, Fall 1994. The other rows use the Sharpe Ratio concept in different ways.

―――

Figure 13–2. Reward/Risk Ratios for Five-Year-Duration Tilts with 60% Forecasting Reliability

	Risk	Reward/Risk Ratio
I. In All-Bond Portfolio: Additional Bond Return = 80 Basis Points		
• Tracking Error	5.00 %	0.16
• Relative Volatility	4.94	0.16
• Increase in Absolute Volatility	2.03	0.39
II. In 60/40 Portfolio: Additional Bond Return = 80 Basis Points		
Additional Portfolio Return = 32 Basis Points		
• Increase in Absolute Volatility	0.18 %	1.78

basis points, as shown in Figure 13–1.[6] The different rows in Figure 13–2 reflect the alternative views of risk that we present in the remainder of this chapter.

Varying Types of Risk

We now consider the various types of risk embodied in Figure 13–2, using the following definitions.

- "Relative return" is the return of the portfolio minus the return of the benchmark.

- "Tracking error" (also known as "root-mean-square error," or RMSE) is the square root of the average of the squared relative returns. It measures the dispersion of the relative returns around zero.

- "Relative volatility" is the standard statistical volatility of the relative returns. It measures the dispersion of the relative returns around their mean.

- By "absolute volatility," we refer to the standard statistical volatility of the annual returns of an asset class or a total portfolio, without regard to a benchmark.

―――――――――――

[6]With an average rate change of 80 basis points and a five-year-duration tilt, the 60% forecaster gains an average of 400 basis points (5 × 80 basis points) 60% of the time and loses the same 400-basis-point average 40% of the time. The net gain is 60% × (+400) + 40% × (−400) = 80 basis points.

Risk Relative to the Asset Class Benchmark

We begin our discussion of risk with tracking error. If the manager kept the duration consistently extended by five years, the tracking error would be 5%. It would remain 5% if he or she always shortened the duration by five years. Now suppose that improved forecasting permits a 100% correction of any wrong duration tilts. This correction changes the negative relative returns to positive ones of the same magnitude, thereby leaving the tracking error unchanged. This result occurs because the tracking error calculation fails to distinguish between positive and negative relative returns. Thus, the tracking error for five-year-duration tilts is 5%, no matter how accurate the forecasting.

If the forecasting is superior, however, more of the relative returns will be positive than negative. The outcomes will therefore group not around zero but around their positive mean value (the expected return shown in Figure 13–1). This revised "centering" will reduce their statistical *volatility*.[7] For the 60% forecaster, the relative returns tend to group around the positive mean of 80 basis points, reducing the relative volatility to 4.94%, as shown in Figure 13–2. The minor difference between relative volatility and tracking error justifies the common use of tracking error to measure risk relative to a benchmark, as long as the mean of the relative returns is small in relation to the tracking error.

Absolute Risk for the Asset Class

However, if the benchmark is only an operational standard for an acceptable balance of return and risk, then the sponsor should also be interested in the *absolute* volatility of the bond portfolio that incorporates the forecasting strategy.

Suppose that departures from a benchmark produce relative returns that are perfectly correlated with the returns of the benchmark itself. Then the absolute volatility of the total returns will be the sum of the benchmark volatility and the relative volatility of the departures. For example, a consistent five-year extension relative to the fixed five-year benchmark (that is, a fixed 10-year portfolio) produces a relative volatility of 5% and an absolute volatility of 10%.

---

[7]Volatility measures the deviations of the differential returns from their mean, rather than from zero. It follows that volatility is a better yardstick in this instance, because it avoids penalizing a bias toward positive returns. Even volatility, however, is an inadequate measure for significantly asymmetrical differential returns; it would be preferable to use a measure that reflects downside risk only. For example, see "Asset Pricing in a Generalized Mean-Lower Partial Moment Framework: Theory and Evidence," W. V. Harlow and R. Rao, *Journal of Financial and Quantitative Analysis*, September 1989; and "Capital Market Equilibrium in a Mean, Lower Partial Moment Framework," V. Bawa and E. B. Lindenberg, *Journal of Financial Economics*, November 1977.

If, however, the correlation between the departures and the benchmark is *imperfect*, the absolute volatility will be less than the sum of the benchmark and relative volatilities because the risks are diversified.[8] Thus, the 60% forecaster produces an absolute volatility of 7.03% (only 2.03% more than the benchmark, as Figure 13–2 showed). This result implies an imperfect correlation (in fact, zero in our model) between the benchmark and the departures called for by the forecasting strategy: the 60% forecaster has a 60% chance of producing positive relative returns whether the bond market (and benchmark return) is weak or strong. The absolute volatility is quite stable at about 7% in the 50% to 65% range of forecasting accuracy, dropping significantly only at much higher levels of accuracy. Interestingly, even a perfect forecaster would incur volatility of 5.84%. Although his return would never trail the benchmark return and never be less than the 7.50% cash return, the volatility still exceeds that of the benchmark, because of the extraordinary performance of the 10-year-duration bonds when rates fall. This "good" volatility highlights the weakness of volatility as a risk measure for asymmetric distributions.

The Reward/Risk Ratio

We can now evaluate in absolute terms the change in the return/risk profile generated by the forecasting strategy. For this purpose, we compute the increment in expected return of the forecasting strategy over the benchmark, divided by the increment in absolute volatility (rather than by the volatility of the differential return). This measure enables the investor to determine whether the new strategy improves on the benchmark, *without penalizing it for merely being different*. Thus, for the 60% forecaster, the 80 basis points of increased return are divided by the increase in absolute volatility of 7.03% – 5.00% = 2.03%. The result is the 0.39 ratio shown in Figure 13–2—a significantly better reward/risk trade-off when viewed in absolute rather than relative volatility terms. Figure 13–3 shows the corresponding values for a range of forecasting percentages.

Varying the Duration Tilts

The foregoing illustrations reflect a fixed five-year-duration adjustment by which the investor responds to the forecast, regardless of its reliability. In

---

[8] A consistent five-year shortening, which is perfectly *negatively* correlated with the benchmark, results in an absolute volatility of zero. See the Appendix to this chapter for the formula used to calculate the absolute volatilities produced by forecasting.

Figure 13–3. Incremental Reward/Risk Ratio for Five-Year-Duration Tilts in an All-Bond Portfolio

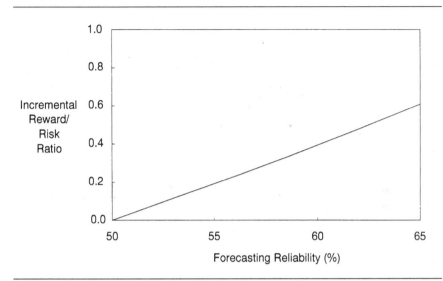

practice, of course, the more confidence the investor has in the forecast, the more heavily he or she would skew the duration. We now consider how much duration tilt a particular level of forecasting reliability would justify. Figure 13–1 implies that any duration tilt is rewarded in expected return terms, as long as the forecast has a better-than-50% chance of being correct. Duration tilts increase volatility, however, regardless of the forecaster's sagacity.[9] We frame the question by arbitrarily supposing that the investor wishes to improve on the benchmark by adding two basis points of expected return for each basis point of absolute volatility—that is, the ratio of incremental reward to incremental risk should equal 2.0.[10] Figure 13–4 illustrates how much of a duration tilt the investor can afford while meeting this reward/risk constraint, for forecasting reliability levels ranging from 50% to 65%.

---

[9]We assume that the investor responds symmetrically to up and down forecasts, which are equally reliable. Of course, the investor could lower volatility by responding only to up forecasts, but this policy would be inconsistent with our use of the benchmark as a neutral duration.

[10]This 2.0 ratio is a stringent constraint. We can show that requiring only a 1.28 ratio is equivalent to requiring that the new portfolio have a 90% shortfall threshold (or 10th-percentile return) that matches that of the benchmark. See Chapter 2.

Figure 13–4. Maximum Duration Tilt and Incremental Expected Return in an All-Bond Portfolio (Incremental Reward/Risk Ratio = 2.0)

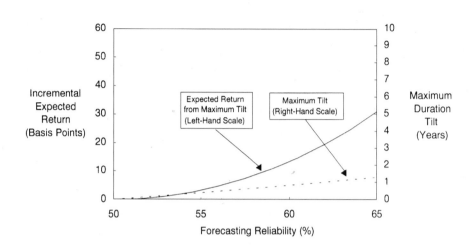

With only 50% forecasting reliability, the investor cannot afford *any* duration tilts relative to the five-year benchmark, because they create unrewarded increases in volatility. A 55% forecaster can afford only a 0.4-year-duration tilt while satisfying the 2.0-reward/risk ratio constraint. Even 65% forecasting reliability, which stretches the bounds of what most market participants would regard as achievable, permits only a 1.3-year tilt.

Figure 13–4 shows that the rewards for forecasting, in the reliability range that seems plausible, are quite modest. The 0.4-year tilts that 55% forecasting justifies would add only three basis points of expected return. Even 60% reliability reaps only a 13-basis-point reward for our admittedly stringent 2.0 reward/risk ratio and one-year forecasting horizon.

TACTICAL DURATION TILTS IN A MIXED PORTFOLIO

Thus far, we have evaluated rate forecasting in the context of a Treasury portfolio in which duration is the exclusive source of risk. In a previous chapter, we discussed the "total portfolio effect," the improvement that can occur in the risk profile of an investment strategy when it is placed in a total portfolio

Figure 13–5. Volatility for Five-Year-Duration Tilts in All-Bond and 60/40 Portfolios

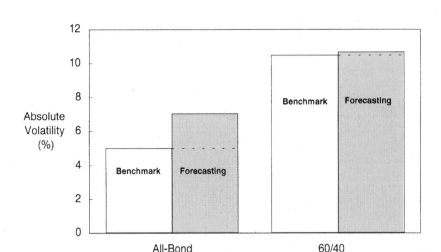

context.[11] Specifically, the reward/risk ratio improves if the strategy involves risk along a dimension that is imperfectly correlated with other larger risks in the total portfolio. We now consider the consequences of duration tilts in a 60% equity/40% Treasury portfolio. We assume that equity returns have an annual volatility of 16% and a 0.35 correlation with bond returns.[12]

Asset Class Risk versus Total Fund Risk

Figure 13–5 contrasts the absolute volatility added by five-year-duration tilts in an all-bond portfolio and a 60/40 portfolio. (We focus on the 60% forecasting level: the results are virtually identical throughout the 50% to 65% forecasting range.) A 60/40 portfolio with a fixed five-year bond duration has a 10.47% annual volatility. When the 60% forecaster uses five-year tilts in the 60/40 portfolio, the volatility rises by only 18 basis points, compared with

---

[11]See Chapter 12.

[12]The 0.35 correlation assumption is representative of the experience of the past decade. The total portfolio effect for rate forecasting is not sensitive to the bond/equity correlation because the returns *added* by rate forecasting are uncorrelated with equity returns.

Figure 13–6. Maximum Duration Tilt and Incremental Expected Return in a 60/40 Portfolio

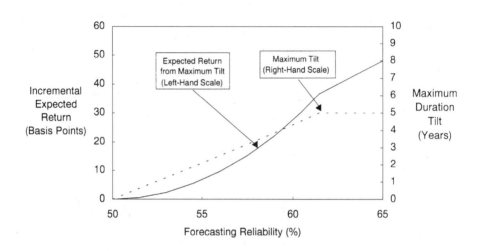

---

203 basis points in the all-bond portfolio. In other words, only 9% of the bond volatility "passes through" to the total portfolio.[13] Meanwhile, as we would expect, 40% of the 80-basis-point incremental return passes through.

We now apply the same reward/risk constraint to the 60/40 portfolio, permitting duration tilts that add two basis points of total portfolio expected return for each additional basis point of absolute volatility. The low pass-through of volatility to the total portfolio naturally improves the reward/risk ratio of the forecasting strategy, allowing greater duration latitude to the forecaster. Figure 13–6 extends the results shown in Figure 13–4 to the 60/40 portfolio; that is, it shows the allowable duration tilts and the corresponding gain in expected *total portfolio* return (40% of the additional bond return).[14] In the all-bond portfolio, the reward/risk constraint limits the duration tilts for a 60% forecaster to 0.82 years, for a return pickup of 13 basis points (see Figure 13–4). In contrast, for the 60/40 portfolio, the constraint becomes quite liberal; the 60% forecaster can adjust the duration by as much as 4.31 years,

---

[13]This 9% pass-through rate is lower than those in Chapter 12, because, as mentioned in the preceding footnote, the volatility added by the forecasting is uncorrelated with equity returns.

[14]To avoid negative durations, we set the maximum permissible tilt at five years. This limit is reached at a 61.5% forecasting level, causing the "kinks" in Figure 13–6.

adding 69 basis points of *bond return* and, as shown in Figure 13–6, 28 basis points of *total portfolio return* (40% × 69).

The investor can afford these larger tilts because of the total portfolio effect. In the all-bond portfolio, these 4.31-year tilts would add 69 basis points of return and 156 basis points of volatility, an unsatisfactory trade-off. When those results are embedded in a 60/40 portfolio, however, the 69-basis-point bond return translates to 28 basis points of total portfolio return—a 40% pass-through—but the 156-basis-point increase in bond volatility adds only 14 basis points of total portfolio volatility—a 9% pass-through, because of risk diversification. The improved risk/return trade-off enables the investor to achieve the required 2.0 ratio (a 28-basis-point return increment divided by a 14-basis-point volatility increment).

Factors That Enhance the Total Portfolio Effect

The latitude for benchmark departures within an asset class grows as the total portfolio becomes more diversified relative to the asset class and to the particular departures being taken. Our illustration is based on a 0.35 correlation of Treasury bonds and equities, which is representative of the past decade's experience with regard to the S&P 500 Stock Index. Further diversification of the risky assets into small-cap stocks, international securities, real estate, and other weakly correlated investments would enhance the total portfolio effect for active bond management, offering the potential for greater return gains without increasing risk at the total fund level. Another factor that can allow greater freedom to the active manager is an imperfect correlation between the primary benchmark and the true objective of the fund. For example, uncertainty concerning the true liabilities that the fund is expected to meet reduces the value of precision in the asset return pattern and improves the reward/risk trade-off for return-seeking departures from the liability benchmark.[15]

A STRATEGIC TILT: INCREASING THE ALLOCATION OF CORPORATE BONDS

We now pass from tactical departures based on a forecasting model to a *strategic* departure from a benchmark. Our new benchmark is an all-bond portfolio, 75% Treasuries and 25% corporates, each component having a five-

---

[15]See Chapter 4.

year duration. The investor expects corporates to outperform Treasuries by 100 basis points annually over the long term and wishes to set the strategic norm for the portfolio at 55% five-year Treasuries and 45% five-year corporates. The investor anticipates an incremental return of 20 basis points annually (20% additional corporates × 100 basis points).

This incremental return carries a "volatility cost." We use the same annual volatility of 100 basis points for Treasuries as before and a 25 basis-point volatility for corporate spreads, which we assume fully captures the effect of credit risk. The additional spread exposure creates 25 basis points of annual volatility relative to the benchmark (20% × five-year duration × 25 basis points). The strategy therefore has a return/risk ratio of 0.8 (20 basis points/25 basis points), measured in terms of its departure from the benchmark.

If the benchmark is not intrinsically vital, but merely a reward/risk standard, however, the investor may simply compare the absolute measurements of the benchmark with the proposed portfolio to determine whether the change gives enough return for its additional absolute risk. This calculation depends on the correlation between spread changes and Treasury rate changes. If we assume that this correlation is zero, the volatility of the benchmark is 5.01% and that of the proposed strategic norm 5.03%, only two basis points higher. When viewed in these terms, the change carries an extraordinarily attractive return/risk ratio of 10.[16]

The incremental volatility of the increased corporate allocation is very small, and it would be smaller still if placed in a 60/40 portfolio. The total portfolio effect depends on a full correlation matrix of Treasury rates, corporate spreads, and equity returns. The effect would be less favorable than in our earlier illustrations if corporate spread changes were highly correlated with equity returns, but generally, the correlation for investment-grade corporates has been quite weak.

CONCLUSION

Diversification traditionally focuses on the mixture of asset classes and subclasses included in the portfolio. In this chapter, we have demonstrated that

---

[16]The correlation between the movements of Treasury rates and investment-grade corporate spreads generally has been substantially negative—for example, –0.44 during 1990–94. Under these conditions, the increased allocation to corporates actually reduces volatility. If volatility is accepted as the only measure of risk, substituting corporates for Treasuries becomes an almost irresistible strategy. The risk of spread exposure can be reduced even further by dollar-duration matching; see Chapter 19; Chapter 20; and *An Application of Spread Immunization in the U.S. Corporate Bond Market*, Raymond Iwanowski, Salomon Brothers Inc, February 1995.

return-enhancing departures from asset class benchmarks also offer diversification benefits. These benefits are commonly overlooked because of a myo-
pic view of benchmark departures in terms of their tracking risk within the
asset class, rather than their effect on the total fund.

We have illustrated both tactical and strategic departures from bond
benchmarks that incur substantial risk relative to the benchmarks, but with
trivial effect on total fund risk. Plan sponsors should recognize that their
individual *asset class* benchmarks rarely embody specific critical fund objectives in themselves; generally, they merely represent standards of the reward/
risk profiles that the sponsors wish to achieve. Asset class benchmarks are
valuable tools for delegating fund management, but they should not take on
a life of their own that distracts from the true overall fund objectives. Thus,
departures that promise positive return increments while retaining satisfactory total fund risk should not be ruled out simply because they differ significantly from the stated benchmarks.

An obvious but important caveat is that benchmark departures must be
justified by a credible expectation of incremental returns, after fees and transaction costs. A *bona fide* structural advantage is needed to justify active departures from asset class benchmarks or the inclusion of exotic asset classes.
Additional volatility without added return does not provide risk diversification—it only provides risk! Our findings should not be read as supporting
rate forecasting in particular or active management generally. Rather, we
argue that a sponsor who does choose to rely on active managers should
consider increasing their latitude to deliver an improvement in total fund
performance.

APPENDIX

In this Appendix, we describe the model for tactical duration tilts. We assume a flat yield curve, subject only to parallel shifts, and use the following definitions:

i = Initial interest rate.

$\tilde{\delta}$ = Change in interest rate, assumed to be normally distributed with zero mean.

σ_i = Standard deviation of interest-rate change.

F = Forecasting percentage, defined as the probability of correctly anticipating the direction of the change in interest rates.

D_B = Benchmark portfolio duration.

D_C = Absolute value of duration tilt based on forecast of interest-rate change.

D = Portfolio duration.

$\tilde{R}$ = Portfolio return.

$\tilde{r}$ = Excess portfolio return = $\tilde{R} - i$.

The investor bases the portfolio duration on the interest-rate forecast. Thus, we assume that the investor lengthens duration from D_B to $D_B + D_C$ when an interest rate decrease is forecast, and shortens duration to $D_B - D_C$ when an increase is forecast. We view F as a conditional probability—the probability that a rate increase was forecast, given that a rate increase occurs (and vice versa for rate decreases). Because the probability of a rate increase is 50%, the probability that rates increase and that the increase was correctly forecast is $0.5F$. Figure 13–A1 highlights the four possible combinations of rate changes and forecast results.

If rates increase, the mean increase is computed as the expected value of the right half of the normal distribution (E $[\tilde{\delta}] = \sigma_i\sqrt{2/\ }$). [17] Likewise, we can compute $E[\delta^2]$ $(= \sigma_i^2)$ for the right half.

Ignoring convexity, we calculate the expected value of $\tilde{r}$ from the returns and probabilities in Figure 13–A1 along with the value of $E[\tilde{\delta}]$ given above:

---

[17] The result $\sigma_i\sqrt{2/\ }$ is obtained by an appropriate integration involving the normal density function over the range from 0 to . Because we are working with only half the distribution, we must multiply the density function by 2 to assure that the total probability is 1.

Figure 13–A1. Probabilities, Durations, and Returns for Four Outcomes

	Forecast	
Rate Change	**Increase**	**Decrease**
Increase	Correct Prediction;	Incorrect Prediction;
	Probability = 0.5F;	Probability = 0.5(1 – F);
	$D = D_B - D_C$;	$D = D_B + D_C$;
	$\tilde{r} = -(D_B - D_C)\|\tilde{\delta}\|$	$\tilde{r} = -(D_B + D_C)\|\tilde{\delta}\|$
Decrease	Incorrect Prediction:	Correct Prediction;
	Probability = 0.5(1 – F);	Probability = 0.5F;
	$D = D_B - D_C$;	$D = D_B + D_C$;
	$\tilde{r} = (D_B - D_C)\|\tilde{\delta}\|$	$\tilde{r} = (D_B + D_C)\|\tilde{\delta}\|$

$$E(\tilde{r}) = -\sigma_i\sqrt{2/}\ [0.5(1 - F)(D_B + D_C) + 0.5F (D_B - D_C)$$
$$- 0.5(1 - F)(D_B - D_C) - 0.5F(D_B + D_C)].$$

Thus,

$$\bar{r} = E(\tilde{r}) = 2\sigma_i\sqrt{2/}\ D_C(F - 0.5), \quad \text{and}$$

$$\bar{R} = E[\tilde{R}] = i + 2\sigma_i\sqrt{2/}\ D_C(F - 0.5). \tag{1}$$

Note that the expected return depends on the forecasting percentage F, but is independent of the benchmark duration D_B for our flat yield curve. When $F = 50\%$, nothing is gained by deviating from the benchmark duration and $\bar{R}$ is simply the yield i. As F increases to 100%, the expected gain per unit of duration tilt approaches 80% ($\sqrt{2/}$) of the inter est-rate volatility.

Using the values of $\tilde{r}$ in Figure 13-A1, and the fact that $E[\tilde{\delta}^2] = \sigma_i^2$, we compute the variance of portfolio return as

$$E[(\tilde{R} - \bar{R})^2] = E[(\tilde{r} - \bar{r})^2] = E[\tilde{r}^2] - \bar{r}^2$$
$$= 0.5\sigma_i^2[(1 - F)(D_B + D_C)^2 + F(D_B - D_C)^2 + (1 - F)(D_B - D_C)^2$$
$$+ F(D_B + D_C)^2] - 4\sigma_i^2(2/)\ D_C^2(F - 0.5)^2.$$

That is,

$$\sigma_R^2 = \sigma_i^2 (D_B^2 + D_C^2 [1 - (8/) (F - 0.5)^2]). \tag{2}$$

If no duration tilts are allowed ($D_C = 0$), portfolio return volatility is simply equal to $\sigma_i D_B$, as expected. If tilts are permitted, return volatility is highest when $F = 50\%$. Thus, an absence of forecasting ability is equivalent to random duration tilts, resulting in a portfolio duration of either $D_B + D_C$ or $D_B - D_C$ and an increase in portfolio variance of $D_C^2 \sigma_i^2$. With perfect forecasting ability, the increase in portfolio variance created by forecasting is about $\frac{1}{3}$ of $D_C^2 \sigma_i^2$.

The expected value and variance of the portfolio return relative to a benchmark return ($\tilde{R}_B$) can be obtained from Figure 13–A1 by substituting $D_B = 0$. We find that

$$E(\tilde{R} - \tilde{R}_B) = \bar{r} = 2\sigma_i \sqrt{2/} \ D_C(F - 0.5), \quad \text{and} \tag{3}$$

$$\sigma^2 (\tilde{R} - \tilde{R}_B) = \sigma_i^2 D_C^2 [1 - (8/)(F - 0.5)^2]. \tag{4}$$

The derivation of the formulas for the expected return and variance of a mixed equity/bond portfolio follows the same lines as for the all-bond portfolio above; it also reflects the interest sensitivity and residual volatility of equity. The formulas are as follows:

$$\bar{R} = w(i + RP) + (1 - w)[i + 2\sigma_i \sqrt{2/} \ D_C(F - 0.5)], \quad \text{and} \tag{5}$$

$$\sigma_R^2 = w^2 \sigma_E^2 + (1 - w)^2 \sigma_i^2 (D_B^2 + D_C^2 [1 - (8/)(F - 0.5)^2])$$

$$+ 2w(1 - w)\rho_{BE}\sigma_i\sigma_E D_B \tag{6}$$

where the new symbols have the following meanings:

w = Equity weight in portfolio.
RP = Equity risk premium.
σ_E = Equity return volatility.
ρ_{BE} = Correlation between bond and equity returns.

Chapter 14

The Hierarchy of Benchmarks: Structuring Retirement Fund Risk

INTRODUCTION

Institutions manage their large diversified investment pools with careful attention to the performance of each individual asset class, as commonly measured against standard market indexes. As we suggested in a recent chapter, this process can sometimes promote operational efficiencies at the asset management level but at the expense of the fund's overall performance.[1]

In this chapter, we outline a top-down approach to asset allocation that flows from the sponsor's overall goals for the fund. We couch our discussion in terms of corporate pension funds, but the process we describe applies equally to public retirement systems, endowments, and other capital pools. Most pension funds have carefully thought-out asset allocations, but a surprising similarity prevails among sponsors with widely divergent business prospects, pension funding status, and corporate financial practice. This similarity suggests that many funds could benefit from greater senior-level strategic input into setting the objectives for what is often a multibillion-dollar corporate enterprise.

In the framework that we present, the fund's objectives flow through a hierarchy of benchmarks that establish goals and accountability at each level of fund management. At the top of the hierarchy is a *policy benchmark*. This benchmark embodies senior management's views regarding asset perfor-

---

[1]See Chapter 12.

mance and risk, surplus control, performance relative to a peer group, and any other critical standards. The policy benchmark describes the target allocation in broad terms but does not reflect any special market views.

Responsibility for performance relative to the policy benchmark then passes to an investment committee.[2] To carry out this responsibility, the committee develops a *strategic benchmark*. This benchmark will likely be more detailed than the policy benchmark. For example, "equity" can be subdivided into domestic large- and small-cap stocks and international. "Bonds" may include Treasuries, corporates, mortgages, and international. The strategic benchmark may express certain limited long-term market views, such as the presumptive superiority of equities, the benefits of international diversification, or the dependability with which spreads can be captured on corporate bonds. This benchmark may thus incorporate some long-term tilts relative to the policy benchmark. Some of these tilts may be encouraged by the "total fund effect," which can improve the reward/risk ratio of an asset class investment strategy when it is viewed in a total portfolio context.[3]

The investment committee implements the asset allocation policy by delegating portions of the strategic benchmark to various inside or outside managers. Each manager is assigned an asset class benchmark that reflects the asset class or subclass within which he or she will be operating. Managers' departures from their benchmarks are limited by how well they foster the attainment of the overall fund objectives, as reflected in the policy benchmark. Through the total fund effect, this overall view supports wider latitude for productive departures from the asset class benchmarks by any *active* managers chosen by the committee—particularly if the excess returns promised by those departures have a low correlation with the total fund returns.

FUNDAMENTAL OBJECTIVES

The top management of the sponsoring institution may set one or more *fundamental objectives* for their funds, including the following:

- **Asset-Only Performance**. Pension funds traditionally seek to maximize asset returns, subject to some measure of asset risk. Modern portfolio theory began with this objective, and it remains primary to

---

[2] In practice, the functions we assign to senior management/investment committee/asset managers may be subdivided or combined in a variety of ways, among committees, individuals, Board of Trustees, and the like.

[3] See Chapters 12 and 13.

most sponsors. Between two strategies with equal expected returns, asset-only investors will opt for the lower asset risk (commonly measured by volatility); between two equally risky strategies, they choose the higher expected return. Without regard to the specific liability, many sponsors note that under *any* conditions, greater fund growth improves the ability to pay benefits.

- **Surplus Performance.** Proponents of asset/liability management argue that the purpose of pension funds is to pay benefits to participants, not to maximize returns. Pension fund performance, therefore, should be evaluated in terms of benefit security. Although high asset returns are always better than low ones, it may be more important to ensure that high asset returns are coincident with high liability returns. Consider a simple example with assets and liabilities both equal to $150 million. The liabilities are volatile and will equal either $100 million or $200 million (with equal probability) at year-end. The sponsor compares the following two investment strategies:

  1. *A liability-matching strategy* produces assets of $100 million in the first case and $200 million in the second. The asset volatility is high, but the liabilities are always covered.

  2. *An asset-only strategy* consistently delivers assets of $155 million. The assets are perfectly stable, but the results can range from a $45-million deficit to a $55-million surplus.

  Because of a multitude of asymmetries in the financial impact of deficits and surpluses, a sponsor with liability concerns may embrace the liability-matching strategy, despite its lower average return *and* greater asset volatility.[4]

- **Performance Relative to Peer Group.** Interfund comparisons are another common performance measure. In addition to providing "safety in numbers," peer group performance indicates the returns achieved by investors with similar objectives, concerns, expertise, and market opportunities. Furthermore, corporate plan sponsors must keep their pension costs in line with those of their competitors. Radical departures from competitive practices may be justified on pure investment grounds, but they entail the risk of incurring pension costs that are materially different from those of competitors.

---

[4]The asymmetries include the confiscatory tax on surplus reversions, contrasted with the sponsor's full liability for deficits; the risk-related premium payable to the Pension Benefit Guaranty Corporation; the required reporting of plan deficits (but not surpluses) on the corporate balance sheet; and the accelerated funding requirements imposed on underfunded plans.

In each of the above areas, management must quantify its objectives so that they reflect reasonable capital market assumptions. Nothing is wrong with *wishing* to earn a 10% return through a market cycle, or to rank consistently in the top quartile of a peer group. However, an investment policy must be grounded in market realities and specific asset allocation possibilities. The investment committee responsible for pension investments should establish a *policy benchmark* that balances the prospect of fulfilling often-conflicting multiple objectives.

THE POLICY BENCHMARK

The policy benchmark is thus an asset allocation that should produce acceptable performance outcomes with regard to each of the objectives, given only "conventional" capital market assumptions, independent of any special market views. The policy benchmark is typically expressed as a simple mix of standard market indexes. For example, we can characterize the benchmark by its equity percentage, assumed to be invested in the S&P 500 Stock Index, and a fixed-income component, assumed to be invested in a broad bond market index with maturity cut-offs to achieve a specified duration. Figure 14–1 illustrates how the policy benchmark derives from the fundamental objectives.

Shortfall constraints are useful in dealing with multiple management objectives. A shortfall constraint represents a critical level of performance that the fund should achieve with a high degree of assurance. For example, the

Figure 14–1. The Policy Benchmark

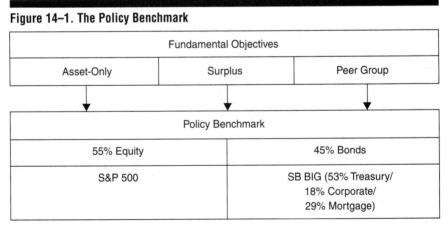

Fundamental Objectives		
Asset-Only	Surplus	Peer Group

Policy Benchmark	
55% Equity	45% Bonds
S&P 500	SB BIG (53% Treasury/ 18% Corporate/ 29% Mortgage)

SB BIG = Salomon Brothers Broad Investment-Grade Bond Index.

sponsor may require a 90% assurance that the one-year return will exceed –3%. A different target may be set for the surplus performance, and yet another for the performance relative to a peer group. Constraints may apply to varying time horizons, although we use one-year horizons for simplicity throughout this chapter. By tightening or loosening each constraint, the pension officer can reflect the relative weight that management attaches to each objective.

In the Appendix to this chapter, we illustrate the derivation of a policy benchmark that satisfies the following three shortfall constraints:

1. 90% assurance that the one-year asset return exceeds –3%.
2. 90% assurance that the one-year surplus return exceeds –8%.
3. 90% assurance that the one-year return relative to a peer group average exceeds –3%.

We show that a portfolio comprising 55% S&P 500 Stock Index and 45% Salomon Brothers Broad Investment-Grade (BIG) Bond Index meets each of these three objectives with some margin. Because this benchmark portfolio provides satisfactory performance characteristics, senior management should regard it as an acceptable standard against which to measure the pension fund management.

From the committee's viewpoint, this 55/45 policy benchmark has the advantage of permitting a range of strategic and tactical departures, while still meeting the three shortfall constraints. For example, under our assumed constraints and capital market characteristics, the Appendix to this chapter shows that the equity percentage could rise to 57.6%, or the bond duration could be set from 3.5 to 9.5 years, on a long-term *strategic* basis. *Tactical* departures from the benchmark also may be taken opportunistically.

THE STRATEGIC BENCHMARK

From the policy benchmark, the investment committee develops the *strategic benchmark*. The policy benchmark expresses management's objectives in terms of a simple mix of standard asset classes and benchmarks. The strategic benchmark, however, can go several steps further, as Figure 14–2 illustrates.

- The strategic benchmark may incorporate the committee's view that a small increase in the equity allocation is a sound *long-term* method of outperforming the policy benchmark, without undue risk. Alternatively, the benchmark may have a flexible mix, geared to the market cycle. (We have not incorporated such adjustments in Figure 14–2.)

Figure 14–2. The Strategic Benchmark

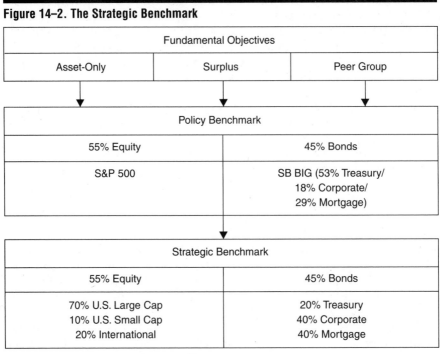

Fundamental Objectives		
Asset-Only	Surplus	Peer Group

Policy Benchmark	
55% Equity	45% Bonds
S&P 500	SB BIG (53% Treasury/ 18% Corporate/ 29% Mortgage)

Strategic Benchmark	
55% Equity	45% Bonds
70% U.S. Large Cap 10% U.S. Small Cap 20% International	20% Treasury 40% Corporate 40% Mortgage

SB BIG = Salomon Brothers Broad Investment-Grade Bond Index.

- Second, and perhaps more important, the strategic allocation *within* asset classes can deviate from the policy benchmark to reflect modest strategic market views that are expected to persist over the long term.[5]

The consequences of various deviations differ markedly for departures in the major risk class (equity) and those in the minor risk class (bonds). A typical departure in the equity component would be to diversify the S&P 500 benchmark into 70% large-cap domestic (perhaps reweighting the style components), 10% small-cap domestic, and 20% international. Conventional market views suggest that this change would produce equal or greater expected returns and less volatility.

---

[5]The policy benchmark should reflect only standard benchmarks that can be replicated by passive portfolios. The strategic benchmark, however, can also reflect investments that may be described as asset management *processes* rather than asset *classes*. For example, a tactical asset allocator may rotate among equities, bonds, and cash, using futures overlays. As another example, the committee may believe that a *passive* hedged foreign bond portfolio offers no intrinsic advantage over domestic bonds, but they may be persuaded that active management can consistently add value in such a portfolio.

When we turn from equity risk to bond risk, the case for latitude relative to the policy benchmark strengthens even further because of what we have labeled the total fund effect in a previous study.[6] This effect is the improvement in the reward/risk profile of an asset class investment strategy, which can occur when it is viewed in a total portfolio context. While the return of an asset class passes through proportionately to the overall fund, diversification effects may greatly dilute the volatility pass-through. For example, when we considered various historical departures that added return and volatility to the bond component of a 60% equity/40% bond portfolio, we found that (as expected) about 40% of the incremental return passed through to the total portfolio. However, only 20% to 25% of the incremental volatility passed through, nearly doubling the reward/risk ratio at the total fund level. Incremental bond risk, therefore, may have a modest impact on the total portfolio risk, and productive departures from the policy benchmark can have considerable appeal.

A common departure from the policy benchmark for the bond component lies in the belief that the market is too rich in short-term Treasuries. These securities are priced by investors seeking liquidity and short-term stability, attributes that pension funds should not value highly. Even intermediate- and long-term Treasuries may be more abundant in the market than in an effectively managed pension fund. Many investors believe that, with little added risk, they can consistently capture credit spreads in a diversified portfolio of corporate securities with suitable quality constraints. The substitution of such securities for Treasuries can dramatically improve the return/risk profiles of the bond portfolios and, to an even greater extent, the profile of the equity/bond portfolio within which they are embedded.[7]

Thus, the strategic benchmark establishes the asset allocation norms that will guide the management of the fund in its quest to outperform top management's policy benchmark. In this quest, the strategic benchmark can incorporate departures founded on stable, long-term market views. The benchmark may of course change when those views or management's objectives change.

CORRELATION OF STRATEGIC AND POLICY BENCHMARKS

In the previous section, we considered how the investment committee could transform the policy benchmark into a strategic benchmark with a superior

---

[6]See Chapter 12.
[7]See Chapter 13.

risk/return profile. This task raises a critical question: *Does the policy benchmark simply represent a standard for the return/risk profile of the fund, or must the fund performance adhere closely to the benchmark?* In other words, do we compare the absolute return and volatility of the fund with the policy benchmark, or do we focus on its tracking error?

If the policy benchmark is simply a risk/return standard, the committee might accept a strategic benchmark that differs radically from the benchmark but offers a comparable or improved balance of risk and return. A 100% foreign portfolio, for example, might occupy a similar, perhaps "more efficient," position in risk/return space. Although it might succeed or fail under entirely different circumstances, its comparable expected return and *absolute* volatility may make it a plausible strategic approach.

On the other hand, if the fund performance is expected to *track* the benchmark closely, the departures from the policy benchmark must be more measured and the strategic portfolio returns must be closely and *reliably* correlated with the policy benchmark. The returns must not only be similar or superior *on average*; they must be reasonably similar *at all times*.

There are important implications for those funds that can use the policy benchmark simply as a gauge of performance, rather than as a tracking straightjacket. Such funds can profitably replace the equity component of the policy benchmark with a combination of risky assets that promises equal or higher expected returns at equal or lesser risk—regardless of the correlations. Broad latitude also remains for the bond component. The strategic benchmark should then encompass diversified departures that are expected to improve upon the return/risk pattern of the policy benchmark, with reduced emphasis on tracking error.

This conclusion will *not* hold for a fund that is tightly constrained with regard to a well-defined benchmark or liability. Such a fund will need to closely match its equity component (if any) to the policy benchmark and exercise rigorous duration control. The strategic benchmark would have to correlate tightly with the policy benchmark. To achieve the necessary tracking, the committee should be mindful of the reliability of asset class or subclass correlations:

1. Correlations among securities of the same asset subclass, which have a fundamental resemblance, are reliably high. For example, a diversified portfolio of large-capitalization U.S. equities will correlate highly with the S&P 500 Index.

2. Correlations among securities of fundamentally different classes or subclasses, such as bonds/equities or U.S. equities/foreign equities, are statistical rather than fundamental. These correlations arise from

economic and market forces that can change gradually or rapidly, and the correlations can be quite unstable.

This distinction does not always hold. All domestic investment-grade bonds are driven largely by Treasury rates, so the correlations between investment-grade bond subclasses are dependably high. Equity subclasses, on the other hand, can be further subdivided into somewhat diverse groupings; there is no categorical definition of "subclass." In general, a sponsor facing a high correlation requirement could not rely substantially on statistical correlations between risky asset subclasses.

ASSET CLASS AND SUBCLASS BENCHMARKS

The investment committee can now parcel out the management of the fund among the various inside or outside managers. Each manager is responsible for managing a portion of the assets against an assigned *asset class benchmark*, which is a component of the strategic benchmark for the overall fund, as depicted in Figure 14–3.

Figure 14–3 illustrates a possible distribution of passive and active assignments. Some managers would simply be engaged to replicate their assigned asset class benchmarks. These assignments may reflect the committee's belief that they cannot obtain any structural advantage in the asset class that would justify the costs and risks of active management. Furthermore, even in an asset class in which the committee anticipates excess returns from active management, they may wish to establish an *indexed core*. This passive portfolio would provide reasonable overall tracking of the asset class benchmark. The committee would then expect its active managers, with only a portion of the asset class, to take *aggressive* tactical departures relative to their benchmarks. The result should be a more focused effort by the managers, and the fund avoids paying active management fees on the passive "deadweight" found in many "semiactive" funds. For example, the "passive" box under the bond asset class in Figure 14–3 replicates portions of the bond component of the strategic benchmark—all of the Treasury portion and half of the others. One manager may be assigned to run this as an index fund, while active specialists manage pure corporate and mortgage funds, reflecting the (arguable) view that active management of the Treasury component is less likely to prove productive.

Another factor should encourage a high level of activity among the active managers—the recognition that performance is ultimately judged not by the asset class returns in isolation, but by the fund's overall combination

Figure 14–3. Distributed Asset Class Benchmarks

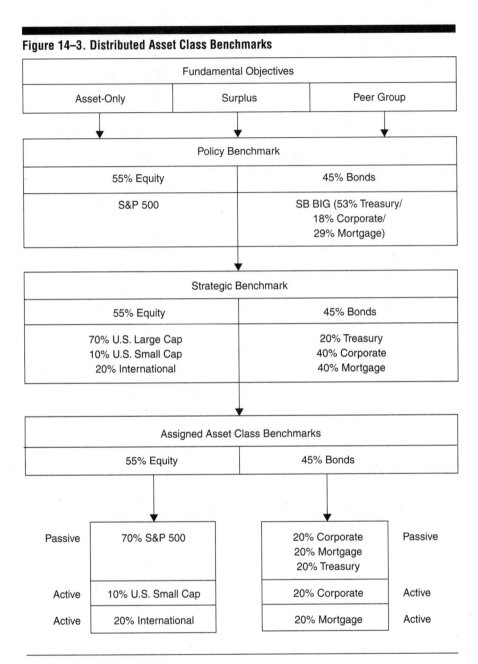

SB BIG = Salomon Brothers Broad Investment-Grade Bond Index.

of returns. The committee should therefore allow considerable latitude for productive departures from the asset class benchmarks because of the total fund effect discussed in the previous section. This effect is even stronger for tactical departures whose correlation with the basic asset class returns is weak—for example, yield-curve or risk premium plays that are generally expected to add value in good and bad markets. Ideally, an actively managed fund should subsume a variety of departures from the asset class benchmarks, each of which promises some incremental expected return. The departures should be weakly correlated, not only with the overall fund but with each other: Managers' bets should neither compound nor cancel each other.[8]

Thus, the strategic asset class benchmarks should serve as a guide and a standard to the asset class managers, but they should not inhibit the productive ventures of those active managers in whom the committee places its confidence. The committee should constrain asset class departures, not in narrow terms of local tracking error, but in the broader context of overall fund performance relative to the policy benchmark.

CONCLUSION

The size and importance of many pension funds call for senior management to articulate explicit objectives for fund performance. In this chapter, we illustrate how these objectives should flow through the following hierarchy of benchmarks that regulate the investment process:

- The *policy benchmark* is a passive mix of standard asset class indexes that best meets the key objectives of the fund, as defined by senior management. These objectives may include goals for asset-only performance, surplus control, and performance relative to a peer group.

- The *strategic benchmark* refines the policy benchmark in two ways:
    1. It can reflect stable long-term views about possible improvements relative to the standard market-weighted benchmarks—for example, by substituting corporate bonds for Treasuries, or by di-

---

[8]For other approaches to structuring the active/passive components of a fund, see "How to Use Security Analysis to Improve Portfolio Selection," Jack L. Treynor and Fischer Black, *The Journal of Business*, January 1973; *Active Portfolio Management*, Richard C. Grinold and Ronald N. Kahn, Probus Publishing, 1995; and "Benchmark Orthogonality Properties," David E. Tierney and Jeffery V. Bailey, *The Journal of Portfolio Management*, Spring 1995.

versifying equities beyond the domestic large-cap universe represented by the "standard" equity benchmarks.

2. It can add active management processes, such as tactical overlays, to the strategic allocation.

- The *assigned asset class/subclass benchmarks* are the components of the strategic benchmark that are delegated to the managers. Some asset classes may be fully passive because the sponsor doubts that active management can add sufficient value. For others, active management may be combined with an indexed core that provides low-cost tracking of the assigned benchmark. The sponsor should then encourage the active managers to be aggressive in their return-seeking departures from the benchmarks, because of the tracking stability of the passive core and the volatility dilution arising from the total fund effect.

APPENDIX

In this Appendix, we illustrate the derivation of a policy benchmark that satisfies multiple shortfall constraints.[9] By a shortfall constraint, we mean a critical level of performance that the fund should achieve with a high degree of assurance. For example, the sponsor may require a 90% assurance that the one-year return will exceed –3%.[10]

Figure 14–A1 illustrates the equity/bond mixes and the associated bond durations that meet a –3% shortfall constraint on one-year asset performance.[11]

The riskless portfolio (all cash; that is, 0% equity and 100% bonds with zero duration) would be at the origin. Departures from the origin introduce

Figure 14–A1. Acceptable Portfolios—Shortfall Threshold Equals –3% Asset Return

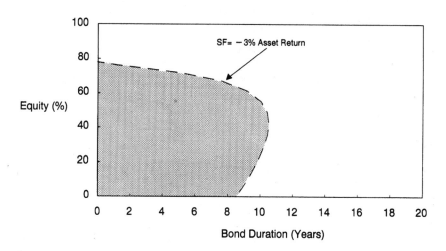

SF = shortfall.

---

[9]For details, see Chapter 3.

[10]It may be preferable to express the minimum return in relation to the 8% riskless rate—that is, the –3% shortfall constraint is equivalent to –11% relative to the one-year rate. Under this formulation, risk posture remains stable when rates change. Achieving a *fixed* minimum return, on the other hand, becomes more difficult in a low interest rate environment. See Chapters 8 and 9.

[11]We assume that returns are normally distributed, as follows: Equity Returns—Mean = 13%, Volatility = 15%, Bond Returns—Mean = 8%, Volatility = 1% × Year-End Duration, Equity/Bond Correlation = 0.35, Liability = 10-Year-Duration Bond. We assume that the initial assets are 130% of the liability.

risk; the shaded area of Figure 14–A1 encompasses the portfolios that meet the –3% shortfall constraint. For example, a portfolio consisting of 77% equity and 23% "cash" (one-year bonds with a year-end duration of zero) has a 90% probability of returning more than –3% in a year. An all-bond portfolio with an 8.6-year duration has the same shortfall risk.

If the sponsor's only concern was the absolute return, without regard to the liabilities or a peer group, the primary benchmark would be selected from the upper portion of the acceptable region, where the equity percentages and therefore the expected returns are the highest. If, however, surplus is also important, the sponsor may also wish to limit the surplus risk.

Surplus risk can be usefully expressed in terms of either the surplus dollars or the funding ratio (assets divided by liability). In this regard, we return to our earlier example, with initial assets and liabilities of $150 million, where the liability at year-end will be either $100 million ("Outcome A") or $200 million ("Outcome B"). Now suppose that two asset/liability management strategies are available, as set forth in Figure 14–A2. Strategy 1 always produces surplus of $15 million—that is, assets of $115 million in Outcome A and $215 million in Outcome B. Strategy 2 always produces a 110% funding ratio—assets of $110 million in Outcome A and $220 million in Outcome B. With both strategies having the same $15 million average ending surplus, which is preferable?

From a *fiduciary* viewpoint, the funding ratio may be the best measure of benefit security. In this sense, Strategy 1 is less stable. Outcome B, with a 107.5% funding ratio, has less margin of safety than the 115% Outcome A ratio; for example, it can absorb less of a future equity downturn, an extension of life expectancy, or a cluster of early retirements. Informed participants may prefer the assured 110% funding ratio of Strategy 2. Their concerns would best be addressed by focusing on the *funding ratio return* (FRR), the percentage change in the funding ratio.[12]

From a *corporate finance* viewpoint, however, the surplus dollars may be more important. After adjustment for income and perhaps excise taxes, they represent a source of shareholder value—as an ultimate cash reversion or a reduction in future contributions. Management may therefore favor Strategy 1, because its consistent $15-million surplus helps to stabilize shareholder wealth.

By law, the fiduciary viewpoint takes precedence over corporate finance considerations. In practice, the two approaches are quite similar. For simplicity, in this example, we assume that the committee accepts the second

---

[12]See Chapter 10.

Figure 14–A2. Two Asset/Liability Management Strategies

	Liability	Assets (Funding Ratio)	
		Strategy 1	Strategy 2
Outcome A	$100 Million	$115 Million (115%)	$110 Million (110%)
Outcome B	200 Million	215 Milion (107.5%)	220 Million (110%)

Figure 14–A3. Acceptable Portfolios—Shortfall Threshold Equals –3% Asset Return, –8% Surplus Return

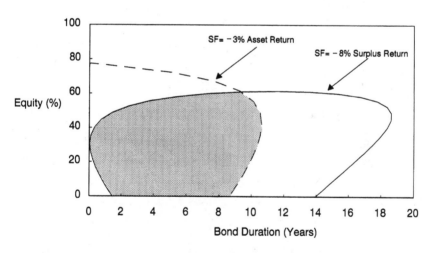

SF = shortfall.

view and uses a surplus return constraint, requiring at least 90% assurance that the *surplus return* (the dollar change in surplus divided by the initial liability) will not be less than –8%.[13] The solid curve in Figure 14–A3 encloses the range of portfolios that satisfy this condition; the curve centers roughly

---

[13]We assume that the assets initially equal 130% of the liability.

Figure 14–A4. Acceptable Portfolios—Shortfall Threshold Equals –3% Asset Return, –8% Surplus Return, –3% Relative to 60/40

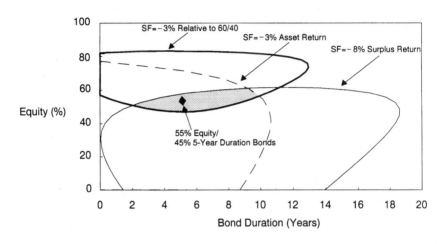

SF = shortfall.

on the riskless portfolio in the surplus context, an all-bond portfolio with a dollar duration that matches that of the liability.

The shaded area encompasses the portfolios that satisfy *both* the asset-only constraint and the surplus constraint. Some of the portfolios that have acceptable asset-only risk have inadequate surplus control, particularly those with low bond durations and high equity exposure. Thus, the highest-returning portfolios that meet the asset-only constraint are ruled out by surplus management considerations.

Now we suppose that the sponsor also wishes to match the performance of its competitors. Given the uncertainty and diversity of the asset allocations, this objective is not a well-defined investment goal. The pension officer may decide to approximate it with what he believes to be the competitors' average allocation—60% equity and 40% five-year-duration bonds.[14] The heavy curve in Figure 14–A4 encircles the range of portfolios that have at least 90% assurance of returning at least –3% relative to the 60/40 peer group target—that is, no more than a 10% chance of a 3% underperformance. (The curve "centers" approximately on the riskless portfolio in this relative return context, 60% equity and 40% five-year-duration bonds.)

---

[14]See Chapters 4 and 5.

The shaded region in Figure 14–A4 now defines the "triple-shortfall port-folios." Each portfolio in this region has at least a 90% chance of meeting each performance hurdle.[15] The highest-returning portfolio in the region, at the upper right-hand corner, comprises 61% equity and 39% nine-year-duration bonds. This portfolio, however, offers little room to maneuver and provides no margin for errors in the capital market assumptions. Also, it positions the bond portfolio at an outlying duration that may offer meager opportunity for yield enhancement.

The investment committee may instead select a more central portfolio as the policy benchmark, such as 55% equity (Standard & Poor's 500 Stock Index) and 45% Salomon BIG Index (approximately five-year duration). This benchmark, indicated by the diamond in Figure 14–A4, comfortably meets the key objectives: Its 10th-percentile asset return is –1.1% (versus a –3% requirement); the 10th-percentile surplus return is –7.6% (versus a –8% requirement); and the 10th-percentile asset return relative to a 60/40 peer group benchmark is –1.2% (versus a –3% requirement). Thus, this portfolio is a satisfactory policy benchmark both in meeting the key objectives and in offering some scope for productive strategic and tactical departures in the fund management.

---

[15]The probability of meeting all three conditions simultaneously will range from 70% to 90%, depending on the correlations among asset, surplus, and peer group performance.

Part II

Yield-Curve Positioning

A Shortfall Approach to Duration Management

INTRODUCTION

Over the past decade, fixed-income portfolio managers have almost universally embraced "duration" as the preeminent predictor of portfolio performance. The popularity of the duration measure stems from its ability to provide an estimate of the price response of fixed-income investments to sudden changes in interest rates. Duration provides more insight into prospective portfolio performance than any other single number, and as a result, selecting a target duration is one of the portfolio manager's most important decisions.

In many investment situations, special committees representing the sponsoring organization establish the maximum risk exposure that is consistent with their investment objectives. For the individuals who are involved in this process, it may be more important to have an approximate risk yardstick whose implications are well understood than to have a more refined theoretical measure that lacks intuitive appeal. Thus, in this chapter, we offer some intuitive solutions to portfolio risk management by providing a simple analytical model that offers a means of both quantifying downside risk and determining the maximum allowable duration within the established risk tolerance.

We will measure risk—not just by return volatility or duration, but also by the probability of shortfall over a predetermined horizon. The "shortfall probability" is a simple measure of downside risk that quantifies the likelihood that a given portfolio strategy will result in a performance "shortfall" relative to a specific return threshold. By transforming this risk measure into a "shortfall constraint," the manager can determine which portfolios can satisfy the minimum return requirements with a given probability.[1]

The shortfall approach can be applied to general investment portfolios that consist of a combination of asset classes, for example, equities, bonds, international securities, and real estate. Moreover, this approach can be generalized to address risks associated with returns measured relative to a specified market benchmark or index. However, to provide a concrete example, we will focus the following discussion on setting the duration of a single-currency fixed-income portfolio.

To simplify the exposition, we first consider the case of a flat yield curve and one-year investment horizon. Later, we relax both of these assumptions. We show how the methodology can be applied to both a multiyear investment horizon and the case of a rising yield curve.

A SIMPLE MODEL FOR BOND RETURNS

Fixed-income portfolio managers typically are faced with a dilemma. From a long-term point of view, there may be many reasons to extend duration. In a liability context, volatility of surplus generally can be minimized by matching the duration of the assets to that of the liabilities. In addition, in a total return context, if the yield curve is fairly steep and positively sloped, the manager may hope to gain higher expected returns by extending maturity/duration. However, regardless of the long-term objective, portfolio performance still must be evaluated at regular intervals over the short term. Thus, we must always consider the short-term consequences of long-term duration targets. Because duration measures the sensitivity of price to changes in interest rates, long-duration instruments will react most violently to rate fluctuations. Sponsors and managers will be elated if the market rallies and their portfolio outperforms the market. However, they will be dismayed if their portfolio underperforms the market. This situation is complicated further by the desire to avoid negative returns, regardless of the market performance. Sponsors are unlikely to be pleased if the portfolio outperforms the market but still suffers a negative return. In a sense, when the market slumps, there is a natural tendency to compare the portfolio results—retroactively—to the risk-free rate.

---

[1]The concept of a shortfall constraint is discussed in greater detail in "Portfolio Optimization with Shortfall Constraints: A Confidence-Limit Approach to Managing Downside Risk," Martin L. Leibowitz and Roy D. Henriksson, *Financial Analysts Journal*, March/April 1989.

Figure 15–1. The Flat Yield Curve

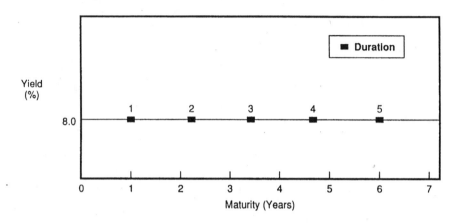

To simplify our study of the impact of rate volatility, we make several assumptions. First, we begin with the assumption that the yield curve is flat, so that bonds of all durations offer precisely the same 8% yield. This yield curve is illustrated in Figure 15–1, where we also indicate the duration associated with various maturities.[2] Our second simplifying assumption is that the expected return over any horizon is equal to the yield. Finally, we avoid reinvestment effects over a one-year horizon by assuming that coupon payments are made annually.

As we move to the right along the yield curve, the expected return over a one-year horizon remains 8%, but the volatility inherent in that return increases. Naturally, over a one-year holding period, a one-year Treasury bill will provide an 8% return. That is, the return volatility is zero, because the security is being held to maturity and there is no price or reinvestment risk. As we move further to the right along the yield curve, the duration increases and the expected return is accompanied by greater volatility as a result of

---

[2]In this chapter, the "duration" generally should be assumed to be the Macaulay duration. When actually computing the sensitivity of price to instantaneous changes in yield, we must use the modified duration. See, for example, *Understanding Duration and Volatility*, Salomon Brothers Inc, September 1985.

increased price variability over the one-year holding period. The impact of yield change on price is illustrated in Figure 15–2 for a four-year-duration bond.

To obtain a more complete picture of return volatility, we must introduce a model of how interest rates change over a one-year horizon. To this end, we assume that interest-rate *changes* follow a normal distribution with a zero mean and a standard deviation of 150 basis points at all points along the yield curve. This distribution of interest-rate changes is illustrated in Figure 15–3 and is generally consistent with the distribution of 12-month rate changes observed over the past 10 years.

As a result of the assumption of a normal distribution, 68% of the rate changes are in the range of plus or minus 150 basis points (that is, within one standard deviation of the mean rate change of 0%). Thus, our normality assumption implies that there is an 84% probability that yields will remain above 6.5% (that is, the expected yield of 8% less 150 basis points).

The distribution of interest-rate changes can be linked to the distribution of returns by means of a convenient approximate formula (see the Appendix to this chapter). For example, if the flat yield curve undergoes a 150-basis-point parallel shift over a one-year horizon, a four-year-duration bond will experience an average absolute deviation of approximately 4.5% from its expected return. In other words, if the yield volatility is 150 basis points, the return volatility will be about 450 basis points. The distribution of interest-rate changes depicted in Figure 15–3 therefore leads to the distribution of returns in Figure 15–4.[3]

THE SHORTFALL RISK CONSTRAINT

Now, we reexamine our return distribution with an eye toward the likelihood of "unacceptable" returns. For example, for the distribution in Figure 15–4, 10% of the returns will be below 2.2%, as illustrated by the shaded region in Figure 15–5. We describe this situation by saying that there is a 10% "shortfall risk" that the return on the four-year-duration bond will fall below a 2.2% threshold. Of course, there is also a 90% probability that the returns will be above 2.2%.

---

[3]For ease of exposition, we show a normal return distribution. In fact, a normal distribution of yield changes leads to a somewhat skewed return distribution, and this skewness increases with convexity. Thus, for example, in the case of an extreme barbell portfolio, there will be a significant departure from normality.

Figure 15-2. The Impact of Yield Changes (One-Year Horizon)

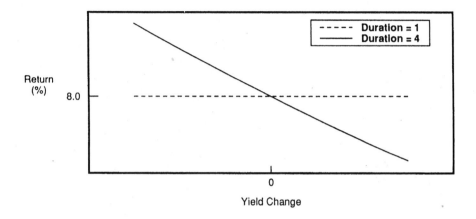

Figure 15-3. The Distribution of Interest Rate Changes (One-Year Horizon)

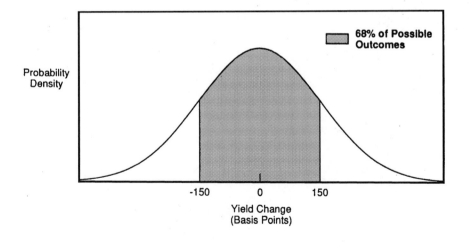

Figure 15–4. The Return Distribution of a Four-Year-Duration Bond (One-Year Horizon)

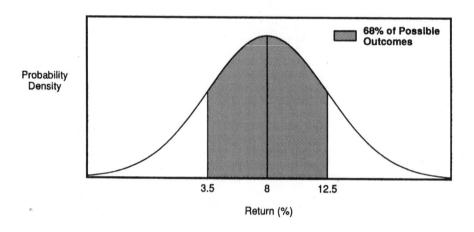

Figure 15–5. The 10th-Percentile Return (Four-Year-Duration Bond)

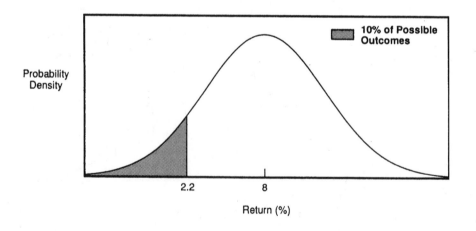

Shortfall risk addresses the "bad side" of risk. In this sense, it provides a more intuitive yardstick and is easier to communicate than the more traditional statistical risk measure, return volatility.[4] In addition, as we shall see, the shortfall risk affords a simple interpretation when viewed in terms of a return/risk diagram.

We introduce the shortfall approach using an example. Suppose that the fund sponsor has specified the following "shortfall constraint":

It is required that there be at most a 10% probability that returns over a one-year horizon fall below a 3% threshold.[5]

Or, equivalently:

It is required that there be at least a 90% probability that returns over a one-year horizon lie above a 3% threshold.

We already have observed that there is a 10% probability that returns on our four-year-duration bond will fall below 2.2% over a one-year horizon. Thus, this bond clearly fails to meet the shortfall constraint, because it will bear a greater than 10% probability that its return will fall below 3%. To fulfill the shortfall constraint, we must create a portfolio with a lower shortfall probability by either shortening duration or increasing expected return.

Because duration lengthens as we move to the right along the yield curve, it follows that the "riskiness" of returns also increases.[6] In Figure 15–6, we illustrate the relationship between expected return and risk by using duration as the risk measure. As indicated earlier, we assume that the expected return and yield are equal.

The impact of duration on shortfall risk is illustrated in Figure 15–7. In this case, we maintain an 8% expected return and superimpose the return

---

[4]The shortfall probability is an incomplete measure of risk, because it fails to provide any indication of how bad the shortfall will be in the event that one should occur. For a more fully developed theory of shortfall analysis that incorporates these "higher" considerations, see "Asset Pricing in a Generalized Mean-Lower Partial Moment Framework: Theory and Evidence," W. V. Harlow and R. Rao, in *Journal of Financial and Quantitative Analysis*, September 1989; and "Capital Market Equilibrium in a Mean, Lower Partial Moment Framework," V. Bawa and E. B. Lindenberg, in *Journal of Financial Economics*, November 1977.

[5]There is no obvious "correct" choice of the appropriate minimum return threshold. Rather, it is likely to be arrived at after consideration of a variety of factors, such as the sponsor's objectives and risk tolerance.

[6]In general, return volatility depends on both duration and the level of interest-rate volatility. Because we have assumed that interest-rate volatility is the same at all points on the yield curve, only duration changes as we move along the yield curve.

Figure 15–6. Expected Return versus Risk (Duration) in the Case of a Flat Yield Curve and One-Year Horizon

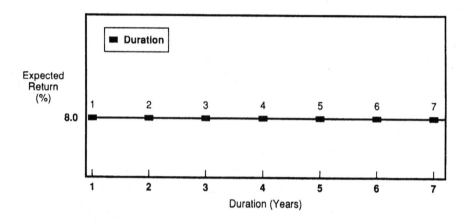

Figure 15–7. Probability of Returns Below 3%: Expected Return = 8%; Duration = 3.6 and 4.0 Years

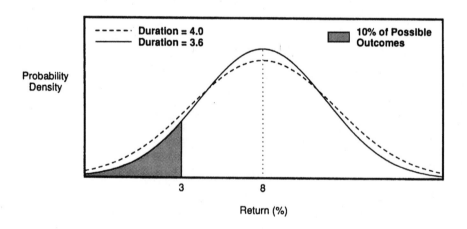

distributions that correspond to durations of 3.6 and 4.0 years. The shorter duration leads to the diminished "spread" of the return distribution. As a result, a decreasing proportion of returns falls below the 3% threshold. In particular, a reduction in the duration from 4.0 to 3.6 years leads to a return distribution in which precisely 10% of the returns fall below the 3% threshold. Any further duration reduction would lead to an even smaller likelihood of returns below 3%. Thus, the maximum permissible duration for the given shortfall constraint is 3.6 years. All longer-duration portfolios will have a greater than 10% probability of returns falling below 3%.

THE SHORTFALL LINE

The impact of changes in expected return on shortfall risk is illustrated in Figure 15–8. We have superimposed the return distributions that correspond to expected returns of 8.0% and 8.8%, while maintaining a four-year duration. Because duration (and hence volatility) is held constant, the shape of the distribution is preserved, while the entire distribution shifts to the right as the expected return increases. Thus, higher expected returns decrease the proportion of returns that fall below the 3% threshold. In particular, when

Figure 15–8. Probability of Returns Below 3%: Duration = 4.0 Years; Expected Return = 8% and 8.8%

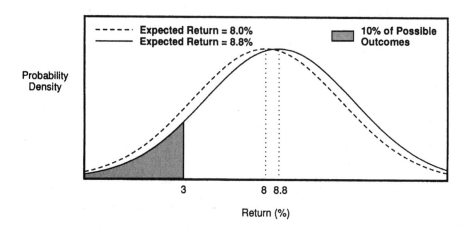

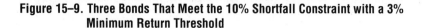

Figure 15–9. Three Bonds That Meet the 10% Shortfall Constraint with a 3% Minimum Return Threshold

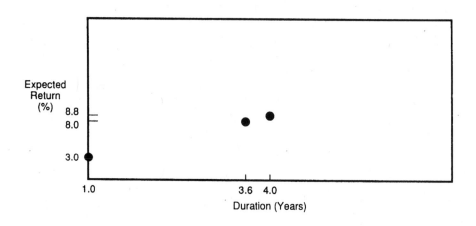

the expected return reaches the 8.8% level, only 10% of the returns fall below the 3% threshold, and the shortfall constraint is fulfilled.

Now we have two expected return/duration combinations that meet the shortfall constraint over a one-year horizon. These two combinations are illustrated as points in Figure 15–9. In addition, a one-year-duration bond with an expected return of 3% would experience no volatility over a one-year holding period. This bond will achieve the 3% minimum return threshold and also is shown as a third point in Figure 15–9.

The fact that the three points just mentioned appear to fall on a straight line is not coincidental. Under fairly general conditions on the return distribution, a straight line will depict the relationship between a portfolio's duration and the expected return required to satisfy a shortfall constraint (see the Appendix to this chapter). This relationship is valid for all yield curves and is illustrated by the "shortfall line" in Figure 15–10.

The shortfall line intercepts the expected return axis at the minimum return threshold (which is 3% in our example). Its slope depends solely on the shortfall probability. All portfolios with return/duration combinations on or above the shortfall line will have at least a 90% probability of achieving a return greater than 3%; that is, they satisfy the shortfall constraint. All points below the line represent return/duration combinations that lead to more than

---

Figure 15–10. The 10% Shortfall Line with a 3% Minimum Return Threshold (One-Year Horizon)

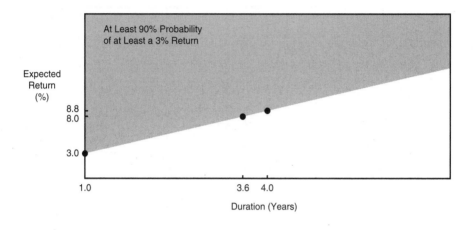

a 10% chance of failing to achieve a 3% return over a one-year horizon; that is, they fail to satisfy the shortfall constraint. In Figure 15–11, we superimpose return distributions at several points along the shortfall line. As we already have seen, as duration lengthens, so does the spread of the distribution, and higher expected returns are required as an offset. Thus, the shortfall line divides the return/risk diagram into two regions: the upper region, where the shortfall constraint is satisfied; and the lower region, where it is not.

DURATION TARGETING WITH A SHORTFALL CONSTRAINT

The shortfall line now can be used to locate portfolios that can be expected to meet or exceed the shortfall constraint. To illustrate how this is done, we make the simplifying assumption that the yield curve represents all investment opportunities. In this case, Figure 15–6 can be interpreted as an "efficient frontier," with risk being measured by duration. In Figure 15–12, we superimpose the 10% shortfall line on this efficient frontier. Because all portfolios that fall on or above the shortfall line fulfill the minimum return requirements, the part of the efficient frontier that falls above this line contains

Figure 15–11. The 10% Shortfall Line with Corresponding Return Distributions

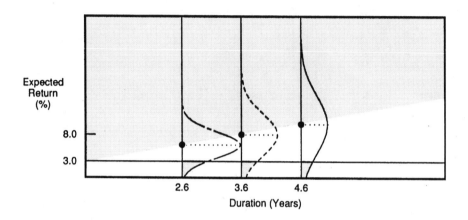

Figure 15–12. The 10% Shortfall Constraint and the Efficient Frontier

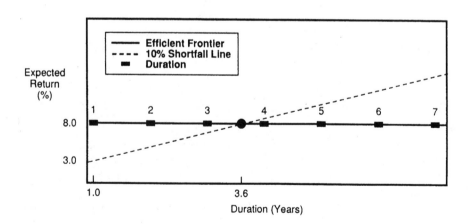

Figure 15–13. The Shortfall Constraint with Varying Shortfall Probabilities

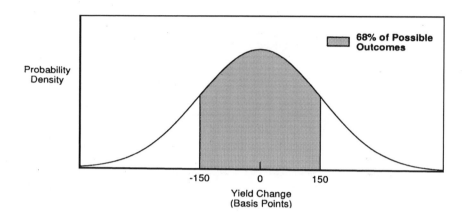

all admissible portfolios. Thus, the longest admissible duration portfolio will be found at the point where the shortfall line "cuts" the efficient frontier. This more general methodology, of course, leads to the same 3.6-year maximum duration as we found earlier.

VARIATIONS IN THE SHORTFALL SPECIFICATION

In this section, we consider the impact of changes in the shortfall probability and in the minimum return threshold on the longest admissible duration. For example, suppose our portfolio manager was willing to tolerate an increase from 10% to 15% in the probability of returns falling below the 3% threshold. This weaker 15% shortfall constraint is represented by a shortfall line that has a lower slope than for the 10% constraint. As a result, the point of intersection between the efficient frontier and the shortfall line moves to the right, and the maximum portfolio duration extends to about 4.2 years. By contrast, a 5% shortfall probability implies a steeper shortfall line that reduces the maximum allowable duration to 3.0 years. These results are illustrated in Figure 15–13.

Figure 15–14. The Shortfall Constraint with Varying Threshold Returns

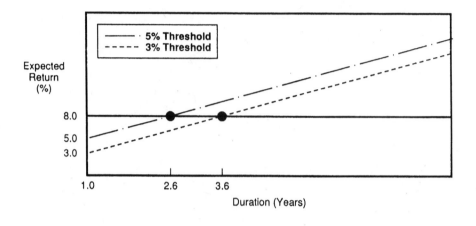

The implication of an increase in the minimum return threshold from 3% to 5% is illustrated in Figure 15–14, where the shortfall probability remains at our original 10% level. Because the shortfall probability does not change, the slope of the shortfall line is the same as for a 10% probability of the return falling below a 3% threshold. The only difference in the two shortfall lines is that the intercept with the return axis has been raised to 5%. This "lifting" of the shortfall line implies that less volatility (that is, less duration) can be tolerated. Thus, the maximum allowable duration now is reduced to about 2.6 years.

SHORTFALL CONSTRAINTS WITH VARYING INTEREST-RATE VOLATILITY

To this point, we have assumed that the interest-rate volatility is 150 basis points per year. Now we consider the impact of changes in the rate volatility assumptions on our duration target. As rate volatility increases, so does the return volatility and, hence, the risk of shortfall. Thus, we should expect that in a high volatility environment, we will have to shorten duration to meet the shortfall constraint.

Figure 15–15. The Impact of Rate Volatility on the Duration Target

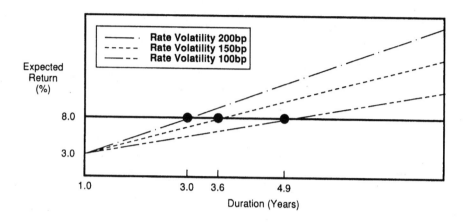

In our shortfall model, as illustrated in Figure 15–15, the slope of the shortfall line increases with greater rate volatility (see the Appendix to this chapter). As the slope increases, the point at which the shortfall line cuts the efficient frontier moves to the left, thereby reducing the maximum admissible duration. For example, if the rate volatility rises to 200 basis points per year, the new shortfall line intersects the efficient frontier at a duration of only 3.0 years, compared with 3.6 years for a rate volatility of 150 basis points per year. Similarly, if the rate volatility drops to 100 basis points per year, the maximum allowable duration increases to 4.9 years.

THE MULTIYEAR INVESTMENT HORIZON: FLAT YIELD CURVE

To this point, we have been considering a one-year investment horizon. To illustrate how the methodology of this chapter can be extended to longer horizons, we now turn our attention to an analysis of a two-year investment horizon. In this case, the 10% shortfall constraint allows for considerably longer-duration portfolios.

Figure 15–16. The One- and Two-Year "Efficient Frontier": Flat Yield Curve

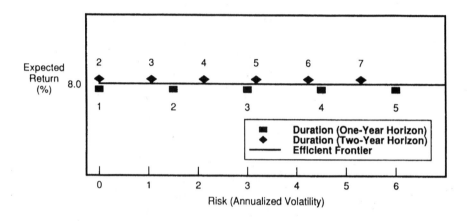

Over multiyear horizons, the relationship between risk, duration, and interest-rate volatility becomes more complicated (see the Appendix for a more detailed discussion). Consequently, it is convenient to depart from the use of duration as our risk measure and return to the more traditional risk measure, the standard deviation of returns. In Figure 15–16, we illustrate the assumed relationship between expected return and risk. On the upper side of the "efficient frontier," we indicate the durations that correspond to various risk levels over a two-year horizon. On the lower side of the "efficient frontier," we do the same for a one-year horizon.

Observe that, for a two-year horizon, at any duration there is a decrease in the volatility of the *annualized* expected return. For example, observe that the annualized return of a four-year-duration bond is less volatile over a two-year horizon than over a one-year horizon. This volatility decrease is the result of two effects. First, price sensitivity declines as the horizon approaches the duration. Second, we implicitly assume that interest rates follow a random walk. Consequently, interest-rate volatility increases fairly slowly as the holding period lengthens and the impact of this volatility on annualized returns actually decreases.

The 10% shortfall line with a 3% minimum return threshold now can be

Figure 15–17. The Multiyear Shortfall Constraint: Flat Yield Curve

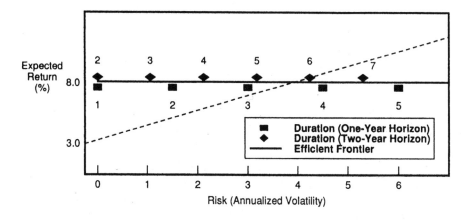

superimposed on the efficient frontier,[7] as illustrated in Figure 15–17. A single shortfall line can be used for both the one- and two-year horizons, because we have used the *annualized* return and *annualized* return volatility as our expected return and risk measures. The admissible portfolios now have a maximum duration of about 5.7 years for a 2-year horizon, compared with only 3.6 years over a 1-year horizon.

The maximum duration that meets the two-year shortfall constraint will, as in the case of a one-year horizon, be sensitive to both the specified shortfall probability and minimum return threshold. Figure 15–18 exhibits the maximum duration under both a 10% and 20% shortfall constraint for a range of threshold returns.

Under similar shortfall constraints, a two-year horizon always leads to a considerably longer permissible duration than a one-year horizon. In addition, the sensitivity of the permissible duration to changes in the return threshold varies with both the shortfall probability and the investment horizon.

---

[7]The equation of the shortfall line must be recast in terms of the standard deviation of returns, which is our new risk measure. The result, which is derived in the Appendix to this chapter, is as follows:

Required Expected Return = Risk Factor × Return Volatility + Threshold Return.

For example, with a 10% shortfall probability and a one-year horizon, the duration decreases by about one-half year for each 100-basis-point increase in return threshold. By contrast, at a 20% shortfall probability (and a one-year horizon), when the return threshold increases by 100 basis points, the maximum permissible duration decreases by about three-fourths of a year.

In addition, observe that as the horizon increases, so does the duration change. For example, at a 20% shortfall probability, a 100-basis-point increase in the threshold return leads to a decrease in duration of about 1.1 years over a 2-year horizon and 1.4 years over a 3-year horizon (not shown in Figure 15–18).

As indicated earlier in this chapter, portfolio managers often labor under different constraints for different investment horizons. For example, suppose that a portfolio manager is fairly risk tolerant over a one-year horizon and can accept a 20% probability of a one-year return less than 3%. This constraint implies a maximum duration of 5.0 years. However, suppose that over a two-year horizon, this same manager can tolerate only a 10% probability of an annualized return below 6%. This second constraint implies a maximum duration of 3.5 years—about 1 1/2 years shorter than the 1-year maximum allowable duration. If we make the static assumption that a single portfolio is bought and held for the entire 2-year period, the maximum acceptable duration that will enable *both* constraints to be fulfilled is 3.5 years.[8] This example illustrates how our analysis can be applied to determine the maximum duration that will fulfill a combination of multiyear constraints. Keep in mind, however, that the analysis is sensitive to the actual shape of the one- and two-year efficient frontiers.

THE RISING YIELD CURVE CASE

Although we have assumed a flat yield curve in the preceding development, the methodology of this chapter can be applied to any yield curve. To illustrate how this is done, assume that the yield curve is positively sloped with a one-year bond yielding 8.0%.

As we move to the right along the yield curve, we again make the assumption that the expected return is equal to the yield. In Figure 15–19, we

---

[8]For an in-depth discussion of the implications of targeted duration strategies where the portfolio is periodically rebalanced to maintain a constant duration, see "Duration Targeting and the Management of Multiperiod Returns," Terence C. Langetieg, Martin L. Leibowitz, and Stanley Kogelman, *Financial Analysts Journal*, September/October 1990. See also *Liability Management—A Developing Country Perspective*, Janet L. Showers, Mark Koenigsberg, and John McClure, presented at The Salomon Brothers Asset and Liability Workshop for Monetary Authorities, May 1989.

Figure 15–18. Maximum Permissible Duration for Varying Constraints (Flat Yield Curve at 8%)

Threshold Return	10% Shortfall Probability		20% Shortfall Probability	
	Horizon 1 Year	Horizon 2 Years	Horizon 1 Year	Horizon 2 Years
0	5.2 Yrs.	7.9 Yrs.	7.3 Yrs.	11.0 Yrs.
1	4.6	7.1	6.5	9.8
2	4.1	6.4	5.7	8.7
3	3.6	5.7	*5.0*	7.6
4	3.1	4.9	4.2	6.5
5	2.6	4.2	3.4	5.4
6	.2.0	*3.5*	2.6	4.2
7	1.5	2.7	1.8	3.1
8	1.0	2.0	1.0	2.0

Figure 15–19. Expected Return versus Risk: Rising Yield Curve and One-Year Horizon

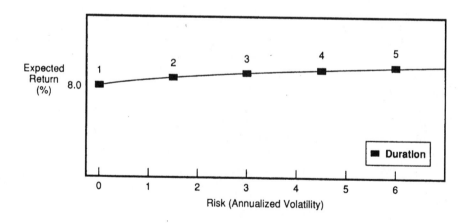

illustrate the "efficient frontier" for a one-year investment horizon. The risk measure is the standard deviation of returns, and the duration at various risk levels is indicated in the figure.

Figure 15–20. The Shortfall Constraint: Rising Yield Curve

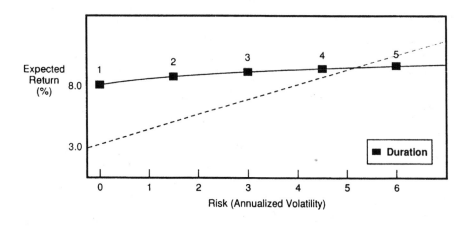

Now, in Figure 15–20, we superimpose the 10% shortfall line with a 3% return threshold on the "efficient frontier" in Figure 15–19. Because all portfolios that fall on or above the shortfall line fulfill the minimum return requirements, the part of the efficient frontier that falls above this line contains all admissible portfolios. Observe that the longest admissible duration is about 4.4 years, more than three-fourths of a year longer than the 3.6-year duration limit in our example of a flat yield curve.

At this point, the extension of the shortfall methodology to arbitrary yield curves is straightforward. It simply requires superimposing the shortfall constraint on the appropriate efficient frontier and then locating the point of intersection with the shortfall line. The same is true for a two-year "efficient frontier" (see Figure 15–21). Observe that the longest admissible duration is about 7.2 years over a 2-year holding period, almost 3 years longer than the duration limit for a 1-year holding period.

SUMMARY AND CONCLUSION

In this chapter, we first showed how a portfolio manager's need to achieve a certain minimum return even in the case of generally poor market performance could be expressed as a shortfall constraint. Then, we demonstrated

Figure 15–21. The Multiyear Shortfall Constraint: Rising Yield Curve

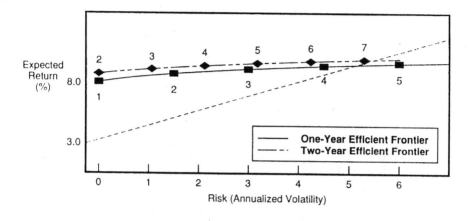

how this shortfall constraint could be used to refine the portfolio duration targeting process over one-year and multiyear horizons. This process allowed for the longest duration consistent with the portfolio risk tolerance.

We also noted that, for a given shortfall constraint, the longest admissible duration is sensitive to the estimated volatility of interest rates. Thus, in a market in which the volatility estimate changes over time, one cannot focus solely on setting a fixed duration limit. In such a context, the shortfall approach provides a natural process for adjusting the duration limit required to meet a specified minimum return threshold.

The actual application of the methodology of this chapter is straightforward once shortfall limits consisting of a minimum return threshold and a shortfall tolerance are set. Often, however, the portfolio manager does not explicitly think in these terms and may not have a well-defined return threshold or shortfall tolerance in mind. In such a case, our model can be used as a tool for testing the impact of various shortfall limits on the maximal permissible duration. In addition, given a duration target, we can back into the implied shortfall probability and gain new insight into the risk inherent in the portfolio's current duration level. Thus, the methodology of this chapter can be helpful in finding a practical resolution to the conflicting objectives that are often encountered in the practice of portfolio management.

APPENDIX

The Babcock Formula for Estimating Annualized Compound Return

If yields undergo an instantaneous parallel shift and remain at the new level until the horizon, the impact of the yield change on returns can be approximated by the following formula:[9]

Return Change ≈ (1 – Duration/Horizon) × Yield Change.

In this formula, the duration is the Macaulay duration, and the return change is the difference between the annualized compound return and the yield to maturity (assuming that the bond under consideration pays annually). The real power of this formula becomes apparent when observing that it holds for horizons that may be *either* shorter *or* longer than the duration.

To illustrate the Babcock formula, assume that a four-year-duration, annual-pay bond yields 8%. If yields undergo a 150-basis-point shift, the formula predicts that the resulting return change over a one-year horizon will be approximately 4.5%.[10]

The Shortfall Line

Suppose we wish to locate all portfolios whose return/risk characteristics are such that there is a probability k that the annualized compound return $\tilde{R}$ will exceed some minimum threshold R_{min}. This requirement can be expressed as follows:

$$P[\tilde{R} \quad R_{min}] = k.$$

This is equivalent to

$$P[(\tilde{R} - \bar{R})/\sigma \quad (R_{min} - \bar{R})/\sigma] = k,$$

---

[9]The return approximation formula was developed by Babcock and is discussed at length in "Duration Analysis: Managing Interest Rate Risk," Gerald O. Bierwag, 1987, Chapter 5. A simplified derivation of this formula is provided in "Duration Targeting and the Management of Multiperiod Returns."

[10]If yields move down by 150 basis points, the actual deviation from the yield to maturity is +4.63. If yields move up by 150 basis points, the actual return deviation is –4.37. The difference in the effects of upward and downward shifts reflects convexity effects that the first order Babcock formula does not take into account. The average absolute deviation is 4.5%, which is in agreement with our estimate.

where $\bar{R}$ is the mean return and σ is the standard deviation of returns. If the quantity to the left of the inequality is a standard normal variate, we can determine a positive value z_k (assuming $k > 0.5$) for the cumulative normal distribution such that

$$P[\tilde{R} \quad R_{min}] = k,$$

provided that

$$(R_{min} - \bar{R})/\sigma = -z_k$$

or

$$\bar{R} = z_k \sigma + R_{min}.$$

The above relationship is satisfied by all portfolios whose return/risk point lies above the "shortfall line" with slope z_k emanating from the minimum return threshold point R_{min} on the return axis. For example, if $k = 0.90$, then $z_k = 1.282$.

The shortfall line can be related to interest-rate volatility and duration by means of the Babcock formula. For example, if the horizon is one year, the Babcock formula predicts the return volatility σ as follows:

$$\sigma = (\text{Duration} - 1) \times \text{Interest-Rate Volatility}.$$

Using this relationship, we can write the shortfall line as:

Required Expected Return = $z_k \times$ (Duration – 1) × Interest-Rate Volatility
+ Threshold Return.

Over a two-year horizon, the interest-rate volatility under the assumption that interest rates follow a random walk is $\sqrt{2}$ times the one-year interest-rate volatility. In this case, by using the Babcock formula, we find the following equation for the shortfall line:

Required Expected Return = $z_k \times$ (Duration – 2)($\sqrt{2}/2$) × One-Year
Interest Rate Volatility + Threshold Return.

Chapter 16

Statistical Duration: A Spread Model of Rate Sensitivity across Fixed-Income Sectors

INTRODUCTION

In an earlier chapter, we used a statistical approach to explore the interest-rate sensitivity of equities as an asset class.[1] By computing a "statistical" duration, based on the correlation between equity returns and the yield movements in U.S. Treasuries, we estimated the duration of equities. These equity studies have proven helpful in conceptualizing the return/risk relationships that are central to asset allocation studies where defined liabilities are present.

In this chapter, we come full circle and explore how this technique can be adapted to find statistical durations in both foreign and domestic fixed-income markets. We use a simple model that treats a fixed-income sector as consisting of generic bonds with prescribed cash flows.[2] At the outset, we consider a single domestic "non-Treasury" sector that trades at some yield

---

[1]See Chapter 6; *A Total Differential Approach to Equity Duration*, Martin L. Leibowitz, Eric H. Sorensen, Robert D. Arnott, and H. Nicholas Hanson, Salomon Brothers Inc, December 1987; and *Total Portfolio Duration*, Martin L. Leibowitz, Salomon Brothers Inc, February 1986.

[2]The precise calculation of duration is straightforward for Treasury securities, but it can be very complex for securities with optional redemption features such as corporate bonds and mortgage-backed securities. For example, see *Beyond Duration: Risk Dimensions of Mortgage Securities*, Michael Waldman, Salomon Brothers Inc, July 1992; *Managing Yield Curve Exposure: Introducing Reshaping Durations*, Thomas E. Klaffky, Y. Y. Ma, and Ardavan Nozari, Salomon Brothers Inc, June 1992; *Effective Duration of Callable Bonds: The Salomon Brothers Term Structure-Based Option Pricing Model*, Mark Koenigsberg and William Boyce, Salomon Brothers Inc, April 1987; and *Evaluating the Option Features of Mortgage Securities*, Michael Waldman, Salomon Brothers Inc, September 1986.

spread to comparable-maturity Treasuries. Changes in the Treasury market will influence the prices of non-Treasuries, both directly through the Treasury yield change and indirectly through induced spread changes. There may be further movement in the yield spread as a result of other factors that are unrelated to the Treasury market, such as changing credit perceptions.

We capture all Treasury-related risk with a cross-sector "statistical duration" measure. This approach adjusts the standard duration to better reflect the impact of both the direct Treasury yield changes and the induced spread changes.[3] The statistical duration may be longer or shorter than the standard duration, depending on such factors as the magnitude of intermarket correlations, the current level of spreads, and the direction in which spreads tend to move. By defining the statistical duration in this way, we help clarify the principle that consistent spread behavior can have an important impact on sensitivity to Treasury rate changes. For example, many market participants believe that spreads should bear a percentage relationship to the level of yields. However, it is not widely appreciated that any such relationship, even if it were stable only over specific time periods, would significantly affect the appropriate duration values for structuring multisector portfolios.

In our model, we regard the non-Treasury–induced spread changes as an intrinsic risk associated with the sector. We show how these Treasury "rate-independent" spread risks can be estimated, and how portfolios can be constructed to minimize such risks. Unlike Treasury-related risks, however, the intrinsic risk of a *single* non-Treasury sector cannot be hedged or "durationed away" through combination with Treasury securities.

Our presentation of the statistical duration is cast in terms of a simplified model based on simulated spread relationships. In actual market situations, the underlying spread/rate relationships usually are difficult to determine and tend to be subject to the special market conditions that exist at specific times. However, we believe that, as a theoretical concept, the statistical duration can prove to be a useful guide in thinking about portfolio construction, particularly within an asset/liability context.

---

[3]The multiplicity of commonly used duration measures can easily lead to confusion. For any non-Treasury asset, we use the term "standard duration" to refer to the commonly used measure of rate sensitivity. For a noncallable bond, the modified duration measures the response to changes in the bond's own yield. For callable corporates and mortgages, an effective duration is used to capture the impact of each security's optional redemption features.

SPREAD EFFECTS

Throughout this chapter, we focus on an example consisting of a non-Treasury fixed-income asset class (referred to as NT) that trades at a positive yield spread to comparable-duration Treasury securities (symbolized by TSY). Both corporate and mortgage securities are examples of such an NT asset class. To make our development more concrete, we make several simplifying assumptions:

- The TSY yield curve is flat, with all securities yielding 5%. (This unrealistic assumption is not restrictive and is used only to simplify our discussion.)
- The NT sector includes securities that trade at spreads ranging from 25 basis points over the short end to 140 basis points over the eight-year point of the flat Treasury curve (see Figure 16–1).
- All yield-curve shifts are parallel so that absolute yield volatility is uniform across maturities. (Thus, any yield spread changes are assumed to apply simultaneously to all maturities within the NT sector.)

Figure 16–1. Yield versus Duration for Non-Treasury and Treasury Securities

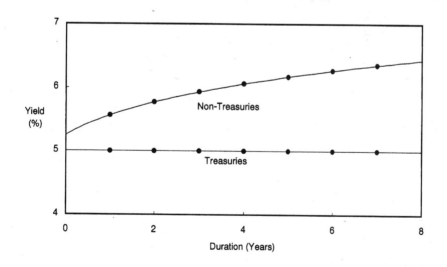

- Investments are evaluated over a one-year horizon, and quoted duration values always refer to the *duration at the horizon*.
- Convexity effects are ignored.

Within this framework, we now proceed to develop a theoretical model of how sector spreads relate to changing TSY rates. As a first step, we observe that, *if sector spreads never change,* a given TSY yield change will produce an identical change in the NT security yield,

NT Yield Change ($\tilde{\delta}_{NT}$) = TSY Yield Change ($\tilde{\delta}_{TSY}$).

We now consider an NT yield change that results from a combination of a TSY yield change and a spread change.

NT Yield Change ($\tilde{\delta}_{NT}$) = TSY Yield Change ($\tilde{\delta}_{TSY}$)
+ Spread Change ($\tilde{\delta}_S$).

For the moment, we assume a perfect correlation between TSY yield changes and spread changes.[4] Specifically, we assume that

Spread Change ($\tilde{\delta}_S$) = Spread Response Coefficient (a)
$\times$ TSY Yield change ($\tilde{\delta}_{TSY}$).

In a more compact form,

$$\tilde{\delta}_S = a\tilde{\delta}_{TSY}.$$

If $a > 0$, spreads will move in the same direction as TSY yield changes, and rising rates will lead to widening spreads (see Figure 16–2). Similarly, falling rates will lead to narrowing spreads. This would be the case, for example, if spreads retained a fixed percentage relationship to the basic TSY rate (although different maturity points could have a different "fixed" percentage spread). In other words, with $a > 0$, TSY market rallies and slumps are accentuated for NTs. Thus, NT security returns will be more volatile than TSY returns for investments with identical standard durations.

When $a < 0$, the impact of TSY rate changes on NT returns is the opposite of that described above. Rising rates lead to narrower spreads; falling rates

---

[4]When spread changes are perfectly correlated with TSY yield changes, NT yield changes also will be perfectly correlated with TSY yield changes.

Figure 16–2. A Deterministic Model of Non-Treasury Spread Changes

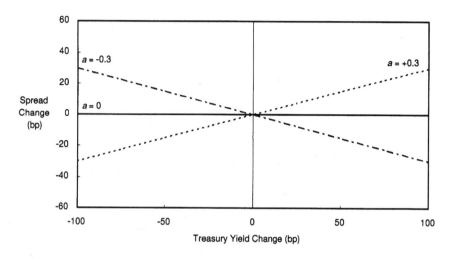

a = spread response coefficient; bp = basis points.

lead to wider spreads. This could be the case, for example, if NT rates are "sticky," or if they are weakly correlated with TSY rates, so that a rise in TSY rates is unlikely to be matched by an equal or greater rise in NT rates.

THE STATISTICAL DURATION CONCEPT

Figure 16–3 shows how the response patterns illustrated in Figure 16–2 translate into incremental returns for four-year-duration TSY and NT securities. The horizontal axis represents the movement in TSY yields. The vertical axis reflects the price response, including the incremental effect of the spread change that is driven by the TSY yield move. We can think of $a = 0$ as a base case in which NT and TSY securities respond identically to rate changes (if they both have a four-year duration relative to TSY yield moves). When spreads widen with higher yields ($a > 0$), the NT's accentuated response is comparable to that of a TSY bond with a duration greater than four years. By the same token, when $a < 0$, the muted response of the NT security matches that of a TSY security with a lower duration than four years.

From Figure 16–3, we see how the NT standard duration can be adjusted to give a "statistical duration" D* that incorporates the spread response. This

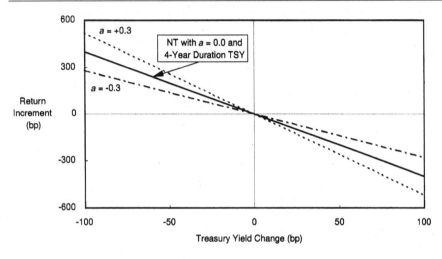

Figure 16–3. Return Gains or Losses for Four-Year-Duration Treasury and Non-Treasury Securities

a = spread response coefficient; bp = basis points; NT = non-Treasury; TSY = Treasury.

statistical duration acts as a "TSY duration surrogate" that more accurately reflects the NT's sensitivity to benchmark TSY rate moves.

With this model, the duration adjustment is given by[5]

$$D^* = (1 + a)D_{NT}.$$

If $a = 0$, spreads do not change, no adjustments are necessary, and $D^* = D_{NT}$.

If $a > 0$, $D^* > D_{NT}$, while for $a < 0$, $D^* < D_{NT}$.

EXPECTED RETURNS AND STATISTICAL DURATION

We now turn to the risk/return trade-offs that apply to NT securities in the context of the spread model described above. In this model, the return vola-

---

[5]If $\tilde{\delta}_{NT} = \tilde{\delta}_{TSY} + \tilde{\delta}_{S}$, and $\tilde{\delta}_{S} = a\tilde{\delta}_{TSY}$, then $\tilde{\delta}_{NT} = (1 + a)\tilde{\delta}_{TSY}$. Because yield changes expand (or contract) by a factor of $(1 + a)$, it is as if the duration has been adjusted by the same factor. Thus, the NT's price change becomes $D_{NT}\tilde{\delta}_{NT} = D_{NT}(1 + a)\tilde{\delta}_{TSY} = D^*\tilde{\delta}_{TSY}$.

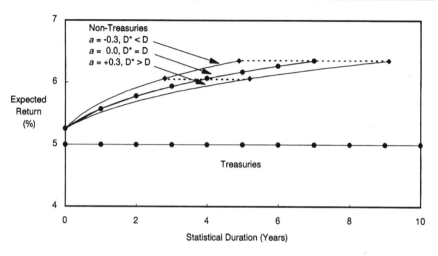

Figure 16–4. Expected Return versus Statistical Duration for Treasury and
Non- Treasury Securities

D* = statistical duration; D = standard non-Treasury duration.

tility of all securities is driven by TSY interest-rate moves and the magnitude
of D*. Therefore, in composing a return/risk diagram, we can use D* as the
horizontal axis.[6]

We assume that the yield can act as a proxy for the expected return over
a one-year investment horizon, and we plot that expected return on the vertical axis.[7] Thus, with our flat-yield-curve assumption for TSY securities, the
expected return curve also is flat. Moreover, for TSYs, D* = D, so no duration
adjustments are needed.

In contrast to the TSY curve, the shape of the NT curve may be altered
dramatically, depending on the value of the spread response coefficient a
(see Figure 16–4). If $a = 0$, D* = D for NTs, and the expected return curve has
the same shape as the yield curve in Figure 16–1. However, when $a > 0$, the
NTs effectively experience a duration expansion, so that at any given level of
expected return, there is increased TSY rate-related volatility. Likewise, if
$a < 0$, there is a duration contraction and a diminished sensitivity to interest-
rate changes.

---

[6]More properly, the risk is D* multiplied by TSY yield change volatility.

[7]See Chapter 21 for a discussion of the relationship between horizon yield curves and expected
return.

Viewing Figure 16–4 from a different vantage point, we observe that when $a > 0$, the rightward shift of the expected return curve results in lower-than-anticipated returns at a fixed level of D*. Similarly, when $a < 0$, there are greater-than-anticipated returns at a fixed level of D*.

STATISTICAL DURATION WITH UNCERTAINTY

To this point, we have assumed that spread changes are completely predictable from TSY yield changes (that is, the correlation ρ is either –1 or 1). In practice, this relationship is never really perfect because many other factors affect spreads. We now turn our attention to that more realistic case in which $-1 < \rho < 1$.

To illustrate how an inter-sector correlation can affect duration, we consider some market examples. Figure 16–5 plots the historical returns for the three-to-seven-year sector of the TSY market against the change in the TSY sector yield. The vertical coordinate is the monthly return increment, computed by subtracting one-twelfth of the yield at the beginning of the month from the total return for the month. The time period is from January 1983 to March 1993. Figure 16–5 also plots a "best fit" regression line through the data points. The closeness of the data points to the line reflects the almost perfect –0.998 correlation between TSY yield changes and incremental returns.

The –3.51 slope of the regression line can be viewed as indicating an empirical duration of 3.51 years. Each 100-basis-point rise in yield results in a 3.51% return decrease. It is interesting to note that, over the 10-year period, the average standard duration was 3.63 years. The deviation between the empirical duration and the standard duration primarily is attributable to the fact that we are averaging over a sector with a four-year maturity span, with the sector composition changing from month to month.

In general, correlations are very high between the incremental returns of any NT sector and the yield changes *within* that sector. However, fixed-income managers should compare the response of all sectors to a common yield change, usually the change in TSY yields.

For the NT sectors, incremental returns are attributable to both changes in TSY rates *and* changes in spreads. Because of these spread effects, the correlation between NT return increments and TSY yield changes will be somewhat weaker than the correlations within the TSY sector. To illustrate these effects, we use data from the Salomon Brothers Broad Investment-Grade (BIG) Bond Index to plot three-to-seven-year "A" corporate return increments against three-to-seven-year TSY yield changes, again using data over the pe-

Figure 16–5. Treasury Return Increment versus Treasury Yield Change (Three-to-Seven-Year Sector; Jan. 83–Mar. 93; Monthly)

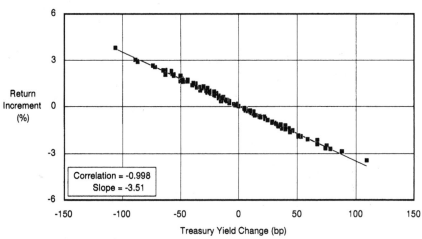

bp = basis points.

Source: Salomon Brothers Broad Investment-Grade (BIG) Bond Index.

riod from January 1983 to March 1993 (see Figure 16–6).[8] The correlation is now weakened to –0.93, compared with the –0.998 TSY to TSY correlation. In this illustration, the empirical duration for the A corporates is 2.56, compared with this sector's average effective duration of 3.17 years.[9] These correlation and duration differences imply that TSY yield changes by themselves are a less reliable predictor of corporate returns than of TSY returns. This greater "noisiness" of the corporate response pattern is evident in Figure 16–6.

The noisiness of the NT response to TSY yield changes is amplified when the NT sector is a foreign fixed-income market. As an example, using data from the Salomon Brothers World Government Bond Index, Figure 16-7 plots the dollar-hedged monthly returns of three-to-seven-year German government bonds against TSY yield changes over the period from January 1985 to March 1993.[10] In this case, the empirical duration is just under one year, reflecting the smaller portion of German bond returns that can be attributed to changes in U.S. rates.

---

[8]The data in Figure 16–6 are taken from Salomon Brothers' *Total Rate of Return Indexes.*

[9]The effective duration for corporates is based on an option-adjusted spread model. The "raw" nominal duration is even larger. See *Effective Duration of Callable Bonds.*

[10]The data in Figure 16–7 are from Salomon Brothers' *International Market Indexes.*

Figure 16–6. "A" Corporate Return Increments versus Treasury Yield Change (Three-to-Seven-Year Sector; Jan. 83–Mar. 93 Sector; Monthly)

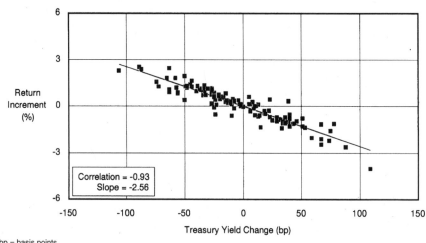

bp = basis points.

Source: Salomon Brothers Broad Investment-Grade (BIG) Bond Index.

A SPREAD MODEL WITH IMPERFECT CORRELATIONS

The historical data in the last section serve to illustrate the "noisiness" that usually exists when returns of an NT sector are plotted against TSY yield changes. This noise results from spread changes that arise *independently* of TSY yield changes. To better understand the impact of such spread changes, we now turn from the correlations between *returns* and yield changes to the correlations between *spread* changes and yield changes, $\rho_{S,T}$.

For illustrative purposes, we construct a simple model of the spread behavior of a hypothetical NT sector. We choose a relatively tight $\rho_{S,T}$ of 0.67, a spread change volatility of 45 basis points, and a TSY yield change volatility of 100 basis points (see Figure 16–8). This choice of parameters results in a spread response coefficient of 0.3, so that the "predicted" spread change is 30% of the TSY yield change:[11]

$$\tilde{\delta}_S \quad 0.3\, \tilde{\delta}_{TSY}$$

---

[11]Changes in NT spreads and NT yields are mathematically related in accordance with the following formulas (see Figure 16–8 for symbol definitions):

Figure 16-7. Hedged German Government Bond Return versus Treasury Yield Change (Three-to-Seven-Year Sector; Jan. 85–Mar. 93; Monthly)

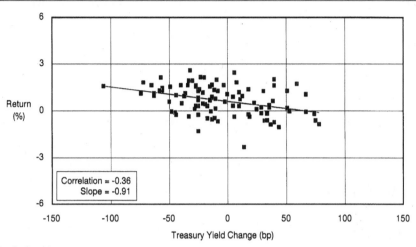

bp = basis points.

Source: Salomon Brothers World Government Bond Index.

The data points in Figure 16–9 illustrate a simulation of 200 outcomes from this spread model. Clearly, there is some spread volatility that is unrelated to TSY yield changes, which we call the "residual" spread volatility. The residual volatility is unpredictable or "unexplained" in the sense that it represents the variation in NT yields that results from market factors other than TSY yield changes. The TSY rate-related volatility and the residual spread volatility combine (but not by a simple addition) to give the overall spread volatility (see Figure 16–8).

The NT security's exposure to TSY yield changes can be represented as follows:

NT Yield Change Volatility $\equiv \sigma_{NT} = \sqrt{\sigma_{TSY}^2 + \sigma_S^2 + 2\rho_{S,T}\sigma_{TSY}\sigma_S}$

Correlation between NT yield change and TSY yield change $\equiv \rho_{NT,T} = (\rho_{S,T}\sigma_S + \sigma_{TSY})/\sigma_{NT}$.

Application of these formulas shows that our spread model implies that σ_{NT} = 134 basis points and that the NT *yield change* correlation $\rho_{NT,T}$ = 0.97. These volatility and correlation values are quite different from those embedded in our historical example. In fact, the lower correlations and NT volatilities that are often observed in practice may lead to weak spread correlations and negative values for the spread response coefficient.

Figure 16–8. Spread Model Assumptions

Name	Value	Symbol	Formula
Correlation between NT Spread Change and TSY Yield Change	0.67	$\rho_{S,T}$	
Spread Response Coefficient	0.30	a	$\rho_{S,T}\sigma_S\sigma_{TSY}$
TSY Yield Change Volatility (Annualized)	100bp	σ_{TSY}	
NT Spread Volatility (Annualized)	45.0bp	σ_S	$\sqrt{(\sigma_{Si})^2 + (\sigma_{S\varepsilon})^2}$
TSY Rate-Related Spread Volatility (Annualized)	30.0bp	σ_{Si}	$\lvert a \rvert \sigma_{TSY}$
Residual Spread Volatility (Annualized)	33.5bp	$\sigma_{S\varepsilon}$	$\sigma_S \bullet \sqrt{1 - \rho_{S,T}^2}$

bp = basis points; NT = non-Treasury; TSY = Treasury.

Figure 16–9. Simulated Non-Treasury Spread Change versus Treasury Yield Change

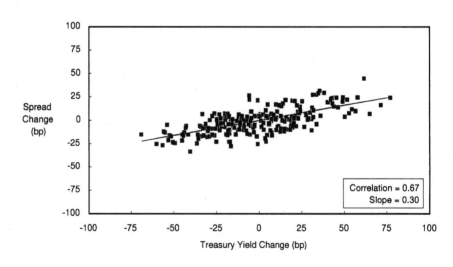

bp = basis points.

Figure 16–10. Return Gains or Losses for Investments in Non-Treasuries (With Spread/Yield Change Correlation = 0.67)

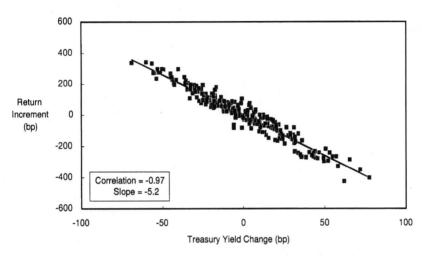

bp = basis points.

$$\text{NT Yield Change} = \text{TSY Yield Change}$$
$$+ \text{TSY Yield-Change-Related Spread Change}$$

$$= \tilde{\delta}_{TSY} + a\,\tilde{\delta}_{TSY}$$

$$= (1 + 0.3)\tilde{\delta}_{TSY}$$

$$= 1.3\tilde{\delta}_{TSY}.$$

In Figure 16–10, the simulated spread changes are projected into return responses for an NT security with a four-year standard duration. The scatter of return points reflects the noisy spread changes derived from our simulated spread model. The "best fit" line drawn through these return points has a slope of –5.2. Thus, we see that the 30% spread impact of TSY yield changes translates into a statistical duration that is 130% of the standard duration (130% of 4 = 5.2).[12] When spread changes are positively correlated with yield changes, there is an implicit "duration expansion," reflecting an increased sensitivity to TSY rates.[13]

PERFECT AND IMPERFECT HEDGES

The scatter of the data points about the return curve in Figure 16–10 stems from the residual spread volatility. This residual volatility is unavoidable and, in contrast to the TSY-related volatility, cannot be hedged with TSYs.[14]

To illustrate this point, we first plot the return volatility of portfolios consisting of a long position in a 5.2-year-duration TSY security and an equal short position in TSY securities with durations ranging from zero to 10 years. Figure 16–11 illustrates the obvious result: When the duration of the short position matches the 5.2-year duration of the long position, the hedge is perfect (that is, it has zero volatility). For TSY durations other than 5.2 years, the yield change sensitivity of the portfolio will equal 5.2 minus the duration of the short position. Consequently, the volatility of this long/short portfolio will increase in direct proportion to the absolute difference between 5.2 and the duration of the shorted TSY, resulting in the "V-shaped" pattern illustrated in Figure 16–11.

We now consider a long position in the 4-year-duration (standard) NT and recall that the imperfect correlation ($\rho = 0.67$) resulted in a D* of 5.2 years. To create a hedged portfolio, we combine the NT with short positions in TSYs of varying duration. The upper curve in Figure 16–11 depicts the volatilities of these hedged portfolios.[15] The best hedge is obtained when the long/short

---

[12]With our spread model, the statistical duration could have been computed directly from the formula

$$D^* = D(nominal) \bullet (1 + \rho \sigma_S / \sigma_{TSY}).$$

Several authors have utilized measures of duration that resemble, but are distinct from, the statistical duration as defined in this chapter. For example, see *Active Total Return Management of Fixed Income Portfolios*, Chapter 11, Ravi E. Dattatreya and Frank J. Fabozzi, Probus, 1989; "Computing Durations for Bond Portfolios," Gerald O. Bierwag, Charles J. Currado, and George G. Kaufman, *The Journal of Portfolio Management*, Fall 1990; and "Multifactor Immunization," Peter D. Noris, in *Fixed Income Analytics*, Chapter 11, Ravi E. Dattatreya, ed., Probus, 1991.

[13]In the example, we showed how a spread relationship could be used to determine a statistical duration. We could also change the point of view and utilize an empirical model of a return/yield relationship to calculate an implicit relationship between spread and yield changes.

[14]In this chapter, we consider all non-interest-related spread volatility to be residual risk. We do not address the complex issue of the correlation between credit risk and spread changes. This interdependence also may affect expected returns for NT securities.

[15]The equation for Figure 16–11 is $\sigma_{Hedge} = \sqrt{[(D^*_{NT} - D_{TSY})\sigma_{TSY}]^2 + [D_{NT}\sigma_{Se}]^2}$. For the TSY versus TSY case, this formula simplifies to $\sigma_{Hedge} = |5.2 - D_{TSY}|\, \sigma_{TSY}$.

Figure 16–11. Volatility of Investments Hedged with Treasury Securities of Varying Duration

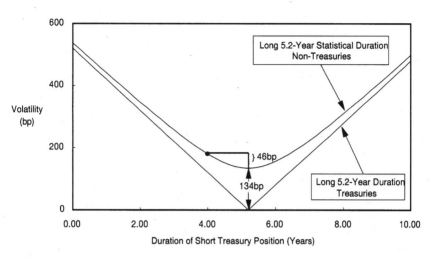

bp = basis points.

portfolio has the least volatility. As we can see, this minimum volatility occurs when the shorting TSY duration matches the NT's *statistical* duration rather than the standard duration. We should expect this result, given the statistical duration's construction as a "Treasury duration surrogate."

However, even with the best TSY short, the NT hedge is not perfect. The residual spread volatility results in a hedge-portfolio volatility that always is greater than zero. In fact, the residual spread volatility translates directly into the minimum residual return volatility of 134 basis points that is shown in Figure 16–11. All other hedges result in return volatilities that are greater than this 134-basis-point minimum. In particular, with the "naive hedge" obtained by shorting a four-year-duration TSY, the return volatility would be 180 basis points, or 46 basis points greater than the minimum value.

In the next section, we show how the residual return volatility can be computed by simply multiplying the *standard* NT duration by the residual spread volatility.[16] This will enable us to plot a new return/risk diagram that reflects the trade-offs associated with NT investments of different maturities.

---

[16]When using more sophisticated option-adjusted spread models, the appropriate factor will be the "spread duration."

TWO DIMENSIONS OF RISK IN NON-TREASURY PORTFOLIOS

In this section, we continue with the NT example of the previous section and recall that

Residual Spread Volatility = 33.5 bp.

This residual volatility adds another dimension of risk to investments in NT securities. Within the context of our hypothetical spread model, the residual spread behavior is independent of any movement in TSY rates. Changes in the residual NT spread are strictly a "within-sector" event. For a given NT security, the price and return impact of these residual spread movements naturally will depend on the NT's *standard* duration.

Thus, the residual return volatility can be approximated by the following formula:

Residual Return Volatility = NT Standard Duration
                            $\times$ NT Residual Spread Volatility.

In fact, when this formula is applied to our example, we obtain the same values as the minimum return volatility observed in Figure 16–11:

Residual Return Volatility = 4 $\times$ 33.5 bp = 134 bp.

Within the context of this model, this value implies that the four-year NT's actual return may differ significantly from what might be expected on the basis of TSY rate movements alone. More precisely, the noise effect from residual spread changes will have a standard deviation of 1.34%. This residual return volatility is an intrinsic characteristic of the NT security.

A NEW RETURN/RISK DIAGRAM

The risk in the NT security has been partitioned into two components—the first captured by the statistical duration and the second represented by the residual return volatility. In this section, we address the question of how this more complex two-dimensional view of risk can be presented in a return/risk diagram.

Consider the three variables that characterize the NT security in our model: (1) expected return, (2) statistical duration, and (3) residual return volatility. From the $a = 0.0$ return curve displayed in Figure 16–4, we see that

Figure 16–12. The Statistical Duration and "Residual Spine" of a Four-Year-Duration NT Security

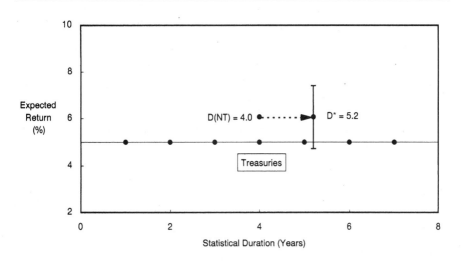

the four-year-duration NT investment offers an expected return that is 106 basis points greater than TSYs. In addition, when properly adjusted, the NT security ends up with a 5.2-year statistical duration (so that it has the same sensitivity to TSY yield changes as a 5.2-year-duration TSY).

However, as shown in the preceding section, our four-year NT security also has a residual return volatility of 1.34% that is unrelated to TSY yield changes. In Figure 16–12, we display this residual volatility as a vertical "spine." This spine extends 1.34% above and below the 5.2-year NT statistical duration point. Note that the lower portion of the spine extends below the TSY return curve, implying that residual volatility may lead to underperformance by the NT security. On the other hand, significant outperformance also is equally likely.[17]

Figure 16–13 takes the above analysis a step further by adding residual volatility spines to the $a = +0.3$ curve that was presented in Figure 16–4. As we extend duration, the length of the spines grows, as does the risk of

---

[17]If the return distribution is normal, there is a 32% probability that the observed deviation from the mean will be greater than one standard deviation. That is, the probability is 16% that the return will fall below 4.72% (6.06% − 1.34%). Likewise, the probability is 16% that the return will exceed 7.40% (6.06% + 1.34%).

underperforming TSYs. For example, as we shift from a four- to a six-year NT standard duration, the statistical duration grows by 50%, from 5.2 to 7.8 years, while the spine width grows from 1.34% to 2.01%.[18]

With Figure 16–13, we now have a two-dimensional representation of the three ingredients of return and risk: expected return, TSY yield sensitivity, and residual risk. This revised return/risk diagram is a graphic reminder of the two facets of risk that must be accommodated as one reaches for enhanced return. While this diagram can be helpful in comparing individual securities, it can prove particularly useful in assembling multisecurity portfolios.

This portfolio application is illustrated in Figure 16–14. The three diagonal lines show how the return/risk characteristics vary as one constructs mixed portfolios of TSY and NT securities. The middle line represents the expected return and statistical duration for portfolios composed of 4-year-duration TSYs (the lower point) and 4-year-duration NTs (with a 5.2-year statistical duration). The midpoint of that line is a portfolio with 50% TSYs and 50% NTs. This 50% mixture portfolio captures 50% of the expected return premium offered by 4-year NTs (53 basis points), and it has a statistical duration of 4.6 years.

The upper and lower lines in Figure 16–14 show how residual return volatility is transferred to mixed portfolios. Residual return risk is always transferred in proportion to the percentage of NT investments. For example, the 50% NT/50% TSY portfolio will capture 50% of the residual return risk (that is, ± 67 basis points), extending the one standard deviation return band from –14 basis points to +120 basis points relative to TSYs.

Thus, with the dual decomposition of risks provided by our model, all three characteristics can be linearly combined to determine the behavior of any multisecurity portfolio. It should be noted that this statement does not hold true for the standard single measures of return volatility.[19] This simple weighting procedure provides for better insights and clearer intuitions when one is constructing fixed-income portfolios.

The above example shows the key role that residual volatility plays in portfolio performance. This volatility cannot be eliminated, but it can be understood and quantified. By including residual volatility spines in a traditional risk/return plot, we gain a new measure of the rewards and risks inherent in NT securities.

---

[18]Recall that we calculate all duration values at the end of a one-year investment horizon.

[19]For a portfolio P consisting of weight w_i of security i, the statistical duration of the portfolio is $(D_p^* = \Sigma w_i D_i^*$ and the portfolio residual return volatility is $\sigma^{(P)}$(Residual Return) $= \Sigma w_i \sigma_i$(Residual Return). The total volatility of the portfolio can be found from the expression

$$\sqrt{(D_p^* \sigma_{TSY})^2 + (\sigma^{(P)}(\text{Residual Return}))^2}.$$

Figure 16–13. Expected Return versus Statistical Duration with Residual Volatility Spines

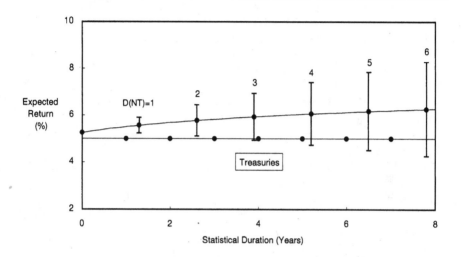

Figure 16–14. Expected Return and Residual Volatility of Non-Treasury/Treasury Portfolios

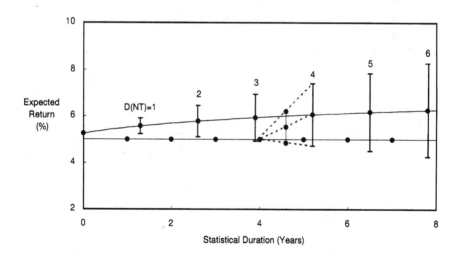

SUMMARY AND CONCLUSION

The relative return of non-Treasury securities and like-duration Treasury securities is determined largely by changing spreads. In this chapter, we show how spread changes can be separated into a Treasury-induced component and a second residual component that is statistically independent of Treasury rate moves. We then can calculate a statistical duration that provides a better estimate of the total sensitivity to Treasury yield changes. Moreover, within the bounds of the reliability of the statistical parameters, the statistical duration can be used to assess the interest-rate risk of mixed portfolios that include one or more non-Treasury sectors.

Investors in non-Treasury securities also must recognize that such securities bear residual risk from other market factors, such as changing credit perceptions, that cannot be "durationed away." Consequently, the expected return gains from non-Treasury securities must be balanced against the uncertainties associated with these residual risks.

As noted at the outset, this chapter presents a simple theoretical model to address the spread/duration problem in generic terms. In dealing with practical problems relating to any given sector, a host of special issues remain to be addressed. Nevertheless, the concepts of statistical duration and residual risk should provide a helpful framework for understanding the risk characteristics of multisector portfolios.

Chapter 17

The Spread Curve and the Risk/Return Decision: Structuring Fixed-Income Portfolios for Treasury Benchmarks

INTRODUCTION

Many fixed-income-portfolio managers face the challenge of providing returns in excess of some market benchmark while operating within a constrained universe of permissible investments. These restrictions may include a required credit quality, as well as bounds on the proportions of various fixed-income sectors, such as mortgages, corporates, and (possibly) foreign bonds.

In this chapter, we introduce a theoretical model for arriving at an "optimal" portfolio for a given Treasury benchmark. To simplify our presentation, we focus on a single non-Treasury sector that has a positive "spread curve" relative to the Treasury yield curve. Changes in the Treasury market will influence the price of non-Treasuries, both directly through the Treasury yield changes and indirectly through induced spread changes. The volatility associated with these Treasury-related spread changes can be captured through a concept that we call "statistical duration." This duration measure adjusts the standard duration to reflect the full impact of Treasury yield changes.[1]

---

[1]For any non-Treasury asset, we use the term "standard duration" to refer to the commonly used measure of rate sensitivity. For a noncallable bond, the modified duration measures the response to changes in the bond's own yield. For callable corporates and mortgages, an effective duration captures the impact of each security's optional redemption features.

Spread changes that are not related to Treasury movements constitute an additional source of return volatility that is intrinsic to the non-Treasury sector. In our theoretical model, this residual volatility depends solely on the market weight and the standard duration of the non-Treasury portfolio. By balancing the residual risk against the yield advantages of non-Treasury securities with various durations, the portfolio manager can determine an optimal portfolio for a given Treasury benchmark. Moreover, this same non-Treasury component will be present in the optimal portfolio for *any* Treasury benchmark. Thus, non-Treasury security selection can be based solely on the manager's absolute risk tolerance, without regard to the measurement benchmark.

STATISTICAL DURATION AND RESIDUAL RISK

In Chapter 16, we introduced a model for spread changes between yields for a non-Treasury fixed-income asset class (referred to as NT) and yields for comparable-duration Treasury securities (symbolized by TSY). In this model, we separated spread changes into two components: TSY interest-rate-related changes and "residual" changes.

In Chapter 16, we showed how the NT standard duration could be adjusted by some factor to account for the increased TSY rate-related sensitivity of NT securities.[2] We made this adjustment by defining a "statistical duration," D^*, that acts as a "TSY duration surrogate." In an example developed in Chapter 16, we described a situation in which this adjustment factor turned out to be 1.3, leading to

$$D^* = 1.3D_{NT}.$$

In this illustration, the NTs effectively experience a duration expansion. For example, for an NT security with a four-year duration, the statistical duration becomes 5.2 years, a significantly greater rate change sensitivity.

---

[2]According to our model, the spread change is some percentage a of the yield change *plus* an unexplained residual. Thus,

NT Spread Change $= a \bullet$ TSY Yield Change + Residual Spread Change.

NT Yield Change $=$ TSY Yield Change + NT Spread Change

$\qquad\qquad\quad = (1 + a) \bullet$ TSY Yield Change + Residual Spread Change.

If $a = 0.30$, the TSY rate-related yield change of an NT security becomes 1.3 times the TSY yield change. Consequently, the statistical duration of an NT security, D^*, is 1.3 times the standard duration, D_{NT}.

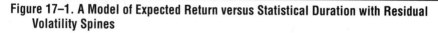

Figure 17–1. A Model of Expected Return versus Statistical Duration with Residual Volatility Spines

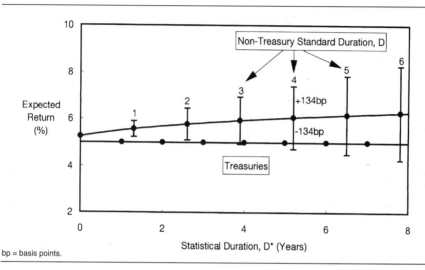

bp = basis points.

For the return dimension, we assume that the positive spread of NT securities translates into an expected return advantage that increases with duration. With this assumption, we can plot expected return versus risk, as measured by the statistical duration. Figure 17–1 plots these return/risk characteristics of NTs and TSYs, while Figure 17–2 outlines the model assumptions. Because the standard TSY duration captures all TSY-related risk, $D = D^*$ for TSYs.

To complete the picture of the performance of NT securities, we must include the residual spread volatility. Figure 17–1 illustrates this residual volatility by attaching vertical spines to the NT return curve. For example, the spine attached to the four-year standard duration NT extends 134 basis points above and below the expected return for that security.[3] (In this chap-

---

[3]In Chapter 16, we used an example in which the TSY yield change volatility was 100 basis points, the TSY rate-related spread volatility was 30 basis points (30% of 100 basis points), and the residual spread change volatility was <u>33.5 basis p</u>oints. These values combine to an overall NT spread change volatility of 45 basis points ($\sqrt{30^2 + 33.5^2}$).

The residual *return* volatility can be approximated from D_{NT} and the residual *spread* volatility as follows:

Residual Return Volatility = NT Standard Duration × Residual Spread Volatility.

If we assume that the residual spread volatility is 33.5 basis points and $D_{NT} = 4$,

Residual Return Volatility = 4 × 33.5 bp = 134 bp.

Figure 17–2. Statistical Duration Model Assumptions

- The yield curve for TSYs is flat, and all securities yield 5%.
- There is only one NT sector available.
- The NT sector includes securities with yield advantages ranging from 25 basis points over the short TSYs to 140 basis points over the eight-year point on the flat Treasury curve.
- The expected returns of TSYs and NTs are set equal to their yields.
- Investments are evaluated over a one-year horizon, and quoted duration values always refer to the *duration at the horizon*.
- All yield-curve shifts are parallel, so absolute yield volatility is uniform across maturities. (Thus, any spread changes are assumed to apply simultaneously to all maturities within the NT sector.)[a]
- Convexity effects are ignored.

[a]Our assumption that the expected return is the same as the yield implies a particular yield curve reshaping at the one-year horizon. The parallel yield-curve shifts are relative to this implicit horizon yield curve. For a detailed discussion, see Chapter 21.

---

ter, we use a convention of describing the spine's size by its half-length, which is the residual volatility.) This illustration implies that a one-standard-deviation adverse spread movement could negate the expected return advantage of the NT security, bringing the return below that of TSYs. Note how the length of the spines grows as we extend the standard duration (and, consequently, the statistical duration)—without a fully compensating increase in expected return. Consequently, as the duration increases, so does the risk of underperformance relative to TSYs.

MAINTAINING A BENCHMARK DURATION WITH MATURITY BARBELLS

In this section, we address the investment options of a portfolio manager who is measured against a four-year-duration TSY benchmark and who must maintain the benchmark rate sensitivity. We also assume that the manager can invest up to 40% of the assets in NT securities.

At the outset, we suppose that the 40% NT investment is the four-year-duration (standard) NT security. This security provides a 106-basis-point advantage over TSYs. Using our spread model, we regard this NT security as having a 5.2-year statistical duration. If the balance of the assets is invested in 4-year-duration TSYs, the portfolio duration will be 4.48 years (60% × 4 +

Figure 17–3. Mixing 40% Non-Treasuries with 60% Treasuries

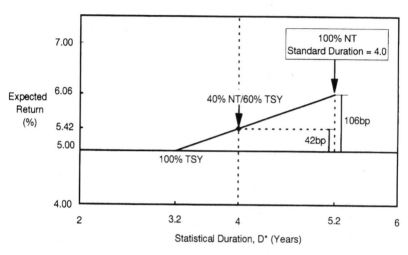

bp = basis points; NT = non-Treasury; TSY = Treasury.

40% × 5.2), exceeding the 4-year-duration benchmark by almost one-half year. In addition, because the portfolio consists of 40% NTs, the manager gains 42 basis points (40% of the 106-basis-point advantage) from the NT investment.

To achieve the 4-year target duration (and avoid TSY-related interest-rate risk), the manager should regard the 4-year-duration NT as having a 5.2-year (statistical) duration and should choose a 3.2-year-duration TSY (60% × 3.2 + 40% × 5.2 = 4.0). This TSY choice does not affect the 42-basis-point return gain because of our flat TSY return curve assumption.

Figure 17–3 illustrates the "geometry" of this portfolio construction. With 40% NTs, we gain the same proportions of both incremental return and duration—40% of the 106-basis-point return increment and 40% of the 2 years of additional statistical duration (5.2-year NTs, compared with 3.2-year TSYs). The resulting "barbell" will have the desired four-year statistical duration and an expected return of 5.42% (40% × 6.06 + 60% × 5.00%).

While the portfolio just described eliminates TSY interest-rate risk relative to the benchmark, it does not eliminate the risk that stems from residual spread volatility.[4] The four-year NT carries 134 basis points of such residual

---

[4]Although our model illustration has only one NT sector, the residual risk could be further reduced by including additional NT sectors whose spreads are only weakly correlated with each other.

risk, and the barbell mixture will retain 40% of that risk, or 53.6 basis points. Figure 17–4 illustrates this transference of residual risk by utilizing the image of the residual spine that we introduced in Figure 17–1. In essence, 53.6 basis points of residual spine are moved to the four-year-duration level. This translation shows that we have matched the duration of the benchmark and gained 42 basis points of expected return—but at the cost of 53.6 basis points of residual risk.

To illustrate the generality of the transference of residual risk, we consider one additional example in which the NT security has a standard duration of two years. According to our illustrative return curve (see Figure 17–1), the expected return spread of the two-year duration NT is 78 basis points, and 40% of this return will be captured in the barbell portfolio.

Because the 2-year NT has a statistical duration of 2.6 years, we must use 60% 4.9-year-duration TSYs in the portfolio to match the 4-year benchmark.[5] The residual risk of the two-year NT is 67 basis points, half the residual risk of the four-year NT. Figure 17–5 shows this residual risk as a vertical spine at the four-year-duration point. As before, we transfer 40% of both the incremental return and the residual risk, bringing us to an expected return of 5.31% and a spine width of 26.8 basis points.

PLOTTING RELATIVE RETURN AGAINST RESIDUAL RISK

A portfolio manager with a four-year-duration TSY benchmark can always match the benchmark return simply by investing 100% in four-year-duration TSYs. To outperform the benchmark, the manager may incur the added risk of NT securities that promise added return. To minimize this risk, we choose TSYs that appropriately offset the *statistical* duration of the NT security, leaving the portfolio's statistical duration at four years. However, the residual performance risk that results from non-interest-related spread risk is unavoidable *within the framework of our model.*

In the preceding examples, we constructed barbell portfolios whose statistical durations match the four-year TSY benchmark. Thus, each barbell portfolio can be expected to move with the TSY benchmark under all parallel shifts of the TSY yield curve. The question is how the investor should

---

[5]The required calculations are as follows:

$$D^* = 1.3D_{NT} = 1.3 \times 2.0 = 2.6.$$

$$\text{TSY Duration} = (\text{Benchmark Duration} - 40\% \text{ of } D^*)/0.6$$

$$= (4 - 40\% \text{ of } 2.6)/0.6 = 4.93.$$

Figure 17–4. The Carryover of Residual Risk into a 40% Non-Treasury/60% Treasury Portfolio

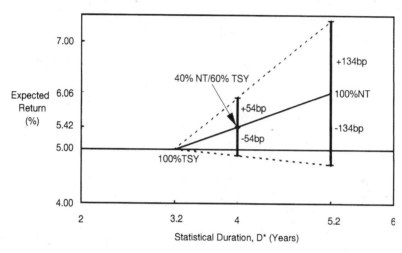

bp = basis points; NT = non-Treasury; TSY = Treasury.

Figure 17–5. Portfolio Impact of 40% Two-Year-Duration Non-Treasuries

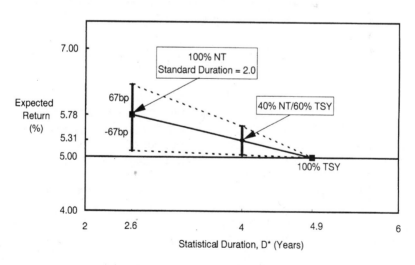

bp = basis points; NT = non-Treasury; TSY = Treasury.

choose between two alternative barbell portfolios. On the one hand, the portfolio with 40% four-year NTs provides the greater return advantage: 42 basis points versus 31 basis points for the two-year NT. On the other hand, the four-year NT portfolio carries a greater residual risk—a spine width of 53.6 basis points versus 26.8 basis points for the two-year NT portfolio. Thus, the choice of the optimal NT security entails a fundamental assessment of the investor's risk/return trade-off.

This risk/return analysis can be facilitated by a simple plot of the relative return advantage against the residual risk associated with each NT security. Each barbell portfolio under consideration contains exactly 40% of the indicated NT security. Hence, for each NT duration, the values plotted in Figure 17–6 correspond to 40% of the NT spread curve (the expected return advantage over TSYs in our hypothetical model) versus 40% of the spine width (the standard deviation of residual risk). For example, the four-year NT portfolio point has a relative return of 42 basis points and a residual risk of 53.6 basis points. The two-year NT portfolio point has a return of 31 basis points and a residual risk of 26.8 basis points.

In Figure 17–6, every NT security is paired in a 40%/60% barbell portfolio; the TSY duration is chosen to minimize risk by achieving an overall statistical duration of 4.0 years. These duration matches should eliminate all relative risk from TSY rate movements. With this risk dimension removed (or "durationed away"), the problem is now reduced to the standard two-dimensional configuration of return versus risk. In essence, Figure 17–6 can be viewed as a "residual" return curve for the NT sector, one that plots *relative* return versus *residual* risk.

A SHORTFALL APPROACH TO RESIDUAL RISK MANAGEMENT

Figure 17–6 provides a simple illustration of the relative return/residual risk trade-off, but it fails to provide insight into how the manager should choose the NT investment. As a step in this direction, suppose that the portfolio manager would like to limit the likelihood of poor performance. Specifically, suppose that the risk threshold is set so that the portfolio has *no more than a 10% probability of underperforming the benchmark by 25 basis points*.

Another way of stating this "shortfall constraint" is that the investor seeks a 90% assurance that the selected portfolio's return will be no more than 25 basis points below that of the TSY benchmark. We can show that such a shortfall constraint divides the return/risk space into two distinct regions: One region consists of portfolios with acceptable return/risk combinations, while the other region represents portfolios that violate the shortfall condition. These

---

Figure 17–6. Incremental Return and Relative Return Risk for the Full Range of Non-Treasury Investments for 40% Non-Treasury/60% Treasury Portfolio

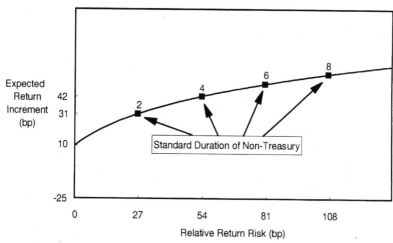

bp = basis points.

---

regions (see Figure 17–7) are separated by a straight line that emanates from the shortfall threshold (–25 basis points in our example) and has a slope determined by the shortfall probability (10% in our example).[6] All investments with return/risk characteristics that place them above the shortfall line will have superior downside performance and will exceed the shortfall constraint. Investments that fall beneath the shortfall line will fail to meet the shortfall constraint.

In our example, the shortfall condition is satisfied for any NT investment with a duration shorter than 3.9 years. In principle, the shortfall constraint could be met by *any* portfolio that has an NT duration of 3.9 years or shorter. However, in our example, the net spread curve rises with duration; thus—all else being equal—the manager likely will select the portfolio that provides the greatest relative return and meets the shortfall constraint. In Figure 17–7, the highest return occurs at the intersection with the shortfall line. By investing 40% of the assets in this 3.9-year-duration NT security, the portfolio manager expects to outperform the benchmark by slightly less than 42 basis points.

---

[6]See Chapter 15.

Figure 17–7. The Shortfall Constraint

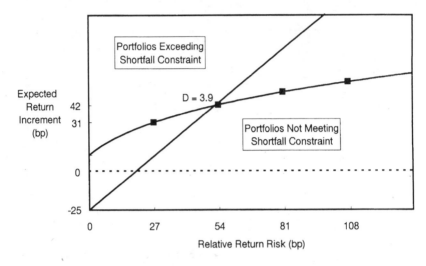

bp = basis points; D = standard duration of non-Treasury.

THE ROLE OF THE TREASURY BENCHMARK

We now return to the 40% NT example illustrated in Figure 17–4, but we change our benchmark to a six-year-duration TSY. With a 4-year standard-duration NT security and a longer-duration benchmark, the duration of the barbell TSY security must be lengthened to 6.5 years (40% × 5.2 + 60% × 6.5 = 6). This new TSY investment ensures that the portfolio and the benchmark have the same TSY rate-related sensitivity.

The new barbell has a return increment of 42 basis points and a residual volatility of 53.6 basis points—identical to the barbell that we constructed earlier to match the four-year TSY benchmark (see Figures 17–3 and 17–4). The only difference is that the residual spine has been moved to the six-year-duration level. From a different perspective, this result should not be surprising. Once all TSY interest-related risk has been "durationed away," only residual risk remains. That risk is transferred in direct proportion to the magnitude of the NT investment. Hence, for 40% NT barbells, a given NT security will always convey the same relative return and residual risk, regardless of the prescribed TSY benchmark.

Figure 17–8. Residual Risk Transfer with a Six-Year-Duration Benchmark (40% Non-Treasury with a Four-Year Duration)

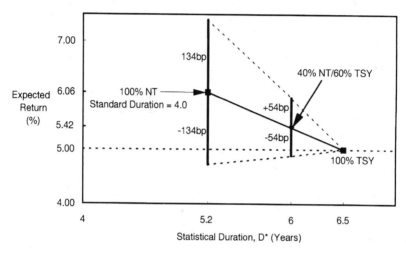

bp = basis points; NT= non-Treasury; TSY = Treasury.

This example shows that the return/risk diagram presented in Figure 17–6 and the shortfall analysis of Figure 17–7 for the four-year TSY benchmark also applies to our six-year-duration TSY benchmark. Thus, for either TSY benchmark, we obtain the same "optimal" NT security—the 3.9-year NT. This benchmark independence implies the following result:

The optimal NT investment for one TSY benchmark will be optimal for *all* other TSY benchmarks.

Recall that we obtained this result under the assumptions of a flat TSY curve and yield curves that are subject only to parallel movements. However, given this framework, fixed-income managers can choose NT investments based solely on the relative returns and residual risks within the NT sector itself. While the benchmark duration is an important determinant of the appropriate TSY component of the barbell, that duration is irrelevant to the return/risk decision.

THE SPECTRUM OF NON-TREASURY PERCENTAGES

Our general strategy for making an NT investment is to create a barbell portfolio to "duration away" TSY rate-related risk relative to a given TSY benchmark. With a flat TSY expected return curve, this strategy enables us to gain
the expected return increment of the NT security, while adding only residual
NT risk.

"Durationing away" is accomplished by choosing the TSY security duration so that the barbell's overall statistical duration equals the benchmark
duration. For moderate proportions of NT investments and intermediate
duration benchmarks, "durationing away" is easy, as we indicate in our earlier examples. In more extreme cases, to complete the required barbell, we
may find ourselves in need of TSYs with very long or even negative durations. A simpler and more direct strategy for "durationing away" is to establish a short position in the appropriate TSYs. For example, the expected return advantage of a 5.2-year statistical duration NT can be "captured" by
going long 5.2-year NTs and shorting an equal dollar amount of 5.2-year
TSYs. This long/short portfolio will have zero TSY rate-related risk while
retaining the residual risk that is intrinsic to the NT sector. Moreover, by
making a further investment in TSYs having the desired benchmark duration, the captured NT spread and the residual risk can be transported to the
benchmark point.[7]

With this ability to "duration away" TSY-related risks, it always should
be possible to reduce the NT investment problem to three key ingredients:
(1) the NT return spread over TSYs, (2) the residual NT spread change volatility, and (3) the market weight of NT investments.

In Figure 17–9, we compare the plots of NT return increment versus residual risk for portfolios with NT allocations fixed at 40%, 80%, and 100%,
assuming that all TSY-related risk has been eliminated. The incremental return and residual risk clearly increase in direct proportion to the NT investment percentage. The extreme case of 100% NTs reflects the full expected
return increment and residual risk associated with each NT security. Note
that the benchmark independence principle applies to this entire family of
curves representing the different NT percentages.

To locate the "optimal" NT portfolio within the bounds of a shortfall
constraint, Figure 17–10 superimposes the shortfall line that we used in Figure 17–7 on the entire family of portfolios plotted in Figure 17–9. Observe

---

[7]This long/short approach should work with yield curves of any shape. However, this simplified
model neglects risks associated with unanticipated yield-curve reshapings.

Figure 17–9. Incremental Return and Residual Risk at Higher Proportions of Non-Treasury Investments

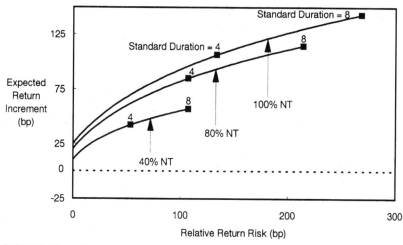

bp = basis points; NT= non-Treasury.

Figure 17–10. Portfolio Selection across the Entire Family of Non-Treasury Investments

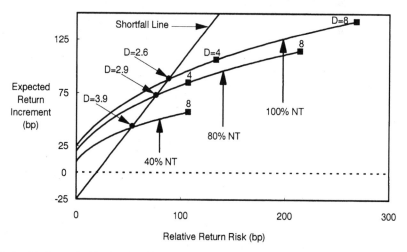

bp = basis points; D = standard duration of non-Treasury; NT= non-Treasury.

that as the NT allocation increases, the allowable duration decreases from 3.9 years at 40% NTs to 2.6 years at 100% NTs.

In practice, portfolio managers often substitute short-term corporates for similar-maturity Treasuries. This behavior is consistent with our finding that higher NT allocations should lead to a greater concentration in the shorter maturities. Recognize that our model assumes a fixed NT percentage, derived from some exogenous constraint such as credit concerns. Without any such constraint, the investor naturally would be driven to a virtually *total* allocation to very short-term NTs. Such a position might appear riskless from a narrow viewpoint, but it could entail outsized credit risks (beyond those captured by the spread variability that forms the basis for our model). When such credit concerns are contained through a prescribed maximum percentage, our model leads to the appropriate solution: an intermediate-maturity position that provides the greatest return improvement within the specified shortfall limit on overall fund performance.

Figure 17–10 essentially completes our presentation of a methodology for selecting NT securities based on their spread, residual volatility, and percentage allocation.

THE ROLE OF THE SPREAD CURVE

In this section, we suggest an alternative portfolio selection process that utilizes only the original return curve in Figure 17–1 and yet can be applied to any percentage allocation. In Figure 17–11, the expected returns of NTs are plotted against their standard duration. Note that this curve can be transformed into the 100% NT curve in Figure 17–10 by simply multiplying the duration by the residual spread volatility.

With residual risk measured by the standard duration, we can also construct a shortfall line based on duration, rather than on volatility.[8] Figure 17–11 plots this shortfall line, emanating from the vertical axis at –25 basis points. Observe that the shortfall line and the spread curve intersect at a

---

[8]With a relative return threshold of –25 basis points and 10% shortfall probability, the equation of the shortfall line is as follows:

Expected Return = –25 + 1.282 • D • Residual Spread Volatility.

When plotting the shortfall line in terms of residual portfolio volatility, we use a horizontal coordinate of D • Residual Spread Volatility and a slope of 1.282. When plotting the shortfall line against duration (D), we use a horizontal coordinate of D and a slope of (1.282 • Residual Spread Volatility). Thus, greater residual spread volatility results in a steeper slope.

Figure 17–11. Using the Initial Spread Curve for Portfolio Selection

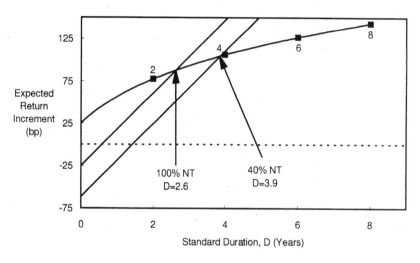

bp = basis points; D = standard duration of non-Treasury.

duration of 2.6 years. Thus, the original spread curve and the 100% NT curve (in Figure 17–10) lead to the same choice for the NT security.

Changes in the allowable NT percentage can be accommodated by appropriately shifting the shortfall line while leaving the spread curve unchanged. For example, suppose that the NT allocation is restricted to 40%. Then, because only 40% of the performance of the NT is transmitted to the portfolio, we can tolerate a lower return threshold for the NT component. For example, a return that is 62.5 basis points below TSYs on 40% of the portfolio provides an overall portfolio return that matches our original threshold of –25 basis points. Note that the lower shortfall line in Figure 17–11 emanates from –62.5 basis points, rather than –25 basis points. This line intersects the spread curve at D = 3.9 years, leading to the same NT selection as in Figure 17–10 with 40% NTs.

In this interpretation of the spread curve, the spread volatility and its relation to TSY changes act as the key to properly sizing the risk dimension. Thus, we see how this statistical duration/residual volatility approach allows the basic spread curve to serve as a consistent framework for addressing NT investment problems under various constraints.

SUMMARY AND CONCLUSION

Managing portfolios of Treasury and non-Treasury securities against a Treasury benchmark entails both duration risk and spread risk. In this chapter, we utilize the concept of statistical duration to reorganize the spread risk into a Treasury-related component and a residual component. This regrouping enables us to create portfolios of Treasury and non-Treasury securities that have the same statistical response to Treasury rate changes as the benchmark. We thereby reduce the non-Treasury investment decision to an assessment of the trade-off between the expected incremental return and the residual risk intrinsic to the non-Treasury sector.

Our key finding is that (within the limitations of the model) the optimal non-Treasury investments will be the same for all Treasury benchmarks. This result adds a new degree of freedom to non-Treasury security selection. More generally, we show that the portfolio manager can focus on the standard spread curve and seek the "best" non-Treasury investment subject to an appropriately rescaled measure of residual risk.

Chapter 18

The Spread Curve and a Mixed-Sector Benchmark: Structuring Fixed-Income Portfolios for Relative Performance

INTRODUCTION

Money managers are usually evaluated by comparing their realized returns over fixed measurement periods with the returns of a previously specified benchmark portfolio. For example, in the fixed-income markets, the manager might be measured against a simple benchmark like an all-Treasury portfolio or a mixed benchmark that includes Treasuries, corporates, and mortgages in the same proportions as the market. To outperform the benchmark allocation, the manager must depart from the benchmark by targeting a different asset mix in terms of the percentages or durations of the component sectors. While such departures from the benchmark are intended to improve performance, they are risky because any nonbenchmark portfolio bears some likelihood of underperformance.

This chapter presents a methodology for constructing portfolios of Treasury (TSY) and non-Treasury (NT) securities that provide the best risk/return trade-off relative to a mixed two-sector benchmark. For illustration, we focus on a benchmark portfolio consisting of 60% five-year-duration TSYs and 40% four-year-duration NTs.

In earlier chapters, we separated NT investment risk into a component that is related to TSY interest-rate movements, and a second residual component that reflects spread changes that are uncorrelated with interest-rate changes.[1] In the context of our model, all NT risk attributable to interest-rate

---

[1] We use the term "interest-rate movements" only to refer to Treasury rate changes. For a detailed discussion of the components of non-Treasury investment risk see Chapters 16 and 17.

movements can be "durationed away" with an appropriate long or short position in TSYs. The result is that only residual spread risk remains. The magnitude of this risk is determined by the NT's residual spread volatility and the "spread duration"—the sensitivity of the total portfolio to spread changes.[2]

The key finding of this chapter is as follows: When managing against a mixed benchmark, the portfolio selection decision can be based on the following factors: (1) the maximum allowable proportion of NT securities in the investment portfolio, (2) the extent to which the manager is willing to risk underperforming the benchmark portfolio, (3) the shape of the spread curve, and (4) the residual spread volatility.

THE SPREAD CURVE

Investment-grade NT securities are attractive to investors because they offer higher yields than comparable-duration TSYs. Figure 18–1 plots yield against duration for a hypothetical NT "spread curve." To simplify our presentation, we use a flat TSY yield curve at 5% and we assume that the NT yield increment climbs from 25 basis points for short-term investments to almost 160 basis points for 10-year-duration NTs. The flat yield curve assumption is not binding, because we can modify our analysis to include more realistic sloped curves.

Figure 18–1 shows a benchmark portfolio consisting of 60% five-year TSYs and 40% four-year NTs. The four-year NT has a yield of 6.06%, a spread of 106 basis points over the TSY yield. With 40% NT investment, the benchmark portfolio gains 40% of this 106-basis-point spread, bringing the portfolio yield to 5.42%.

The duration of the mixed benchmark is 4.6 years, 0.4 year shorter than the TSY duration.[3] More generally, all portfolios comprised of five-year TSYs and four-year NTs are located along a straight line between the five-year TSY point and the four-year NT point. As the NT percentage increases, the portfolio spread increases proportionately while the portfolio duration decreases, moving toward the four-year duration of the NT investment.

---

[2]Spread duration is defined in "Spread Duration: A New Tool for Bond Portfolio Management," Martin L. Leibowitz, William S. Krasker, and Ardavan Nozari, *The Journal of Portfolio Management*, Spring 1990.

[3]The benchmark duration is the weighted average of the NT duration and the TSY duration: 40% × 4 years + 60% × 5 years = 1.6 years + 3.0 years = 4.6 years.

Figure 18–1. An Illustrative Spread Model

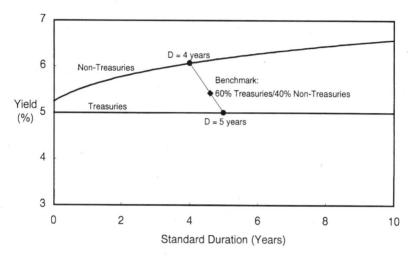

D = standard duration.

We now address the expected return and risk of NT investments, assuming a one-year investment horizon. A comprehensive return forecast entails taking a view on future yield curve reshapings. However, for modeling purposes, we take the expected return over a one-year horizon to be the same as the initial yield.[4] Thus, as with the TSY yield curve, the expected return curve for TSYs is flat, and we express the expected return of NT investments as a spread over TSYs (see Figure 18–2).

The standard measure of investment risk is the volatility or standard deviation of returns. For NT securities, this risk can be separated into two "orthogonal" (independent) components: (1) interest-rate risk and (2) residual risk that is uncorrelated with interest-rate movements.

The *interest-rate risk* is the NT return volatility that is directly attributable to TSY rate changes. We approximate this volatility as the product of the volatility of interest-rate changes and the "statistical" duration of the NT

---

[4]This simplification embodies several assumptions. First, we neglect credit losses. Second, we assume no changes in spreads beyond the spread changes required to maintain each security's yield level over the one-year horizon. In general, the one-year return of a fixed-income security will equal its initial yield if the year-end yield is also the same as the initial yield. For a detailed discussion of the relationship between horizon yields and expected returns, see Chapter 21.

Figure 18-2. The Non-Treasury Risk/Return Trade-Off

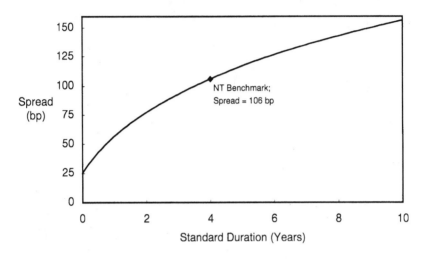

bp = basis points; NT= non-Treasury.

security.[5] Such interest-rate-related return volatility is avoidable because it can be "durationed away" by taking an appropriate position in TSYs.

In contrast to interest-rate risk, NT *residual risk* cannot be avoided.[6] With a one-year investment horizon, residual risk (or "residual return volatility") results from "unanticipated" year-end spread changes. We can approximate the residual risk of each NT security by the product of its residual *spread* volatility and its NT standard duration (D_{NT}).[7] If we assume all unanticipated spread changes result from parallel shifts of the spread curve at year-end, then all NT securities will have the same spread volatility. Hence, the residual return volatility for each NT security will increase in direct proportion to its D_{NT}.

---

[5]The statistical duration is calculated as the standard duration multiplied by an adjustment factor that represents the interest-rate-related spread changes. For details of this calculation see Chapter 16.

[6]We may be able to further reduce residual risk by including additional NT sectors with spreads that are weakly correlated to spreads in the first NT sector. In this chapter, however, we focus on a single NT sector, so that no reduction in residual risk is possible.

[7]NT Residual return volatility = Standard duration × Residual spread volatility, where Residual spread volatility = $\sqrt{1 - \rho^2}$ × Standard deviation of spread changes, with ρ being the correlation between interest-rate changes and spread changes.

Figure 18–3. Non-Treasury Duration Required to Match a 1.6-year Spread Duration

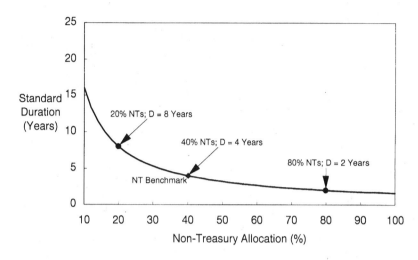

D = standard duration; NT= non-Treasury.

Thus, with parallel shifts, D_{NT} can serve as a proxy for NT residual volatility. A *portfolio's* residual volatility can then be determined from the spread duration, $w_{NT}D_{NT}$, where w_{NT} represents the NT percentage allocation. In our example, the spread duration of the benchmark portfolio is 1.6 years (40% × 4 years). If we assume a 33.5-basis-point residual spread volatility, the residual return volatility for the benchmark portfolio will be approximately 53.6 basis points (1.6 × 33.5 basis points). As we will see in subsequent sections, this statistical characterization enables us to balance the reach for increased portfolio spread against the associated increase in residual risk.

To match the residual risk of the benchmark, the portfolio manager must match the spread duration. This match can be accomplished with any appropriate combination of NT duration and percentage—for example, an 80% allocation to two-year NTs (80% × 2 years = 1.6 years) or a 20% allocation to eight-year NTs (see Figure 18–3).

In our example, increasing the NT allocation leads to a greater portfolio spread (see Figure 18–4), even when the duration is shortened to maintain a spread-duration match. Thus, a manager reaps a greater portfolio spread as the NT percentage is increased. Ultimately, all else being equal, a maximum

Figure 18–4. Portfolio Spread in Spread-Duration-Matched Portfolios

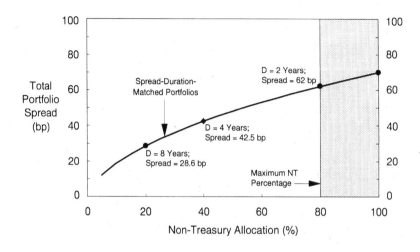

bp = basis points; D = standard duration; NT= non-Treasury.

spread of 70 basis points is obtained with 100% 1.6-year NTs.[8] However, with vastly different NT percentages, all things are obviously *not* equal.

A high NT percentage portfolio will suffer approximately the same price erosion as the benchmark as long as its spread duration is matched to the 1.6-year spread duration of the benchmark. In other words, within the context of our model, the spread-duration-matched portfolios in Figure 18–4 are all "risk-free" in terms of performance relative to the benchmark. However, many other risk factors, such as negative credit events, changing supply and demand, refundings and/or prepayment uncertainties can lead to adverse spread curve reshapings that are not captured in our model. In general, these "exogenous" risks escalate with higher NT percentages. Therefore, it is hardly surprising that, in practice, the portfolio manager is likely to find himself constrained by some specified maximum allowable NT percentage.

In Figure 18–4, we took this maximum NT percentage to be 80%. Within the context of our example, the manager would obtain the greatest portfolio spread by moving directly to this maximum 80% NT allocation. At this NT percentage, a duration of 2.0 years provides the "riskless match" to the 1.6-

---

[8]With unusually shaped spread curves, the portfolio spread may not always increase with increasing NT percentage.

Figure 18–5. Portfolio Spread versus Non-Treasury Spread Duration at Varying Proportions of Non-Treasury Investments

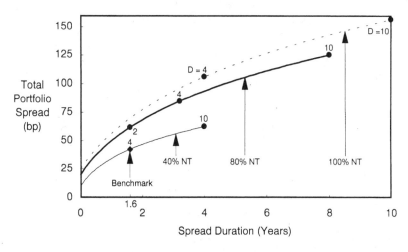

bp = basis points; D = standard duration; NT= non-Treasury.

year spread duration of the benchmark portfolio. From the original spread curve in Figure 18–2, the two-year NT is seen to carry a spread of 78 basis points. Hence, with an 80% allocation of two-year NTs, the total portfolio provides a spread advantage of 62 basis points (= 80% × 78 basis points), which is the value displayed in Figure 18–4.

The spread-duration-matched 80% NT portfolio is attractive because it is "risk-free," at least in our narrow sense. However, when we restrict ourselves to this portfolio, we do not take full advantage of the risk/return trade-off available with a positively sloped spread curve. Figure 18–5 shows that with a fixed 80% NT allocation, the total portfolio spread widens as the spread duration increases. The extent of this widening can be seen to be greater for high NT percentages than it is for low NT percentages. Of course, any spread-duration lengthening beyond the strict 1.6-year spread-duration match will have the consequence that the portfolio will no longer be "risk-free"— parallel spread movements will expose the portfolio to some degree of underperformance relative to the benchmark. In the following sections, we shall explain how this mismatch can be controlled so as to provide an acceptable balance between incremental spread and the associated residual risk.

THE BENCHMARK SHORTFALL CONSTRAINT

To match the performance of a benchmark *exactly*, the manager must buy the full benchmark portfolio. In contrast, to outperform the benchmark, the manager must adjust the duration and/or the proportion of NTs, thereby departing from the benchmark allocation. Consequently, the resulting "active" portfolio will carry some risk of underperforming the benchmark.

Portfolio managers can use a "shortfall constraint" to control this relative performance risk. To illustrate, we continue to focus on the 40% four-year-duration NT/60% five-year-duration TSY benchmark. We allow for the possibility that the investment portfolio will return less than this benchmark, but we seek reasonable assurance that significant underperformance will be infrequent. Specifically, we apply the following shortfall constraint: The investment portfolio can have only a 10% probability of underperforming the benchmark by more than 25 basis points. We refer to the –25-basis-point tolerance as the *shortfall threshold*.

At first, we consider only a 40% NT allocation for the investment portfolio, so we focus on the lowest curve in Figure 18–5. Portfolios that fulfill the shortfall constraint are located within the "V-shape" in Figure 18–6.[9] The vertex represents a portfolio with the same 1.6-year spread duration as the 40/60 benchmark portfolio, but with a spread of 17 basis points over TSYs. This vertex point is chosen so that its spread is exactly 25 basis points lower than the 42-basis-point benchmark spread. Because of the spread-duration match, spread changes will have the same price impact on both the benchmark and the vertex portfolio. Thus, the spread gap is "locked in" and the vertex portfolio will provide a total portfolio return that is 25 basis points less than the benchmark.[10] The vertex point represents the lowest portfolio spread that is consistent with the –25-basis-point shortfall constraint. A spread-duration-

---

[9]It can be shown that the width of the shortfall "V" decreases as the residual spread volatility increases. Thus, a residual volatility greater than our assumed 33.5 basis points will lead to a more restricted choice of portfolios. For a derivation of the construction of the shortfall "V," see "Portfolio Optimization under Shortfall Constraints: A Confidence Limit Approach to Managing Downside Risk," Martin L. Leibowitz and Roy D. Henriksson, *Financial Analysts Journal*, March/April 1989. The points within the shortfall region provide a balance between spread and duration that meets the shortfall requirements. In practice, not all of the combinations represented by the standard region can be realized in the financial markets. In our example, all the points along the NT curve are realizable.

[10]Recall that the "lock-in" is based on the following assumptions: the yield curve is flat, there are no yield-curve reshapings, and unexpected spread changes are uniform across the yield curve. The analysis can be readily generalized to sloped yield curves, but the adjustments for nonparallel shifts are more complex.

Figure 18–6. The Region of Acceptable Shortfall Portfolios with 40% Non-Treasuries

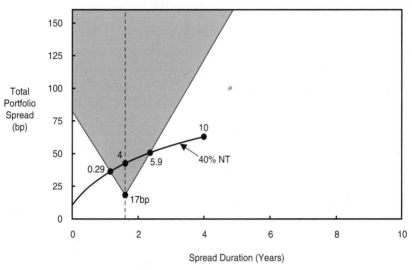

bp = basis points; D = standard duration; NT= non-Treasury.

matched portfolio with any lower spread will underperform the benchmark by more than 25 basis points.

Portfolios along the vertical center line of the "V" have the same spread duration as the benchmark. As we move up this vertical line, both the portfolio spread and the NT percentage increase. In contrast, portfolios along either arm of the "V" do not match the spread duration of the benchmark. However, these portfolios still meet the shortfall constraint because they add enough portfolio spread to compensate for the incremental volatility. The symmetry of the "V" reflects the fact that the magnitude of the duration gap determines the incremental volatility, regardless of whether the mismatch is in a positive or a negative direction.

Points in the shaded interior of the "V" represent NT investments that exceed the shortfall requirement. For example, spread-duration-matched portfolios along the vertical line have a 0% probability of falling below the –25-basis-point relative shortfall threshold. As we move horizontally away from the center line, the portfolio spread remains constant, but the spread-duration mismatch increases. Consequently, the probability of failing to meet the shortfall threshold increases as we move toward the arms of the "V."

The points at which the "V" intersects the 40% NT curve represent the extremes of allowable duration. Figure 18–6 shows that the NT investment duration can be extended to 5.9 years or shortened to 2.9 years. If there are no other considerations, the manager naturally will prefer the longer-duration portfolio (with a positively sloped spread curve) because it offers 50 basis points of total portfolio spread, 8 basis points more than the benchmark itself. For this reason, we will refer to the portfolio with 5.9-year NTs as the "optimal portfolio."

As shown earlier, increasing the NT allocation provides even more dramatic improvements (see Figure 18–7) than extending duration. Suppose that, as indicated earlier, the NT allocation is constrained to a maximum of 80%. With an 80% NT allocation, the duration-matched portfolio (with two-year-duration NTs) provides a spread of 62 basis points, substantially higher than the spread available from any 40% NT allocation that meets the shortfall constraint. However, the optimal shortfall portfolio for the 80% NT spread curve provides an even greater spread than the duration-matched portfolio. At the optimal point, the NT standard duration is 3.9 years, the spread duration is 3.1 years, and the portfolio spread is 85 basis points—43 basis points greater than the benchmark portfolio spread.[11]

Comparing Optimal Shortfall Portfolios to Spread-Duration-Matched Portfolios

For our example, we find that at any NT allocation, the standard NT duration of the optimal shortfall portfolio is greater than that for the spread-duration-matched portfolio (see Figure 18–8). Moreover, the spread difference between the *optimal* portfolio and the *duration-matched* portfolio grows rapidly as the NT percentage increases (see Figure 18–9).

---

[11]Because we have taken the expected return curve to be the same as the initial yield curve, we have referred to both the NT yield advantage and the NT return advantage as the "spread." More generally, the shape of the NT expected return curve could be driven by some expected movement in yield spreads, in which case the shape of the return spread curve would differ significantly from our basic example. If a uniform widening of yield spreads was anticipated, the expected return curve would take the form of a downward rotation of the original spread curve around the zero duration point, and the optimal duration would shift to the shorter duration of the left arm of the "V." In contrast, a uniform spread narrowing would generate an upward rotation, resulting in an expected return curve that is significantly more positively sloped than the initial yield curve. In this case, the shortfall "V" will encompass a much wider range of expected returns. However, the spread-duration-matched portfolios always remain "risk-free," including when spread changes are expected. In turn, within the context of our model, this implies that the maximum NT percentage should generally be maintained, even in the face of an expected spread *widening*. In fact, given a sufficiently large anticipated widening, the optimal portfolio would be the maximum NT percentage with the shortest duration "V-intersect." (In certain situations, the initial spread curve can be used in conjunction with alternative market expectations. For example, an investor might want to establish a spread-duration tilt based on his or her *subjective* market views, but still exercise a more *objective* degree of risk control based on shortfalls relative to the static spread curve.)

Figure 18–7. Shortfall Portfolios with a 40% or an 80% Non-Treasury Allocation

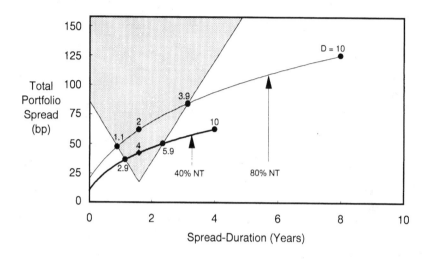

bp = basis points; D = standard duration; NT= non-Treasury.

Figure 18–8. Standard Duration of Non-Treasuries in Optimal Shortfall Portfolios

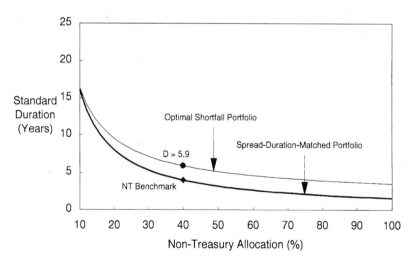

D = standard duration; NT= non-Treasury.

Figure 18–9. Spread Gains from Non-Treasuries in Optimal Shortfall Portfolios

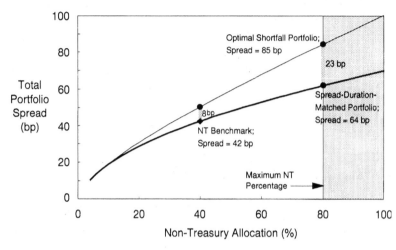

bp = basis points; NT= non-Treasury.

With a positively sloped spread curve subject only to parallel shifts, our analysis clearly points to the optimal shortfall portfolio. However, when spread-curve reshapings are considered, the spread-duration-matched "bullet" portfolio may be too risky for some investors. In fact, there are less risky ways of gaining some of the additional return that NT investments offer. As long as a positive spread can be captured with short-duration NTs, investors will find movement toward the maximum NT percentage to be advantageous. For example, a less risky 80% NT allocation can be achieved with a barbell portfolio that is equally divided between four-year-duration and short-duration NTs. This portfolio will have the same 1.6-year spread duration as the benchmark. Moreover, the 40% four-year NT is the only portfolio component that is sensitive to spread movements of any kind! Thus, with *any* spread curve reshaping, the portfolio should precisely track the performance of the benchmark.

In our spread curve (see Figure 18–2), NT securities with zero horizon duration have a 25-basis-point spread advantage over TSYs. Consequently, a 40% four-year-duration/40% 0-year-duration NT portfolio will have a 10-basis-point advantage (40% of 25 basis points) over the benchmark portfolio. For comparison, recall that the 80% two-year NT investment had a 22-basis-point advantage, while the optimal shortfall portfolio had a 45-basis-point advantage.

Benchmark Duration Independence

Throughout this section, we have not mentioned the duration of TSYs in the benchmark portfolio. The reason for this omission is that as long as the TSY curve is subject only to parallel movements, the NT investment decision is independent of the benchmark duration. To illustrate this independence, we suppose that the sensitivity of 4-year-duration NTs to TSY rate changes is reflected in a 5.2-year statistical duration. If the benchmark TSY duration is 5.0 years, the total portfolio duration will be 5.08 years, the weighted average of these two durations.

Using this total portfolio duration, the portfolio manager can invest at any point along the NT spread curve according to the following strategy:

1. Buy a 100% 5.08-year TSY portfolio;
2. Buy the optimal NT securities in accordance with the shortfall criterion given above; and
3. Short TSY securities with the same duration as the statistical duration of the NT securities. The dollar value of the long NT position and the short TSY position should be the same.[12]

This strategy captures the NT spread while matching the benchmark portfolio duration. The same approach could be used for *any* benchmark duration, and the selection criteria for NT investments would be unchanged. Within the context and limitations of our model, the optimal NT security can then be found by reaching for the maximum NT spread gain within the duration bounds set by the shortfall constraint.

OPTIMAL PORTFOLIO SELECTION USING A SINGLE SPREAD CURVE

In the previous section, separate spread curves were plotted for a 40% and an 80% NT allocation. To find an optimal shortfall portfolio, we restricted the space of acceptable portfolios to those within a fixed shortfall "V." These plots are convenient for illustrative purposes, but they fail to capture the continuum of possible NT allocations. Another drawback to the previous approach is that the duration of the optimal portfolio cannot be directly read from the horizontal "spread-duration" axis. To overcome both of these limi-

---

[12]This theoretical strategy neglects the cost of shorting over extended investment horizons.

tations and to gain additional insights into the available portfolio choice, we now show how a *single* spread curve can be used to locate optimal shortfall NT portfolios for *any* NT percentage.

We begin with the NT spread curve from Figure 18–2. Then, for any specified NT percentage, we plot a "V" that cuts off the segment of the curve having the acceptable NT durations. While the shape of the "V" is the same for all NT percentages, the location of the "vertex portfolio" varies.[13] For any NT percentage, the vertex point must provide a *total portfolio spread* that falls 25 basis points below the 42-basis-point spread of the benchmark portfolio. Thus, for any NT percentage, the vertex point must provide a total portfolio spread of 17 basis points (= 42 − 25) over TSYs.

A 40% NT Allocation

As an example, we first restrict the investment portfolio to the same 40% NT allocation as the benchmark (see Figure 18–10). Then, we translate the required total portfolio spread of 17 basis points into a corresponding spread for the NT component. With a 40% allocation, the required NT spread is 43 basis points (= 17/0.40). This determines the vertical placement of the vertex.

We set the horizontal placement of the vertex so that the vertex spread duration matches the 1.6-year benchmark spread duration. Thus, the vertex is located at an NT duration of 4 years (40% × 4 years = 1.6 years). This "vertex portfolio" locks in 25 basis points of underperformance relative to the benchmark.

Figure 18–10 also shows that the shortfall "V" intersects the spread curve at durations of 2.9 years and 5.9 years—the same duration values that were found for the 40% NT curve in Figure 18–6. Thus, Figures 18–10 and 18–6 select the same portfolios.

An 80% NT Allocation

If the percentage of NTs in the investment portfolio differs from the benchmark, two adjustments must be made to the vertex position (see Figure 18–11). As an example, consider the maximal 80% NT allocation. In this case, the vertex duration must be set to two years in order to coincide with the 1.6-year benchmark value (80% of 2 years = 1.6 years). We also set the

---

[13]The slope of the arms of the "V" is determined from the residual spread volatility (33.5 basis points) and the shortfall percentile. In our example, we set our shortfall probability at 10%. Assuming that all return distributions are normal, the 10th-percentile return is located 1.282 standard deviations below the mean. Under these assumptions the slope is ± 1.282 × 33.5 = ±42.95.

Figure 18–10. The Shortfall Constraint for 40% Non-Treasury Portfolios

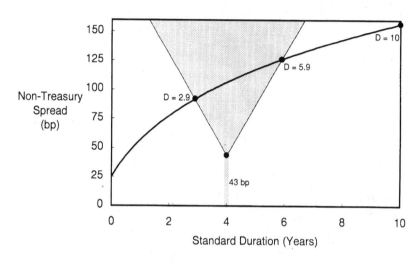

bp = basis points.

Figure 18–11. The Shortfall Constraint for 80% Non-Treasury Portfolios

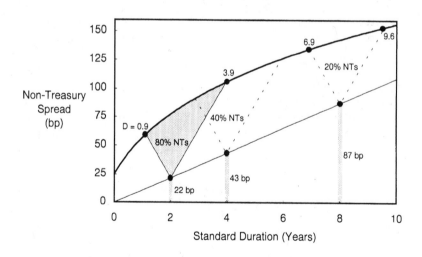

bp = basis points; D = standard duration; NT= non-Treasury.

spread at the vertex to reflect the NT percentage. Because the vertex point must provide a total portfolio spread advantage of 17 basis points over TSYs, the vertex NT security must now have a spread of 22 basis points (80% of 22 = 17). These duration and spread adjustments lead to a downward and left-ward shift of the vertex point. At the new vertex location, the "V-region" includes a duration band from 0.9 year to 3.9 years. The optimal duration is 3.9 years, the same value as in Figure 18–7.

Figure 18–11 also shows that the vertex points for the 40% and 80% NT allocation fall on a line that extends from the origin (the zero-duration, zero-spread point).[14] If the NT allocation is less than 40%, a spread-duration match is achieved with a longer duration than the benchmark. Thus, with a 20% NT allocation, the "V" moves upward to the 8-year duration point (40% × 8 years = 1.6 years), and the optimal duration is found to be 9.6 years.

PORTFOLIO SELECTION UNDER TIGHTER SHORTFALL CONDITIONS

In the previous section, we observed that the vertex points for shortfall regions were located on a straight line. For a given benchmark (40% four-year-duration NTs were used in our example), the slope of that vertex line depends on the benchmark spread duration and the minimum spread (which is determined from the shortfall threshold of –25 basis points). Figure 18–12 illustrates the effect of tightening the shortfall threshold from –25 basis points to –15 basis points. Note that the vertex line rotates about the origin, increasing its slope. As a result, all shortfall "Vs" move vertically upward, reflecting the more restrictive shortfall constraint. As the shortfall "Vs" move closer to the spread curve, the duration gap shrinks, and the optimal shortfall portfolio moves closer to the spread-duration-matched portfolio. For example, with a 40% NT, the optimal duration shrinks from 5.9 years for the –25-basis-point shortfall threshold to 5.2 years for the –15-basis-point shortfall threshold.

Also, note that the new vertex line intersects the spread curve at the 8.6-year duration point. The shortfall "V," with its vertex at that intersection

---

[14]Two conditions must be satisfied at a vertex point: (1) the spread duration of the portfolio must = 1.6 years, the spread duration of the benchmark; and (2) the spread of the portfolio must be precisely 17.4 basis points, the minimum spread to meet the shortfall constraint. We now can find the NT spread at the vertex from the ratio of (2) to (1) as follows:

(NT weight × NT spread)/(NT weight × NT duration) = 17.4/1.6 = 10.875,   or

NT spread = 10.875 × NT duration.

The above expression represents a straight line through the origin with slope 10.875.

Figure 18–12. Shortfall Constraints with Low Risk Tolerance

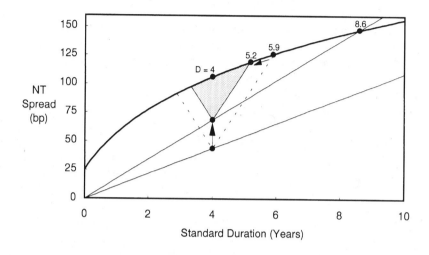

bp = basis points; D = standard duration; NT= non-Treasury.

point, can be shown to correspond to an 18.6% NT allocation.[15] With this allocation, the "V" will include only one point of the spread curve (i.e., the vertex), and only one NT duration (8.6 years) will meet the shortfall constraint. With percentages lower than 18.6%, the "Vs" will all lie *above* the spread curve. Thus, for very low NT percentages there are *no* NT securities that satisfy the shortfall constraint.

SUMMARY AND CONCLUSION

Portfolios of Treasury and non-Treasury securities are subject to both interest-rate risk and residual spread risk. The interest-rate risk reflects the price response to changes in Treasury rates, while the residual spread risk derives from spread changes that are unrelated to Treasury rates. Investors who manage against a mixed Treasury/non-Treasury benchmark must take both these risks into account. However, with the help of the statistical duration

---

[15]With an NT duration of 8.6 years at the vertex intersection point, a spread-duration match will occur only with an 18.6% NT allocation (18.6% × 8.6 years = 1.6 years). Thus, the tangent "V" must correspond to an 18.6% NT allocation.

concept, investors can address these two sources of risk as separate problems. This separation implies that, under the assumptions of our model, the Treasury benchmark will not influence the choice of an optimal non-Treasury investment.

In this chapter, we first focus on non-Treasury investments that have the same spread duration as the benchmark. We then show that, in general, improved portfolio returns can be attained by proceeding to the maximum permissible non-Treasury percentage, while maintaining the spread-duration match. Such spread-duration-matched portfolios can increase return without adding residual risk from parallel shifts of the spread curve.

However, even at the maximum non-Treasury percentage, the spread-duration-matched portfolio does not take full advantage of a positively sloped spread curve. By departing from a spread-duration match, we can find non-Treasury investments that provide a higher expected return with limited relative performance risk. Specifically, we use a shortfall constraint to control the likelihood that an investment portfolio will significantly underperform the benchmark. This formulation enables us to find the optimal non-Treasury investment by looking *only* at the spread curve for the non-Treasury sector.

While the model of spread behavior developed in this chapter is rather simplistic, the optimization technique provides a number of insights that should prove valuable in choosing portfolios that balance the trade-off between the incremental spread and the associated risks.

Chapter 19

Spread Immunization: Portfolio Improvements through Dollar-Duration Matching

INTRODUCTION

Today's fixed-income markets offer portfolio managers a wide array of high-quality investment opportunities. In the U.S. market, investors can choose Treasury (TSY) securities of virtually any maturity, from 30 days to 30 years. Investors seeking higher-than-Treasury yields can select non-Treasury (NT) securities such as mortgages and investment-grade corporates. In reaching for yield, however, investors must accept a variety of risks such as those associated with mortgage prepayments, corporate credit developments, and changing intermarket spreads. In the international markets, the differences in the shapes of foreign and domestic yield curves form the basis of many investment opportunities. By hedging currency risk, U.S. investors can treat foreign fixed-income securities as another class of dollar-based NT investments.

In this chapter, we view the portfolio manager as having an initial portfolio with a specified duration and fixed (nonzero) proportions of TSY and NT securities.[1] We then show how investors can take advantage of the spread of NT yields relative to TSY yields. The primary strategy is to improve the portfolio's yield while maintaining the original portfolio's sensitivity both to TSY rate changes and to spread changes. This balance is maintained by keep-

---

[1]An early version of the strategies described in this chapter was introduced at the Salomon Brothers Central Bank Seminar, May 26, 1994, in a lecture by Martin L. Leibowitz, entitled "Managing Relative to a Multicurrency Benchmark."

ing the total portfolio duration (TPD) and the "spread duration" of the NT component equal to the initial values.[2] With this duration-matching strategy, the new portfolio will have the same response as the original to parallel shifts of the TSY curve (assuming constant spreads). Thus, relative to the initial portfolio, the new portfolio will be "immunized" against parallel TSY curve shifts. Moreover, by spread-duration matching the NT components, we can also achieve a form of "spread immunization" against parallel *spread curve* shifts.

Our key finding is that, with certain positively sloped return curves, the investor can improve the portfolio yield by shifting toward higher percentages of lower-duration NTs, balanced by a correspondingly lower percentage of longer-duration TSYs. We also show how to identify the "best" points on the respective yield curves for these weight shifts and how the resulting gains can be quickly estimated.

THE INITIAL PORTFOLIO

Throughout this chapter, we assume a one-year investment horizon and an initial portfolio consisting of 60% TSYs and 40% NTs. Because we focus on the total return over the one-year period, we are primarily concerned with the interest-rate sensitivity at year-end. Thus, we focus only on the horizon duration, which we assume to be four years for the TSY component and five years for the NT component.

We compute the total portfolio duration (TPD) as the weighted average of the two durations:[3]

TPD = (60% × 4 Years) + (40% × 5 Years) = 4.4 Years.

The 4.4-year TPD measures the horizon sensitivity to unexpected changes in TSY yields, assuming that the spread between TSY and NT yields does not change. Any such change in spreads will further affect the return of the NT component.

---

[2]For the NTs in a portfolio, spread duration = weight × duration. The spread duration multiplied by the total dollar value of the portfolio (that is, the dollar duration) is a measure of the dollar impact of changes in NT spreads. In this chapter, we use the terms "spread duration" and "dollar duration" interchangeably.

[3]In this chapter, for simplicity, we assume that spread changes are independent of yield changes. However, the spread-duration matching technique as developed in this chapter will achieve the desired spread immunization for *any* statistical relationship between spread and yield changes (assuming only parallel shifts). A methodology for adjusting the TPD when spread changes are directly related to yield changes is developed in Chapter 16.

Figure 19–1. Flat Yield Curves for Intermediate-Duration Treasury and Non-Treasury Securities

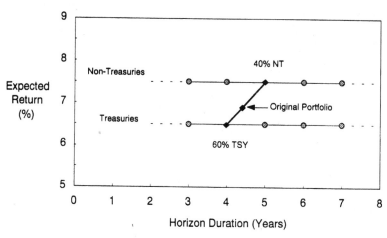

NT= non-Treasury; TSY = Treasury.

This sensitivity to spread changes is measured by the spread duration (the product of the relative weight and duration of the NTs).[4] For the original portfolio,

Spread Duration = 40% × 5 Years = 2 Years.

Turning to the return dimension, Figure 19–1 illustrates a hypothetical situation in which the TSY curve is flat at 6.50% throughout the intermediate sector, and the curve is expected to remain at that level over the one-year investment horizon. Under these special conditions, the expected return is the same as the yield.[5]

In Figure 19–1, the NT spread is a flat 100 basis points, bringing the yield of NTs to 7.50%. If spreads do not change, the return also will be 7.50%. We emphasize that we are only focusing on horizon durations between three and seven years.

---

[4]See "Spread Duration: A New Tool for Bond Portfolio Management," Martin L. Leibowitz, William S. Krasker, and Ardavan Nozari, *The Journal of Portfolio Management*, Spring 1990.

[5]More generally, forecasts of expected return reflect the anticipated horizon yield curve that results from factors such as parallel yield shifts, yield-curve "persistence," and/or yield-curve reshaping. However, for simplicity of exposition, throughout this chapter we will use the terms "yield" and "expected return" synonymously. See Chapter 25.

Figure 19–1 shows the original portfolio positioned at a point that is 40% of the distance between the four-year-duration TSY point and the five-year-duration NT point. The duration at this point is 4.4 years and the expected return is 6.90%.

PORTFOLIO RESTRUCTURING WITH FLAT RETURN CURVES

When return curves are flat and NTs have a return advantage over TSYs, the portfolio manager can increase the expected portfolio return by increasing the exposure to NTs. In practice, however, the NT allocation is likely to be restricted to some maximum level. This limitation protects against excessive credit risk.

As an example, we assume that there is an overriding limitation that constrains the manager to no more than 60% NTs. If the NT weight was shifted to this maximum 60% level, the duration of NTs would have to be shortened to maintain the original level of spread risk. More precisely, the manager must keep the spread duration at two years. This can be accomplished by setting the duration of the NTs to 3.33 years. With this duration choice,

Spread Duration = 60% × 3.33 Years = 2 Years.

With 60% of assets now in NTs, only 40% is left to invest in TSYs. Because the TSY percentage has been lowered from 60% to 40%, the TSY duration must be increased from 4 years to 6 years in order to maintain the original 2.4-year, TSY-only duration (60% × 4 years = 40% × 6 years = 2.4 years). By keeping the duration sensitivity on both curves at their initial settings, we have also maintained the original TPD of 4.4 years.

Figure 19–2 illustrates the new portfolio and shows the return pickup. More precisely,

New Portfolio Return = (40% × 6.50%) + (60% × 7.50%) = 7.10%

Original Portfolio Return = 6.90%

Expected Return Gain = 7.10% – 6.90% = 20 Basis Points.

The restructuring in Figure 19–2 shows that 20 basis points of return can be gained without change in either overall interest-rate risk (as measured by the TPD) or spread risk, as long as unexpected changes in horizon yields or spreads result from parallel shifts of either the yield curve or the spread curve (or both).

Figure 19–2. Portfolio Restructuring with Flat Return Curves

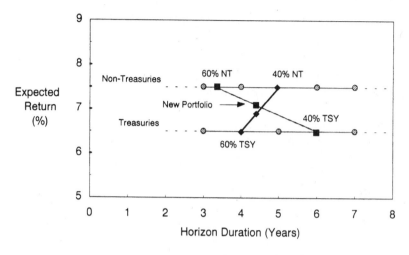

NT= non-Treasury; TSY = Treasury.

We note that the 20-basis-point gain is precisely the 20% difference between the new and the old NT allocation (60% – 40%), multiplied by the
uniform 100-basis-point yield spread. Later, we show that a similar result
holds under more general conditions. We also note that the analysis does not
address many other factors that can significantly affect returns. For example,
investment-grade corporates are subject to credit risk and liquidity costs,
and substantial diversification is required to achieve a reasonably "safe" return. In the mortgage market, prepayment risk, model risk, and negative
convexity can seriously affect the returns. More generally, the shift in
weightings may alter the overall maturity structure and lead to new problems with convexity and/or vulnerability to nonparallel curve reshapings.

RESTRUCTURING WITH A SLOPED NON-TREASURY RETURN CURVE

Figure 19–3 illustrates the intermediate portion of a sloped NT yield curve
together with a flat TSY curve. In this new example, the original portfolio is
the same as in the first example—a flat TSY curve at 6.50% and the five-year

NT at 7.50%. However, the NT curve's slope lowers the return of the new portfolio's 3.33-year NT to 7.39%. Thus,

New Portfolio Return = (40% × 6.50%) + (60% × 7.39%) = 7.03%

Expected Return Gain = 7.04% – 6.90% = 14 Basis Points.

This example shows that the slope of the curves can have a significant effect on the size of potential gains.

Figure 19–4 illustrates an interesting facet of this spread-duration matching process. The upper line is drawn through the 3.33- and 5-year NT points and projected leftward to the return axis, intersecting that axis at 7.17%. The same construction was made through the four- and six-year TSY points, resulting in a horizontal line at the 6.50% return level. The 67-basis-point difference between these two intersection points can be used to compute the return gain: The 14-basis-point return gain is the product of the 20% weight change and this 67-basis-point "projected spread."

Return Gain = (Change in NT Allocation) × Projected Spread

= (60% – 40%) × (7.17% – 6.50%)

= 20% × 67 Basis Points

= 14 Basis Points.

The above formula can be shown to hold in general (see the Appendix to this chapter for more detail). Thus, the return gain from restructuring with dollar-duration matching is determined by only two factors. The first factor is the NT percentage allocation. The second factor is the "projected spread," based on the relative positions of the four relevant duration points. Using this approach, we can see at a glance whether significant yield improvement can be achieved from this form of portfolio rebalancing.

PORTFOLIO RESTRUCTURING WITH TWO RISING RETURN CURVES

The methodology of the preceding section can be applied generally. To illustrate this application, Figure 19–5 shows two hypothetical rising curves. The first portfolio we consider is the same as in our previous example: 60% 4-year TSYs/40% 5-year NTs, rebalanced to 40% 6-year TSYs/60% 3.33-year NTs.

In Figure 19–5, the steepness of the TSY curve is advantageous because there is a return gain as the TSY duration is extended from four years to six

Figure 19–3. Portfolio Restructuring with a Sloped Non-Treasury Curve

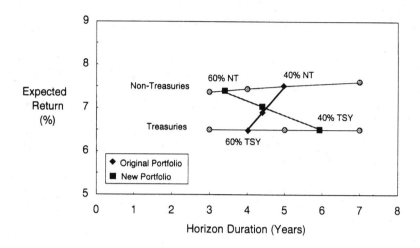

NT = non-Treasury, TSY = Treasury.

Figure 19–4. Estimating the Return Gain from the Projected Spread

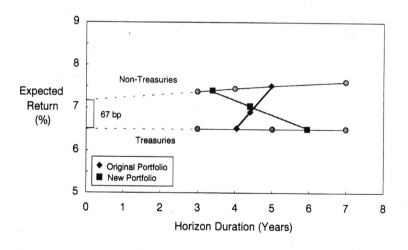

bp = basis points.

Figure 19–5. Portfolio Restructuring with Two Rising Yield Curves

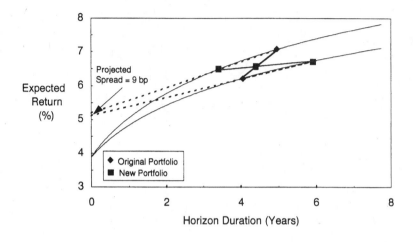

bp = basis points.

Figure 19–6. The Components of Portfolio Restructuring

Original Allocation	Restructuring	Calculation of Gain (Loss)	Gain (Loss)
60% TSY @ 6.20%	40% TSY @ 6.75%	40% × (6.75% − 6.20%)	22.0bp
	20% NT @ 6.45%	20% × (6.45% − 6.20%)	5.0
40% NT @ 7.08%	40% NT @ 6.45%	40% × (6.45% − 7.08%)	−25.2
Final Portfolio	40% TSY/60% NT		1.8

bp = basis points; NT= non-Treasury; TSY = Treasury.

years. Figure 19–6 traces out this process, showing that the gain occurs in two ways. The 40% of assets that remain in TSYs provide a higher return than at the outset. The 20% of TSYs that are shifted into NTs also add return, because the return of 3.33-year NTs is greater than the return of 4-year TSYs.

In contrast to the TSY curve, the steepness of the NT curve works against investors. As the original 40% 5-year NT investment is traded for 3.33-year NTs, we move down the NT curve and give up return. The result is that the

Figure 19-7. Portfolio Restructuring with a 60% Two-Year Treasury/40% Seven-Year Non-Treasury Benchmark

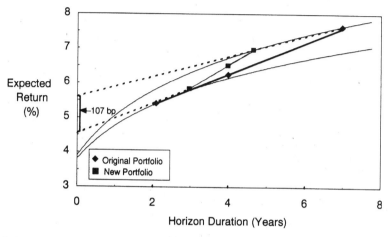

bp = basis points.

gains and losses almost exactly balance, and the portfolio rebalancing is virtually return-neutral. The lack of a significant return from the weight shift can also be gleaned from the negligible projected spread derived from extending the lines between the "shift points" on each curve.[6]

The reason that we have not picked up return with the sloped curves is that we are focusing on the wrong part of the curve. Suppose, for example, that the original portfolio consists of 60% two-year TSYs/40% seven-year NTs. This portfolio has an expected return of 6.31%, a TPD of 4 years, and a spread duration of 2.8 years (40% of 7 years). The portfolio components are situated on the flatter portion of the NT curve and on the steeper portion of the TSY curve (see Figure 19–7). Thus, the gains from moving *up* the TSY curve will dominate the losses incurred by moving *down* the NT curve.

---

[6]In this example, we have shown smoothly rising return curves that reflect the fact that credit spread tends to increase with maturity. The smooth-curve idealization is not restrictive because the return gain only depends on the four duration points relevant to the initial and restructured portfolios. We also note that the actual shape of the individual yield curves is more important than the structure of the nominal NT spreads. For example, if the TSY curve were flat and we maintained the same NT spreads as in Figure 19–5, the projected spread (and the corresponding return pickup) would be much greater than in Figure 19–5.

Figure 19–8. Portfolio with Equal Weightings of Treasuries and Non-Treasuries

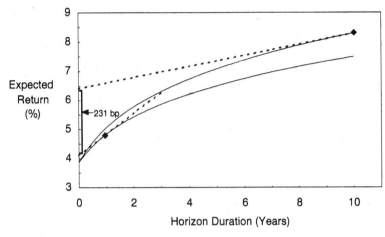

bp = basis points.

Figure 19–7 illustrates the result of increasing the NT allocation to 60% while maintaining the same total portfolio duration and the same spread duration. This is accomplished by shortening the NTs to a 4.67-year duration and extending the TSY duration to 3 years. Although the two yield curves are the same as in Figure 19–5, where we only picked up 2 basis points, we are now able to gain 21 basis points. This greater return pickup can be seen by observing that the projected spread in Figure 19–7 is much wider than in Figure 19–5.

GENERAL PORTFOLIO STRUCTURES

The examples in the preceding section indicate that a strategy of spread immunization and preservation of TPD works best when the portfolio components are located on the flattest part of the NT curve on the one hand and on the steepest part of the TSY curve on the other hand. In this section, we show that this result holds for a general range of positively sloped yield curves.[7]

[7]More specifically, we require continuous yield curves with a positive first derivative and negative second derivative at all points. This requirement assures that yields increase with duration, and that the yield curve is concave down. It is also possible to generalize our results to yield curves where the second derivative changes sign—that is, the concavity changes from down to up.

In Figure 19–8, we assume a "laddered" portfolio with equal dollar investments in TSYs and NTs with maturities of 1, 3, 5, 7, and 10 years. Given the same return curves as in Figure 19–7, we look for potential rebalancings that bring the maximum gains in expected return while preserving total portfolio duration and spread risk. To this end, we have constructed tangent lines at the 1-year TSY point and at the 10-year NT point. These lines are then extended leftward until they meet the vertical axis, leading to a projected spread of 231 basis points. This projected spread is important because, as in the simple example of Figure 19–4, it can be used to estimate the gains from rebalancing.

For example, suppose we focus on just two components of our laddered portfolio, the 1-year TSY (at 4.82%) and the 10-year NT (at 8.30%). We can view these two bonds as forming an equally weighted portfolio, with a TPD of 5.5 years (50% × 1 year + 50% × 10 years) and an expected return of 6.56% (50% × 4.82% + 50% × 8.30%). If we increase the NT allocation by 20% and shorten duration (to preserve spread duration), the portfolio return gain can be approximated as follows:[8]

Return Gain ≈ (Change in NT Allocation) × Projected Spread

= (70% − 50%) × 231 Basis Points

= 46 Basis Points.

This pickup from adding NTs is the greatest that can be achieved with any pairing of TSY and NT securities in the laddered portfolio. At shorter NT durations, the tangent line becomes steeper, leading to a smaller projected spread and diminished return pickup. Similarly, at longer TSY durations, the tangent line becomes flatter, again resulting in a smaller projected spread. These findings confirm and generalize the observations of the preceding section. Maximum return pickups are achieved when the benchmark portfolio is an extreme barbell, with the NT component at the flattest part of the curve and the TSY component at the steepest part of the curve.

There may be many opportunities for return improvements in the laddered portfolio. For example, suppose we focus on another extreme pairing of bonds (not shown in Figure 19–8), the 10-year TSY (at 7.50%) and the 1-year NT (at 5.04%). The TPD of this pairing is 5.5 years (as in the prior

---

[8]In this example, the precise return gain is 39 basis points. Because the approximation is derived under the assumption of a small change in allocation, the accuracy of the approximation declines as the change in weight increases. For comparability, all our examples have been based on a 20% increase in the NT allocation. As indicated earlier, such a large increase in NT exposure may significantly change the convexity, credit risk, and yield-curve reshaping risk of the portfolio. To avoid such risks, changes in the NT allocation may be more tightly constrained.

example) and the expected return is 6.27%. In this case, we are on the steepest part of the NT curve and the flattest portion of the TSY curve. Reasoning similar to the first example shows that we should be able to increase return by *decreasing* the allocation to NTs. Thus, we now *increase* the TSY allocation by 20% and find that we can maintain TPD and spread duration with a portfolio of 70% 7.14-year TSYs (at 7.00%) and 30% 1.67-year NTs (at 5.56%). This new portfolio has 6.57% expected return, 30 basis points *greater* than the original portfolio.

If we were to make *both* of the portfolio shifts described above, we would have picked up return while maintaining the same overall percentage allocation to NTs, the same TPD, and the same spread duration.[9] Under the starting assumption of equal 10% weighting of investments along the 10 points of the two return curves, our restructuring would have gained approximately 14 basis points (1/5 × [39 basis points + 30 basis points]).

In these examples, we have looked at extremal portfolios, where we naturally expect to be able to achieve the greatest gains. Less extreme pairings in our ladder will also result in gains, but more modest ones. Thus, if the spread immunization approach is applied iteratively throughout the ladder, we will develop a portfolio with considerable return advantages. We will also maintain the initial portfolio sensitivity to *parallel* shifts in *both* the yield curve and the spread curve.

If this process of weight-shifting and dollar-duration matching were continued indefinitely, the portfolio would ultimately collapse to a bullet portfolio. However, at some point, the iterative process would run into one or more exogenous portfolio constraints, such as the maximum NT weight, prescribed maturity/duration "buckets," or minimum convexity requirements. The optimal portfolio improvement is achieved by sequentially pursuing the most productive allowable weight/duration shift until all potential degrees of freedom have been eliminated.

From another vantage point, suppose the initial portfolio coincided with a prescribed benchmark index. Then the revised portfolio could be viewed as an "inner index" that would provide generally superior performance as long as the model conditions were met. This inner index—with its higher proportion of NTs (corporate and/or mortgage securities)—could then function as an improved neutral posture, thereby serving as a base for incremental active management.

---

[9]If the first restructuring step brings substantial return gains but exceeds the maximum NT allocation, a less productive second shift, designed to restore the maximum, may be desirable. In fact, if preservation of the NT maximum is critical, we may even be willing to give up some return when making a subsequent portfolio shift.

A more complete portfolio restructuring requires sophisticated software that can choose from the full spectrum of TSY and NT securities in order to create "optimal" portfolios that satisfy "customized" constraints on convexity, credit quality, and vulnerability to yield-curve reshapings.

CONCLUSION

Fixed-income-portfolio managers generally are restricted to a very narrow band about the duration of a preestablished benchmark. To exceed the benchmark return, the manager must be able to take advantage of relative value opportunities that exist both within the TSY market and in markets for other NT securities such as mortgages or corporates.

In this chapter, we introduce a methodology for quickly determining points on both the TSY and NT return curves where the maximum benefit can be gained from shifting the weight of NTs. This rebalancing is subject to the requirement that no change is to be made in either the total portfolio duration or in the spread duration.

In our analysis, we assume a positively sloped yield curve that tends to flatten at longer maturities. For simple barbell portfolios consisting of one TSY and one NT position, we find that higher-return portfolios can be structured by increasing the allocation to NTs but shortening their duration to maintain the same exposure to parallel movement in spreads. In order to retain the same total duration for the overall portfolio, the duration of the now lower-weighted TSY must then be lengthened.

More typically, fixed-income portfolios incorporate a spectrum of maturities. By viewing various combinations as separate barbell portfolios, we find that it is possible to systematically restructure the portfolio and pick up substantial added return. In all cases, we tend to increase duration on the steep part of one curve while decreasing duration along the flat part of the second curve. The new portfolio will have a somewhat different maturity structure than the original portfolio but the same duration and the same spread sensitivity. Thus, this portfolio restructuring can be viewed as an important step in the direction of creating an "optimal" fixed-income allocation.

APPENDIX

In this Appendix, we derive the relationship between projected spread and return gain that is discussed in the body of this chapter. Our goal is to calculate the return gain that can be achieved by rebalancing a portfolio of TSY and NT securities. The return gain results from increasing the allocation to NTs while adjusting the duration of TSYs and NTs to maintain the initial spread duration and TPD.

Using the symbols defined in Figure 19–A1, the TPD and initial spread duration are as follows:

$$\text{TPD} = wD_{NT} + (1 - w)D_{TSY}$$

$$\text{Spread Duration} = wD_{NT}.$$

The requirement of constant spread duration implies that

$$wD_{NT} = (w + \Delta w)(D_{NT} + \Delta D_{NT}).$$

Figure 19–A1. Definition of Variables

	Initial Value	Change in Value	Final Value
NT Weight	w	Δw	$w + \Delta w$
NT Expected Return	R_{NT}	ΔR_{NT}	$R_{NT} + \Delta R_{NT}$
NT Duration	D_{NT}	ΔD_{NT}	$D_{NT} + \Delta D_{NT}$
TSY Weight	$1 - w$	$-\Delta w$	$1 - (w + \Delta w)$
TSY Expected Return	R_{TSY}	ΔR_{TSY}	$R_{TSY} + \Delta R_{TSY}$
TSY Duration	D_{TSY}	ΔD_{TSY}	$D_{TSY} + \Delta D_{TSY}$
Portfolio Expected Return	R_P	ΔR_P	$R_P + \Delta R_P$
Portfolio Duration	TPD	ΔD_P	$D_P + \Delta D_P$

NT= non-Treasury; TSY = Treasury.

Solving the above equation for ΔD_{NT}, we find that

$$\Delta D_{NT} = -\left(\frac{\Delta w}{w + \Delta w}\right) D_{NT}. \tag{1}$$

With the spread duration constant, the TPD will be unchanged if the TSY "spread duration," $(1 - w)D_{TSY}$, is unchanged. Using this spread-duration constraint, as we did for D_{NT}, we then find that

$$\Delta D_{TSY} = \frac{\Delta w}{1 - (w + \Delta w)} D_{TSY}. \tag{2}$$

We now turn to our primary concern—changes in expected return. At the outset,

$$R_p = wR_{NT} + (1 - w)R_{TSY}.$$

After restructuring,

$$R_p + \Delta R_p = (w + \Delta w)(R_{NT} + \Delta R_{NT}) + (1 - w - \Delta w)(R_{TSY} + \Delta R_{TSY}).$$

Thus,

$$\Delta R_p = \Delta w R_{NT} + (w + \Delta w)\Delta R_{NT} - \Delta w R_{TSY} + (1 - w - \Delta w)\Delta R_{TSY}$$

$$= \Delta w(R_{NT} - R_{TSY}) + (w + \Delta w)\Delta R_{NT} + (1 - w - \Delta w)\Delta R_{TSY}. \tag{3}$$

The above relationship can be simplified by making use of the following observations:

- The chord passing through the initial and final NT points, (D_{NT}, R_{NT}) and $(D_{NT} + \Delta D_{NT}, R_{NT} + \Delta R_{NT})$, has slope

$$m_{NT} = \Delta R_{NT} / \Delta D_{NT}. \tag{4}$$

- The chord passing through the initial and final TSY points has slope

$$m_{TSY} = \Delta R_{TSY} / \Delta D_{TSY}. \tag{5}$$

We utilize (4) and (5) in (3) and find that

$$\Delta R_p = \Delta w (R_{NT} - R_{TSY}) + (w + \Delta w)\Delta D_{NT} m_{NT} + (1 - w - \Delta w)\Delta D_{TSY} m_{TSY}. \tag{6}$$

Next, we substitute (1) and (2) in (6),

$$\Delta R_p = (R_{NT} - R_{TSY})\Delta w - D_{NT} m_{NT}\Delta w + \Delta w m_{TSY} D_{TSY}$$

$$= [(R_{NT} - D_{NT} m_{NT}) - (R_{TSY} - D_{TSY} m_{TSY})]\Delta w. \tag{7}$$

The expressions $(R_{NT} - D_{NT} m_{NT})$ and $(R_{TSY} - D_{TSY} m_{TSY})$ are the y-intercepts of the lines that include the chords through the two NT points and the two TSY points, respectively. The difference between these two intercepts is the projected spread discussed in the text. Thus, equation (7) shows that

Return Change $= \Delta R_p =$ Projected Spread $\times \Delta w$.

Chapter 20

Yield-Curve Positioning for Multisector Bond Portfolios

INTRODUCTION

Many fixed-income-portfolio managers face the challenge of outperforming a benchmark consisting of a fixed proportion of Treasury (TSY) and non-Treasury (NT) securities. The manager usually is limited to small deviations from the total portfolio duration (TPD) of the benchmark and modest departures from the TSY/NT benchmark proportion. In this context, the "intuitive response" is to maximize the NT allocation while extending duration as far as possible along a rising NT spread curve. The remaining TSY investment is then repositioned to maintain the TPD.

In this chapter, we show that this intuition of moving to maximal NT weight and duration can be misleading. Moreover, we develop a general methodology for finding the optimal NT allocation and duration for *any* spread curve and *any* underlying TSY curve. We find that this optimal position *cannot* be located by examining the spread curve alone. Even with identical spread curves, different TSY curves can lead to vastly different results.

Three other findings are important: (1) with a strongly rising TSY curve, the optimal portfolio is sometimes attained by moving *down* the NT curve; (2) if the benchmark portfolio consists of short-duration NTs, the optimal portfolio may reflect *decreased* NT weight; and (3) under some conditions, one *should not* go to either the NT weight limit or the NT duration limit—intermediary positions can often be optimal.

OPTIMAL PORTFOLIO STRUCTURE 1: MAXIMUM NT WEIGHT AND MAXIMUM SPREAD-DURATION RISK

At the outset, we consider a flat TSY yield curve and a positively sloped NT yield curve based on the assumption that the yield spread of NTs over TSYs increases with duration. For simplicity, we regard the yield as the expected return over the investment holding period.[1] In all examples, we use the following conventions:

- The holding period for all investments is one year.
- The duration of a fixed-income security is the duration at the end of the one-year holding period.

Under these assumptions, Figure 20–1 displays a benchmark portfolio containing short-duration TSYs and long-duration NTs. Specifically, the benchmark comprises 60% 2-year-duration TSYs and 40% 8.25-year-duration NTs. This composition results in the following portfolio characteristics:

TPD $= 0.60 \times 2 \text{ Years} + 0.40 \times 8.25 \text{ Years} = 4.5 \text{ Years}$

Expected Return $= 0.60 \times 6.50\% + 0.40 \times 7.24\% = 6.80\%.$

Throughout this chapter, we assume that any changes in yields result from parallel shifts of the TSY curve and/or the spread curve. We do not address yield-curve or spread-curve reshaping risk. Within this simplified model, with the concavity illustrated in Figure 20–1, bullet NT allocations will dominate barbells. For example, an NT portfolio consisting of equal weights of short-duration NTs and long-duration NTs would not be optimal. The barbell portfolio would be expected to underperform a bullet portfolio that is concentrated at the average of the two durations.

We now assume that the portfolio manager is restricted to the benchmark TPD but may take two types of "risk departures" from the benchmark: (1) a shift in NT weight that creates some tolerable difference in credit and liquidity, and (2) an extension or contraction in NT duration that results in some allowable change in sensitivity to spread changes (that is, some degree of spread-duration risk).[2]

---

[1]This assumption is one of convenience only. Our analysis applies for any set of expected return forecasts. For a more complete discussion of the relationship between horizon yield and horizon return, see Chapters 21 and 25.

[2]The spread duration is the NT weight multiplied by the NT duration. Thus, the initial spread duration is 3.30 years (40% × 8.25 years). In an earlier chapter, we considered weight shifts, but we required that the benchmark spread duration be maintained. For a more detailed discussion, see Chapter 19.

Figure 20–1. Benchmark Portfolio with a Flat Treasury Curve

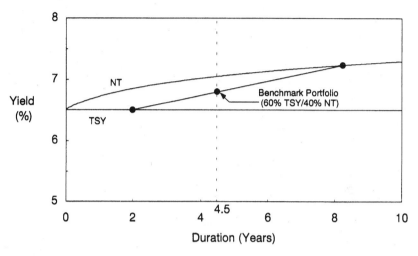

NT= non-Treasury; TSY = Treasury.

In the example of Figure 20–1, we permit a maximum weight change of 20% (in either direction) and a maximum spread-duration change of 1.2 years.[3] We then try to create a TPD-matching portfolio that has the maximum "yield" (expected return). Because the long-duration NTs have higher yields than the short-duration TSYs, we pick up yield by maximally increasing the NT weight from 40% to 60%. However, given these revised weightings, to maintain both the TPD and spread duration at benchmark levels, we decrease the NT duration from 8.25 years to 5.5 years (see Figure 20–2) and increase the TSY duration from 2 to 3 years.[4]

As the NT duration decreases, we slide down the NT curve, and the NT yield decreases by 13 basis points (from 7.24% to 7.11%). This modest yield decrease results because we are operating on the flat part of the NT curve.

---

[3]In practice, the manager may have unlimited latitude to decrease the NT allocation, possibly increasing the TSY allocation to 100% in adverse markets. Thus, the limitations on NT weight decrease may be manager-imposed rather than sponsor-imposed.

[4]When the NT weight increases by 20%, the spread duration associated with 8.25-year NTs increases by 1.65 years (20% × 8.25 years) to 4.95 years. To maintain the initial 3.30-year spread duration with 60% NTs, we decrease the NT duration to 5.50 years (3.30 divided by 60%). We also increase the TSY duration to 3 years so that the TPD is 40% × 3 years + 60% × 5.5 years = 4.5 years, the same as the benchmark TPD.

Figure 20–2. Increasing Return through a Weight Shift with a Flat TSY Curve

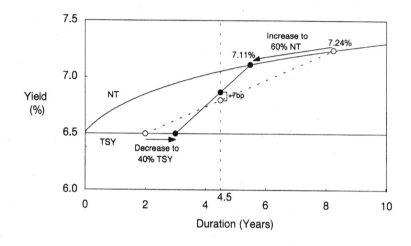

bp = basis points; NT= non-Treasury; TSY = Treasury.

We lose 13 basis points only on the original 40% NT allocation. However, we gain 61 basis points (7.11% – 6.50%) by shifting 20% of the portfolio from TSYs to NTs. Because the TSY curve is flat, there is no change in yield when we shift the remaining 40% TSYs to the three-year-duration point. In summary, we achieve the following changes:

Loss from Decreased NT Yield = 40% × –13 bp = –5.2 bp

Gain from Shift to NTs   = 20% × 61 bp   = 12.2 bp

Gain from Increased TSY Yield = 40% × 0 bp   = 0.0 bp

Net Portfolio Gain   = 7.0 bp.

We can increase our return still further by taking full advantage of the allowable 1.2-year deviation between the spread duration of the new portfolio and the benchmark. Maintaining the NT weight at 60%, we can extend the NT duration from 5.5 years to 7.5 years and increase spread duration by 1.2 years. Because this extension brings the spread duration to 4.5 years (that

---

Figure 20–3. A Portfolio with Maximum NT Weight and Maximum Spread-Duration Mismatch

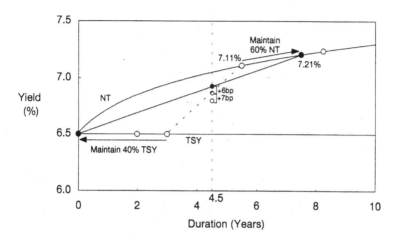

bp = basis points; NT= non-Treasury; TSY = Treasury.

---

is, the spread duration equals the TPD), we now must decrease the TSY duration to 0 years to maintain the TPD at 4.5 years (see Figure 20–3). The shift up the NT curve adds another 6 basis points (above the 7-basis-point gain achieved by the weight shift), bringing the portfolio yield to 6.93%, 13 basis points higher than the benchmark. For these yield curves, constraints, and benchmark, we can demonstrate that 6.93% is the maximum portfolio yield available.

In summary, with a flat TSY curve, we maximize yield at the "double-max" point—maximum NT weight and maximum spread-duration mismatch. It may seem logical to always move to such a double-max point, regardless of the yield-curve configuration. However, we now show that the double-max does not always provide the optimal yield.[5]

---

[5]In the Appendix to this chapter, we show that a "single-max" is always part of the optimal solution—we always utilize the maximum weight or the maximum spread duration, but not necessarily both.

OPTIMAL PORTFOLIO STRUCTURE 2: MAXIMUM NT WEIGHT SHIFT BUT PARTIAL USE OF ALLOWABLE DURATION MISMATCH

In the previous section, we considered a rising NT curve and flat TSY curve. In this case, the shape of the *spread* curve totally determined the yield enhancement. With a sloped TSY curve, however, the shapes of both *yield* curves are more significant than the spread curve itself. The reason is that when restructuring portfolios, the spread between the yield of the NT security and the yield of the TSY security is primary, even when those securities have different maturities. In contrast, the spread curve only gives the yield spread between NT and TSY securities of the same maturity. With a flat TSY curve, all TSYs have the same yield, so the spread curve carries all relevant information.

As an illustration, Figure 20–4 shows a sloped TSY curve. The NT curve is formed by adding the NT spreads shown in Figure 20–1. We also consider the same benchmark portfolio as in the previous section: 60% 2-year TSYs and 40% 8.25-year NTs. The portfolio characteristics in this new environment are as follows:

TPD   = 0.60×2 Years + 0.40×8.25 Years = 4.5 Years

Expected Return = $0.60 \times 5.43\%$ + $0.40 \times 7.94\%$ = 6.43%.

Figure 20–4 shows that the slope of the TSY curve significantly affects the return of the benchmark. For comparison, we recall that in Figure 20–1, where the TSY curve was flat at a 6.5% yield, the benchmark portfolio yield was 6.80%, 30 basis points higher than the TSY yield at the 4.5-year-duration point. In Figure 20–4, however, the TSY yield rises from 3.9% at the zero-duration point to 6.36% at the 4.5-year-duration point. For these curves, the 6.43% portfolio yield is only 7 basis points higher than the 4.5-year TSY yield.

We now show how the rising TSY curve influences the yields of restructured portfolios, even with the identical NT spread curve. We assume the same constraints as in the previous section: (1) the maximum NT weight change is 20%, (2) the maximum spread-duration change is 1.2 years, and (3) the TPD is unchanged. As in the previous section, we first maximize the NT allocation while holding the spread duration constant. We increase the NT weight from 40% to 60% (see Figure 20–5), shorten the NT duration from 8.25 years to 5.50 years to preserve spread duration, and extend the TSY duration from 2 years to 3 years to preserve the TPD.

Figure 20–4. The Benchmark Portfolio with a Sloped TSY Curve[a]

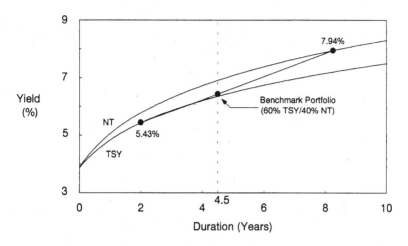

[a]The scale in this figure is much broader than in Figure 20–2. Consequently, the small spread at the zero-duration point (while the same as in Figure 20–2) is not visible in this figure. NT = non-Treasury; TSY = Treasury.

Figure 20–5. Increasing Return through a Weight Shift with Rising TSY Curve

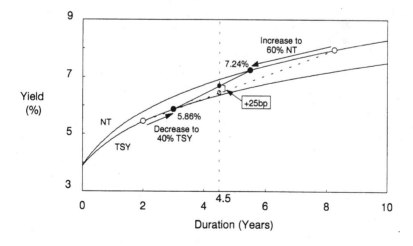

bp = basis points; NT= non-Treasury; TSY = Treasury.

Figure 20–5 shows that we pick up 25 basis points by shifting to the maximum NT weight, far more than the 7 basis points that we gained when the TSY curve was flat. The additional gain is attributable to the shape of the TSY and NT curves. In shifting weight to NTs, we moved down the NT curve to a 5.5-year duration, and the yield of the NT security decreased by 70 basis points (from 7.94% to 7.24%). This yield give-up applies only to original 40% NT allocation. When we replace 20% TSYs by NTs, we gain the 181-basis-point spread between 5.5-year NTs and 2-year TSYs (7.24% – 5.43%). We also gain yield when we move up the TSY curve from the two-year point (5.43%) to the three-year point (5.86%).

Loss from Decreased NT Yield = 40% × –70 bp = –28.0 bp

Gain from Shift to NT   = 20% × 181 bp = 36.2 bp

Gain from Increased TSY Yield = 40% × 43 bp   = 17.2 bp

Net Portfolio Gain   = 25.4 bp.

These calculations show that the relative steepness of the TSY curve in comparison to the NT curve (as shown by the gain from the shift from short TSYs to longer NTs) is more important than the loss from sliding down the NT curve. In addition, we make considerable gains when we move up the TSY curve. We also note that, although Figures 20–1 and 20–4 are based on the same spread curve, the portfolio gains with a rising TSY curve are far greater than with a flat curve.

Our next step is to use the 1.2-year spread-duration flexibility. In the previous example, we increased the NT duration and kept the TPD constant by making an offsetting decrease in the TSY duration. The TSY duration decrease, from three years to zero, was costless because of the flat TSY curve. In our current example, the same strategy would entail a substantial yield give-up, as we would move down the steepest portion of the curve. This yield decrease cannot be offset by the gain achieved by moving along the relatively flat part of the NT curve from the 5.5-year point to the 7.5-year point. Thus, with a rising TSY curve, we should not move to the maximum spread duration. It also turns out that we should not move to the minimum spread duration.[6]

---

[6]The minimum spread duration of 2.1 years (3.3 years – 1.2 years) is attained by moving down the NT curve to the 3.5-year-duration point. See the Appendix to this chapter for details on locating the optimal spread duration.

Figure 20–6. The Parallel Slope Solution for a Rising TSY Curve

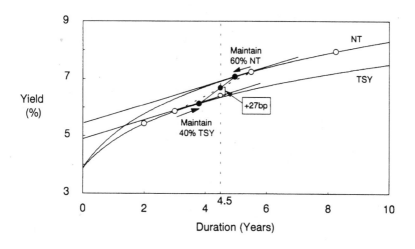

bp = basis points; NT= non-Treasury; TSY = Treasury.

The optimal solution is simply a *moderate decrease* in spread duration. In Figure 20–6, we show that the optimal solution is found at the pair of points on the TSY and NT curves where the slopes are parallel and the TPD remains at 4.5 years. At this "balance" point (NT duration = 4.97 years; TSY duration = 3.81 years), we pick up a modest 2 basis points beyond the 25 basis points gained by a weight shift, bringing the total yield enhancement to 27 basis points. More generally, with other yield-curve shapes, the gain from the spread-duration shift associated with the "parallel slope" portfolio may turn out to be comparable to (or greater than) the gain from shifting weight.

OPTIMAL PORTFOLIO STRUCTURE 3: UTILIZING MAXIMUM SPREAD RISK AND MODERATE NT WEIGHT SHIFT

In this section, we maintain the same yield curves as in the previous section, but we use a new benchmark portfolio with 40% short-duration NTs (1.13 years) and 60% intermediate-duration TSYs (6.75 years). With this configuration, the TSY yield is greater than the NT yield (see Figure 20–7).

Figure 20–7. A Benchmark Portfolio with Short-Duration NTs

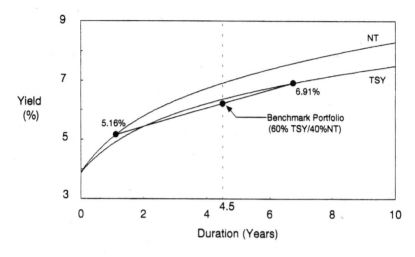

NT= non-Treasury; TSY = Treasury.

$$\text{TPD} = 0.60 \times 6.75 \text{ Years} + 0.40 \times 1.13 \text{ Years} = 4.5 \text{ Years}$$

$$\text{Expected Return} = 0.60 \times 6.91\% + 0.40 \times 5.16\% = 6.21\%.$$

We continue to maintain the TPD at 4.5 years and allow a 20% NT weight change, but we now restrict the spread-duration risk to 0.5 year.

Figure 20–7 shows that with short-duration NTs, the 4.5-year-duration benchmark portfolio yield is less than the yield of a bullet portfolio of 4.5-year TSYs. Such a portfolio can arise in a variety of ways. For example, a typical NT/TSY investment portfolio is likely to include a spectrum of durations, ranging from very short to fairly long. In that context, we can view Figure 20–7 as a "subportfolio" or *portion* of a benchmark, taken from the short end of NTs and the long end of TSYs. The goal then is to find a portfolio that outperforms this benchmark portion.

Because the TSY yield is greater than the NT yield, we use our weight flexibility to *increase* the TSY allocation. At the same time, we maintain the TPD by shortening the TSY duration and lengthening the NT duration. We also utilize our 0.5-year spread-duration flexibility to further extend the NT duration. With both sources of flexibility, it can be shown that the resulting optimal portfolio is attained by using the maximum spread duration, but we

Figure 20–8. Optimal Portfolio at "Pincer" Point

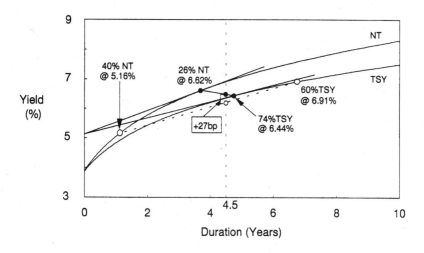

bp = basis points; NT= non-Treasury; TSY = Treasury.

only increase the TSY weight by 14.4%, rather than by the permissible 20%.[7] This restructuring results in a total gain of 27 basis points—15 basis points from the weight shift and 12 basis points from rolling up the NT curve and taking spread-duration risk (see Figure 20–8).

An important feature of the optimal portfolio in Figure 20–8 is its location at points whose tangents meet at the vertical return axis. This "pincer-like" structure represents the third possible form for the optimal solution.

Characterization of Optimal Solutions

We summarize by noting that in the preceding examples, we have seen three types of optimal solutions: (1) the "double-max" (Figure 20–3), (2) the parallel slope (Figure 20–6); and (3) the pincer (Figure 20–8). As shown in the Appendix to this chapter, the optimal portfolio for yield maximization will always fall into one of these three categories. Moreover, within each category, the solution is unique.

---

[7]The initial spread duration = 0.40 × 1.13 years = 0.45 year. With the NT allocation reduced to 25.6% (40% – 14.4%) at a 3.71-year duration, the final spread duration = 0.256 × 3.71 years = 0.95 year, representing a 0.5-year spread duration extension. See the Appendix to this chapter for details of the optimization procedure.

For example, for a given TPD and NT weight, it turns out that there is precisely one position where the NT and TSY curves have parallel slopes. This position provides the maximum yield associated with *any* spread duration. In other words, there is no advantage in pursuing higher spread durations than the value associated with the unique "parallel slope point." We also find that for a given TPD and spread duration, there is a unique weight shift that leads to a "pincer-point" structure between the two curves. This pincer point corresponds to the maximum portfolio yield that can be obtained by *any* level of weight shift. Thus, this pincer-point weight shift will be optimal provided that the shift falls within permissible weight transfer bounds.

CONCLUSION

This chapter shows that with rising TSY and NT yield curves, the spread between NTs and TSYs of like maturity is not the most important factor in determining an optimal portfolio structure. With a sloped TSY curve, the important factors are the spread between NT and TSY investments of different maturities and each investment's position along the relevant curve. For example, when rebalancing a portfolio by shortening along the NT curve and extending along the TSY curve, we would prefer the *shortening* movement to be along the *flat* part of the NT curve (thereby giving up little yield), while the *extension* should be along the *steep* part of the TSY curve.

If the yield curves are reasonably smooth, we have the surprising result that there are only three possible locations at which the maximum yield can be attained: (1) at a pair of NT and TSY duration points at which the tangents to the yield curves are parallel, (2) at NT and TSY durations for which the tangents intersect at the same zero-duration point, or (3) at a "double-max" point where both the maximum weight shift and extremal spread-duration risk are utilized. Moreover, as shown in the Appendix to this chapter, the solution point in each case is unique.

APPENDIX

In this Appendix, we derive a general formula that shows how shifts in NT weight and/or spread duration affect the return of a portfolio of TSY and NT securities. Figure 20–A1 summarizes the symbols we use in our derivation.

Figure 20–A1. Symbol Definitions

	Weight	Yield	Duration
Treasury (TSY)	$1 - \omega$	y_T	D_T
Non-Treasury (NT)	ω	y_{NT}	D_{NT}
Portfolio	1	y_P	TPD

For a portfolio, both the yield and TPD can be computed as the weighted average of the yields and durations of the assets that comprise the portfolio. Thus,

$$y_P = \omega y_{NT} + (1 - \omega) y_T, \quad \text{and} \tag{1}$$

$$TPD = \omega D_{NT} + (1 - \omega)D_T. \tag{2}$$

We assume a simple yield-curve model in which the TSY and NT yields are expressed as differentiable functions of duration. Symbolically,

$$y_{NT} = f(D_{NT}), \quad y_T = g(D_T)$$

$$y'_{NT} = f'(D_{NT}), \quad y'_T = g'(D_T).$$

We also represent infinitesimal changes in weight and duration by the differential quantities $d\omega$, dD_{NT} and dD_T. When changes in the portfolio yield or duration are the result of small shifts in weight or duration, the portfolio changes can be found by taking the total differential of (1) and (2). First we focus on yield changes.

$$dy_P = \omega dy_{NT} + y_{NT}d\omega + (1 - \omega)dy_T - y_Td\omega$$

$$= (y_{NT} - y_T)d\omega + \omega dy_{NT} + (1 - \omega)dy_T. \tag{3}$$

We note that, in general, if $y = f(D)$ then $dy = f'(D)dD = y'\, dD$. Using this result in (3), dy_p can be expressed solely in terms of $d\omega$, dD_{NT}, and dD_T

$$dy_p = (y_{NT} - y_T)\, d\omega + \omega y'_{NT}\, dD_{NT} + (1 - \omega)y'_T\, dD_T. \qquad (4)$$

We interpret (4) as the change in yield that results when a small amount of weight ($d\omega$) is shifted from TSYs to NTs; the NT point is shifted from (D_{NT}, y_{NT}) to ($D_{NT} + dD_{NT}$, $y_{NT} + f'[D_{NT}]dD_{NT}$); and the TSY point is shifted from (D_T, y_T) to ($D_T + dD_T$, $y_T + g'[D_T]dD_T$).

To further simplify (4), we turn to (2) and require that weight and duration shifts do not change the TPD.

$$0 = d(TPD) = d[\omega D_{NT} + (1 - \omega)\, D_T]$$

$$= d[\omega D_{NT}] + d[(1 - \omega)D_T]. \qquad (5)$$

The first term in brackets, ωD_{NT}, is the spread duration of the NT investment. Thus, $d[\omega D_{NT}]$ is the small change in spread duration that occurs as a result of a change in NT weight and duration. For convenience, we introduce the following symbol:

$$\varepsilon = d[\omega D_{NT}]. \qquad (6)$$

Using (6) and the condition (5), we develop a formula for dD_T in terms of ε and $d\omega$.

$$0 = \varepsilon + d\left[(1 - \omega)D_T\right]$$

$$0 = \varepsilon + (1 - \omega)dD_T - D_T d\omega$$

$$dD_T = \frac{-\varepsilon + D_T d\omega}{1 - \omega} \qquad (7)$$

By expanding (6), we also obtain a relationship that gives dD_{NT} in terms of ε and $d\omega$.

$$\varepsilon = d[\omega D_{NT}]$$

$$= \omega dD_{NT} + D_{NT} d\omega$$

$$dD_{NT} = \frac{\varepsilon - D_{NT} d\omega}{\omega} \tag{8}$$

Substituting (7) and (8) in (4) expresses portfolio yield changes in terms of weight shifts and spread-duration shifts as follows:

$$dy_P = (y_{NT} - y_T)d\omega + y'_{NT}(\varepsilon - D_{NT}d\omega) + y'_T(-\varepsilon + D_T d\omega)$$

$$= [(y_{NT} - D_{NT}y'_{NT}) - (y_T - D_T y'_T)]\,d\omega + (y'_{NT} - y'_T)\varepsilon. \tag{9}$$

The coefficients of $d\omega$ and ε have a very simple and intuitive interpretation. Because y'_{NT} is the slope of the tangent line to the yield curve $y_{NT} = f(D_{NT})$ at the point (D_{NT}, y_{NT}), the expression $y_{NT} - D_{NT} y'_{NT}$ represents the y-intercept, b_{NT}, of the tangent line drawn at (D_{NT}, y_{NT}). Likewise, $y_T - D_T y'_T$ represents the y-intercept, b_T, of a tangent line to the TSY curve at the point (D_T, y_T). Thus,

$$dy_P = (b_{NT} - b_T)d\omega + (y'_{NT} - y'_T)\,\varepsilon. \tag{10}$$

This last equation is rich in information and can be interpreted through several separate cases as follows:

Case I. If $b_{NT} - b_T = 0$, the tangent lines intersect at the point of contact with the vertical axis, creating the "pincer" pictured in Figure 20–8. Weight changes at a pincer have no effect on portfolio yield because in equation (10) the coefficient of $d\omega = 0$. Thus, if a pincer is reached before the maximum (or minimum) allowable weight shift is reached, there is no gain from further weight shifts.[8]

---

[8]If $b_{NT} - b_T > 0$, then $(b_{NT} - b_T)\,d\omega$ provides a good approximation to the yield gain that results from a small increase in NT weight. Geometrically, the distance between the y-intercepts of the tangent lines approximately represents the yield gain per unit of weight shift for any benchmark portfolio. If $b_{NT} - b_T < 0$, the same observations apply to a weight shift from NTs to TSYs. See Chapter 19 for more detail.

Case II. If $y'_{NT} - y'_T = 0$, the tangent lines to the TSY and NT curves are parallel (see Figure 20–6). At such a parallel tangent point, spread-duration changes, as represented by ε, have no effect because in equation (10) the coefficient of ε is zero. Thus, if a parallel tangent point is reached before all spread-duration flexibility has been utilized, further spread durations will add risk but not return.[9]

Case III. If neither a pincer nor a parallel tangent point is reached, we continue to add (or subtract) NT weight and spread duration. The optimal solution then occurs at a "double-max" point as in Figure 20–3.

In summary, Cases I through III describe all the situations depicted in the body of this chapter. Equation (10) also implies that at least a "single-max" point will be part of any optimal solution. For example, if a pincer is reached (Case I) and the maximum spread-duration shift has not been utilized, then improvements can still be gained by adjusting the spread duration. The reason is that, at a pincer, the tangents, by definition, are not parallel, so the second term in equation (10) will not be zero. Similar comments apply to weight shifts at a parallel tangent point (Case II).

Uniqueness of the "Pincer"

The pairs of points at which the tangents form a pincer are unique for a specified TPD and spread duration. To prove this, we show that the initial spread between the intersection points of the two tangent lines decreases monotonically as the NT weight increases. We assume that the TPD and spread duration are held constant and that the concavity of the NT and TSY curves is downward, as depicted in Figure 20–4.

The concavity assumption implies that the second derivatives of y_{NT} and y_T are negative. The constant-spread-duration assumption means that $\varepsilon = 0$ so the second term in equation (10) drops out. Thus,

$$dy_P = F(D_{NT}, D_T)d\omega, \tag{11}$$

where $F(D_{NT}, D_T)$ represents the initial spread between intersection points. Specifically,

$$F(D_{NT}, D_T) = b_{NT} - b_T$$
$$= [y_{NT}(D_{NT}) - D_{NT}y'_{NT}(D_{NT})] - [y_T(D_T) - D_T y'_T(D_T)]. \tag{12}$$

---

[9] If $y'_{NT} - y'_T > 0$, then $(y'_{NT} - y'_T)\varepsilon$ approximates the yield gain from a small increase in spread duration (see footnote 8).

To rebalance a portfolio, we shift weight to NTs from TSYs, and adjust durations to preserve TPD and spread duration. We have already noted that a pincer occurs whenever $F(D_{NT}, D_T) = 0$. To determine how F varies with ω we first compute the total differential from equation (12).

$$
\begin{aligned}
dF &= \frac{\partial F}{\partial D_{NT}} dD_{NT} + \frac{\partial F}{\partial D_T} dD_{NT} \\
&= (y'_{NT} - y'_{NT} - D_{NT} y''_{NT}) dD_{NT} - (y'_T - y'_T - D_T y''_T)\, dD_T \\
&= -D_{NT} y''_{NT} dD_{NT} + D_T y''_T dD_T.
\end{aligned}
\tag{13}
$$

Using equations (7) and (8) with ε set to zero in (13), we find that

$$
dF = \left[\frac{D^2_{NT} y''_{NT}}{\omega} + \frac{D^2_T y''_T}{1 - \omega} \right] d\omega.
\tag{14}
$$

Because y''_{NT} and y''_T are negative by assumption,

$$
\frac{dF}{d\omega} < 0
\tag{15}
$$

Thus, F decreases monotonically as NT weight increases. Hence, for a given TPD and spread duration, there is at most one point at which $F = 0$, implying that if a pincer exists, it is unique.

It is important to realize that this uniqueness applies across the full range of NT durations and weights. That is, for a given TPD and spread duration, there is at most one NT weight and duration (and one corresponding TSY weight and duration) at which a pincer occurs. This uniqueness implies that if the maximum allowable NT weight is greater than the NT weight at the pincer point, then the pincer point is optimal (for the given spread duration). Likewise, if the maximum weight is less than the pincer weight, then the optimal point is the maximum weight point.

Uniqueness of the Parallel Tangent Point

If, instead of holding the spread duration constant we hold the NT weight constant, then observations similar to those above apply to the parallel tangent solution. As spread duration increases, the difference between the slopes of the tangent lines can be shown to decrease monotonically. Thus, there can be at most one point at which the slopes are equal and the tangent lines are parallel. As a consequence, the unique optimal spread-duration point occurs at either a parallel tangent point or a preset maximum point.

Part III

Global Fixed-Income Investments

Chapter 21

Global Fixed-Income Investing: The Impact of the Currency Hedge

INTRODUCTION

Although many investors have expected significant convergence of the global fixed-income markets over time, these markets persist in going their separate ways. Yield curves range from inverted to sharply positive, with widely divergent interest-rate movements. This climate creates continued interest and opportunity in international fixed-income investing. In this chapter, we present a framework for determining hedged cross-currency returns, with particular focus on the effects of the hedge period. We show that the hedge serves not merely to reduce currency exposure; it actually converts some or all of the foreign investment to a synthetic domestic investment. In particular, the hedge period plays a key role in selecting the segment of the foreign yield curve to which the investor is exposed.

We do not address the decision about whether to hedge at all. Many investors believe that foreign investments do not need to be hedged, because currency exposure provides additional diversification, averages out over time, or can be managed to enhance return. The currency risk and the hedged return risk are largely separable, however, and we find it more enlightening to treat them separately. Accordingly, we deal only with hedged investments in this chapter.[1]

---

[1] The pros and cons of hedging international fixed-income investments are discussed in *Currency Hedging and International Diversification: Implications of a World Reserve Currency Effect*, Vilas Gadkari and Mark Spindel, Salomon Brothers Inc, November 1989.

We begin by showing how yield curves can be related to return curves in both domestic and foreign markets. Next, we review the mechanics of currency hedging and show how a foreign return curve is translated into domestic currency for varying hedge periods. We then discuss "interest-rate parity," a condition that generally governs currency exchange forward rates. Under interest-rate parity, a foreign zero-coupon note with a currency hedge expiring at its maturity produces the same return as a domestic zero-coupon note with the same maturity. Finally, we build on this principle to show that the hedged return of a generalized foreign investment is the return of a domestic zero-coupon note (with a maturity equal to the hedge period) *plus* the excess return of the foreign investment relative to a foreign zero-coupon note (with a maturity that also matches the hedge period).

RETURN CURVES

We begin with a hypothetical interest-rate spot curve, whose one-to-five-year segment we show in Figure 21–1.[2]

Now consider an investor with a one-year investment horizon. At each maturity, the yield level on the spot curve specifies the performance that a zero-coupon note will deliver over its lifetime, barring default. Over a one-year period, however, the investment performance is uncertain, because it is determined not only by the initial yield curve, but also by the yield curve at the end of the year. The year-end yield curve cannot be forecast with certainty, and the investor must decide what return patterns are likely to emerge. We now discuss three return curves that are commonly used in scenario analysis: (1) the initial yield to maturity, (2) the rolling yield, and (3) the flat return curve.[3]

1. Yield to maturity. The first return pattern that comes to many investors' minds is given by the spot curve itself. In other words, each security's one-year return is its yield to maturity, as shown by the heavy solid line in Figure 21–2. For example, it seems natural that a two-year zero-coupon note with a

[2]As explained in the Appendix to this chapter, the curve used in this type of analysis should reflect the rates at which private activity in the currency markets can be financed (interbank rates), because these rates generally determine the currency exchange forward rates. Throughout this chapter, we assume that investments at these rates carry no credit risk.

[3]For a more detailed discussion of these three curves, see the Appendix to this chapter; also see *Total Return Management*, Martin L. Leibowitz, Salomon Brothers Inc, 1979; and *Effects of Alternative Anticipations of Yield-Curve Behavior on the Composition of Immunized Portfolios and on Their Target Returns*, Lawrence Fisher and Martin L. Leibowitz, JAI Press, 1983.

Figure 21–1. Hypothetical Spot Curve

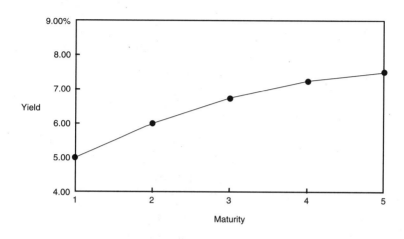

6% yield to maturity will return 6% in the first year. Figure 21–2 shows, however, that such a return pattern requires a substantial reshaping of the yield curve. A note will produce a first-year return that equals its yield to maturity only if its year-end yield equals its initial yield—even though the note is one year shorter. For example, the two-year note returns 6% in the first year only if at year-end—when it has shortened to a one-year note—the one-year spot rate has risen from 5% to 6%. Thus, the year-end yield curve must consist of the initial yield curve shifted one year to the left, as shown in Figure 21–2.

2. Rolling yield. We have seen that securities return their yield to maturity over a one-year period only if the yield curve shifts one year to the left. A different return pattern results if the yield curve remains unchanged at year-end. With our positive yield curve, this scenario produces one-year returns that exceed the initial yields. These excess returns are derived from the capital gains that are generated by "rolling down the yield curve" as the securities age and are repriced at the lower yields that correspond to their shortened maturities. We refer to these returns as "rolling yields." Figure 21–3 shows the rolling yield curve for the one- to five-year notes. For example, the two-year note has an initial yield to maturity of 6%. If the yield curve is unchanged at year-end, the note is repriced at the *one-year* yield of 5%. The

Figure 21–2. Yield Curve Reshaping for Return Curve Equal to Yield to Maturity

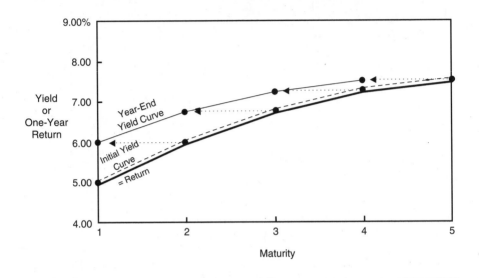

Figure 21–3. Rolling Yield Return Curve for Unchanging Yield Curve

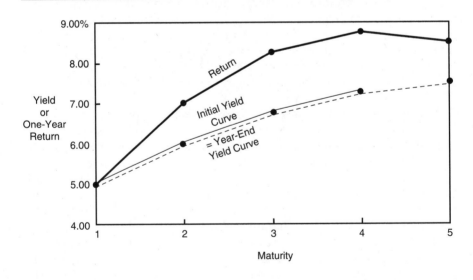

Figure 21–4. Yield Curve Reshaping for Flat Return Curve

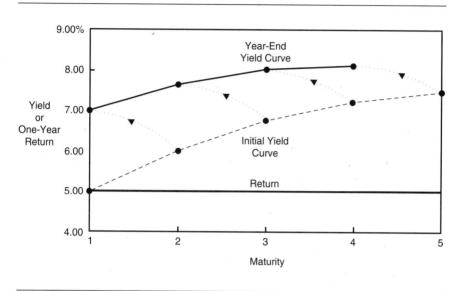

appreciation that results from this repricing raises its first-year return above the 6% initial yield to a rolling yield of approximately 7%.

3. Flat return curve. A third return curve occurs when securities of all maturities produce the same one-year return as a one-year security, or 5% in our example.[4] For the 6% two-year note to return only 5% in the first year, it must suffer depreciation by being repriced at a year-end yield *greater* than 6%. Figure 21–4 shows the yield curve reshaping that produces this return pattern.

Figure 21–5 brings together the return curves for these three scenarios.

We now adopt the perspective of an international investor who seeks enhanced portfolio returns through foreign investment. We assume that the initial foreign yield curve is given in Figure 21–1 and that the initial domestic yield curve is flat at 10%. We further assume that both yield curves remain unchanged at year-end; thus, the domestic one-year return curve is flat at 10%, and the foreign return curve consists of the rolling yields in Figure

---

[4]The flat return curve underlies the forward securities market; it will result if the one-year forward rates implied by the initial yield curve become the actual spot rates at year-end. The flat return curve omits the liquidity premium that many yield-curve models add as maturity lengthens.

Figure 21–5. Three Possible Return Curves

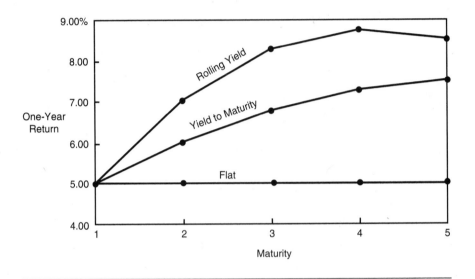

21–3. We do not propose the rolling yield as a standard assumption; it offers a convenient "base case" against which to measure the effect of yield curve changes during the year. In practice, an investor's assumed return curves can come from any source, including his or her own views of potential yield-curve shifts. The results that we present are general and apply to any other assumed return curve.

CURRENCY TRANSLATION

We consider two types of currency transaction. An investor entering the currency exchange market today with no prior contract would exchange currency at the **spot** exchange rate. Alternatively, an investor may enter into a **forward** contract to exchange fixed amounts of currency at a specified future date. For example, an investor who wishes to hedge a one-year foreign investment could sell the anticipated foreign proceeds one year forward for a fixed amount of domestic currency and thus avoid having his or her investment return affected by changes in spot exchange rates.

Hedged investment returns are governed largely by the relationship between currency exchange spot and forward rates known as "interest-rate parity." Interest-rate parity, which we discuss further in the Appendix to this chapter, describes the market conditions under which a hedged foreign investment in a one-year (or an n-year) zero-coupon note produces the same return over its life as a domestic investment in a comparable note.

We use an example to illustrate interest-rate parity and to develop additional insights into global fixed-income investing. Given our assumed flat domestic return curve, an investor could invest one unit of domestic currency locally at 10% in a one-year zero-coupon note, which would produce proceeds of 1.10 units at maturity. Alternatively, the investor could purchase a foreign one-year zero-coupon note (see Figure 21–6).

On the basis of the assumptions in Figure 21–6, the investor could change a unit of domestic currency into two units of foreign currency, purchase a foreign one-year note, and enter into a currency exchange forward contract to sell the anticipated note proceeds at the end of one year for 0.5238 domestic unit per foreign unit. After one year, he or she would receive the note proceeds and fulfill the currency contract, producing the transaction sequence shown in Figure 21–7 and ending with the same 1.10 domestic units that the domestic investment returned. (We use $\mathcal{D}$ to represent units of domestic currency and $\mathcal{F}$ to indicate foreign currency.)

Because our example uses a currency exchange forward rate that reflects interest-rate parity, the domestic investment and the hedged foreign investment produce the same 10% domestic return. In essence, the hedged currency gain (0.5238/0.5000) precisely compensates for the interest-rate advantage that is lost by investing in foreign rates (1.10/1.05). A different forward

---

Figure 21–6. Assumptions for Hedged Investment in a Foreign One-Year Note

Description	Illustrative Value
One-Year Spot Interest Rates	
Domestic	10%
Foreign	5
Initial Currency Exchange Rates[a]	
Spot Rate (Domestic Units per Foreign Unit)	0.5
Spot Rate (Foreign Units per Domestic Unit)	2.0
One-Year Forward Rate (Domestic Units per Foreign Unit)	0.5238

[a]The spot rate (0.5 domestic unit per foreign unit) is arbitrary, and the reciprocal spot rate (2.0 foreign units per domestic unit) necessarily follows. We chose the forward rate of 0.5238 to satisfy interest-rate parity, as defined in the Appendix to this chapter.

Figure 21–7. Transaction Sequence for Hedged Investment in a Foreign One-Year Note

Initial Action	Initial Cash Flow	Cash Flow after One Year
Exchange One Domestic Currency Unit for Two Foreign Units.	$-\mathcal{D}1.00$ $+\mathcal{F}2.00$	
Buy Foreign One-Year Note Yielding 5%.	$-\mathcal{F}2.00$	$+1.05 \times \mathcal{F}2.00 = +\mathcal{F}2.10$
Sell Anticipated Note Proceeds One Year Forward.		$-\mathcal{F}2.10$ $+0.5238\mathcal{D}/\mathcal{F} \times \mathcal{F}2.10 = +\mathcal{D}1.10$
Total	$-\mathcal{D}1$	$+\mathcal{D}1.10$

exchange rate would cause the one-year domestic and foreign returns to diverge, creating an arbitrage opportunity that would be exploited until interest-rate parity was satisfied.

ONE-YEAR HEDGE

We have shown how a hedged foreign one-year note produces the same domestic currency return as a domestic one-year note. We now consider the one-year domestic currency return produced by hedged foreign investments other than the one-year note. These investments may differ from the one-year note in any respect—for example, maturity, coupon, or credit risk; they can even be equities. Because their one-year returns cannot be known in advance, the currency exposure cannot be hedged precisely. We arbitrarily assume that the investor continues to use a one-year hedge on the amount that a foreign one-year note would produce. The investor will experience a currency translation gain or loss on any difference between the actual foreign return and the hedged amount. For example, if the foreign one-year note earns 5% and the actual foreign investment earns 6%, the principal plus 5% of the return is converted at the forward exchange rate under the hedge. The remaining 1% excess return, however, must be converted at the new spot exchange rate, which may reduce or enhance the 1% excess.

To engage in a one-year hedged foreign investment, the investor carries out the opening transactions set forth in the previous section. The closing transactions are the same as before, but the investor is left with a residual foreign currency position corresponding to the return excess or shortfall earned by the foreign investment relative to the foreign one-year note. This residual currency position is a long position if the foreign investment has outperformed the foreign one-year note and a short position if it has underperformed the note (that is, the forward contract obligates the investor to pay more foreign currency than he actually has).[5] This residual position then is closed out at the new spot exchange rate. Because the excess return was generated on foreign currency bought at the initial spot rate and is reconverted at the year-end spot rate, it is increased (or decreased) by the percentage change in currency spot rates.

The total return in domestic currency terms is then a **domestic base return** *plus* a **foreign excess return** relative to a **foreign base return.**

- The **domestic base return** is the domestic one-year spot interest rate.
- The **foreign excess return** is measured against a **foreign base return** of the foreign one-year note. The foreign excess return then is increased or decreased by the percentage change in currency spot exchange rates.

For a hedged investment in a foreign one-year note, there is no foreign excess return. Thus, the total return is the return of the domestic one-year note, or 10% in our illustrative return curves. We now consider investments in longer-dated foreign notes with a one-year hedge. For convenience, we reproduce the assumed domestic and foreign return curves, each in its own local currency, in Figure 21–8.

For a one-year hedged investment in a foreign two-year note, the return is the **domestic base return** of a domestic one-year note (10%) *plus* the **foreign excess return** of the foreign two-year note over the **foreign base return** of the foreign one-year note, adjusted by the percentage change in currency spot rates. This excess return is 2% (that is, the 7% from the two-year note *minus* the 5% from the one-year note). The return in domestic terms therefore is 12% (10% *plus*

---

[5]In Figure 21–7, at the end of one year, the investor had exactly the 2.10 foreign units that he was obligated to deliver. If the foreign investment unexpectedly produced a return of zero, he would have had only 2.0 foreign units and would have to buy 0.1 more at the new spot rate to meet his obligation under the forward contract.

Figure 21–8. Illustrative Domestic and Foreign Return Curves in Local Currency Terms

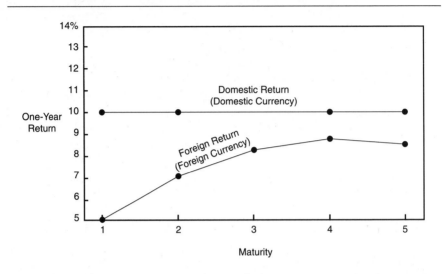

Figure 21–9. Domestic and Foreign Return Curves with a One-Year Hedge

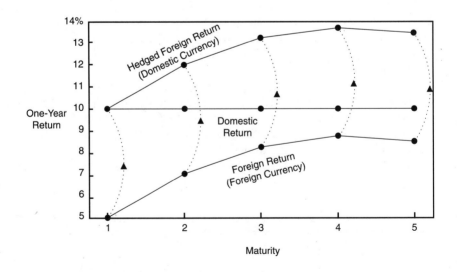

2%), ignoring any currency spot rate change.[6] Similar relationships exist for other foreign notes; thus, the return curve of foreign investments expressed in domestic currency terms is as shown in Figure 21–9.

Figure 21–9 shows that the foreign return curve in Figure 21–8 undergoes essentially a parallel shift upward when we use a one-year hedge and measure the return in domestic, rather than foreign, currency terms. We have seen that the hedged foreign one-year note produces the same domestic return as the domestic one-year note. Therefore, the point that represents the foreign one-year note moves up to occupy the same position as the domestic one-year note. The other foreign securities move up to maintain their return advantage over the foreign one-year note. Figure 21–9 shows an expanded universe of securities with returns denominated in domestic currency. In the next section, we will see how varying the hedge period brings about a further expansion.

LONGER HEDGES

We now generalize our results to a longer hedge—for example, three years.[7] The investor remains concerned, however, about one-year performance measurement.

We modify the reasoning of the preceding section by first assuming that the foreign investment is a three-year zero-coupon note. We then can recast the example shown in Figure 21–7 to cover a three-year period, using the three-year currency exchange forward rate based on interest-rate parity. After a three-year holding period, the domestic proceeds of the hedged foreign three-year zero-coupon note are the same as those of a domestic three-year zero-coupon note. Thus, we can regard the hedged foreign three-year zero-coupon note as a synthetic domestic three-year note. This synthetic three-

---

[6]The change in currency exchange spot rates represents a "second-order" effect on the total return because the currency change is multiplied only by the *excess* foreign return relative to the foreign one-year rate. For example, a 10% currency spot rate change would add 20 basis points to the 12% return on the hedged two-year note (10% currency gain *times* 2% foreign excess return). Of course, if the entire transaction were unhedged, the currency change would apply not only to the excess return, but also to the full principal, creating substantial added volatility. In our examples, we assume that the currency spot rate change is zero; a modest nonzero assumption would have no visible effect. (For example, the return curve shift in Figure 21–9 would depart from parallel by a few basis points.)

[7]Note that even a long-term investor may choose a short-term hedge that is rolled over each time that it expires. The selection of a hedge period may be based on liquidity considerations or tactical views about currency exchange rates, as well as the domestic and foreign yield and return curve relationships that we explore in this chapter.

year note has the same return as the domestic three-year note over *any* interim period. (In the Appendix to this chapter, we show how the foreign note and the currency hedge are repriced after one year to produce this equality.)

Thus, if the foreign investment is a three-year zero-coupon note with a three-year hedge, the investor's one-year return equals the one-year return of a domestic three-year note. Now suppose that the foreign investment is some other security or portfolio and that the investor continues to use the three-year hedge described above. The alternative foreign investment produces an incremental (or decremental) return that must be translated at the new currency exchange spot rate. Then, the investor's one-year return in domestic terms again can be expressed as the **domestic base return** *plus* the **foreign excess return** relative to the **foreign base return**, where "base return" refers to the one-year return of a three-year zero-coupon note in the indicated currency.[8] (The foreign excess return is modified by the percentage change in currency exchange spot rates; we ignore this second-order currency effect in the remainder of this chapter.)

We can generalize the relationship as follows:

One-Year Return of Foreign Investment with n-Year Hedge

= One-Year Return of Domestic n-Year Zero-Coupon Note

+ (One-Year Return of Actual Foreign Investment

− One-Year Return of Foreign n-Year Zero-Coupon Note).

Figure 21–10 illustrates this equation schematically. The hedged foreign return, the right-hand bar, is built by starting with the one-year return of the domestic n-year zero-coupon note. On top of this, we place the excess return of the actual foreign investment over the one-year return of the foreign n-year zero-coupon note.

Figure 21–11 shows how the investor's foreign return curve shifts when he or she uses a three-year hedge and changes the currency in which returns are measured from foreign to domestic. Using a three-year hedge on a for-

---

[8]Note that both the domestic and foreign bases are zero-coupon notes based on the financing rates for dealer activity in the currency markets. The actual foreign investment, however, is *not* restricted to zero-coupon notes but instead may carry coupons and different credit exposure. Also note that this formulation holds for hedge periods *shorter* than one year. For example, suppose that the investor uses a rolling one-month hedge. For each month, the return will consist of a **domestic base return** of domestic one-month paper *plus* a **foreign excess return** measured against a **foreign base return** of foreign one-month paper. We then determine the return for a one-*year* measurement period by compounding the individual hedged monthly returns of the foreign securities.

Figure 21–10. Domestic Return of Foreign Investment with an *n*-Year Hedge

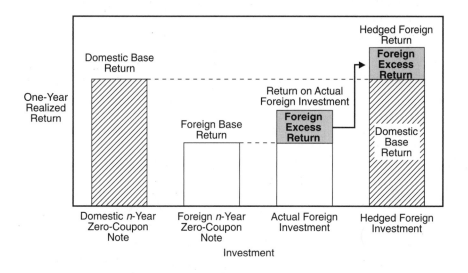

Figure 21–11. Domestic and Foreign Return Curves with a Three-Year Hedge

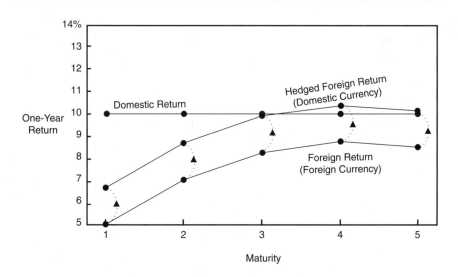

eign three-year zero-coupon note converts it to a synthetic domestic three-year note. Other foreign notes (as well as other types of investments not represented on that curve) retain their return advantages or disadvantages relative to the foreign three-year note.

A comparison of Figures 21–11 and 21–9 illustrates the effect of lengthening the term of the hedge. As the hedge period moves from one year to three years, the investor loses the benefit of the steepness of the foreign curve between one and three years. The lengthening results in a domestic base return equal to that of the domestic three-year note, rather than the domestic one-year note; because the domestic one- and three-year notes have the same 10% return in our illustration, this change has no effect. However, the lengthening of the hedge also requires that the foreign excess return be measured against a base of the foreign three-year zero-coupon note (an 8.3% return in Figure 21–8), rather than the foreign one-year note (a 5% return). Thus, the overall effect of lengthening the hedge is to lower the hedged foreign return by 3.3%. In other words, during a one-year measurement period, the investor receives the rewards (and risks) of the domestic return curve up to a point defined by the hedge period and the rewards (and risks) of the foreign return curve from that point to the maturity of the actual foreign investment.[9]

For example, we use the local currency returns shown in Figure 21–8 and suppose that the investor has purchased a foreign five-year note that returns 8.5% in foreign currency terms during the year. The returns with one- and three-year hedges appear in Figure 21–12.

CONCLUSION

Most investors treat foreign fixed-income securities as a separate asset class from domestic securities and regard currency hedging as a means of regulating the volatility that can arise from currency exchange rate fluctuations. In this chapter, we show that a currency hedge may be thought of as a mecha-

---

[9]An interesting way of measuring the effect of the hedge period is to rearrange the terms in our formulation of the hedged foreign return as follows:

Hedged Foreign Return = One-Year Return of Actual Foreign Investment

+ (One-Year Return of Domestic n-Year Zero-Coupon Note

− One-Year Return of Foreign n-Year Zero-Coupon Note).

This revision shows that the optimal hedge period (with hindsight) is the maturity for which the domestic zero-coupon note outperformed the foreign zero-coupon note by the widest margin. Using this hedge would result in the greatest upward shift of the hedged foreign curve shown in Figures 21–9 and 21–11.

Figure 21–12. One-Year Returns of a Foreign Five-Year Note with One- and Three-Year Hedges

Domestic Base Return +		Foreign Excess Return				= Total Return
		Foreign Base		Actual Foreign Investment		
Security	Return	Security	Return	Return	Excess Return	
One-Year Hedge						
One-Year Zero	10.0%	One-year zero	5.0%	8.5%	3.5%	13.5%
Three-Year Hedge						
Three-Year Zero	10.0%	Three-year zero	8.3%	8.5%	0.2%	10.2%

nism for partially converting foreign securities into domestic securities. A currency-hedged foreign bond actually is a hybrid of a foreign *and* a domestic bond; the length of the hedge determines how much of the return is based on the foreign market and how much is based on the domestic market. If the foreign security is a zero-coupon note maturing at the expiration of the hedge, there is no foreign exposure; if the foreign security is quite different, the exposure to foreign return patterns can be significant.

Investors who wish to limit their intermarket risk thus can choose a cautious approach to foreign markets. These investors can pursue modest incremental foreign returns on a limited segment of the foreign return curve, by using a hedge that converts most of the foreign return into that of a targeted domestic bond. Other investors may prefer an aggressive approach—for example, rolling short-term hedges against long-term foreign securities—that exposes them to substantial risks and rewards based on the performance of the foreign markets. Given the variety of foreign yield curves and interest-rate movements, these choices can greatly enrich an investor's opportunity set. In future chapters we will explore the opportunities and risks associated with yield-curve changes in the domestic and foreign markets.

APPENDIX

In this Appendix, we develop the formulas that underlie the three return curves that we discussed in the opening section. We then explain interest-rate parity and show that a foreign n-year zero-coupon note with an n-year hedge offers the same year-to-year return in domestic terms as a domestic n-year zero-coupon note. Finally, we extend that demonstration to derive the general relationship between domestic and hedged foreign returns that we discuss in this chapter.

Figure 21–A1 shows the notation that we use in this Appendix. In general, upper-case letters represent variables denominated in domestic currency, and lower-case letters represent the corresponding variables in foreign-currency terms. Parenthetical superscripts show the length of the period covered by a spot interest rate or a currency exchange forward contract; and subscripts indicate the date at which the variable is measured.

First, we derive an expression for the one-year return on an n-year zero-coupon note. An investment of $\mathcal{D}\,1$ promises a cash flow after n years of $\mathcal{D}\,(1 + I_0^{(n)})^n$. Its value after one year is determined by discounting that flow for the remaining $n - 1$ years, using the $(n - 1)$-year yield at year-end, $I_1^{(n-1)}$:

Figure 21–A1. Symbols Used in Appendix

	Domestic	Foreign
Currency Units	$\mathcal{D}$	$\mathcal{F}$
Currency Exchange Rates[a]		
Exchange Rates at Time 0		
• n-Year Forward Rate	$F^{(n)}$	
• Spot Rate	S_0	
Exchange Rate at Time 1		
• Spot Rate	S_1	
Interest Rates		
• n-Year Spot at Time 0	$I_0^{(n)}$	$i_0^{(n)}$
• $(n-1)$-Year Spot at Time 1	$I_1^{(n-1)}$	$i_1^{(n-1)}$
One-Year Realized Rates of Return		
• n-Year Zero-Coupon Bond	$\tilde{R}^{(n)}$	$\tilde{r}^{(n)}$
• Generalized Foreign Investment	$\tilde{R}$	$\tilde{r}$

[a]Domestic units per foreign unit.

Value of n-Year Zero-Coupon Note after One Year $= \mathcal{D} \dfrac{(1 + I_0^{(n)})^n}{(1 + I_1^{(n-1)})^{n-1}}$.

Because the initial investment was $\mathcal{D} 1$, the one-year return is

$$\tilde{R}^{(n)} = \frac{(1 + I_0^{(n)})^n}{(1 + I_1^{(n-1)})^{n-1}} - 1. \tag{1}$$

Similarly,

$$\tilde{r}^{(n)} = \frac{(1 + i_0^{(n)})^n}{(1 + i_1^{(n-1)})^{n-1}} - 1. \tag{2}$$

We now use equation (1) to analyze three return curves: the yield to maturity; the rolling yield; and the flat return curve.

Yield to Maturity

For this return curve, the one-year return equals the initial yield to maturity:

$$\tilde{R}^{(n)} = I_0^{(n)}.$$

Substituting in equation (1), we get

$$I_0^{(n)} = \frac{(1 + I_0^{(n)})^n}{(1 + I_1^{(n-1)})^{n-1}} - 1, \quad \text{which can be solved to give}$$

$$I_1^{(n-1)} = I_0^{(n)}. \tag{3}$$

That is, the $(n-1)$-year spot rate at year-end equals the initial n-year spot rate, and the note's yield to maturity does not change. Because the year-end spot rate for each maturity equals the initial spot rate at the maturity one year greater, the entire curve shifts one year to the left, as shown in Figure 21–2.

To illustrate the yield-curve relationships embedded in our three return curves, we use the two-year 6% zero-coupon note from Figure 21–1. The two-year note is convenient for this purpose because its second-year return, which

---

Figure 21–A2. Annual Returns on Two-Year Zero-Coupon Note

Basis of Return Curve	Yield to Maturity of Two-Year Zero-Coupon Note	First-Year Return	Second-Year Return	Year-End One-Year Spot Rate
Yield to Maturity	6.00%	6.00%	6.00%	6.00%
Rolling Yield	6.00	7.01	5.00	5.00
Flat Return Curve	6.00	5.00	7.01	7.01

---

equals the one-year spot rate that prevails at year-end, must compound with its first-year return to equal 6% annually. The first line of Figure 21–A2 shows that if the first-year return equals the initial 6% yield to maturity, the two other rates are all 6%.

Rolling Yield

The rolling yield curve shows the return if the initial yield curve is unchanged at year-end; the defining relationship is as follows:

$$I_1^{(n-1)} = I_0^{(n-1)}.$$

Substituting that relationship in equation (1), we find that the one-year return is given by

$$\tilde{R}^{(n)} = \frac{(1 + I_0^{(n)})^n}{(1 + I_0^{(n-1)})^{n-1}} - 1. \tag{4}$$

Applying this formula to our two-year note, we find the following first-year return:

$$\tilde{R}^{(2)} = \frac{(1 + I_0^{(2)})^2}{(1 + I_0^{(1)})^1} - 1 = \frac{(1.06)^2}{1.05} - 1 = 7.01\%.$$

The second line of Figure 21–A2 summarizes this result by showing a first-year return of 7.01%. Another route to the same result is to observe that the *second-year* return of the two-year note must be 5%, because the note has shortened to a one-year note at year-end, for which the yield is 5%. Because its two-year sequence of returns must compound to 6% annually, the first-year return must equal 7.01%, because $1.0701 \times 1.05 = 1.06^2$.

Flat Return Curve

We define the flat return curve as one for which all securities have one-year returns equal to the one-year spot rate:

$$\tilde{R}^{(n)} = I_0^{(1)}.$$

Equation (1) then becomes

$$I_0^{(1)} = \frac{(1 + I_0^{(n)})^n}{(1 + I_1^{(n-1)})^{n-1}} - 1, \quad \text{which can be rearranged to give}$$

$$I_1^{(n-1)} = \left[\frac{(1 + I_0^{(n)})^n}{(1 + I_0^{(1)})} \right]^{\frac{1}{n-1}} - 1. \tag{5}$$

Equation (5) defines the new yield curve at year-end shown in Figure 21–4, which consists of the forward rates embedded in the initial yield curve. By substituting the appropriate values in equation (5), we find that the two-year note returns 5% during the first year if the one-year spot rate resets to 7.01% at year-end:[10]

$$I_1^{(1)} = \left[\frac{(1 + I_0^{(2)})^2}{(1 + I_0^{(1)})} \right]^{\frac{1}{1}} - 1 = \frac{(1.06)^2}{1.05} - 1 = 7.01\%.$$

The third line of Figure 21–A2 shows this result, which can be verified by noting that this two-year return sequence compounds to equal the two-year yield of 6% annually ($1.05 \times 1.0701 = 1.06^2$).

---

[10] The reappearance of the 7.01% rate that we saw as the rolling yield is not coincidental. It results from the fact that the rolling yield on an n-year note equals the implied $(n-1)$-year forward one-year rate, as equation (4) shows.

Interest-Rate Parity

We now turn our attention to interest-rate parity. The interest rates referred to in Figure 21–A1 underlie interest-rate parity—that is, they are the rates at which dealer activity in the currency exchange markets can be financed (interbank rates).

Consider the sequence of transactions shown in Figure 21–A3 resulting from the purchase of a foreign n-year zero-coupon note and an n-year forward sale of the expected foreign currency proceeds.

Figure 21–A3. Interest Rate Parity

Initial Action	Initial Cash Flow	Cash Flow after n Years
Exchange One Domestic Currency Unit.	$-\mathcal{D}\,1$ $+\mathcal{F}\,(1/S_0)$	
Buy Foreign n-Year Zero-Coupon Note.	$-\mathcal{F}\,(1/S_0)$	$+\mathcal{F}\,(1/S_0)(1 + i_0^{(n)})^n$
Sell Anticipated Note Proceeds n Years Forward.	None	$-\mathcal{F}\,(1/S_0)(1 + i_0^{(n)})^n$ $+ \mathcal{D}(1/S_0)(1 + i_0^{(n)})^n F^{(n)}$
Total	$-\mathcal{D}1$	$+ \mathcal{D}\,(1/S_0)(1 + i_0^{(n)})^n F^{(n)}$

We note that by investing the original $\mathcal{D}\,1$ in a domestic n-year zero-coupon note, the investor could obtain proceeds of $\mathcal{D}\,(1 + I_0^{(n)})^n$ after n years. If the hedged investment in a foreign zero-coupon note shown in Figure 21–A3 produces proceeds different from that amount, opportunities for risk-free arbitrage profits exist. If the proceeds in Figure 21–A3 *exceed* $\mathcal{D}\,(1 + I_0^{(n)})^n$, an investor can execute the transaction sequence after borrowing the initial $\mathcal{D}\,1$ for n years; his repayment of $\mathcal{D}\,(1 + I_0^{(n)})^n$ after n years would leave him a positive net cash return with no outlay or risk. If the proceeds are *less than* $\mathcal{D}\,(1 + I_0^{(n)})^n$, the investor could engage in similar transactions with the currencies reversed, beginning by borrowing $\mathcal{F}\,1$, and again show a risk-free profit. In either case, these arbitrage activities would restore the equilibrium condition under which the proceeds of the hedged foreign investment in Figure 21–A3 equal those of the comparable domestic investment. The equality is given by equation (6):

$$\mathcal{D}(1 / S_0) (1 + i_0^{(n)})^n F^{(n)} = \mathcal{D}(1 + I_0^{(n)})^n. \tag{6}$$

Thus, under interest-rate parity, a hedged foreign zero-coupon note produces the same ending cash flow and, therefore, the same return over its life as a domestic investment in a comparable note.

More commonly, interest-rate parity is expressed in terms of the relationship between currency exchange spot and forward rates:

$$F^{(n)} = S_0 \left[\frac{(1 + I_0^{(n)})}{(1 + i_0^{(n)})} \right]^n. \tag{7}$$

Note that Figure 21–7 is simply the one-year case of Figure 21–A3. With an initial currency spot exchange rate of 0.5 domestic unit per foreign unit and domestic and foreign one-year spot interest rates of 10% and 5%, respectively, we find that $F^{(1)} = 0.5 \times (1.10/1.05) = 0.5238$. The foreign currency forward premium captured in the hedge (from 0.5 to 0.5238 domestic unit per foreign unit) compensates for the lower foreign interest rate.

Thus, we have shown that the return over the life of a foreign n-year zero-coupon note with an n-year currency hedge equals the return of an n-year domestic zero-coupon note, because both provide the same net domestic cash flow after n years (with no interim cash flow). It follows that the foreign note and its hedge must have the same value at all times as the domestic note; a divergence at any time would violate interest-rate parity for the period from that time until maturity and would permit a risk-free arbitrage profit for that period. (In the next illustration, we show how the security and currency positions can be valued separately to arrive at this intuitive result.)

We conclude that a foreign n-year zero-coupon note with an n-year hedge has the same return over any period as a domestic n-year zero-coupon note.

Return on Generalized Foreign Investment with n-Year Hedge

We now examine the return on a generalized hedged foreign investment, which is not restricted to zero-coupon notes (or even to bonds). We continue to use an n-year hedge, but the ultimate foreign proceeds are unknown at the time that the hedge is established. We assume that the hedge amount is based on the foreign n-year spot interest rate—that is, the amount of foreign currency sold n years forward is the amount that would be received after n years if the foreign investment were an n-year zero-coupon note.

414

Chapter 21

To determine the one-year domestic return on a generalized hedged foreign investment, we observe the transaction sequence shown in Figure 21–A4. The investor initially acquires the hedged position as in Figure 21–A3. The first two columns of symbols in Figure 21–A4 are similar to those of Figure 21–A3; the value of the foreign investment after n years is unknown, and we have used equation (6) to simplify the last entry in the second column.

We have added a column to show the position after one year. The investor retains the foreign investment, which has a value based on a first-year return of $\tilde{r}$. The investor also retains a currency position under the forward exchange contract, to be settled $n-1$ years later. The currency position has two parts: an obligation to pay the amount of foreign currency originally specified, and a right to receive the specified domestic currency payment. We value these two future cash flows by discounting each at the $(n-1)$-year spot interest rates that prevail in the respective currencies one year after the initial transaction.

Figure 21–A4. Generalized Foreign Investment with n-Year Hedge

Initial Action	Initial Cash Flow	Cash Flow after n Years	Value after 1 Year
Exchange Domestic Currency Unit.	$-\mathcal{D}1$ $+\mathcal{F}(1/S_0)$		
Buy Foreign Security.	$-\mathcal{F}(1/S_0)$	Unknown	$+\mathcal{F}(1/S_0)(1+\tilde{r})$
Sell Foreign Currency n Years Forward.	None	$-\mathcal{F}(1/S_0)(1+i_0^{(n)})^n$	$-\mathcal{F}(1/S_0)(1+i_0^{(n)})^n/(1+i_1^{(n-1)})^{n-1}$
		$+\mathcal{D}(1/S_0)(1+i_0^{(n)})^nF^{(n)}$ [that is, $+\mathcal{D}(1+I_0^{(n)})^n$]	$+\mathcal{D}(1+I_0^{(n)})^n/(1+I_1^{(n-1)})^{n-1}$

The investor's position after one year, which in our notation is $\mathcal{D}(1+\tilde{R})$, is the sum of the three terms in the last column of Figure 21–A4.

$$\mathcal{D}(1+\tilde{R}) = \mathcal{F}(1/S_0)(1+\tilde{r}) - \mathcal{F}(1/S_0)(1+i_0^{(n)})^n/(1+i_1^{(n-1)})^{n-1}$$
$$+ \mathcal{D}(1+I_0^{(n)})^n/(1+I_1^{(n-1)})^{n-1}. \qquad (8)$$

By using the definitions of $\tilde{R}^{(n)}$ and $\tilde{r}^{(n)}$ in equations (1) and (2), we can simplify equation (8):

$$\mathcal{D}(1 + \tilde{R}) = \mathcal{F}(1 / S_0)(1 + \tilde{r}) - \mathcal{F}(1 / S_0)(1 + \tilde{r}^{(n)}) + \mathcal{D}(1 + \tilde{R}^{(n)}).$$

At year-end, each unit of foreign currency can be converted into S_1 units of domestic currency based on the currency exchange rate at year-end. Using $\mathcal{F}1 = \mathcal{D}1 \bullet S_1$ at year-end, we have

$$\mathcal{D}(1 + \tilde{R}) = \mathcal{D}(S_1 / S_0)(1 + \tilde{r}) - \mathcal{D}(S_1 / S_0)(1 + \tilde{r}^{(n)}) + \mathcal{D}(1 + \tilde{R}^{(n)})$$

$$= \mathcal{D}[(1 + \tilde{R}^{(n)} + (\tilde{r} - \tilde{r}^{(n)})(S_1 / S_0)].$$

The one-year return is therefore given by

$$\tilde{R} = \tilde{R}^{(n)} + (\tilde{r} - \tilde{r}^{(n)})(S_1 / S_0).$$

This is our primary result: The one-year return (in domestic currency) of an n-year hedged foreign investment is the one-year return of the domestic n-year zero-coupon note, plus the foreign excess return relative to the return of the foreign n-year zero-coupon note, modified by the change in currency exchange spot rates.

Chapter 22

Interest-Rate Risks in Currency-Hedged Bond Portfolios

INTRODUCTION

In an earlier chapter,[1] we described a framework for hedged global fixed-income investing. We showed how the hedged return of a foreign fixed-income investment is determined by the domestic return curve, the foreign return curve, and the length of the hedge. In this chapter, we explore the risks and rewards associated with domestic and foreign yield-curve shifts and consider how an investor can protect against, or capitalize on, various changes in global interest-rate levels and relationships.[2] We show that the currency hedge partitions the total interest-rate exposure between the domestic and foreign yield curves, and we quantify the effect of joint movements in the two yield curves and changes in the intermarket spreads. This analysis gives rich insights into the effects of adjusting portfolio duration and hedge length as interest rates change in different ways.

---

[1]See Chapter 21. That chapter contains a more detailed discussion of the principles that are summarized and the formulas that underlie all calculations in the following sections.

[2]For another view of foreign bond volatility, see "Measuring the Risk of Foreign Bonds," *The Journal of Portfolio Management*, Steven I. Dym, Winter 1991; and "Global and Local Components of Foreign Bond Risk," *Financial Analysts Journal*, Steven I. Dym, March/April 1992.

RETURN CURVES WITH NO YIELD-CURVE CHANGES

Figure 22–1 shows the illustrative domestic and foreign spot interest rates that we use in this chapter. The yields are shown in local currency—that is, domestic bonds all yield 10% in domestic currency, and foreign bonds yield 5.0%–7.5% in foreign currency.

Each yield in Figure 22–1 represents the average annual return that an investor who holds a zero-coupon note of the indicated maturity would receive over the lifetime of the note. The *one-year* return of each note, however, is uncertain and depends on both the initial and year-end yield. Figure 22–2 shows what the one-year returns would be if the yield curves remain unchanged at year-end. These returns are known as "rolling yields"; they include, for the positive foreign curve, both the stated yield of each note and the price appreciation as maturity shortens and the note moves to a lower yield. For example, the two-year note returns its initial yield of 6% *plus* the appreciation that results when it is repriced at year-end as a 5% one-year note. We use these rolling yields as a base from which to measure the effect of yield-curve changes.[3]

Now suppose that an investor buys a foreign zero-coupon note and hedges the currency risk through a forward sale of the anticipated proceeds. The one-year investment return will depend on the length of the hedge. Figures 22–3A and 22–3B show how the one-year foreign return translates into a domestic currency return with a one-year hedge and a three-year hedge.

Figure 22–3A portrays the effect of the one-year hedge. Based on the principle known as "interest-rate parity," a foreign one-year zero-coupon note with a one-year currency hedge becomes a synthetic domestic one-year note and produces the same return in domestic currency. Under this principle, the one-year currency hedge must offer a premium of 5% to compensate for the yield advantage of the domestic note over the foreign note (10% versus 5%). Therefore, as the measurement basis changes from foreign to domestic currency, the hedged foreign one-year note combines a 5% currency return with a 5% local interest return to produce the same 10% return as the domes-

---

[3]The approach in this chapter uses the rolling yield as a reference point and then considers the effect of changes *from the initial yield curves*. An alternative method for gauging the effect of yield-curve changes is to use as a reference point any specific set of year-end yield curves and corresponding one-year returns. We then could measure how those returns would be affected by changes in the yield curves *relative to the reference set*, rather than relative to the initial yield curves. In this chapter, we use the initial yield curve as the reference year-end yield curve because of its simplicity, but our results can easily be transformed into the alternative method.

Figure 22–1. Domestic and Foreign Spot Interest-Rate Curves

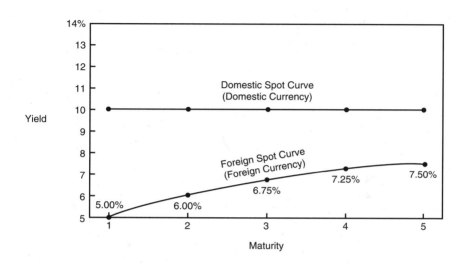

Figure 22–2. Domestic and Foreign Return Curves with Yield Curves Unchanged

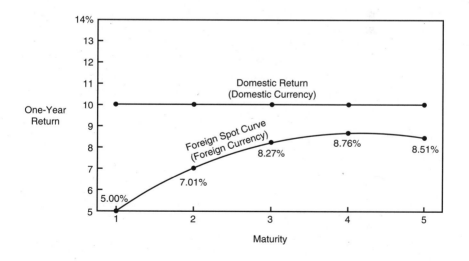

Figures 22–3A and 22–3B. Translating a Foreign Return Curve into Domestic Currency

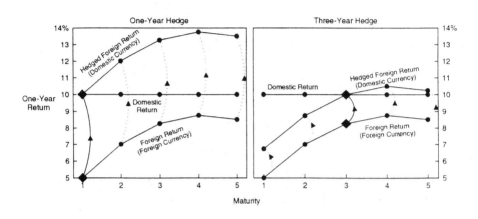

tic one-year note. Thus, the foreign one-year note moves up to occupy the position of the domestic one-year note in Figure 22–3A.

Suppose that the foreign investment is something different—for example, a five-year note. With the illustrative returns of Figure 22–2, the investor earns an incremental 3.51% over the return of the one-year note (8.51% versus 5.00%). This 3.51% increment gives him a total *hedged* return of 13.51%, compared with the 10% hedged return of the foreign one-year note.[4] All one-year hedged foreign investments capture the same 5% currency premium; thus, all points on the hedged foreign return curve maintain their relationship to the one-year note, producing the parallel shift seen in Figure 22–3A.

Figure 22–3B shows that the effect of a three-year hedge is similar to that of a one-year hedge. Now, however, the hedged foreign *three-year* note becomes a synthetic domestic *three-year* note, providing a different anchor point

---

[4]We assume that the currency hedge is based on the anticipated proceeds of the foreign one-year note, so any excess proceeds are unhedged and must be converted at the new spot exchange rate; thus, the incremental (or decremental) return relative to the foreign one-year note should be adjusted by the percentage change in currency exchange spot rates during the year. As we show in the Appendix to this chapter, this adjustment generally has a small "second-order" effect, typically a few basis points; in this chapter, we assume that the unhedged currency change is zero except where we address it explicitly in the Appendix.

for the translated foreign return curve.[5] (A three-year hedge is quite long by currency exchange market standards, but long-term hedges can be developed through a series of swaps. Although it is unusual to consider a currency hedge that is longer than the security that creates the currency risk, we show later in this chapter that such a strategy makes sense under certain conditions.)

Generalizing from these two examples, we can use the following expression for the hedged return of a foreign security, which we refer to as the *Basic Hedged Return Formula*:

Hedged Foreign Return $\approx$ Domestic Hedge Point Return
+ (Foreign Investment Return – Foreign Hedge Point Return),

where "hedge point return" means the return of a zero-coupon note whose maturity equals the length of the currency hedge.[6]

We now assume that the investor has selected a foreign investment and is considering how long a hedge to use. Rather than view the entire return curve, we focus on the foreign three-year zero-coupon note with a range of hedge periods. Figure 22–4 sets forth the one-year domestic currency return

Figure 22–4. Hedged Return of Three-Year Zero-Coupon Note

		Hedge Period			
		1 Year	2 Years	3 Years	4 Years
Hedged Rolling Yield					
(1) Domestic Zero-Coupon Rolling Yield	+	10.00%	10.00%	10.00%	10.00%
(2) Foreign Investment Rolling Yield	+	8.27	8.27	8.27	8.27
(3) Foreign Zero-Coupon Rolling Yield	–	5.00	7.01	8.27	8.76
(4) Hedged Rolling Yield = (1) + (2) – (3)		13.27%	11.26%	10.00%	9.50%

---

[5]Now the currency hedge is based on the anticipated proceeds that the foreign *three-year* note would produce, and the hedged return is determined by the one-year performance of the actual foreign security and the repricing of the hedge at year-end.

[6]As explained in a previous chapter, these hedge point returns always refer to zero-coupon notes whose yields equal the rates at which dealers finance their activity in the currency markets (interbank rates). The actual foreign investment, however, can be any type of security, although our illustrations use the zero-coupon return curve.

of the foreign three-year note with hedges that vary in length from one to four years. First, we use the Basic Hedged Return Formula to develop the hedged rolling yields—the hedged returns that would result if the domestic and foreign yield curves do not change. Under these conditions, as indicated in Figure 22–2, the domestic zero-coupon note for any maturity returns 10%, the foreign three-year note returns 8.27% in foreign currency terms, and the foreign zero-coupon note corresponding to each hedge produces the returns in Line (3).

SENSITIVITY OF HEDGED FOREIGN INVESTMENTS TO INTEREST-RATE CHANGES

A key determinant of return on a fixed-income investment is its duration, or sensitivity to interest-rate movements. A hedged foreign investment presents an unusual problem in defining duration, because its return can be affected by interest-rate movements in both domestic and foreign currencies. We can verify this dual exposure by noting that the first term on the right-hand side of the Basic Hedged Return Formula can be affected by changes in the domestic yield curve, and the other two terms are subject to foreign yield-curve changes. In this section, we show how a hedge partitions the duration of a foreign security between the two yield curves. (The Appendix to this chapter presents a more detailed explanation.)

To determine the effect of interest-rate changes, we need to know how such changes affect the three returns on the right-hand side of the Basic Hedged Return Formula. For example, consider the second term: the return of the foreign investment in its own currency. If the foreign yield curve does not change over the course of the year, the foreign investment earns its rolling yield, providing our reference point. If the yield curve undergoes a parallel shift, we can approximate the one-year return as the rolling yield *minus* the change in interest rates *multiplied* by the duration of the investment.[7] By using similar relationships for the other returns in the Basic Hedged Return Formula, we develop Figure 22–5, which shows the effect of interest-rate changes on the hedged foreign return.

The first column of Figure 22–5 lists the local return components that total to the hedged foreign return. As the signs indicate, it may be helpful to regard the investment as a combination of

---

[7]To simplify the presentation, we limit yield-curve changes to parallel shifts. We use the duration at the one-year horizon, ignoring any interim reinvestment.

- A long position in a domestic zero-coupon note with a maturity equal to the hedge length;
- A long position in the foreign investment; and
- A short position in a foreign zero-coupon note with a maturity equal to the hedge length.[8]

The middle column of Figure 22–5 shows the duration of each component in its local currency. The final column indicates the effect of a change in interest rates on each of the three component positions and on the total return.

Comparing the second line in Figure 22–5 with the fourth line, we see how the interest-rate exposure of the foreign investment varies when we shift our focus from the *foreign* currency return to the hedged *domestic* currency return. The foreign investment's local return is exposed to foreign interest-rate changes to the extent of its duration. The fourth line shows that when the return is hedged, the exposure to interest-rate changes is partitioned between domestic and foreign rates as follows:

- The investor has the domestic exposure of a long position in a hedge-length zero-coupon note, so the sensitivity to domestic interest-rate change is equal to the hedge length; and
- The investor has the foreign exposure of a long position in the foreign investment and a short position in a hedge-length zero-coupon

Figure 22–5. Effect of Interest-Rate Changes on the Hedged Foreign Return

Return Component	Duration	Effect of Change in Interest Rates
(1) + Domestic Hedge Point Return	Hedge Length	− Domestic Rate Increase × Hedge Length
(2) + Foreign Investment Return	Duration	− Foreign Rate Increase × Duration
(3) − Foreign Hedge Point Return	Hedge Length	− (− Foreign Rate Increase × Hedge Length)
(4) Total Hedged Foreign Return		− Domestic Rate Increase × Hedge Length
		− Foreign Rate Increase × (Duration − Hedge Length)

[8]As this relationship implies, the investor can synthesize the hedged foreign investment by taking the long and short positions enumerated here. He or she does not need a separate currency contract, because the offsetting effect of the long and short foreign positions minimizes the currency exposure.

note, so the sensitivity to foreign interest-rate changes is equal to the duration *minus* the hedge length.

By sensitivity, we mean the number of basis points by which the return decreases for each one-basis-point increase in the interest rate. It may be useful to think of these sensitivities as a "domestic duration" and a "foreign duration," although we avoid those labels because of their ambiguity in this context. When we use the term "duration" in the remainder of this chapter, we refer exclusively to the local duration of the foreign investment.

This interpretation reveals the diversification benefits of foreign investments, as mediated by the hedge period. The foreign investment by itself is exposed only to the foreign yield curve. By hedging, a domestic investor can shift some or all of that exposure to the domestic market as she chooses. For example, she can choose a hedge with a length that matches the duration of the foreign investment. Such a hedge substantially converts the investment into a synthetic domestic investment of the same duration. Thus, it shifts virtually *all* the exposure from the foreign yield curve to the domestic yield curve. A very short hedge leaves most of the foreign exposure unchanged. A hedge with a length equal to half the duration allocates half the exposure to each yield curve.

If the two yield curves move in lockstep, the allocation of exposure between them has no effect on the hedged return: with both markets behaving identically, exposure to one market is the same as exposure to the other. If the markets are imperfectly correlated, however, the two exposure components combine to produce a risk that is less than the duration of the foreign investment would indicate—a relationship that we will examine in a later chapter. With decorrelated markets, splitting the interest-rate exposure between the two markets reduces the volatility substantially.

The value of breaking down the interest-rate exposure into its components arises from the different ways that investors may think about changes in global interest-rate levels and relationships. An investor may have strong views or concerns about the domestic market, or the foreign market, or both; he may anticipate a global rate change; or he may hold a conviction about the prospective convergence or divergence of domestic and foreign rates. To understand the sensitivities of his portfolio, he may analyze interest-rate changes in a variety of ways. For example, suppose that domestic rates increase by 100 basis points and foreign rates by 150 basis points. The investor may regard this pair of changes as

- An increase of 100 basis points in domestic rates and an increase of 150 basis points in foreign rates; or

- An increase of 100 basis points in domestic rates and an increase of 50 basis points in the foreign/domestic spread; or

- An increase of 150 basis points in foreign rates and an increase of 50 basis points in the foreign/domestic spread.

We now consider each of these viewpoints as they apply to the hedged three-year note.

Separate Assessments of Domestic and Foreign Interest-Rate Changes

This approach would be natural for an investor who forms independent views of the two markets, as is appropriate for weakly correlated markets. Such an investor would regard our illustrative change as a 100-basis-point domestic rate increase and a 150-basis-point foreign rate increase. With this approach, we would quantify the effect of rate changes as follows:

Effect of Interest-Rate Changes

$\approx$ – Domestic Rate Increase $\times$ Hedge Length

– Foreign Rate Increase $\times$ (Duration – Hedge Length)

Figure 22–6 develops the results for the three-year note. It begins with the hedged rolling yields from Figure 22–4. It then shows the approximate domestic and foreign rate sensitivities of the hedged investment for each hedge period. Because we are considering one-year returns, the duration and hedge lengths are measured at the one-year horizon. Therefore, the domestic sensitivity equals the initial hedge length reduced by one year, while the foreign sensitivity equals the duration of the three-year note (two years, at the one-year horizon) *minus* the reduced hedge length.

Finally, Figure 22–6 shows the estimated effect both of the rate increase in each market separately and of the overall change. The estimates are based on the product of the rate change in each currency and the corresponding rate sensitivity.

The first column in Figure 22–6 indicates that the one-year hedge, with a domestic sensitivity of zero, allocates all interest-rate risk to the foreign yield curve.[9] Therefore, the 100-basis-point domestic rate increase would not af-

---

[9]This risk allocation can be verified by applying the Basic Hedged Return Formula to the one-year hedge. The first and third terms on the right-hand side of the Basic Hedged Return Formula describe the one-year return of a one-year note, which is invariant for yield-curve shifts. The only variable term is the second, the return of the foreign three-year note in its own currency, which carries all the risk.

Figure 22–6. Hedged Return of Three-Year Zero-Coupon Note—Domestic and Foreign Rate Sensitivity

| | Hedge Period | | | |
	1 Year	2 Years	3 Years	4 Years
Hedged Rolling Yield	13.27%	11.26%	10.00%	9.50%
Sensitivity to Rate Changes at Year-End				
Domestic Rates	0	1	2	3
Foreign Rates	2	1	0	−1
Estimated Effect of Rate Changes				
Domestic Rates + 100 bps	0 bps	−100 bps	−200 bps	−300 bps
Foreign Rates + 150 bps	−300	−150	0	+150
Total	−300 bps	−250 bps	−200 bps	−150 bps

bps = basis points.

---

fect the 13.27% rolling yield, while the 150-basis-point foreign rate increase would lower the return by an estimated 300 basis points, to 10.27%. (All estimates in this section come within five basis points of the exact returns; discrepancies arise from our using an unmodified duration and ignoring convexity.)

The second column in Figure 22–6 shows the two-year hedge, with a rolling yield of 11.26%. The two-year hedge divides the duration of the three-year note equally between the domestic and foreign markets, because at the one-year horizon, we have a two-year note with a one-year hedge. The estimated return after the rate changes is the 11.26% rolling yield less 250 basis points, or 8.76%.

In the third column, the three-year hedge converts the foreign three-year note into a synthetic domestic three-year note, so foreign rate changes are irrelevant, and all exposure is to the domestic yield curve.[10] The 100-basis-point increase in domestic rates produces an estimated return of 8%.

The last column of Figure 22–6 demonstrates the value of the dual rate exposure analysis when the foreign investment is *shorter* than the hedge pe-

---

[10]Again, the Basic Hedged Return Formula shows this conversion: the last two right-hand terms cancel each other out, leaving only the return of the domestic three-year note.

Figure 22–7. Domestic and Foreign Rate Sensitivity of Hedged Foreign Three-Year Note

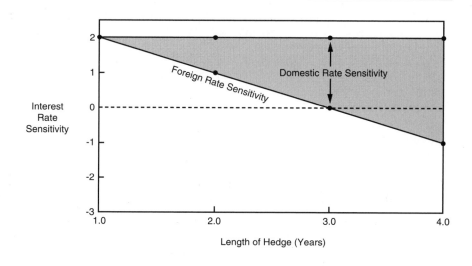

riod. The year-end duration of two years is "split" into a domestic sensitivity of 3.0 and a *negative* foreign sensitivity of –1.0. (The –1.0 sensitivity equals the duration of two years *minus* the year-end hedge length of three years—the foreign exposure is that of a long position in a three-year note and a short position in a four-year note.) A 100-basis-point increase in domestic rates, therefore, *reduces* the hedged return by an estimated 300 basis points. The 150-basis-point increase in foreign rates, however, *increases* the return by an estimated 150 basis points because of the negative foreign rate sensitivity. The 9.50% rolling yield thus is reduced to an estimated 6.50% by the domestic rate increase and then increased to 8.00% by the foreign increase—a surprising result, as the foreign rate increase contributes *positively* to the hedged return! The positive effect occurs because the foreign rate rise improves the performance of the foreign three-year note *relative to the foreign base* (or effective short position) of the four-year note. An investor thus can act on a bearish view of foreign bond markets, not by withdrawing from them, but by lengthening the currency hedge beyond the portfolio duration.

Figure 22–7 portrays the domestic and foreign rate sensitivities shown in Figure 22–6. The exposure of the hedged investment to foreign interest rates is at its maximum when the hedge is shortest and is replaced by exposure to domestic rates as the hedge lengthens. An investor who views foreign rates more positively than domestic rates should favor a shorter hedge, while one who is more positive on domestic rates should use a longer hedge.

Separate Assessments of Joint Rate Moves (Based on Domestic Rates) and Intermarket Spread Changes

An investor who thinks of domestic and foreign rates as associated rather than independent may prefer this second viewpoint, which looks at joint rate moves and spread changes. This approach is analogous to how investors typically view their domestic markets. For example, suppose that U.S. Treasury rates rise from 7% to 8% and corporate rates from 8.00% to 9.50%. Many investors would characterize that movement as a 100-basis-point rise in Treasury rates and a 50-basis-point widening of the corporate-Treasury spread and analyze the effects in those terms. Similarly, an investor could view our illustrative change as a 100-basis-point increase in domestic rates and a 50-basis-point increase in intermarket spreads. (Because corporate-Treasury spreads are always positive, investors can speak unambiguously of their widening or narrowing. Spreads between domestic and foreign rates, however, can be positive or negative, so we arbitrarily define the intermarket spread change as the foreign rate change *minus* the domestic rate change.)

With this approach, we restate the effect of interest-rate changes as follows:

Effect of Interest-Rate Changes

$\approx -$ Domestic Rate Increase $\times$ Duration

$-$ Spread Change $\times$ (Duration $-$ Hedge Length).

Figure 22–8 illustrates how we would estimate the effect of rate changes on the return of the hedged three-year note.

Figure 22–8 presents interest-rate sensitivities in a slightly different format from Figure 22–6. Because the first component of the interest-rate change is a hypothetical "global" rate movement equal to the domestic change, the first sensitivity shown is the response to a joint domestic and foreign rate change, which we refer to as the joint rate sensitivity. This sensitivity is the sum of the domestic and foreign sensitivities in Figure 22–6; the underlying equation shows that this *sensitivity to a joint rate change is simply the duration of the foreign investment*, independent of the hedge period.

The second component is a spread change, consisting of an incremental 50-basis-point increase in the foreign rate. The second sensitivity, therefore, is simply the sensitivity to foreign rate changes from Figure 22–6. The total estimated effects are, of course, the same as those shown in Figure 22–6.

It is interesting to observe that the hedge period does not affect the joint rate sensitivity; the hedged foreign three-year note loses about 200 basis points of value for each 100-basis-point increase in domestic and foreign rates, regardless of the hedge length. A uniform worldwide increase in rates would affect *all* two-year-duration bonds by the same amount, regardless of the currency in which they are denominated or how the currency exposure is hedged. An investor who wishes to act on an anticipated global increase in interest rates has little choice but to shorten duration; adjusting the currency hedge will not help. An investor who anticipates that the foreign/domestic spread will increase, however, can lengthen the currency hedge to the point at which the hedged foreign investment *benefits* from the rise—beyond three years, where the spread sensitivity turns negative.

Figure 22–9 depicts the joint and spread sensitivities from Figure 22–8. The joint rate sensitivity is invariant for changing hedge periods. The spread sensitivity is at its maximum for the shortest hedge; it declines to zero when the hedge length equals the duration, because we then have, in effect, a domestic security; thereafter, it turns negative. An investor who anticipates a

Figure 22–8. Hedged Return of Three-Year Zero-Coupon Note—Domestic Rate and Spread Sensitivity

| | Hedge Period | | | |
	1 Year	2 Years	3 Years	4 Years
Hedged Rolling Yield	13.27%	11.26%	10.00%	9.50%
Sensitivity to Rate Changes at Year-End				
Domestic and Foreign Rates Jointly	2	2	2	2
Spread (Incremental Foreign Rate Change)	2	1	0	−1
Estimated Effect of Rate Changes				
Domestic Rates + 100 bps	−200 bps	−200 bps	−200 bps	−200 bps
Spread + 50 bps	−100	−50	0	+50
Total	−300 bps	−250 bps	−200 bps	−150 bps

bps = basis points.

Figure 22–9. Joint Rate and Spread Sensitivity of Hedged Foreign Three-Year Note

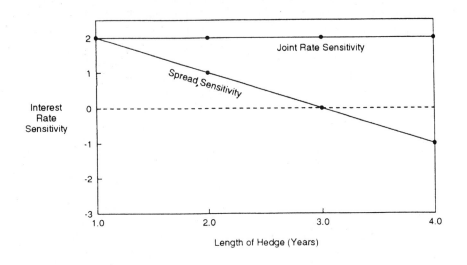

spread increase (foreign rates rising relative to domestic rates) would favor a longer hedge for its negative sensitivity to spreads.

Separate Assessments of Joint Rate Moves (Based on Foreign Rates) and Intermarket Spread Changes

This approach is similar to the second approach in considering the two rate changes together rather than independently. We now, however, take the foreign rate change as the primary component of interest-rate movement—a perspective that may appeal to an investor who focuses on the foreign market. The other component is the spread change that results from a deviation of the domestic rate move from the foreign move. The investor would view the change as a 150-basis-point foreign rate increase and a 50-basis-point spread increase. The effect of the interest-rate realignment under this approach is as follows:

Effect of Interest-Rate Changes

     $\approx$ – Foreign Rate Increase × Duration

     – Spread Increase × (– Hedge Length)

Figure 22–10. Hedged Return of Three-Year Zero-Coupon Note—Foreign Rate and Spread Sensitivity

	Hedge Period			
	1 Year	2 Years	3 Years	4 Years
Hedged Rolling Yield	13.27%	11.26%	10.00%	9.50%
Sensitivity to Rate Changes at Year-End				
Domestic and Foreign Rates Jointly	2	2	2	2
Spread	0	−1	−2	−3
Estimated Effect of Rate Changes				
Foreign Rates + 150 bps	−300 bps	−300 bps	−300 bps	−300 bps
Spread + 50 bps	0	+50	+100	+150
Total	−300 bps	−250 bps	−200 bps	−150 bps

bps = basis points.

Figure 22–10 shows the effect of rate changes from this perspective.

The format of Figure 22–10 is similar to that of Figure 22–8. The sensitivity to joint rate changes is again 2.0, regardless of the hedge period. Note, however, that the spread sensitivity is now uniformly negative. This occurs because we now base the joint rate move on the foreign rate change, and we attribute spread changes to a differential change in domestic rates. An *increase* in the intermarket spread, therefore, is driven by a relative *decrease* in the domestic rate (which *must* boost returns), rather than a relative increase in the foreign rate (which *generally* lowers returns).

ACTING ON INTEREST-RATE VIEWS

We now use the models developed in the previous section to summarize the actions that an investor should take in anticipation of various yield-curve changes.

First, suppose that the investor anticipates general rate stability (although she remains unwilling to accept currency risk). Having selected the foreign investment portfolio, she should set the hedge period at the maturity for which the domestic zero-coupon note has the greatest rolling yield advantage over the foreign zero-coupon note. The reason for this strategy is that the investor wishes to maximize the upward shift of the foreign return curve (see Figures 22–3A and 22–3B). In addition, note that the Basic Hedged Return Formula can be written as

Hedged Foreign Return

≈ Foreign Investment Return

+ (Domestic Hedge Point Return – Foreign Hedge Point Return),

which shows the need to select the hedge point that maximizes the excess of the domestic zero-coupon return over the foreign zero-coupon return.

Now suppose that the investor anticipates specific changes in rates. We arbitrarily adopt the second of the three viewpoints that we have presented— that interest-rate changes can be treated as a combination of a joint change equal to the domestic change and a change in the foreign/domestic spread.

Figure 22–11 presents appropriate responses to various combinations of anticipated rate changes. We base the responses on the sensitivities to joint rate changes and spread changes, as developed previously:

Sensitivity to Joint Rate Changes ≈ Duration

Sensitivity to Spread Changes ≈ Duration – Hedge Length

Then, we identify the adjustments that the investor should make to the duration of his foreign position and the length of the currency hedge. The two question marks in Figure 22–11 indicate that the investor's views about joint rates and spreads give conflicting direction about the advisable duration adjustment. If he believes that the net effect on foreign rates is an increase, he should shorten duration; if a decrease, he should lengthen. Ambiguity is also present where two alternatives are shown for adjusting the hedge. For example, suppose the investor expects joint rates to rise but has no view on spreads. He clearly should shorten duration, thereby reducing exposure to the expected foreign yield-curve increase. He then *may* decide to shorten the hedge, transferring some of the exposure reduction to the domestic yield-curve exposure.

A final question is how an investor should act if he or she expects non-parallel yield-curve reshapings. For these changes, the investor can find guidance in the Basic Hedged Return Formula, as reformulated at the start of this section. The return of the foreign investment can be modeled by conventional single-market methods that accommodate full yield-curve specification. The investor should then choose the hedge length that he or she expects

Figure 22–11. Acting on Interest-Rate Views

Interest-Rate Expectations		Action	
Joint Rates	Foreign/Domestic Spread	Duration	Hedge
No View	No View	None	None
No View	Increasing	Shorten	Lengthen
No View	Decreasing	Lengthen	Shorten
Increasing	No View	Shorten	None or Shorten
Increasing	Increasing	Shorten	Lengthen
Increasing	Decreasing	?	Shorten
Decreasing	No View	Lengthen	None or Lengthen
Decreasing	Increasing	?	Lengthen
Decreasing	Decreasing	Lengthen	Shorten

will maximize the excess of the domestic hedge point return over the foreign hedge point return. The hedge length, therefore, should be set to reflect the investor's view on the maturity range in which the foreign/domestic spread changes would be most favorable to domestic returns.

CONCLUSION

In this chapter, we explain how a currency hedge apportions the interest-rate exposure of a foreign fixed-income security between the domestic and foreign markets. With imperfectly correlated markets, the partitioning of interest-rate exposure can reduce risk by diversifying the exposure between the two currencies. We have shown how various gauges of interest-rate sensitivity can measure the exposure, and we concluded by enumerating the strategies by which an investor can act on interest-rate views. Although we focus on parallel yield-curve shifts, we indicate how our framework can be used to pinpoint the portions of the yield curve that affect the hedged return. To active managers with views more specific than the parallel yield-curve shifts, the combination of hedge selection and security selection permits plays on precisely targeted yield-curve segments. In the next two chapters, we will go beyond the scenario analysis in this chapter to explore the more general risk characteristics of hedged foreign fixed-income portfolios.

APPENDIX

Interest-Rate Sensitivities

In this Appendix, we derive formulas for the various interest-rate sensitivities set forth in the chapter. We develop these sensitivities by using the Babcock Approximation Formula[11] to express returns in terms of initial yields, changes in yield, and duration.

Figure 22–A1 shows our notation. We use capital letters to express results denominated in domestic currency and lowercase for foreign currency. Returns marked with a tilde (~) are uncertain, while those without a tilde are rolling yields—the returns that would occur if interest rates do not change.

Figure 22–A1. Symbols Used in Appendix

	Domestic	Foreign
Currency Exchange Rates (Domestic Units Per Foreign Unit)		
• Spot Rate at Time 0	S_0	
• Spot Rate at Time 1	S_1	
Interest Rates		
• n-Year Spot at Time 0	$I_0^{(n)}$	$i_0^{(n)}$
• $(n-1)$-Year Spot at Time 1	$I_1^{(n-1)}$	$i_1^{(n-1)}$
One-Year Realized Rates of Return		
• n-Year Zero-Coupon Bond	$\tilde{R}^{(n)}$	$\tilde{r}^{(n)}$
• Generalized Foreign Investment (Duration = D)	$\tilde{R}$	$\tilde{r}$
Rolling Yield (One-Year Realized Return If Interest Rates Do Not Change)		
• n-Year Zero-Coupon Bond	$R^{(n)}$	$r^{(n)}$
• Generalized Foreign Investment	R	r

In an earlier chapter,[12] we derived the following formula for the one-year return of an n-year hedged foreign investment:

---

[11]See "Duration as a Link between Yield and Value," Guilford C. Babcock, *The Journal of Portfolio Management*, 1984.

[12]See Chapter 21.

$$\tilde{R} = \tilde{R}^{(n)} + (\tilde{r} - \tilde{r}^{(n)})(S_1 / S_0).$$

This equation is the exact version of the Basic Hedged Return Formula, including the second-order currency effect that we show in this Appendix to be minor. We drop the currency adjustment and use the approximate form:

$$\tilde{R} \approx \tilde{R}^{(n)} + (\tilde{r} - \tilde{r}^{(n)}). \tag{1}$$

Next, we determine the effect of interest-rate changes on each of the three returns on the right-hand side of equation (1). We can estimate the return of a fixed-income security for a specified holding period by using the Babcock Approximation Formula:

Holding Period Return $\approx$ Yield

$$+ \left[1 - \frac{\text{Duration}}{\text{Holding Period}} \right] \times \text{Change in Yield}.$$

We apply this formula to the first term on the right-hand side of equation (1), $\tilde{R}^{(n)}$, the one-year return of the domestic n-year zero-coupon note (which has a Macaulay duration equal to n):

$$\tilde{R}^{(n)} \approx I_0^{(n)} + (1 - n / 1)(I_1^{(n-1)} - I_0^{(n)})$$

$$\approx I_0^{(n)} - (n - 1)(I_1^{(n-1)} - I_0^{(n)}). \tag{2}$$

The rolling yield for this note, $R^{(n)}$, can be approximated by substituting $I_0^{(n-1)}$ for $I_1^{(n-1)}$ in equation (2) (that is, assuming that interest rates do not change during the year):

$$R^{(n)} \approx I_0^{(n)} - (n - 1)(I_0^{(n-1)} - I_0^{(n)}). \tag{3}$$

We now rewrite equation (2) by adding and subtracting $I_0^{(n-1)}$ within the last set of parentheses:

$$\tilde{R}^{(n)} \approx I_0^{(n)} + (n - 1)(I_1^{(n-1)} - I_0^{(n-1)} + I_0^{(n-1)} - I_0^{(n)})$$

$$\approx I_0^{(n)} - (n - 1)(I_0^{(n-1)} - I_0^{(n)}) - (n - 1)(I_1^{(n-1)} - I_0^{(n-1)}).$$

The first part of the right-hand side of this equation is the rolling yield $R^{(n)}$ as expressed in equation (3), so we now can express the return in terms of the rolling yield, the hedge length, and the change in interest rates during the year.

$$\tilde{R}^{(n)} \approx R^{(n)} - (n-1)(I_1^{(n-1)} - I_0^{(n-1)}) \tag{4}$$

We are considering only parallel yield-curve shifts, and we use $\tilde{\delta}_I$ to represent the change in the $(n-1)$-year spot rate during the year, or the change in *any* domestic spot rate. (Similarly, we will use $\tilde{\delta}_i$ for the change in foreign interest rates.) Equation (4) becomes

$$\tilde{R}^{(n)} \approx R^{(n)} - (n-1)\tilde{\delta}_I. \tag{5}$$

We can derive similar relationships for the other two returns in equation (1)—$\tilde{r}$, the return of the foreign investment, and $\tilde{r}^{(n)}$, the return of the foreign n-year zero-coupon note:

$$\tilde{r} \approx r - (D-1)\tilde{\delta}_i, \text{ and} \tag{6}$$

$$\tilde{r}^{(n)} \approx r^{(n)} - (n-1)\tilde{\delta}_i. \tag{7}$$

Substituting equations (5), (6), and (7) in equation (1), we obtain an expression for $\tilde{R}$, the hedged return of the foreign investment:

$$\tilde{R} \approx R^{(n)} + (r - r^{(n)}) - \tilde{\delta}_I(n-1) - \tilde{\delta}_i(D-n). \tag{8}$$

The one-year hedged rolling yield, R, is the hedged return that would result if both domestic and foreign interest rates do not change during the year. In the unchanging rate case,

$$\tilde{\delta}_I = \tilde{\delta}_i = 0,$$

$$\tilde{R} = R, \quad \text{and}$$

$$R \approx R^{(n)} + (r - r^{(n)}).$$

Thus, the first portion of equation (8) can be replaced by R to give

$$\tilde{R} \approx R - \tilde{\delta}_I(n-1) - \tilde{\delta}_i(D-n). \tag{9}$$

Equation (9) shows that the hedged return has a sensitivity to domestic interest-rate changes equal to the length of the hedge at the one-year horizon. The sensitivity to foreign rate changes is the duration of the foreign investment *minus* the length of the hedge.

When $\tilde{\delta}_I = \tilde{\delta}_{I'}$ the sensitivity to this joint domestic and foreign rate change can be found by substituting $\tilde{\delta}_J$ for $\tilde{\delta}_I$ and $\tilde{\delta}_i$ in equation (9):

$$\tilde{R} \approx R - \tilde{\delta}_J(n-1) - \tilde{\delta}_J(D-n)$$

$$\approx R - \tilde{\delta}_J(D-1), \tag{10}$$

so the sensitivity to a joint rate change is the duration *minus* one.[13]

When both domestic and foreign yield curves undergo equal parallel shifts, there is no change in the spread of a foreign rate over a domestic rate. In the case of unequal parallel shifts, the intermarket spread will change. We can view changes in domestic and foreign rates as occurring in either of two ways:

1. A joint change (that is, equal parallel shifts) equal to the domestic change, immediately followed by a spread change caused by a further change in the foreign rate relative to the domestic rate.

2. A joint change equal to the foreign change, and a spread change caused by a further change in the domestic rate relative to the foreign rate.

With the first view, we attribute a change in the spread to a change in the foreign rate alone. That is, the foreign rate charge is split into two parts: a move identical to the domestic rate move, the effect of which is folded into the joint rate sensitivity, and an incremental move to establish the spread change. Thus, under this view, the sensitivity to a spread change is the sensitivity to a foreign rate change—the duration of the foreign investment *minus* the length of the hedge.

With the second view, we attribute a change in the spread to an opposite change in the domestic rate (for example, a 100-basis-point increase in the spread is due to a 100-basis-point decrease in the domestic rate). Then, the sensitivity to a spread change is the negative of the sensitivity to a domestic rate change as shown in equation (9): *minus* the length of the hedge at the one-year horizon.

---

[13]In this chapter, we refer to $(D-1)$ as the year-end duration. In fact, the Babcock formula uses the Macaulay duration and relies on the Macaulay duration minus one to approximate the year-end modified duration; this approximation is quite accurate for a par bond, but less so for a zero-coupon bond. The most accurate approximation for the hedged foreign return will be obtained by using year-end modified durations for all returns.

Effect of Changes in Currency Exchange Spot Rates

Unless the investor has hedged the foreign cash flows precisely, he has some exposure to currency exchange rate fluctuations. As we stated in arriving at equation (1), this exposure has little effect on the returns of an investor who has based his hedge on a reasonable approximation. Figure 22–A2 illustrates this point.

Figure 22–A2 displays the effect of a substantial strengthening of the foreign currency under the scenario used in Figure 22–3B: The investor uses a three-year hedge based on the anticipated proceeds of a foreign three-year zero-coupon note, and we assume that the yield curves do not change. The solid line shows the one-year hedged foreign return curve if currency exchange spot rates do not change during the year, and the nearby dashed line shows the return curve if the foreign currency strengthens by 20%.

Our foreign hedge point is a three-year zero-coupon note, denoted by the diamond. For this investment, the hedge is exact and currency fluctuations have no effect;[14] the investor earns a foreign currency return of 8.27% (based on Figure 22–2) and a hedged return of 10%, regardless of the new currency exchange spot rate.

If the foreign investment is a four-year note, rather than a three-year note, the foreign currency return would be 8.76%, rather than 8.27%, a 0.49% advantage. If the currency exchange spot rate is unchanged at year-end, the 0.49% foreign advantage translates into a 0.49% advantage in domestic currency return as well, for a 10.49% total return. If the foreign currency has appreciated by 20%, however, the advantage is magnified by the favorable exchange rate and becomes 0.59% (120% × 0.49% to a 10.59% total), a 10-basis-point improvement.

On the other hand, if the foreign investment is a note shorter than three years, the investor finishes the year with *less* foreign currency than the holder of a three-year note. If the foreign currency has strengthened, that disadvantage is magnified. The result, as Figure 22–A2 shows, is that securities with excess returns relative to the foreign hedge point have those excess returns increased by the percentage strengthening of foreign currency, and shortfalls also are increased. Weakening of the foreign currency has the opposite effect; excess foreign returns or shortfalls relative to the hedge point return are lessened.

---

[14]More precisely, over a one-year period, currency fluctuations have *offsetting* effects on the unhedged value of the three-year note and the repricing of the three-year hedge.

Figure 22–A2. Effect of 20% Strengthening of Foreign Currency

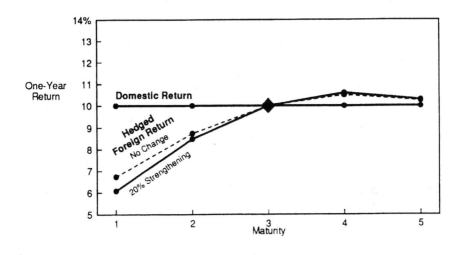

Chapter 23

The Volatility of Hedged Global Fixed-Income Investments

INTRODUCTION

In earlier chapters,[1] we developed a framework for hedged global fixed-income investing. We showed how the hedge provides a baseline return and partitions the interest-rate risk between domestic and foreign markets.

In this chapter, we explore the return volatility associated with these interest-rate risks. First, we examine the significance of the correlation between the domestic and foreign markets. With imperfectly correlated markets, the hedge can provide diversification benefits that significantly reduce the effect of interest-rate volatility (in addition to eliminating the effect of currency volatility). These diversification benefits are present, however, only when the length of the hedge falls between the length of the performance measurement period and the duration of the foreign portfolio. When the hedge is longer than the foreign duration—sometimes a desirable tactic, as we show—we find counterintuitive risk/return curves, which may violate the expectation that volatility rises with duration.

---

[1]See Chapters 21 and 22. For another view of foreign bond volatility, see "Global and Local Components of Foreign Bonds Risk," Steven I. Dym, *Financial Analysts Journal*, March/April 1992; and "Measuring the Risk of Foreign Bonds, Steven I. Dym, "*The Journal of Portfolio Management*, Winter 1991.

EXPECTED RETURN

In the two previous chapters, we developed the *Basic Hedged Return Formula* for foreign investments:

Hedged Foreign Return $\approx$ Domestic Hedge Point Return
+ (Foreign Investment Return
− Foreign Hedge Point Return),   (1)

where "hedge point return" signifies the return of a zero-coupon note whose maturity equals the length of the currency hedge.[2] For example, a foreign five-year note with a three-year hedge would produce the same return as the following combination:

- A long position in a domestic three-year zero-coupon note;
- A long position in a foreign five-year note; and
- A short position in a foreign three-year zero-coupon note.

Figure 23–1 shows the domestic and foreign expected returns that we use in this chapter. The returns are shown in local currency—that is, domestic bonds all have a 10% expected return in domestic currency, and foreign bonds are expected to provide foreign currency returns ranging from 5.00% to 7.50%.[3] We use a one-year horizon throughout this chapter.

Applying the Basic Hedged Return Formula to Figure 23–1, we can determine the expected hedged foreign return curves. Figures 23–2A and 23–2B depict these curves for one- and three-year hedges, respectively.

Figure 23–2A shows the effect of the one-year hedge. Based on the principle of "interest-rate parity,"[4] a foreign one-year zero-coupon note with a

---

[2]See Chapter 21. This approximation assumes that the currency exposure is hedged by the forward sale of foreign currency in an amount equal to the proceeds that would be produced by a zero-coupon note for the length of the hedge. (In the exact formula, the parenthetical expression is modified by the change in currency exchange spot rates during the measurement period, a "second order effect" that we have shown to be minor and will not consider in this chapter.) By "hedge point returns," we refer to the returns on zero-coupon notes whose yields equal the rates at which dealers finance their activity in the currency markets (interbank rates). The actual foreign investment, however, can be any type of security, although our illustrations use the zero-coupon notes.

[3]These expected return curves duplicate the yield-to-maturity curves that we used in Chapter 20. The flat domestic return curve is a convenience, not a restriction of the model. The expected returns can be based on any theoretical or tactical model without altering the approach in this chapter.

[4]When interest-rate parity prevails, currency forward exchange rates are at levels that equalize the hedged yield of a riskless foreign security to the yield of a domestic security with the identical payoff pattern.

Figure 23–1. Domestic and Foreign Expected Return Curves

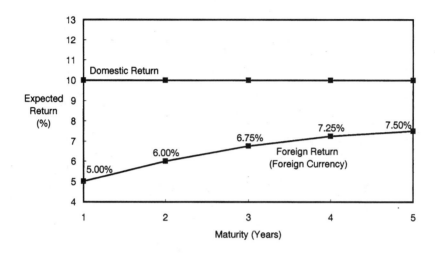

Figures 23–2A and 23–2B. Translating Foreign Return Curves into Domestic Currency

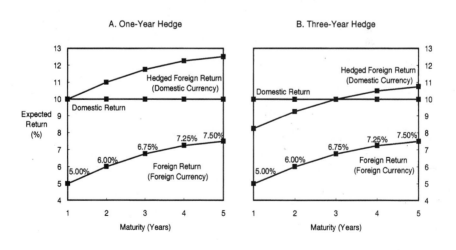

one-year currency hedge becomes a synthetic domestic one-year note. Under this principle, the one-year currency hedge must offer a 5% premium to compensate for the yield advantage of the domestic note over the foreign note (10% versus 5%). Therefore, as the measurement basis changes from foreign to domestic currency, the hedged foreign one-year note combines a 5% currency return with a 5% local interest return to produce the same 10% return as the domestic one-year note. Thus, the foreign one-year note moves up to occupy the position of the domestic one-year note in Figure 23–2A.

Now suppose that the foreign investment is a five-year note. With the illustrative returns of Figure 23–1, the investor earns an incremental 2.50% over the foreign-currency return of the one-year note (7.50% versus 5.00%). When added to the 10% *hedged* return of the foreign one-year note, this 2.50% increment provides a total *hedged* return of 12.50%.[5] All one-year hedged foreign investments capture the same 5% currency premium; thus, all points on the hedged foreign return curve maintain their relationship to the one-year note, producing the parallel shift illustrated in Figure 23–2A.

Figure 23–2B shows that the effect of a three-year hedge is similar to the effect of a one-year hedge.[6] Now, however, the hedged foreign *three-year* note becomes a synthetic domestic *three-year* note, providing a different anchor point for the translated foreign return curve. The foreign five-year note carries a 0.75% return increment over the foreign three-year note. Hence, with a three-year hedge, the five-year note's hedged return becomes 10% *plus* 0.75%, or 10.75%.

---

[5]We assume that the currency hedge is based on the anticipated proceeds of the foreign one-year note; thus, any excess proceeds are unhedged and must be converted at the new spot exchange rate. Accordingly, the incremental (or decremental) return relative to the foreign one-year note should be adjusted by the percentage change in currency exchange spot rates during the year. This adjustment is the small "second order" effect to which we referred previously.

[6]A three-year hedge is quite long by currency exchange market standards, but long-term hedges can be developed through a series of swaps. Although it is unusual to consider a currency hedge that is longer than the security that creates the currency risk, we show later in this chapter that this strategy can make sense whenever the domestic expected return curve is more positively sloped than the foreign curve. The three-year currency hedge is based on the anticipated proceeds that the foreign *three*-year note would produce, and the hedged return is determined by the one-year performance of the actual foreign security and the repricing of the three-year hedge at year-end.

Most currency hedges use much shorter hedges than we illustrate here, rolling monthly or three-month hedges. For example, suppose that we use a one-month hedge for a five-year note. The Basic Hedged Return Formula shows that the return in any month would be the return of a domestic one-month note, *plus* the return of a foreign five-year note, *minus* the return of a foreign one-month note. Over the course of a year, the one-month returns would compound to give *approximately* the one-year return from rolling domestic one-month notes, *plus* the one-year return on the foreign five-year note, *minus* the one-year return from rolling foreign one-month notes. In any case, hedging practically eliminates currency risk.

VOLATILITY WITH PERFECT DOMESTIC/FOREIGN CORRELATION

With the Basic Hedged Return Formula, we can proceed to calculate the volatility of the hedged foreign return. (See the Appendix to this chapter for the formula used.) In this chapter, we focus on the variables specific to cross-currency fixed-income investing. For the returns within each market, we use the following simplified assumptions:

- Yield-curve shifts are parallel. (Although we do not explicitly address the risk of yield-curve reshapings, our framework can accommodate them, because the Basic Hedged Return Formula pinpoints the segments of the yield curve that can affect the return.)

- Interest-rate movements in each currency are normally distributed, with a standard deviation of 1% annually.

- One-year bond returns equal the initial yield *minus* the product of the change in yield and the year-end modified duration.

We now test the effect of differing domestic/foreign interest-rate correlations. We begin by assuming that domestic and foreign interest rates are perfectly correlated, as shown in Figures 23–3A and 23–3B, for the one- and three-year hedges.

In Figures 23–3A and 23–3B, the horizontal axis reflects volatility (that is, the standard deviation of return), rather than maturity. Thus, the foreign return curve presents a risk/return profile for foreign investors who remain in their own currency; the other two curves show risk/return profiles for domestic investors. Despite the change in the x-axis from maturity to volatility, Figures 23–3A and 23–3B reveal expected return curves with the same shape as shown in Figures 23–2A and 23–2B. For the two local return curves in each graph, the shape holds constant as we shift from maturity to volatility (because of the linear relationship between maturity and volatility that holds for zero-coupon bonds). For the hedged foreign return curve, a restatement of the Basic Hedged Return Formula is useful:

Hedged Foreign Return ≈ Foreign Investment Return

+ (Domestic Hedge Point Return

− Foreign Hedge Point Return).   (2)

**Figures 23–3A and 23–3B. Domestic and Foreign Expected Return Curves
                   (Correlation = 1.0)**

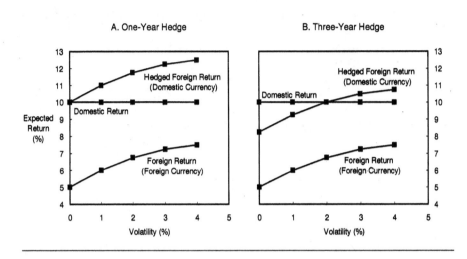

Under our assumptions of equal domestic and foreign rate volatility and perfect correlation, the volatilities of the two hedge point returns offset each other. For example, suppose we have a 100-basis-point increase in domestic rates. Under our assumptions, foreign rates similarly will increase by 100 basis points. The domestic rate increase will lower the domestic hedge point return by a certain amount, and the foreign rate increase will lower the foreign hedge point return by a like amount. Overall, the offsetting changes in the two hedge point returns do not affect the hedged foreign return; only the change in the foreign investment return has an effect. Under these assumptions, therefore, the hedged return of a foreign bond has essentially the same volatility as its foreign currency return.

Another way to view the volatilities in Figures 23–3A and 23–3B is through the sensitivity of the hedged foreign return to domestic and foreign interest rates:[7]

Sensitivity to Domestic Interest-Rate Change Only
$\approx$ Hedge Length,   and   (3)

_____

[7]See Chapter 22 for a full development of these formulas.

Sensitivity to Foreign Interest-Rate Change Only
$$\approx \text{Foreign Investment Duration} - \text{Hedge Length}, \quad\quad (4)$$

where the hedge length and the duration are determined at the end of the measurement period. By "sensitivity," we mean the number of basis points by which the return decreases for each one-basis-point increase in the interest rate (a definition similar to "duration"). In our simple illustration, with a 1.0 correlation and equal domestic and foreign interest-rate volatilities, the domestic and foreign interest-rate changes must be equal. The sensitivity of the hedged return to the (joint) interest-rate change, then, is the sum of the domestic and foreign sensitivities given in equations (3) and (4) above, which is the foreign investment duration—the same as the sensitivity of the foreign investment return. Under these assumptions, the volatility of the foreign return measured in foreign currency is the same as the volatility of the return hedged into domestic currency.

IMPERFECT DOMESTIC/FOREIGN CORRELATION

When we drop the artificial assumption of perfect correlation, the hedge has more interesting effects on the volatilities. Figures 23–4A and 23–4B illustrate the expected return curves when the domestic and foreign rates are uncorrelated (correlation = 0.0).

The hedged return curve for the one-year hedge illustrated in Figure 23–4A is unchanged from that shown in Figure 23–3A, because the hedge length shortens to zero at year-end. Hence, by equations (3) and (4), there is no sensitivity to domestic rates, and the sensitivity to foreign rates is based on the foreign investment duration. All of the volatility, then, is that of the foreign bond in foreign currency, as in Figure 23–3A. This example illustrates a general rule: For a measurement period equal to the hedge period, the volatility of the hedged return equals that of the local foreign return.

In contrast to the one-year hedge, the three-year hedge shown in Figure 23–4B reshapes the foreign expected return curve substantially. To understand the reshaping, we first observe that the foreign three-year note continues to serve as the "anchor point"; with a three-year hedge, a foreign three-year note is a synthetic domestic three-year note. As the foreign investment departs from this perfectly hedged three-year note, a second source of volatility is added to the underlying volatility of the domestic three-year note— the return differential between the foreign three-year note and the actual foreign investment.

**Figures 23–4A and 23–4B. Domestic and Foreign Expected Return Curves
(Correlation = 0.0)**

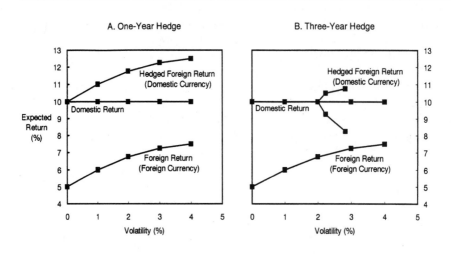

For example, consider a foreign five-year note with a three-year hedge. Based on equations (3) and (4), the hedged return has a domestic sensitivity of approximately 2.0 (the year-end hedge length) and a foreign sensitivity of about 2.0 (the year-end duration of 4.0 *minus* the year-end hedge length of 2.0).[8] If the domestic and foreign interest rates were perfectly correlated, these sensitivities could be added, giving a total sensitivity of 4.0 and a return volatility of about 4%, as in Figure 23–3B. However, because we are now assuming a correlation of zero, splitting the interest-rate exposure between the two yield curves offers a diversification benefit, and the return volatility is reduced to 2.8%.[9] Hence, a leftward contraction of the portion of the return curve above three years occurs in Figure 23–4B.

Now consider a foreign one-year note with a three-year hedge. The hedged return has the same 2.0 domestic sensitivity as that of a five-year note, but the foreign sensitivity is –2.0. If the interest rates were perfectly

---

[8]More precisely, the year-end foreign exposure is that of a four-year note two years forward (apart from any coupon flow during the first two years). This formulation identifies the specific yield-curve segment on which the investor has foreign exposure.

[9] $\sqrt{0.02^2 + 0.02^2} = 0.028$.

correlated, the sensitivities would partially offset each other, producing a net volatility of zero, as in Figure 23–3B. However, because the rates are uncorrelated, the sensitivities combine, rather than offset each other, again giving a return volatility of about 2.8%.

Another way of understanding Figure 23–4B is to think in terms of the long and short positions implied by the hedge, explained following equation (1). A hedged foreign five-year note is equivalent to a long position in a domestic three-year note, a long position in a foreign five-year note, and a short position in a foreign three-year note.

This combination produces positive durations in both currencies. If the two yield curves move in lockstep, as in Figure 23–3B, volatility is maximized; if they are uncorrelated, a diversification benefit reduces the volatility.

For a hedged foreign one-year note, the domestic position retains a positive duration, but the foreign position has a negative duration (short a three-year note and long a one-year note). If the yield curves move together, as in Figure 23–3B, these durations offset one another, eliminating volatility. If the yield curves are uncorrelated, however, the offset is lost, and the investor is exposed to two diverse interest-rate movements. The high volatility of a three-year hedged one-year note illustrates a well-known principle: A hedged position suffers greater volatility as the correlation between the long position (domestic hedge point) and short position (foreign hedge point) declines.

Figures 23–5A and 23–5B show the expected return curves when the domestic and the foreign rates have a correlation of 0.75, as we will assume for the remainder of this chapter. (Correlation between the interest rates of countries with close economic ties can be as high as 0.75, while more distantly related markets will have correlations below 0.50.)

GAINING RETURN WITH A LONGER HEDGE

In our illustrations thus far, the one-year hedge has dominated the three-year hedge, as a comparison of the hedged return curves in all of the A and B graph pairs shows. This dominance reflects our use of a flat domestic return curve and a positive foreign return curve. Figures 23–6A to 23–7B illustrate that the three-year hedge becomes attractive when the domestic curve remains flat and the foreign expected return curve inverts—the result of an inverted yield curve and/or a bearish rate view.[10]

---

[10]This is a single case that illustrates the general conditions under which lengthening the hedge improves return: The lengthening takes place over an interval on which the domestic return curve has a more positive slope than the foreign curve. See Chapter 21.

Figures 23–5A and 23–5B. Domestic and Foreign Expected Return Curves
(Correlation = 0.75)

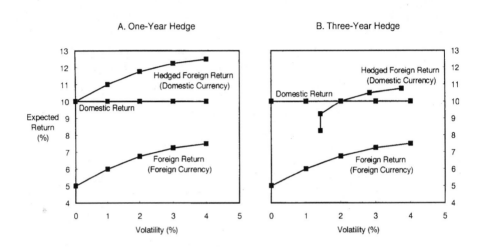

A. One-Year Hedge

B. Three-Year Hedge

Figures 23–6A and 23–6B. Translating Foreign Returns into Domestic Currency
(Inverted Foreign Curve)

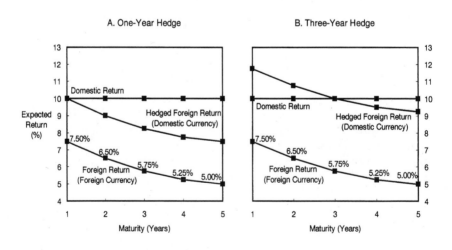

A. One-Year Hedge

B. Three-Year Hedge

Figures 23–7A and 23–7B. Domestic and Foreign Expected Return Curves (Inverted Foreign Curve)

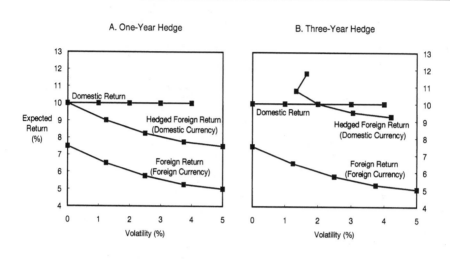

Figures 23–6A and 23–6B show the expected return as a function of *maturity*, similar to Figures 23–2A and 23–2B. Figure 23–6B uses a three-year hedge, which "anchors" the hedged foreign return curve at the three-year point. This hedge gives a much greater "lift" to the foreign curve than the one-year hedge, which anchors the hedged foreign curve at the one-year point. The result is uniformly superior expected returns for the three-year hedge.

Figures 23–7A and 23–7B shift the curves into risk/return space, using a 0.75 correlation. The result is similar to Figures 23–5A and 23–5B, except that the inversion has placed the shorter foreign notes above, rather than below, the longer notes. Under these conditions, short-term foreign notes with a long-term hedge could be the asset of choice.[11] An investor can design even better portfolios by mixing appropriate domestic securities with these long-hedged short-maturity foreign notes.

---

[11]See Chapter 22.

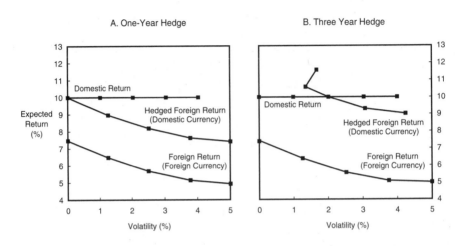

Figures 23–8A and 23–8B. Domestic and Foreign Expected Return Curves with Differing Interest-Rate Volatilities

Notes: Domestic Interest-Rate Volatility = 1%; Foreign Interest-Rate Volatility = 1.25%; and Correlation = 0.75.

DIFFERING DOMESTIC AND FOREIGN VOLATILITIES

We continue with the inverted foreign return curve and permit the domestic and foreign volatilities to differ, raising the foreign interest-rate volatility from 1% to 1.25%. We retain a 1% domestic interest-rate volatility and a 0.75 correlation. Figures 23–8A and 23–8B display the results for one- and three-year hedges.

With the one-year hedge underlying Figure 23–8A, the effect of the higher foreign interest-rate volatility is straightforward: The volatility of each foreign security, hedged or unhedged, rises in proportion to the increase in interest-rate volatility. This effect is evident in the rightward stretch of the foreign return curves from Figure 23–7A to Figure 23–8A.

The three-year hedge in Figure 23–8B has a more complex effect. As before, the hedged foreign three-year note coincides with the domestic three-year note. For foreign securities longer than three years (those *below* the domestic curve), the higher foreign volatility extends the hedged return curve compared with Figure 23–7B.

For foreign securities shorter than three years, the volatility curve has the same "snapback" that we have seen in earlier graphs. The effects are particularly complex for securities shorter than the hedge, because *correlated* foreign rate movements potentially offset the effect of domestic rate movements, while *independent* or *uncorrelated* movements of foreign rates can increase volatility.

CONCLUSION

In this chapter, we have shown how various factors interact to determine the volatility of hedged foreign bonds. One- to three-month hedges are commonly used to eliminate currency exposure, but significantly longer hedges can further reduce volatility through diversification effects that depend on the intermarket correlation.

If reliable intermarket correlations can be found—either long term or for occasional stable periods—our framework can help to identify the rewards and risks of various currency hedges and portfolio selection strategies. Under these conditions, the volatility of a hedged foreign investment can be partitioned into two sources. Part of the volatility can be attributed to domestic interest-rate movements (either directly, or indirectly through the statistical relationship between foreign and domestic rates). Independent or uncorrelated movements of foreign rates cause the remainder of the volatility. Understanding the impact of these risk components is especially important when managing a hedged foreign portfolio against a domestic benchmark. We will analyze these differential volatility effects further in the next chapter.

APPENDIX

In this Appendix, we derive the formula used to approximate the return volatility of hedged foreign investments.

From the Basic Hedged Return Formula,[12] we can derive the following approximation for the one-year return of a hedged foreign investment, assuming that all yield-curve shifts are parallel:[13]

$$\tilde{R} \approx \mu - \tilde{\delta}_I(n-1) - \tilde{\delta}_i(D-n) \tag{1}$$

where

$\tilde{R}$ = Realized one-year return.

μ = Expected one-year return.

$\tilde{\delta}_I$ = Realized change in domestic yield curve *minus* expected change in domestic yield curve.

$\tilde{\delta}_i$ = Realized change in foreign yield curve *minus* expected change in foreign yield curve.

n = Length of currency hedge.

D = Macaulay duration of foreign investment.

We now let σ_R = Standard deviation of hedged return. By definition,

$$\sigma_R^2 = E[(\tilde{R} - \mu)^2]. \tag{2}$$

Substituting equation (1) in equation (2), we can write

$$\sigma_R^2 \approx E[(-\tilde{\delta}_I(n-1) - \tilde{\delta}_i(D-n))^2]$$

$$= (n-1)^2 E[\tilde{\delta}_I^2] + (D-n)^2 E[\tilde{\delta}_i^2] + 2(n-1)(D-n)\, E[\tilde{\delta}_I \tilde{\delta}_i]$$

$$= (n-1)^2\, \sigma_I^2 + (D-n)^2\, \sigma_i^2 + 2(n-1)(D-1)\, \rho\sigma_I\sigma_i,$$

---

[12]For a derivation of the Basic Hedged Return Formula, see Chapter 21.

[13]In an earlier chapter, we derived a special case of this formula in which both expected yield-curve changes are zero and the expected return is the rolling yield. See Chapter 22. The more general form given above incorporates forecast interest-rate changes, which may, of course, be zero.

where

σ_I = Standard deviation of one-year domestic interest-rate change.

σ_i = Standard deviation of one-year foreign interest-rate change.

ρ = Correlation of domestic and foreign interest-rate changes.

Chapter 24

The Duration of Hedged Global Fixed-Income Investments

INTRODUCTION

Many fixed-income investors have turned to foreign bonds to enhance returns and to reduce risk through diversification. In previous chapters, we developed a framework for analyzing currency-hedged investments in global bond portfolios.[1] In this chapter, we examine how to measure the duration of global investments and to assess the risks associated with foreign/domestic spread movements.

Duration is widely recognized as the most important factor in fixed-income-portfolio performance. Duration risk accounts for so large a proportion of fixed-income volatility that many investors view bond risk as one-dimensional, related almost exclusively to changes in domestic government rates, with minor residual risks relating to spread changes, yield-curve reshapings, and other factors. Thus, fixed-income investors often structure their portfolios to control their sensitivity to domestic interest rates.

In this context, foreign bonds create two novel and significant problems for the domestic investor. Domestic rate changes explain—at best—only a portion of the volatility of foreign bonds. The uncertain response of foreign bonds to domestic interest rates thus causes a loss of duration control. Accompanying this loss is the introduction of a new residual risk that arises from independent changes in foreign/domestic spreads.

---

[1]See Chapters 21, 22, and 23.

In this chapter, we show how duration control can be achieved through the concept of *statistical duration*. In the previous chapters, we showed that a hedged foreign bond can be synthesized by a combination of specific domestic and foreign securities. Statistical duration reflects the standard duration of the domestic component *and* the response of the foreign component to domestic rates. Thus, statistical duration measures the response of the hedged foreign bond to domestic rates and can guide the investor in incorporating hedged foreign bonds in a duration target.

Although duration risk can be controlled by using our methodology, foreign bonds still contain significant residual risk beyond the impact of domestic rate movements. This residual volatility relates to changes in foreign interest-rate spreads that arise from an imperfect foreign/domestic interest-rate correlation. The exposure to such changes can be quantified through an appropriately modified version of the *spread duration* concept.[2]

The residual volatility associated with these spread changes represents the "cost" that investors must weigh against the excess returns that they seek in the foreign bond markets. This "volatility cost" can be mitigated by the diversification benefits that stem from the weak correlation of foreign/domestic spreads with other volatility sources in the fixed-income sector and/ or the total portfolio.

EXPECTED RETURN

The Basic Hedged Return Formula for foreign investments that we developed in previous chapters is as follows:

Hedged Foreign Return $\approx$ Domestic Hedge Point Return

+ (Foreign Investment Return

– Foreign Hedge Point Return),   (1)

where "hedge point return" signifies the return of a zero-coupon note whose

---

[2] This split of volatility into statistical duration and spread duration components is a specific application of our methodology for analyzing the volatility of a fixed-income sector in terms of its sensitivity to a base rate (for example, a government rate) and a spread (for example, a corporate spread to the government rate). See Chapter 16. A different view of statistical duration was introduced in "An Asset Allocation Framework for Central Bank Reserve Fund Management," Vilas Gadkari, Henrik J. Neuhaus, and Mark W. Spindel, in *Asset and Liability Management: Concepts and Strategies for Monetary Authorities,* Salomon Brothers Inc, 1989.

Figure 24–1. Domestic and Foreign Expected Return Curves

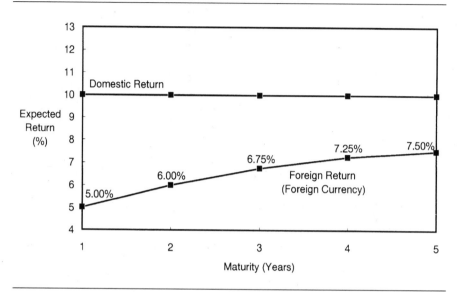

maturity equals the length of the currency hedge.[3] For example, a foreign five-year note with a three-year hedge would produce the same return as the following combination:

- A long position in a domestic three-year zero-coupon note;
- A long position in a foreign five-year note; and
- A short position in a foreign three-year zero-coupon note.

Figure 24–1 shows the domestic and foreign expected returns that we use in this chapter. The returns are shown in local currency—that is, domestic bonds all have a 10% expected return in domestic currency, and foreign

---

[3]See Chapter 21. This approximation assumes that the currency exposure is hedged by the forward sale of foreign currency in an amount equal to the proceeds that would be produced by a zero-coupon note for the length of the hedge. (In the exact formula, the parenthetical expression is modified by the change in currency exchange spot rates during the measurement period, a "second order effect" that we have shown to be minor and will not consider in this chapter.) By "hedge point returns," we refer to the returns on zero-coupon notes whose yields equal the rates at which dealers finance their activity in the currency markets (interbank rates). The actual foreign investment, however, can be any type of security, although our illustrations use the zero-coupon notes.

Figures 24–2A and 24–2B. Translating Foreign Return Curves into Domestic Currency

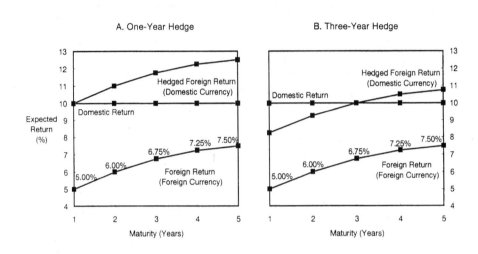

bonds are expected to provide foreign currency returns ranging from 5.00% to 7.50%.[4] We use a one-year horizon throughout this chapter.

Applying the Basic Hedged Return Formula to Figure 24–1, we can determine the expected hedged foreign return curves. Figures 24–2A and 24–2B depict these curves for one- and three-year hedges, respectively.

Figure 24–2A shows the effect of the one-year hedge. Based on the principle of "interest-rate parity,"[5] a foreign one-year zero-coupon note with a one-year currency hedge becomes a synthetic domestic one-year note. Under this principle, the one-year currency hedge must offer a 5% premium to compensate for the yield advantage of the domestic note over the foreign note (10% versus 5%). Therefore, as the measurement basis changes from foreign to domestic currency, the hedged foreign one-year note combines a 5% currency return with a 5% local interest return to produce the same 10%

---

[4]These expected return curves duplicate the yield-to-maturity curves that we used in Chapter 21. The flat domestic return curve is a convenience, not a restriction of the model. The expected returns can be based on any theoretical or tactical model without altering the approach in this chapter.

[5]When interest-rate parity prevails, currency forward exchange rates are at levels that equalize the hedged yield of a riskless foreign security to the yield of a domestic security with the identical payoff pattern.

return as the domestic one-year note. Thus, the foreign one-year note moves up to occupy the position of the domestic one-year note in Figure 24–2A.

Now suppose that the foreign investment is a five-year note. With the illustrative returns of Figure 24–1, the investor earns an incremental 2.50% over the foreign-currency return of the one-year note (7.50% versus 5.00%). When added to the 10% *hedged* return of the foreign one-year note, this 2.50% increment provides a total *hedged* return of 12.50%. All one-year hedged foreign investments capture the same 5% currency premium; thus, all points on the hedged foreign return curve maintain their relationship to the one-year note, producing the parallel shift illustrated in Figure 24–2A.

Figure 24–2B shows that the effect of a three-year hedge is similar to the effect of a one-year hedge.[6] Now, however, the hedged foreign *three-year* note becomes a synthetic domestic *three-year* note, providing a different anchor point for the translated foreign return curve. The foreign five-year note carries a 0.75% return increment over the foreign three-year note. Hence, with a three-year hedge, the five-year note's hedged return becomes 10% *plus* 0.75%, or 10.75%.

RELATIONSHIP BETWEEN DOMESTIC AND FOREIGN INTEREST-RATE CHANGES

We have seen that a hedged foreign bond can be regarded as a combination of domestic and foreign securities. Therefore, it seems to be a simple matter to break out the total volatility into a portion that is dependent on domestic rates alone and another portion that depends only on foreign rates. In an

---

[6]A three-year hedge is quite long by currency exchange market standards, but long-term hedges can be developed through a series of swaps. Although it is unusual to consider a currency hedge that is longer than the security that creates the currency risk, we have shown that this strategy can make sense whenever the domestic expected return curve is more positively sloped than the foreign curve. (See Chapter 23.) The three-year currency hedge is based on the anticipated proceeds that the foreign *three-year* note would produce, and the hedged return is determined by the one-year performance of the actual foreign security and the repricing of the three-year hedge at year-end.

Most currency hedges use much shorter hedges than we illustrate here, rolling monthly or three-month hedges. For example, suppose that we use a one-month hedge for a five-year note. The Basic Hedged Return Formula shows that the return in any month would be the return of a domestic one-month note, *plus* the return of a foreign five-year note, *minus* the return of a foreign one-month note. Over the course of a year, the 12 one-month returns would compound to give *approximately* the one-year return from rolling domestic one-month notes, *plus* the one-year return on the foreign five-year note, *minus* the one-year return from rolling foreign one-month notes. In any case, hedging practically eliminates currency risk.

Figure 24–3. Foreign versus Domestic Interest-Rate Change

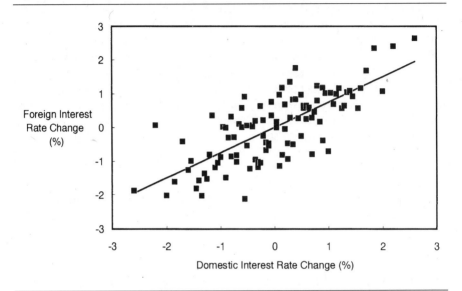

earlier chapter, we developed the following interest-rate sensitivities for the hedged return:[7]

Sensitivity to Domestic Interest-Rate Change Only
    $\approx$ Hedge Length,   and   (2)

Sensitivity to Foreign Interest-Rate Change Only
    $\approx$ Foreign Investment Duration – Hedge Length,   (3)

where the hedge length and the duration are determined at the end of the measurement period. By "sensitivity," we mean the number of basis points by which the return decreases for each one-basis-point increase in the interest rate (similar to "duration").

If the domestic and foreign rates are correlated, the response of the bond to a change in domestic rates becomes more complicated. The hedged return reflects the following: (1) the domestic component, which responds directly to the domestic rate change; and (2) the foreign component, which responds

---

[7]See Chapter 22.

to the foreign rate change. The foreign rate change, in turn, can be split into two parts: the change that is implied by the domestic rate change—based on the domestic/foreign rate correlation—and the "independent" spread change. Thus, we must examine more closely the relationship between domestic and foreign rates.

Figure 24–3 presents the results of 100 simulations of interest-rate changes. We assume that both domestic and foreign interest rates are distributed normally with annual volatility (standard deviation) of 1% and that the domestic/foreign interest-rate correlation is 0.75. (Correlations between the interest rates of countries with close economic ties can be as high as 0.75, while more distantly related markets will have much lower correlations.)

Each point in Figure 24–3 represents the domestic and foreign interest-rate changes that correspond to a single simulation. Figure 24–3 includes a regression ("best fit") line that has a slope, denoted by β, of 0.75.[8]

For any specified domestic rate change, we can expect a foreign rate change of β multiplied by that change; we refer to this expected foreign rate change as the *implied foreign rate change*.[9] For example, under our current assumptions, a 100-basis-point increase in domestic rates implies a foreign rate increase of 75 basis points.

This implied foreign rate change also entails an *implied foreign/domestic spread change*. In our example, the 100-basis-point increase in domestic rates and the implied 75-basis-point increase in the foreign rate would result in a 25-basis-point decrease in the spread of foreign rates over domestic rates. Stated another way, we can look at the implied foreign rate change as being composed of the domestic rate change (*plus* 100 basis points) *plus* the implied spread change (*minus* 25 basis points).

In general, the actual foreign rate change will differ from the implied value because of imperfect foreign/domestic rate correlations. Similarly, the actual spread change will differ from the implied spread change. We call this difference the *unexplained spread change* to distinguish it from the spread change that is expected based on the domestic rate change. In Figure 24–3, as we have stated, a 100-basis-point rise in domestic rates leads to an *implied* spread change of –25 basis points. If the spread actually increases by 10 basis points, we have an unexplained spread change of +35 basis points.

---

[8]The slope can be shown to equal the correlation multiplied by the ratio of the foreign rate volatility to the domestic rate volatility. For now, we assume that the rate volatilities are equal; thus, β equals the correlation.

[9]We use the term "implied," rather then the usual statistical term "predicted," to distinguish between the foreign rate change that is likely in light of the domestic rate change and the foreign rate change that an investor may predict *a priori* on other grounds.

STATISTICAL DURATION

The duration of a domestic bond provides an excellent gauge of how the bond's performance will be affected by changes in domestic interest rates. To capture the expected response of a hedged *foreign* bond to changes in *domestic* rates, we use the concept of *statistical duration*. We also show how to evaluate the residual return volatility that is not explained by domestic interest-rate risk.

For example, consider a foreign five-year zero-coupon note with a three-year hedge. Figure 24–4 plots the one-year hedged return of this security against the change in domestic interest rates, based on the simulation that underlies Figure 24–3.

To analyze this return pattern, we first restate our earlier formulation, derived from the Basic Hedged Return Formula. A foreign five-year zero-coupon note with a three-year hedge is equivalent to the following combination:[10]

- A long position in a domestic three-year zero-coupon note;
- A long position in a foreign five-year note; and
- A short position in a foreign three-year zero-coupon note.

The only direct effect of a change in domestic rates on this combination is on the domestic three-year note, which has a year-end duration of two years. For example, a 100-basis-point increase in domestic interest rates would decrease the return of the domestic three-year note by about 200 basis points.

Figure 24–5 superimposes a line corresponding to this two-year duration on the simulated results—obviously a poor fit. The difficulty is that this approach limits us to considering the domestic position only, because the domestic rate change has no *direct* effect on the foreign positions.

We can improve the model by using a statistical approach, which recognizes that the domestic rate change likely will be reflected to some extent in foreign rates; the change in foreign rates then would have a further effect on the overall hedged return. With our foreign interest rate β of 0.75, for example, a 100-basis-point increase in domestic rates would produce an im-

---

[10]We focus on a three-year hedge in this section of the chapter and do not display results for a one-year hedge. With our one-year horizon, the one-year notes that would appear in the above formulation have no volatility; the investor faces only the volatility of the foreign investment (without currency exposure). The investment can then be modeled similarly to any domestic nongovernment bond using the approach in Chapter 16.

Figure 24–4. Hedged Foreign Return versus Domestic Interest-Rate Change

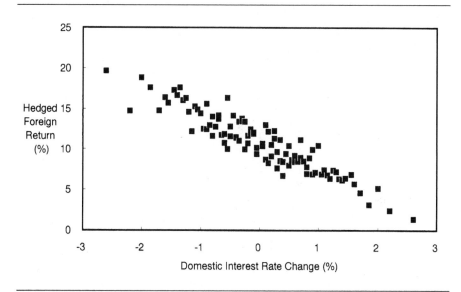

Figure 24–5. Hedged Foreign Return Modeled by Duration of Domestic Position

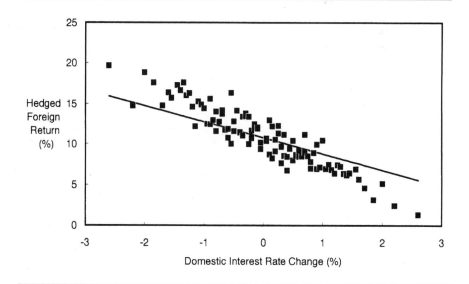

plied foreign rate increase of 75 basis points. This 75-basis-point increase would lower the hedged return by a further 150 basis points [the 75-basis-point increase *multiplied by* the five-year foreign investment duration *minus* the three-year hedge length, as per equation (3)].

With this insight, we can better quantify the effect of a domestic rate change on the hedged return. We must recognize both the direct effect on the domestic position and the "pass-through" effect on the foreign positions. We use the term *statistical duration* to refer to the sum of these two effects (see the Appendix to this chapter for derivation):

Statistical Duration = Hedge Length (*the direct effect*)

$$+ \text{(Foreign Investment Duration} - \text{Hedge Length)}$$

$$\times \text{Foreign Interest Rate } \beta \text{ (\textit{the pass-through effect}). (4)}$$

Thus, the statistical duration of the hedged five-year note is

$$2.0 + (4.0 - 2.0) \times 0.75 = 3.5 \text{ years.}$$

Figure 24–6 compares the simulated returns to those predicted by using the statistical duration and shows a much-improved fit.

Figure 24–6. Hedged Foreign Return Modeled by Statistical Duration

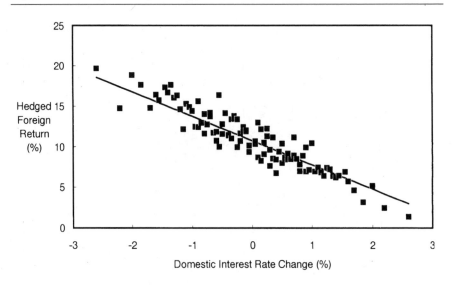

SPREAD DURATION

As we have seen, the statistical duration line has reasonably good explanatory power, at least for these highly correlated interest rates. Figure 24–7 plots the "noise" in the hedged returns—the portion of the returns not explained directly or indirectly by the change in domestic rates, which we refer to as the *residual returns*. (The residual returns can also be seen as the deviations from the duration line in Figure 24–6.)

The change in domestic rates explains all of the return of the domestic position and, through the domestic/foreign interest-rate correlation, a portion of the return on the foreign positions. Usually, however, the foreign interest-rate change is not exactly as was implied by the domestic change. Therefore, we would expect to find some noise in modeling the total returns solely in terms of domestic rate changes. The residual returns have no recognizable pattern in Figure 24–7, which relates them to domestic interest rates. We can see a clear pattern, however, in Figure 24–8, which plots these residual returns against the *unexplained spread change*.

The *unexplained spread changes* arise from independent foreign rate changes. Thus, we would expect their effect on the hedged return to be proportional to the foreign rate sensitivity given in equation (3)—the foreign

Figure 24–7. Portion of Hedged Foreign Return Not Explained by Statistical Duration

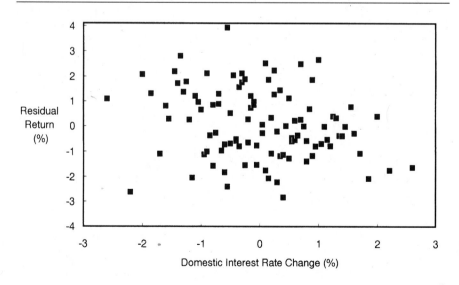

Figure 24–8. Residual Return versus Unexplained Spread Change

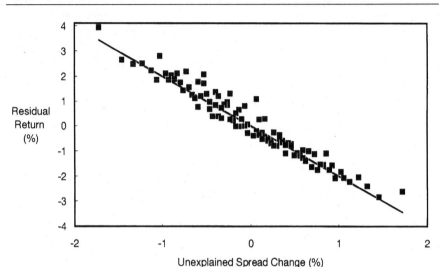

investment duration *minus* the hedge length, two years in our example. The residual returns in Figure 24–8 fit quite well with the line whose slope is –2.0, corresponding to the two-year sensitivity. (The imperfect fit reflects the convexity effects that can arise over the one-year measurement period.)

We refer to this sensitivity as the *spread duration*. The spread duration is simply a standard duration in local interest terms—the foreign investment duration *minus* the hedge length—applied to spread changes. Thus, for each one-basis-point *unexplained spread increase*, the hedged return decreases by the number of basis points given by the *spread duration*.

This analysis traces the complex behavior of a hedged foreign bond to two fundamental sources:

- Its exposure to domestic rates, given by its *statistical duration*; and

- Its exposure to "unexplained" changes in foreign/domestic interest-rate spreads, given by its *spread duration*.[11]

---

[11]As we show in the Appendix to this chapter, the volatility of this residual noise is the product of the spread duration and a fraction of the foreign interest-rate volatility. The fraction is $\sqrt{1 - \rho^2}$, where ρ is the domestic/foreign interest-rate correlation. Because these two sources of volatility by definition are uncorrelated, the total volatility is the square root of the sum of the squares of these two volatilities.

Figures 24–9A and 24–9B. Statistical Duration of Hedged Foreign Investments

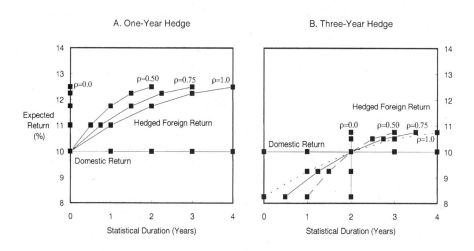

ρ = domestic/foreign interest-rate correlation.

The remaining volatility—deviations from the line in Figure 24–8—solely reflects our use of duration to determine the effect of interest-rate changes without considering convexity. Thus, the hedged foreign return can be estimated as the return of a domestic bond with a **statistical duration** given by equation (4), *plus* a residual term based on the **spread duration** *multiplied by* the **unexplained spread change**.

STATISTICAL DURATION AND RESIDUAL VOLATILITY ALONG THE FOREIGN YIELD CURVE

In this section, we test the effect of varying correlations on the volatility components of the entire one- to five-year foreign yield curve. Figures 24–9A and 24–9B replot the return curves from Figures 24–2A and 24–2B in terms of their year-end statistical duration, rather than maturity. (The markers on the curves represent the year-end maturity, which equals the duration in local terms for these zero-coupon notes.) We show the curves under alternative assumed correlations ranging from zero to one and maintain the 1% volatilities for domestic and foreign interest rates.

For domestic securities, the statistical duration is simply the standard duration, because we have defined *statistical duration* as a measure of the response to domestic rates.[12]

For the hedged foreign returns with a one-year hedge (see Figure 24–9A), the statistical duration patterns are still straightforward. When the correlation is 1.0 and domestic and foreign interest-rate volatilities are equal, foreign securities have exactly the same response to domestic rates (expressed by statistical duration) as to foreign rates (expressed by the standard duration in local terms) because the rates move in lockstep. Thus, in this perfect correlation case, the statistical duration equals the standard duration. As the correlation drops, foreign securities become less sensitive to domestic rates, because only a percentage of the domestic rate change (given by the correlation) is typically passed through to the foreign rates.

With a 0.75 correlation, therefore, the year-end statistical duration is only 75% of the local foreign duration. Hence, the entire 0.75 correlation curve shifts leftward in comparison to the 1.0 correlation curve.

The leftward contraction continues as the correlation drops to 0.50. When the correlation reaches zero, foreign rates have no response to domestic rate changes. The domestic position, a one-year note, also is unresponsive to changes in domestic rates over our one-year measurement period. Thus, the statistical duration is zero for all maturities.

The three-year hedge creates a more complex pattern. When the correlation is 1.0 (with equal domestic and foreign rate volatilities), the statistical duration equals the standard duration, because the two durations measure responses to two rates that move in lockstep.

For the 0.75 correlation, we can think in terms of the security combination: long a domestic three-year note, long the foreign investment, and short a foreign three-year note. The domestic component has a year-end duration (both standard and statistical) of two years. On average, the foreign rates reflect 75% of the domestic rate change. Thus, the foreign component adds (or subtracts) an incremental (or decremental) statistical duration equal to 75% of the difference between the durations of the long foreign investment and the short foreign three-year note. Thus, as we have seen, the five-year note has a statistical duration of

$$2.0 + 0.75 \times (4.0 - 2.0) = 3.5 \text{ years,}$$

---

[12]In Chapter 16, we split the domestic market into two sectors: government and nongovernment. Here we simplify by assuming a single domestic rate structure. A precise formulation would reflect the imperfect correlation between government rates and the rates on which the hedge is based (interbank rates).

Figures 24–10A and 24–10B. Statistical Duration and Residual Volatility

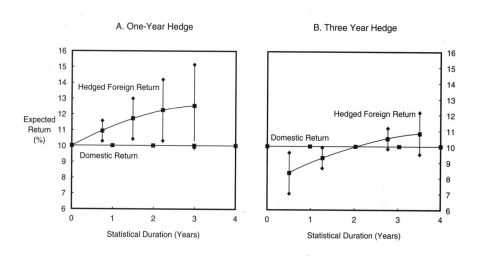

while the one-year note has a statistical duration of

$$2.0 + 0.75 \times (0.0 - 2.0) = 0.5 \text{ year.}$$

The 0.50 correlation curve continues the contraction of the foreign component's statistical duration. The overall statistical duration of both long- and short-duration foreign investments shifts further toward the two-year duration of the domestic component.

The zero correlation eliminates any response of the foreign component to domestic rates. The total sensitivity of the hedged position to domestic rates lies in the domestic component and equals the year-end hedge length of two years. The statistical duration is thus 2.0 for all maturities.

In Figures 24–10A and 24–10B, we focus on the 0.75 correlation curves. We add a "spine" for each foreign security, showing its residual return volatility—the volatility relating to unexplained spread changes. The residual return volatility is proportional to the absolute value of the spread duration. Therefore, it increases in proportion to the absolute difference between the foreign investment duration and the hedge length.

In Figure 24–10A, the spines lengthen as we move out on the foreign curve. By the time we reach the five-year note, the spine is long enough to reach just below the domestic curve. Thus, despite the 250-basis-point expected return advantage of the note relative to domestic securities, an adverse spread change of one standard deviation can drive its return below the domestic curve. Favorable spread changes can result in an equally substantial *increase* in its return advantage.

The three-year hedge produces a more interesting pattern. Recall that a foreign three-year note with a three-year hedge is a synthetic domestic three-year note. Thus, it has no exposure to foreign rates or spreads, and its spread duration and residual volatility are zero. If the foreign investment departs by one year from the three-year hedge duration, one year of (positive or negative) spread duration and the corresponding residual volatility are introduced. A two-year departure doubles the spread duration and the residual volatility, as shown by the lengthening of the spines as the foreign investment moves to the one- or five-year note. Shortening the foreign duration below the three-year hedge length thus has two contrary effects on volatility: It decreases the statistical duration and, consequently, the volatility associated with domestic rate changes, while it increases the residual volatility related to spread changes.

The breakdown of volatility into its statistical and spread duration sources is particularly critical to an investor whose performance is measured against a domestic benchmark. The statistical duration risk relates solely to domestic rates and can be controlled by appropriate adjustments in the domestic component of the total portfolio.[13] The spread risk, portrayed by the spines, however, is intrinsic to the foreign sector and must accompany any foreign rate exposure. When mixed with various types of domestic spread risk that the investor may be taking, the inherent riskiness of the foreign exposure may be moderated somewhat by diversification effects.

This analysis of statistical and spread durations also provides insight into some of the paradoxical volatility curve shapes that we developed in an earlier chapter.[14] Figure 24–11 plots expected returns against total return volatility, with foreign interest-rate volatilities of 1% and 1.5%. The higher foreign rate volatility increases both the (absolute) statistical duration of the foreign component of return and the residual return volatility.[15] For foreign notes exceeding three years, the higher foreign rate volatility adds both sta-

---

[13]See Chapter 16.

[14]See Chapter 23.

[15]The statistical duration of the foreign component increases in proportion to the foreign interest β, which rises from $0.75 \times 1\% / 1\% = 0.75$ to $0.75 \times 1.5\% / 1\% = 1.125$. The residual return volatility is the spread duration multiplied by a constant fraction ($\sqrt{1 - \rho^2}$) of the foreign rate volatility.

Figure 24–11. Expected Return and Volatility of Hedged Foreign Investments (Three-Year Hedge; Correlation = 0.75)

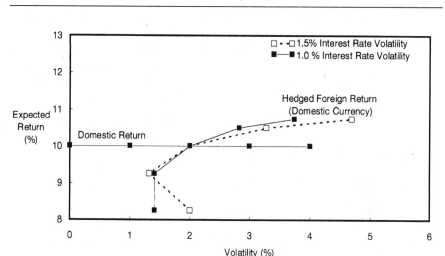

tistical duration and residual volatility, stretching the return curve to the right. (With a one-year hedge, the entire foreign return curve from one year up would be stretched to the right.)

For shorter notes, the reshaping is more complex. The domestic side of the hedge has a two-year duration (standard and statistical). The foreign position has negative statistical duration (long a foreign one- or two-year note and short a foreign three-year note). The higher foreign rate volatility is *helpful* in providing more negative statistical duration to reduce the overall statistical duration and to mute the response to domestic rate changes. However, it *increases the residual volatility*, because the spread duration is exposed to a larger spread volatility. The balance of these two effects explains the nonintuitive reshaping of the short portion of the curve.

CONCLUSION: MANAGING AGAINST A DOMESTIC BENCHMARK

We have shown that a hedged foreign bond can be modeled as a domestic bond with a specified duration and with a residual term that depends on the spread duration (the foreign investment duration *minus* the hedge length). When managing against a domestic benchmark, an investor can control or eliminate the domestic interest-rate exposure through judicious selection of the hedge length or the duration of the domestic allocation of the portfolio. This process leaves only a residual risk, stemming from foreign rate exposure that is unrelated to domestic rate movements. Thus, by using the measures that we have developed in this chapter, the investor can base the foreign investment decision on the balance between this residual risk and the associated return increment.

APPENDIX

In an earlier chapter,[16] we developed the following approximation for the volatility of a hedged foreign bond:

$$\sigma_R^2 \approx (n-1)^2 \, \sigma_I^2 + (D-n)^2 \, \sigma_i^2 + 2(n-1)(D-n)\rho \, \sigma_I \sigma_i, \tag{1}$$

where

$\quad {}_R \quad$ = Standard deviation of one-year hedged return.

$\quad n \quad$ = Length of currency hedge.

$\quad \sigma_I \quad$ = Standard deviation of one-year domestic interest-rate change.

$\quad D \quad$ = Macaulay duration of foreign investment.

$\quad \sigma_i \quad$ = Standard deviation of one-year foreign interest-rate change.

$\quad \rho \quad$ = Correlation of domestic and foreign interest-rate changes.

We now wish to split the volatility given by equation (1) into two components, one relating to domestic interest-rate changes (including correlated spread changes) and one relating to residual foreign rate or spread changes. If we regress foreign rate changes against domestic rate changes, we obtain a regression line with a slope that we call β; we can show that

$$\beta = \rho\sigma_i \, / \, \sigma_I. \tag{2}$$

Substituting equation (2) into equation (1) and rearranging terms, we obtain

$$\sigma_R^2 \approx (n-1)^2\sigma_I^2 + (D-n)^2 \, \sigma_i^2 + 2(n-1)(D-n)\beta\sigma_I^2$$

$$= (n-1)^2\sigma_I^2 + 2(n-1)(D-n)\beta\sigma_I^2 + (D-n)^2\rho^2\sigma_i^2 + (D-n)^2(1-\rho^2)\sigma_i^2$$

$$= (n-1)^2\sigma_I^2 + 2(n-1)(D-n)\beta\sigma_I^2 + (D-n)^2\beta^2\sigma_I^2 + (D-n)^2(1-\rho^2)\sigma_i^2,$$

so

$$\sigma_R \approx \sqrt{[(n-1) + (D-n)\beta]^2\sigma_I^2 + (D-n)^2 \, (1-\rho^2) \, \sigma_i^2}. \tag{3}$$

---

[16]See Chapter 23.

Equation (3) can be thought of as expressing the volatility of the following two-bond portfolio:

- One "bond" has duration $[(n - 1) + (D - n)\beta]$ (*the statistical duration*), exposed to an interest rate with volatility σ_I (domestic rate volatility).

- The other "bond" has duration $(D - n)$ (*the spread duration*), exposed to an interest rate with volatility $\sigma_i \sqrt{1 - \rho^2}$ (*residual foreign rate or spread volatility*), where the correlation between domestic rate changes and residual spread changes is zero.

Chapter 25

Global Fixed-Income Investments: The Persistence Effect

INTRODUCTION

Investment strategies are founded on a wide range of philosophies about the financial markets. Some investors rely on explicit views about market direction, such as interest-rate forecasts or tactical assessments of risk premiums. More skeptical investors may accept the efficient market hypothesis and focus on long-term asset allocation as the key to achieving their goals. Others may steer a middle path by avoiding "macro" forecasts, while making use of more modest assumptions about financial market behavior.

In this chapter, we focus on the decision making of this last investor group. Within the context of a foreign bond portfolio, we explore the implications of accepting or rejecting the view that forward rates necessarily give the best predictions of future yield-curve shapes and currency exchange rates. We define a *persistence factor* that reflects the expectation that rates will remain at their current levels: A persistence assumption of 1 means that spot rates are expected to persist, while a persistence assumption of 0 means that they are expected to give way to forward rates. The persistence model can aid in evaluating the risk/return trade-offs that investors face in their pursuit of superior returns. For example, under a persistence assumption of 1, an investor generally expects to be rewarded for extending duration when the yield curve is positive. However, a persistence assumption of 0—meaning that forward rates will be realized—eliminates any incentive to pursue higher-yielding securities. Thus, *all* investment decisions rely on an assumption, perhaps implicit, about persistence.

Figure 25–1. Domestic and Foreign Spot Interest-Rate Curves

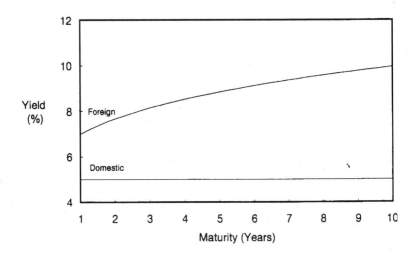

YIELD CURVES AND EXPECTED RETURN CURVES

Figure 25–1 depicts an illustrative set of domestic and foreign annualized spot interest rates. The yields are shown in local currency. For the 1- to 10-year maturity range, domestic bonds all yield 5% in domestic currency, and foreign bonds yield from 7% to 10% in foreign currency.

Each yield in Figure 25–1 represents the average annual return that an investor who holds a zero-coupon note of the indicated maturity would receive during the lifetime of the note. The one-year return of each note with a maturity greater than one year, however, is uncertain and depends not only on the initial yield curve, but on the year-end yield curve as well.

Projecting a one-year return, therefore, requires assumptions about the level and shape of the year-end yield curve. For the moment, we ignore tactical views about the general level of yields or major yield-curve reshapings. Instead, we focus on potential yield-curve changes that may flow from the basic structure of the curve. We consider the following three views:[1]

---

[1] For a more detailed discussion of the relationship between yield curves and return curves, see Chapter 21.

1. The yield curve remains unchanged. We identify this view with a persistence factor of 1, meaning that the current spot rates persist.

2. The yield curve reshapes to produce the forward rates.[2] This reshaping generates the same one-year returns for all (riskless) securities, regardless of maturity. For the positive foreign yield curve, rates would rise, so that capital losses on the bonds longer than one year would force their one-year returns down to the 7% level of the one-year note.[3] For the flat domestic curve, the forward rates equal the spot rates. For an inverted curve, the forward rates would be below the spot rates.

    We identify a persistence factor of 0 with this view that the yield curve will evolve into its forward rates—that is, spot rates have no tendency to persist. In this chapter, we consider yield curves that can be characterized by a single persistence factor that lies between 0 and 1. This range generates a substantial, though not exhaustive, spectrum of yield-curve reshapings.[4] Our model, however, does not depend on a uniform persistence factor but can accommodate any expected year-end yield curve.

3. A third view of yield-curve evolution illustrates a *nonuniform* persistence factor: the view that the yield curve reshapes so that each security's 1-year return equals its yield to maturity.[5] The resulting yield curve would generally lie between those defined by persistence factors of 0 and 1. For our illustrative yields, the persistence factor would range from 0.50 to 0.65 for various maturities.

---

[2]We use the terms "forward rates" and "forward curve" to refer specifically to the implied yields one year forward on all securities.

[3]For the illustrative foreign curve shown in Figure 25–1, the one-year rate is 7%. The two-year note yields 7.7% to maturity, so its first- and second-year returns must compound to 1.077^2. If the two-year note returns only the one-year rate of 7% in the first year, it must return 8.4% in the second year ($1.07 \times 1.084 = 1.077^2$); that is, the one-year rate must reset from 7% at the beginning of the first year to 8.4%—the forward rate—at year-end.

[4]Mathematically, the year-end yield is given by the following:

Persistence Factor × Initial Spot Rate + (1 − Persistence Factor) × Forward Rate.

Investors may anticipate persistence factors outside the 0–1 range. For example, with a positively sloped yield curve, the forward curve is above the spot curve. A persistence factor of 0 implies that the rate will not persist but will move up to the forward rate. A *negative* persistence factor anticipates an upward movement *beyond* the forward rate. On the other hand, a persistence factor of 1 implies that the spot rate will persist and not give way to the forward rate. A persistence factor greater than 1 suggests that the forward rate is a contraindicator and the rate will tend to *decline*.

[5]If the two-year note returns its 7.7% yield the first year, then it must also return 7.7% the second year; that is, the one-year rate must reset from 7% at the beginning of the first year to 7.7% at year-end. This rate is approximately halfway between the spot and forward rates.

Figure 25–2. Year-End Curves with Varying Persistence Levels

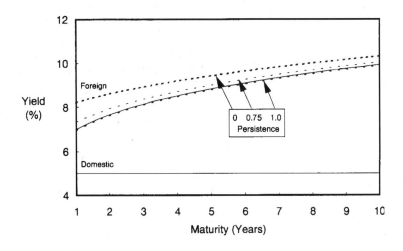

Figure 25–2 portrays three possibilities for the year-end foreign spot curve that reflect the following uniform persistence factors:[6]

- The upper dashed line (persistence = 0), representing the forward rates.

- The lower dashed line (persistence = 1), representing a continuance of current rates.

- An intermediate line (persistence = 0.75), representing a compromise view that gives greater weight to the current rates than to forward rates.

ONE-YEAR RETURN CURVES

Figure 25–3 develops the one-year returns that would result from the year-end yield curves shown in Figure 25–2:

---

[6]Three different curves appear for the foreign market. Because the domestic curve is flat, all persistence factors leave the domestic curve unchanged.

Figure 25–3. One-Year Return (Local Currency) with Varying Persistence

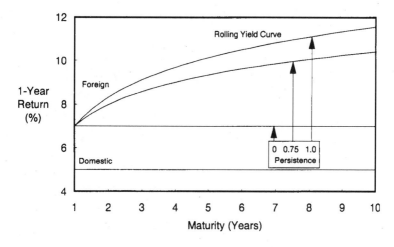

- A persistence of 0, meaning that the year-end yield curve consists of the current implied forward rates, automatically produces a flat return curve at the 7% level of the initial one-year yield. An investor who assumes a persistence of 0 would therefore have no motivation to move out on the yield curve.

- A persistence of 1 produces the rolling yield curve. For our positive yield curve, these one-year returns exceed the initial yields. The excess returns are generated by "rolling down the yield curve." As the securities age, they are repriced at the lower yields that correspond to their shortened maturities. The resulting appreciation boosts the return above the initial yield level.[7] With a positive yield curve, an investor anticipating a persistence of 1 would expect to be rewarded for extending duration, at least until the roll-down effects diminish.

---

[7]Repricing the 7.7% two-year note to a 7% yield after one year gives 0.7% appreciation (a 70-basis-point yield decline at a one-year duration), for a total first-year return of 8.4% (7.7% yield + 0.7% appreciation). For a detailed discussion, see *Total Return Management*, Martin L. Leibowitz, Salomon Brothers Inc, January 1979.

The reappearance of the 8.4% rate that we observed earlier to be the forward rate is not coincidental. It can be shown that the rolling yield on an n-year note equals the implied $(n-1)$-year forward one-year rate.

Figure 25–4. Expected One-Year Return: Local Currency

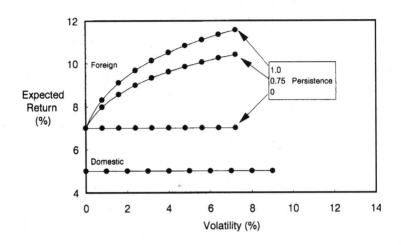

- A persistence of 0.75 generates a return curve lying between the other two.

VOLATILITY

We now illustrate the effect of uncertainty. We treat the year-end yield curves portrayed in Figure 25–2 as *expected* curves, and we assume that yield changes are normally distributed around the expected level. For illustration, we assume that domestic yield changes and foreign yield changes have annual volatilities (standard deviations) of 1% and 0.8%, respectively. We ignore convexity and approximate the return volatility of a security as the product of the interest-rate volatility and the security's duration at the one-year horizon (the maturity *minus* one year for the zero-coupon notes that we are considering).

Figure 25–4 plots the expected one-year returns against the return volatility. The markers indicate horizon durations of 0–9 years, corresponding to maturities of 1–10 years. Because we assume that volatility is proportional to duration, the shape of the curves is quite similar to that shown in Figure

25–3; the foreign curves contract leftward relative to the domestic curve because of the lower foreign yield change volatility.

HEDGED FOREIGN RETURNS

Thus far, we have considered returns in local currency only. We now translate the foreign currency returns into domestic currency. First, we illustrate the translation for an investor who has fully hedged the currency risk. The hedging investor acquires foreign currency at the current *spot exchange rate* and enters into a contract to exchange the expected foreign proceeds at the end of one year for domestic currency. The contractual rate is known as the *forward exchange rate.* In an earlier chapter, we developed the following approximation for the one-year hedged return of a foreign *n*-year security:[8]

Domestic Return ≈ Foreign Return on *n*-Year Security

+ (Domestic One-Year Spot Interest Rate

– Foreign One-Year Spot Interest Rate).

In this expression, the first term on the right-hand side is the local foreign return of the *n*-year security. As shown in our earlier chapter, the parenthetical expression equals the currency return that is built into the hedge—for our illustrative yield curves, 5% – 7% = –2%. This –2% currency return results from selling the foreign currency at a forward rate that is 2% below the spot rate.[9]

Figure 25–5 illustrates the translation into domestic currency for the foreign expected return curve from Figure 25–4 with a persistence of 0.75. The upper curve, showing the foreign expected return in *foreign* currency, is the same as in Figure 25–4. The *hedged* return curve is given by a parallel shift, down to the point where the foreign and domestic one-year notes coincide. The 2% downward shift reflects the currency depreciation that is locked in by the hedge.[10]

---

[8]See Chapter 21.

[9]Under the principle of *interest-rate parity,* the 2% currency loss compensates for the 2% advantage of the one-year foreign spot rate (7%) over the one-year domestic spot rate (5%). Thus, a foreign one-year note with a one-year currency hedge would produce the same 5% return as a domestic one-year note.

[10]In our example, the entire hedged foreign return curve offers a spread over the domestic curve. For other curve shapes and hedge lengths, this relationship may not hold.

Figure 25–5. Expected One-Year Return: Local Currency and Hedged into Domestic Currency

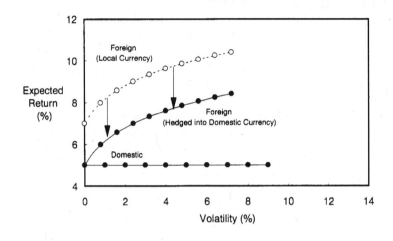

UNHEDGED FOREIGN RETURNS

If the investor does not employ a currency hedge, the domestic value of the foreign investment at the one-year measurement date will be determined by the actual exchange rate at year-end. The total return is approximately the sum of the local foreign investment return and the percentage change in the currency exchange spot rate.[11] First, we assume that the forward exchange rate embedded in our illustrative hedge represents the expected year-end spot rate, so the *expected* currency return is –2%. Under this assumption, the expected currency return equals the currency return implied by the hedge, so the expected total unhedged return equals the expected hedged return.

However, the volatility of the unhedged return is quite different from that of the hedged return because of the exposure to currency fluctuations.

---

[11]More precisely, the total return equals:

(1 + Local Foreign Investment Return) × (1 + Percentage Change in Currency Rate) – 1.

To simplify the discussion, we ignore the cross term (Local Foreign Investment Return × Percentage Change in Currency Rate), which has a relatively small *expected* value.

Figure 25–6. Expected One-Year Return in Domestic Currency: Hedged and Unhedged

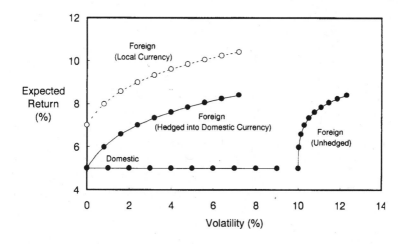

We assume that the currency exchange rate has an annual volatility of 10%. We also assume that these currency movements are uncorrelated with the foreign investment returns.[12] Figure 25–6 compares the hedged and unhedged returns under these conditions.

Because we have assumed the same expected currency return (–2%) for the hedged and unhedged positions, the "height" (expected return) of each security remains the same when the hedge is removed. The currency exposure, however, shifts the return curve far to the right by increasing the total volatility. A hedged foreign one-year note (with a horizon duration of zero) has an assured one-year return of 5% and a volatility of zero. If the note is unhedged, the volatility of the *local return* is zero, but the currency exposure introduces a 10% volatility into the unhedged domestic return. For securities of longer durations, the local return volatility has a more complex effect. The

---

[12]The existence of a strong correlation between currency returns and the local foreign investment returns would be important. A negative correlation would reduce the volatility of the unhedged foreign return: A strong local investment performance would tend to be countered by currency losses, and a weak local return would likely be compensated by currency gains. Conversely, a positive correlation would increase volatility, because currency performance would tend to compound the strength or weakness of the foreign bond market.

incremental local volatility adds relatively little to the total volatility, because uncorrelated volatilities (local return volatility and currency volatility) are not additive.[13] The result is a steep unhedged return curve.

Figure 25–6 demonstrates that an investor who believes that the currency persistence is 0 (spot rates move to the forward rates over the investment horizon) is strongly motivated to hedge. Failure to hedge incurs risk without an expected reward.

In Figure 25–6, the spot exchange rate evolves into the forward rate, producing a –2% expected currency return. If instead, we expect no change in the spot rate, the expected currency return is zero. As we did with the yield curves, we illustrate a range of possibilities based on a *currency persistence factor,* which can vary from 1 (when the spot exchange rate is expected to persist) to 0 (when the spot rate is expected to move to the forward rate).[14] Within this range, the expected unhedged return can vary from equaling the local foreign return (no change in the spot exchange rate) to equaling the expected hedged return (the spot exchange rate changes as anticipated by the hedge). This currency return range, which by no means exhausts the possibilities, is portrayed in Figure 25–7.

The lower right-hand curve, repeated from Figure 25–6, reflects currency persistence of zero—that is, the currency exchange rate is expected to move to its forward rate, duplicating the –2% return of the hedge. When we raise the currency persistence factor to 1, the expected currency return becomes 0%. This 2% improvement shifts the expected return curve upward by 2%; the unhedged expected return now equals the foreign local currency return because the local return is expected to be translated into domestic currency at an unchanged currency rate.

---

[13]A security that is exposed to two uncorrelated sources of volatility has a total volatility equal to the square root of the sum of the squares of the two volatilities. For example, the foreign two-year note, with a one-year horizon duration, has a volatility of 0.8% in local currency. When this local volatility combines with 10% currency volatility, the total volatility becomes $\sqrt{0.8\%^2 + 10\%^2} = 10.03\%$; the incremental volatility added by the 0.8% local volatility is only 0.03% (10.03% for the two-year note minus 10% for the one-year note).

One can also view the unhedged return curve as a rightward shift of the hedged return curve, where the one-year note shifts a full 10%, while each successively longer note shifts less. Currency exposure thus adds substantial volatility to short-duration foreign investments and somewhat less to long-duration investments.

[14]In "Tactical Currency Allocation," Robert D. Arnott and Tan K. Pham, *Financial Analysts Journal,* September–October 1993, the authors indicate that currency exchange rates tend to move away from the forward rates—that is, they show persistence factors greater than 1.

Figure 25–7. Expected 1-Year Return in Domestic Currency: Varying Currency Persistence

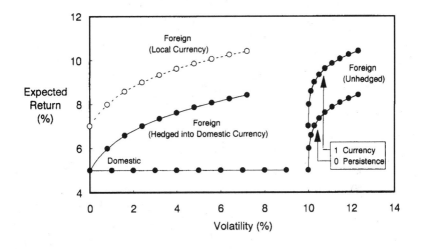

GLOBAL FIXED-INCOME PORTFOLIOS

Thus far, we have limited our discussion to 100% foreign bond portfolios. We now add some brief comments on mixed domestic/foreign portfolios. The dashed lines in Figure 25–8 show combinations of domestic five-year-duration notes and foreign five-year-duration notes, both hedged and unhedged. We assume that domestic and foreign interest rates have a correlation of 0.4. The unhedged returns are based on a currency persistence factor of 1 and therefore incorporate a 0% currency return, in contrast to the –2% hedged currency return. All other assumptions are the same as those underlying Figure 25–7.

Figure 25–8 highlights the combinations of 85% domestic/15% foreign notes. When hedged, this combination has an expected return of 5.4% and a volatility of 4.5%. Thus, the investor can gain 40 basis points of expected return relative to the five-year-duration domestic note, while lowering volatility. This seeming advantage, however, may be negated by a loss of domestic duration control and by tracking error relative to a domestic benchmark.

Without a currency hedge, the 85%/15% mix provides an even greater expected return of 5.7%, while the volatility increases to 4.8%. In this example, however, an investor who is willing to increase the foreign allocation

Figure 25–8. Mixed Domestic/Foreign Portfolios

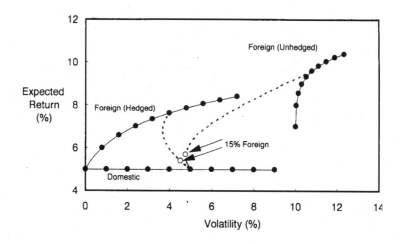

well beyond 15% can match this expected return with a hedged portfolio that has lower volatility.

CONCLUSION

In this chapter, we have used a global fixed-income context to illustrate the concept of spot rate persistence. We observed that if an interest-rate curve has zero persistence, all fixed-income securities priced on that curve will produce the same return over a one-year period—namely, the one-year yield. Under this condition, higher-yielding securities do not provide any higher expected one-year returns. Thus, an investor who believes that the rate persistence is 0 has no incentive to accept duration risk. In an absolute return framework, this investor should hold cash; when managing against a benchmark, he or she should hold the benchmark duration. On the other hand, a positive yield curve with a persistence of 1 does imply a reward for extending duration and accepting interest-rate risk. A willingness to pursue higher-yielding securities must therefore be based on an assumption, perhaps implicit, that interest-rate persistence is not zero.

A similar statement can be made about currency risk. If currency exchange spot rates have a persistence of zero, the expected unhedged currency return equals the return implicit in a currency hedge. Investors would have no reason to accept currency exposure, because the expected currency return could be "locked in" through a hedge. Only the anticipation of non-zero persistence justifies the acceptance of currency risk.

Under the principle of interest-rate parity, a currency persistence of zero equalizes fixed-income returns *across* currencies. Similarly, interest-rate persistence of zero equalizes returns *within* currencies. *Any* yield-seeking behavior, then, implies some expectation that forward rates will not be fully realized. The concept of spot rate persistence can make such expectations explicit and aid in evaluating their credibility and consequences.

Index